MUHLENBERG

WITHDRAWN

The Romantic Tradition in American Literature

The Romantic Tradition
in American Literature

Advisory Editor

HAROLD BLOOM
Professor of English, Yale University

ESSAYS AND REVIEWS

CHIEFLY ON

THEOLOGY, POLITICS, AND SOCIALISM

O[RESTES] A. BROWNSON

ARNO PRESS
A NEW YORK TIMES COMPANY
New York • 1972

Reprint Edition 1972 by Arno Press Inc.

Reprinted from a copy in The Princeton
University Library

The Romantic Tradition in American Literature
ISBN for complete set: 0-405-04620-0
See last pages of this volume for titles.

Manufactured in the United States of America

༄༅༄༅༄༅༄༅༄༅༄༅༄༅

Library of Congress Cataloging in Publication Data

Brownson, Orestes Augustus, 1803-1876.
 Essays and reviews, chiefly on theology, politics,
and socialism.

 (The Romantic tradition in American literature)
 Reprint of the 1852 ed.
 I. Title. II. Series.
AC8.B724 1972   201'.1   72-4954
ISBN 0-405-04626-X

ESSAYS AND REVIEWS

CHIEFLY ON

THEOLOGY, POLITICS, AND SOCIALISM.

BY

O. A. BROWNSON, L.L. D.

NEW YORK:
D. & J. SADLIER & Co. 164 WILLIAM-STREET.
BOSTON:—128 FEDERAL-STREET.
MONTREAL, C. E:
CORNER OF ST. FRANCIS XAVIER AND NOTRE-DAME STREETS.
1852.

Entered according to Act of Congress in the year 1852,
BY D. & J. SADLIER & CO.
In the Clerk's Office of the District Court of the United States, for the Southern District of New York.

Stereotyped by VINCENT L. DILL,
128 Fulton-street, N. Y.

CONTENTS.

	PAGE.
PREFACE,	v
THE CHURCH AGAINST NO-CHURCH,	1
THE EPISCOPAL OBSERVER VERSUS THE CHURCH,	69
THORNWELL'S ANSWER TO DR. LYNCH, (April, 1848.)	100
THORNWELL'S ANSWER TO DR. LYNCH, (October, 1848.)	168
PROTESTANTISM ENDS IN TRANSCENDENTALISM,	209
PROTESTANTISM IN A NUTSHELL,	234
AUTHORITY AND LIBERTY,	262
POLITICAL CONSTITUTIONS,	293
WAR AND LOYALTY,	321
THE HIGHER LAW,	349
CATHOLICITY NECESSARY TO SUSTAIN POPULAR LIBERTY,	368
LEGITIMACY AND REVOLUTIONISM,	386
NATIVE AMERICANISM,	420
LABOR AND ASSOCIATION,	444
SOCIALISM AND THE CHURCH,	479

PREFACE.

The following essays and reviews are republished from *Brownson's Quarterly Review*. They have been subjected to a rigid revision, but are reproduced as originally published, excepting a few verbal corrections, the suppression of a few superfluous sentences, and the omission of some paragraphs which have lost their interest.

It is very possible that in selecting these articles for republication, I have not chosen those which the student of theology or philosophy would have recommended, nor even those which I myself regard as the least unworthy of my writings during the past seven or eight years; but essays of a somewhat abstruse and metaphysical nature, though they may be tolerated in a periodical where they appear along with others of a less unpopular cast, will hardly find in these times readers if published in a volume by themselves. I have selected such articles as have seemed to me best adapted to the tastes of the general reader, and the most likely to be useful to the public at large, whether Catholic or Protestant.

The reader must not expect too much from these articles, and must be content to take them for what they are,—simply articles originally written for a Quarterly Review. They are by no means separate and complete treatises on the several topics they discuss. But, if read in connection, in the order in which I have arranged them, they may, perhaps, be found to give a tolerably full view of the argument for the Church and against Protestantism, of the origin and constitution of Government, the principles of Authority and Liberty, the sacredness of Law, the duty of Loyalty, and the madness and danger of modern Socialism.

If any one looks over this volume for something new, original, or striking he will, most likely, be disappointed. I have not labored to present novel or startling speculations on theology, philosophy, ethics, or politics, but simply to ascertain the principles and doctrines of the Church of God, and to apply them to the great practical questions of the day. My aim has been to bring up anew the old and too often forgotten truth, not to bring out a novel theory. From first to last I think and write as a man many centuries behind his age.

The articles before being printed in the Quarterly Review were submitted to the revision of a competent theologian, and I have no reason to suppose that they contain anything not in accordance with Catholic faith and morals; but they are as a matter of course republished with submission to the proper authority, and I shall be most happy to correct any error of any sort they may contain the moment it is brought authoritatively to my notice. It is not my province to teach; all that I am free to do is to reproduce with scrupulous fidelity what I am taught.

Religion is for me the supreme law; it governs my politics, not my politics it. I never suffer myself to inquire whether such or such a religion favors or not such or such a political order; for if there is a conflict the political must yield to the religious. I therefore have not labored to show that the Church is favorable or unfavorable to monarchy, to aristocracy, or to democracy. I do not find that she erects any particular form of Government into an article of faith,—the monarchical no more than the democratic, the democratic no more than the monarchical. Any one of these particular forms may be legal government, and when and where it is the good Catholic is bound to support it, and forbidden to conspire to subvert it. The republican order is the legal order here, and I owe it civil obedience. I am the citizen of a republic, and therefore a republican citizen; I am a Catholic, therefore a loyal citizen, and no radical or revolutionist, either for my own country or any other.

My Catholic friends, who have been frequently disturbed by hearing it alleged that Catholicity is anti-republican and incompatible with popular institutions, will find no direct attempt to refute so silly, nay, so absurd an objection. I respect my religion, and even the great body of my own countrymen, too much to undertake to do that. But they will find that I have attempted, not unsuccessfully perhaps, to prove that without the Catholic religion it is impossible permanently to sustain popular institutions, or to secure their free and salutary operations. Indeed no form of government can be secure or operate well without the Church. Without Catholicity you can have, in principle at least, only despotism or anarchy. All that our countrymen find in our institutions has been adopted from England, and inherited from Catholic ancestors.

I seldom throw a sop to Cerberus. I have made no attempt to propitiate popular opinion by pandering to popular prejudice. I was not born to be a courtier, either of king or people. I seek to enlighten public opinion, not to echo it; and I always say, in a plain, straight forward way, what I am convinced ought to be said, leaving popularity or unpopularity to look out for itself. But if my language is free, bold, and sometimes severe, I would fain hope that it is never inconsiderate, rash, or gratuitously offensive.

I shall be found to have seldom indulged in frothy declamations about liberty, the rights of man, and the dignity of human nature. There are enough others to do that. I assert my liberty in my practice; I exercise my rights as a man, and I aim to show my respect for the dignity of human nature in my deportment. Liberty is, no doubt, threatened in this country, but the danger comes chiefly from the side of license, and is best averted, not by common place declamations for the largest liberty, but by asserting and maintaining the supremacy of Law.

I have shown no sympathy with the various classes of fanatics with which the country teems,—philanthropists, reformers, as they call themselves. They have become as troublesome as the frogs of Egypt, and are far more dangerous. They strike at the root of all individual liberty and manly independence of character, and are doing their best to revive the absurd and despotic legislation of the early Colonial times of New England. Of Christian Charity, that supernatural virtue which loves God supremely and its neighbor as itself for God's sake, we cannot have too much; but of the whimpering sentiment of philanthropy, which an unbelieving age substitutes for it, and which is the love of all men in general and the hatred of every man in particular, unless a criminal, we cannot have too little. Charity redeems the world, and gives us a heaven on earth; philanthropy effects no good, and tramples down more good by the way in going to its object, than it could possibly effect in accomplishing it.

Whatever the imperfections of these articles, and

no one can be more sensible of their imperfections than I am, there is this to be said in their favor, that they are the production of no youthful aspirant seeking notoriety by paradox and excentricity, nor of an old man soured by disappointment, and seeking to vent his spite upon an unoffending world. I have lived in the world, and shared its vicissitudes, but I have no wrongs to complain of, no sense of injustice rankling in my bosom. I have no mortified ambition, and have attained to more than in the most ardent dreams of my youth I ever aspired to. I am contented with my lot in the world, and have no desire to change it. Conviction, not desperation, led me into the Church, and I have found a thousand times more than I expected. It is true, in my youth and early manhood I held and published views very different from those set forth in this volume, and this fact will have its weight against whatever I may now say. But it is no crime to grow wiser with years, and to profit by experience or by the grace of God. The deliberate convictions of a man of mature age are worth more than the crude speculations of impetuous and inexperienced youth. But there is nothing in these essays and reviews that rests on my personal authority; they are to be taken for what they are worth, without any reference to the much or little respect due to their author.

Much has been said first and last in the newspapers as to the frequent changes I have undergone, and I am usually sneered at as a weathercock in religion and politics. This seldom disturbs me, for I happen to know that most of the changes alleged are purely imaginary. I was born in a Protestant community, of Protestant parents, and was brought up, so far as I was brought up at all, a Presbyterian. At the age of twenty-one I passed from Prebyterianism to what is sometimes called Liberal Christianity, to which, I remained attached, at first under the form of Universalism, afterwards under that of Unitarianism, till the age of forty-one, when I had the happiness of being received into the Catholic Church. Here is the sum total of my religious changes. I no doubt experienced difficulties in defending the doctrines I professed, and I shifted my ground of defence more than once, but not the doctrines themselves.

I was during many years, no doubt, a radical and a socialist, but both after a fashion of my own. I held two sets of principles, the one set the same that I hold now, the other the set I have rejected. I supposed the two sets could be held consistently together, that there must be some way, though I never pretended to be able to discover it, of reconciling them with each other. Fifteen years' trial and experience convinced me to the contrary, and that I must choose which set I would retain, and which cast off. My natural tendency was always to conservatism, and democracy, in the sense I now reject it, I never held. In politics, I always advocated, as I advocate now, a limited government indeed, but a strong and efficient government. Here is the sum total of my political changes. I never acknowledged allegiance to any party. From 1838 to 1843, I acted with the Democratic party, because durring those years it contended for the public policy I approved; since then I have adhered to no party. No party as such ever had any right to count on me, and most likely none ever will have. I do not believe in the infallibility of political parties, and I always did and probably always shall hold myself free to support the men and measures of any party, or to oppose them, according to my own independent convictions of what is or is not for the common good of my country.

But after all, this is not a matter worth taking any notice of. I am not anxious to prove that I have always acted consistently, and have never changed my opinions. Charges may be alleged against me that are not true, but the public is not likely to believe anything worse of my life before I became a Catholic than I do myself. I was a Protestant, and had the virtues and the vices of Protestants, and probably was not much better nor much worse than the average of my class. I was, of course, all unworthy to be a Catholic, and in myself am now all unworthy of the confidence of Catholics. There is no question of that; and if the truth or falsity of my writings depended on my own merits or demerits, they would deserve not a moment's consideration. I have referred to the subject only as an act of justice to my Catholic friends, who have so generously given me their hearts. But I certainly had errors, gross and inexcusable errors, and I beg the public to accept this volume as a slight token of my sincere repentance, and of my earnest wish to do all in my power to atone for them.

I respectfully lay this humble volume at the feet of the Venerable Prelates and Clergy of the United States, not as worthy of their patronage, or even of their notice, but as a mark of filial reverence and submission, and of profound and lively gratitude for their kind encouragement, and generous and uniform support of my humble labors in the cause of Catholic truth.

I would also inscribe it to my Protestant countrymen. They will find in it many resons why I have ceased to be a Protestant, but none I hope, for believing that I have lost any of my former interest in them, or that their welfare here or hereafter is less dear to me than ever it was. My sympathies with my fellow men, which, perhaps, are livelier and deeper than some suppose, have been quickened and expanded, not deadened and contracted, by my conversion to Catholicity. I have said nothing in the following pages in wrath; I have spoken only in love.

Placing this volume, though all unworthy, with devout gratitude, and tender love, under the protection of Our Blessed Lady, as I do myself and all my labors and interests, I send it forth to the public, hoping that it may contain a fit word fitly spoken for some earnest mind struggling to emancipate itself from error, and to burst into " the glorious liberty of the children of God."

THE AUTHOR.

Mount Bellingham,
    Maunday Thursday, 1852.

ESSAYS AND REVIEWS.

THE CHURCH AGAINST NO-CHURCH.*

APRIL, 1845.

The Journal, the title of which we have here quoted, is the ably conducted organ of the American Unitarians. As a periodical, it is one in which we take no slight interest; for it is conducted by our personal friends, and through its pages, which were liberally opened to us, we were at one time accustomed to give circulation to our own crude speculations and pestilential heresies. We introduce it to our readers, however, not for the purpose of expressing any general opinion of its character, or the peculiar tenets of the denomination of which it is the organ; but solely for the purpose of using the article which appeared in the January number, headed *The Church*, as a text for some remarks in defence of the Church against No-Churchism, or the doctrine which admits the Church in name, but denies it in fact, so prevalent in our age and community.

All Protestant sects, just in proportion as they depart from Catholic unity, tend to No-Churchism; and the Unitarians, who

---

* The Christian Examiner and Religious Miscellany, January, 1845.— Art. VI. The Church.

are the Protestants of Protestants, and who afford us a practical exemplification of what Protestantism is and must be, when and where it has the sense, the honesty, or the courage to be consequent, have already reached this important point. They cannot be said, in the proper sense of the word, to believe in any church at all. They see clearly enough, that, if they once admit a church at all, in any sense in which it is distinguishable from no-church, they can neither justify the Reformers in seceding from the Catholic Church, nor themselves in remaining aliens from its communion. They have, therefore, the honesty and boldness to deny the Church altogether, and to admit in its place only a voluntary association of individuals for pious and religious purposes; in which sense it is on a par with a Bible, Missionary, Temperance, or Abolition society, with scarcely anything more holy in its objects, or more binding on its members.

The *Christian Examiner*, in the article we have referred to fully authorizes this statement; and though it by no means discards the sacred name of *Church*, it leaves us nothing venerable or worth contending for to be signified by it. The controversies, for the next few year, it thinks, will, not improbably, revolve around the question of the Church. "What, then," it asks, "is the Church? what is its authority? what its importance? what its true place among Christian ideas or influences?" These are the questions; and its purpose in the article under consideration is to offer a few remarks which may indicate a true answer to them, especially the last.

In answer to the question, What is the Church? the writer replies, "It is the whole company of believers, the uncounted and wide-spread congregation of all those who receive the Gospel as the law of lfe. It is coëxtensive with Christianity; it is the living Christianity of the time, be that more or less, be it expressed in one mode of worship or another, in one or another variety of internal discipline. The Church of Christ comprehends and is composed of all his followers."—pp. 78, 79.

The answer to the question, What is the importance of the Church? is not very clearly set forth. Perhaps this is a point on which the writer has not yet obtained clear and distinct views. It is, probably, one of those points on which "more light is to break forth." The *place* of the Church among Christian ideas and influences also is not very definitely determined; but it would appear that the sacred writers had two ideas,—for they were not, like our modern reformers, men of only one idea,—and these two ideas were, one the Church, the other the individual soul. We do not mean to say that the writer really intends to teach that the Church is an *idea*, for a "company of believers" can hardly be called an *idea*, nor can the individual soul; but he probably means to teach that the sacred writers had two ideas, or rather two points of view, from which they contemplated this company of believers,—the one collective, the other individual.

"They loved to collect—in idea—the members of Christ, *as they styled them*, under one idea, and present them in this relation of unity to their readers. Thus viewed, the Church became the *emblem* of Christian influences and Christian benefits. It expressed all Christ had lived for, or died for. He had loved it, and given himself for it. It was 'the pillar and ground of the truth.' It was the 'body' of which he was the head."—p. 79.

This unity, however, is purely ideal; that is, imaginary. The only unity really existing consists merely in the similar sentiments, hopes, and aims of the individual members. But

"There was another idea on which the Apostles insisted still more strenuously, that of the individual soul. They taught the importance of the individual soul. Around this, as the one object of interest, were gathered the revelations and commandments of the Gospel. Personal responsibleness—in view of privileges, duties, sins, temptations—was their great theme. They preached the Gospel to the soul in its individual exposure and want. It is the peculiarity of our religion, its vital peculiarity, that it makes the individual the object of its address, its immediate and its final action. Christianity divested of this distinction becomes powerless, and void of meaning. It contradicts and subverts itself."—*Ib.*

Here, then, are two ideas,—the idea of the *company*, and the idea of the *individual;* and the first idea is to be held subordinate to the second; which, we suppose, means that the end of Christianity is the redemption and sanctification of the individual soul, and that the Church is to be valued only in so far as it is a means to this end,—a doctrine which we do not recollect to have ever heard questioned. The *place* of the Church is, therefore, below the individual, and being only the effect of the operation of Christianity in the hearts of individuals, as the writer tells us farther on, its importance must consist solely in the reaction of the example of Christians on those not yet converted, and in the aid and encouragement union among professed Christians gives to one another in their strivings after the Christian life. This, as near as we can come at it, is the *Christian Examiner's* doctrine.

The writer throws in one or two remarks, in connexion with his general statement, to which we cannot assent. "It has been maintained," he says, " that the Church is the principal idea in the Gospel. It has been *generally* supposed that the individual exists for the Church. Ecclesiastical writers have contended, and the people have admitted, that the rights of the Church were stronger than the rights of the members, that the prosperity of the Church must be secured at the expense of the believer's peace and independence; that, in a word everything must be made to yield to the Church."—p. 80. The writer must have drawn on his imagination for his facts. Ecclesiastical writers have never contended, nor have the people admitted, any such thing. The doctors of the Church have always and uniformly taught that the Church exists for the individual, not the individual for the Church, and that she is to be submitted to solely as the means in the hands of God of redeeming and sanctifying the individual soul. This is wherefore Catholics so earnestly contend for the Church, so willingly obey her commands, and so cheerfully lay down their lives in her defence.

The question of a conflict of rights between the Church and the individual, which the *Christian Examiner* regards as *the* great question of the age, is no question at all; for there never is and never can be a conflict of rights. It has never been held by any one of any authority in the ecclesiastical world, that the *rights* of the Church are stronger than the *rights* of the members, and that the rights of the members must yield to those of the Church. Rights never yield; claims may yield, but not rights. Establish the fact that this or that is the right of the member, and the Church both respects and guaranties it; but where she has the right to teach and command, she does not come in conflict with individual rights by demanding submission, for there the individual has no rights. To hold him, within the province of the Church, to obedience, is only holding him to obedience to the rightful authority. When the law says to the individual, "Thou shalt not steal," it infringes no right; because the individual has not, and never had, any right to steal.

But passing over this, we may say, the *Christian Examiner* holds, that, in the usual sense of the term, our blessed Saviour founded no church; he merely taught the truth, and, by his teaching, life, sufferings, death, and resurrection, deposited in the minds and hearts of men certain great seminal principles of truth and goodness, to be by their own free thought and affections developed and matured. The Church is nothing but the mere effect of the development and growth of these principles. "It is but a consequence" of the effect of Christianity upon those who are "separately brought under its influence." These, taken collectively, are the Church. These organize themselves in one way or another, adopt for their social regulation and mutual progress such forms of worship or internal discipline as are suggested by the measure of Christian truth and virtue realized in their hearts. This is all the church there is. If you ask, What is its authority? the answer is, "A fiction, a fiction which has cheated millions and ruined multitudes, but a fiction still." —p. 83. This, in brief, is the church theory of *Liberal* Christians, in fact, the theory virtually adopted by the great body of the Protestant world, and the only theory a consistent Protestant can adopt, if not even more than he can consistently adopt.

The insufficiency of this theory it is our purpose in the following essay to point out, by showing that with it alone it is impossible to elicit an act of faith. We shall begin what we have to offer by defining what it is we mean by the Church, and what are the precise questions at issue between us and No-Churchmen. We do this, because the *Christian Examiner* and its associates do not seem to have any clear or definite notions of what it is we contend for, when we contend for the authority, infallibility, and indefectibility of the Church, or what it is of which we really predicate these important attributes.

The word *church*, it is well known, is used in a variety of senses. The Greek ἐκκλησία, *ecclesia*, rendered by the word *church*, taken in a general way, means an assembly, or congregation, whether good or bad, for one purpose or another; but is for the most part taken in the Scriptures and the Fathers in a good sense, for the Church of Christ. The English word *church*, said to be derived from Κύριος and οἶκος, *the Lord's house* would seem to designate primarily the place of worship; but as οἶκος, like our English word *house*, may mean the family as well as the dwelling or habitation, the word *church* may not improperly be used to designate the Lord's family, the worshippers as well as the place of worship; in which sense it is a sufficiently accurate translation of the Greek ἐκκλησία, as generally used by ecclesiastical writers.

1. By the Church we understand, then, when taken in its widest sense, without any limitation of space or time, the whole of the Lord's family, the whole congregation of the faithful, united in the true worship of God under Christ the head. In this sense it comprehends the faithful of the Old Testament,—not only those belonging to the Synagogue, but also those out of it, as Job, Melchisedech, &c.,—the blest, even the angels, in heaven, the suffering in purgatory, and those on the way. As

comprehending the blest in heaven, it is called the Church Triumphant; the souls in purgatory, the Church Suffering; believers on the way, the Church Militant; not that these are three different Churches, but different parts, or rather states, of one and the same Church. But with the Church in this comprehensive sense we have in our present dscussion nothing to do. The question obviously turns on the Church Militant.

2. The Church Militant is defined by Catholic writers to be "The society of the faithful, baptized in the profession of the same faith, united in the participation of the same sacraments, and in the same worship, under one head, Christ in heaven, and his Vicar, the Sovereign Pontiff, on earth." But even this is too comprehensive for our present purpose,—to indicate at once the precise points in the controversy between us and No-Churchmen.

3. We must distinguish, in the Church Militant, between the *Ecclesia credens*, the congregation of the faithful, and the *Ecclesia docens*, or congregation of pastors and teachers.

The Church, as the simple congregation of believers, taken exclusively as *believers*, is not a visible organization, nor an authoritative or an infallible body. On this point we have no controversy with the *Christian Examiner*; for we are no Congregationalists, and by no means disposed to maintain that the supreme authority in the Church, under Christ, is vested in the body of the faithful. The authority of the Church in this sense we cheerfully admit is "a fiction," "a mischievous fiction," as the history of Protestantism for these three hundred years of its existence sufficiently establishes.

When we contend for the Church as a visible, authoritative, infallible, and indefectible body or corporation, we take the word *church* in a restricted sense, to mean simply the body of pastors and teachers, or, in other words, the bishops in communion with their chief. We mean what Protestants would, perhaps, better understand by the word *ministry* than by the word *church*,—although this word *ministry* is far from being exact, as it designates functions rather than functionaries, and, when used to designate functionaries, includes the several orders of the Christian priesthood,—not merely the bishops or pastors, who alone, according to the Catholic view, constitute the *Ecclesia docens*. Nevertheless, to avoid the confusion the word *church* is apt to generate in Protestant minds, we shall sometimes use it, merely premising that we use it to express only the body of pastors and teachers, by whom we understand exclusively the bishops, in communion with their chief, the Pope.

Now, the question between us and No-Churchmen turns precisely on this *Ecclesia docens*. Has our blessed Saviour established a body of teachers for his Church, that is, for the congregation of the faithful? Has he given them authority to teach and govern? Has he given to this body the promise of infallibility and indefectibility? If so, which of the pretended Christian ministries now extant is this body? These are the questions between us and No-Churchmen, and they cover the whole ground in controversy. There is now no mistaking the points to be discussed.

I. We take it for granted that the writer in the *Christian Examiner* admits, or intends to admit, the divine origin and authority of the Christian religion, and that the name of Jesus is the only name "given under heaven among men whereby we must be saved." We shall take it for granted that he holds the Christian religion to be, not merely preferable to all other religions or pretended religions, but the only true religion and way of salvation. We are bound to do so, for. he is a Doctor of Divinity, a professedly Christian pastor of a professedly Christian congregation, and it would be discourteous on our part to reason with him as we would with a Jew, Pagan, Mahometan, or Infidel. We are bound to assume that he holds, or at least intends to hold, that the Gospel of our Lord Jesus Christ is the only law of life, without obedience to which no one can be saved; and, since he makes Christianity and the Church coextensive, that out of the pale of the Church *as he defines it*, there is no salvation. The Church, he says, comprehends and is composed of all the followers of Christ. No one, then, who is not in the Church is a follower of Christ. If the Gospel of Christ be the only law of life, no one not a follower of Christ can be saved. Consequently, no one not a member of the Church of Christ can be saved.

To deny this is to reject Christianity altogether, or to fall into complete indifferency. If men can be saved, or be acceptable to their Maker, in one religion as well as in another, wherein is one preferable to another? If the Christian revelation was not necessary to our salvation, why was it given us, and why are we called upon to believe and obey it? why did God send his only begotten Son to make it, and why was it declared to be of such inestimable value to us? If Jesus Christ taught that salvation is attainable in all religions, or in any religion but his own, why were the Apostles so enraptured with the Gospel, and why did they make such painful sacrifices for its promulgation? If they had not been taught to regard it as the only way of salvation, their conduct is unaccountable; and if it be not the only way of salvation, they and their Master can be regarded only as a company of deluded fanatics, whose labors, sacrifices, and cruel deaths may indeed excite our pity, but cannot command our respect. We shall presume the writer in the *Christian Examiner* sees all this as well as we, and therefore shall presume that he holds with us, that all mankind are bound to worship God, that there is but one true way of worshipping God, and therefore but one true religion, and that this true religion is the Christian religion. He who does not admit this much can by no allowable stretch of courtesy be called a Christian. This premised, we proceed.

In order to be saved, to enter into life, or to become acceptable to God, one must be a Christian. To be a Christian, one must be a *believer*. No one is a Christian who is not a follower of Christ. Every follower of Christ, according to the *Christian Examiner*, is a member of the Church of Christ. But, according to the same authority, the Church is a company of *believers*. Therefore a Christian must be a believer. He who is a believer is a believer because he believes something. Therefore, in order to be a Christian, it is necessary to believe something.

The *Christian Examiner* must admit this conclusion; yet some Unitarians have the appearance of denying it. A short time since, we read an article in a Unitarian newspaper, written by a distinguished Unitarian clergyman, in which the writer maintains, that, although faith is indispensable to the Christian character, belief is not; yet he fails to define what that faith is which excludes or does not include belief. The late Dr. Channing, in his *Discourse on the Church*, objects to all forms, creeds, and churches, and declares that the essence of all religion is in supreme love to God and universal justice and charity towards our neighbour. Yet we presume he wishes this fact, to wit, that this is the essence of all religion, should be assented to both by the will and the understanding. But this is not a fact of science, evident in and of itself. It depends on other facts which are matters of belief, and therefore must itself be an object of belief. Not a few Unitarian clergymen of our acquaintance understand by faith *trust* or *confidence* (*fiducia*), and contend, that, when we are commanded to *believe* in Christ, in God, &c., the meaning is, that we should *trust* or *confide* in him. To believe in the Son is to confide in him as the Son of God. But I cannot confide in him as the Son of God, unless I believe that he is the Son of God; I cannot confide in God, unless I believe that he is, and that he is the protector of them that trust him. Where there is no belief, there is and can be no confidence. Confidence always presupposes faith; for where there is no belief that the trust reposed will be responded to, there is no trust; and the fact, that the one trusted will preserve and not betray the trust, is necessarily a matter of faith, of belief, not of knowledge. Faith begets confidence, but is not it; confidence is the effect or concomitant of faith, but can never exist without it. So, however these may seem to deny the necessity of belief, they all in reality imply it, presuppose it.

Moreover, all Unitarians hold, that, to be a Christian, one

must be a follower of Christ. Their radical conception of Christ is that of a teacher, of a person specially raised up and commissioned by Almighty God to teach, and to teach the truth. But one cannot be said to be the follower of a teacher, unless he believes what the teacher teaches. Therefore, to be a Christian, one must be a believer.

This, again, is evident from the Holy Scriptures. "For without faith," says the blessed Apostle Paul, "it is impossible to please God." Heb. xi. 6. So our blessed Saviour: "He that believeth and is baptized shall be saved; but he that believeth not shall be condemned." St. Mark, xvi. 16. "He that believeth in the Son hath eternal life; but he that believeth not the Son shall not see life; but the wrath of God abideth on him." St. John, iii. 36. This is sufficient to establish our first position, namely, that, in order to be a Christian, it is necessary to be a believer, that is, to believe *somewhat*.

This *somewhat*, which it is necessary to believe, is not falsehood, but truth. What we are required to believe is that for not believing which we shall be condemned. But God is a God of truth, nay, truth itself, and it is repugnant to reason to assume that he will condemn us for not believing falsehood. The belief demanded is also essential to our salvation; for it is said, " He that believeth not shall be condemned." But it is equally repugnant to reason to maintain that a God of truth, who is truth, can make belief in falsehood essential to salvation. Therefore the belief demanded, as to its object, is truth, not falsehood.

The truth we are required to believe is the revelation which Almighty God has made us through his Son, Jesus Christ, or in other words, the truth which Jesus Christ taught or revealed. The belief in question is *Christian* belief, that which makes one a Christian believer, a follower of Jesus, a member of the " uncounted and wide-spread congregation of all those who receive the Gospel as the law of life." But one can be a *Christian* believer only by believing Christian truth; and Christian truth can be no other truth, if different truths there be, than that taught by Jesus Christ. Jesus Christ, according to the confession of Unitarians themselves, was a teacher of truth, and a teacher of nothing but truth. Then all he taught was truth. Therefore, to be truly a Christian believer, truly a follower of Christ, it is necessary to believe, explicitly or implicitly, *all* the truth he taught. Hence, the commission to the Apostles was to teach all nations, and to teach them to observe *all things whatsoever* their Master had commanded them. St. Matt. xxviii. 20.

The truth which Jesus Christ taught or revealed appertains, in part, at least, to the *supernatural* order. By the supernatural order we understand the order above nature, that is, above the order of creation. All creatures, whether brute matter, vegetables, animals, men, or angels, are in God, and without him could neither be, live, nor move. But God has created them all "after their kinds," and each with a specific nature. What is included in this nature, or promised by it, although having its origin and first motion in God, is what is meant by *natural*. Supernatural is something above this, and superadded. God transcends nature, and is supernatural; but regarded solely as the author, upholder, and governor of nature, he is natural, and hence the knowledge of him as such is always termed *natural theology*. But as the author of grace, he is strictly supernatural; because grace, though having the same origin, is above the order of creation, is not included in it, nor promised by it. It is, so to speak, an excess of the Divine Fulness not exhausted in creation, but reserved to be superadded to it according to the Divine will and pleasure. Thus God may be said to be both natural and supernatural. As natural, that is, as the author, sustainer, and governor of nature, he is naturally intelligible, according to what Saint Paul tells us, Rom. i. 20. *Invisibilia enim ipsius, a creatura mundi, per ea quæ facta sunt intellecta, conspiciuntur; sempiterna quoque ejus virtus, et divinitas:* "For the invisible things of God, even his eternal power and divinity, from the creation of the world, are clearly seen, being understood by the things that are made." But as supernatural, that is, as the author of grace, he is not naturally intelligible, and can be known only as supernaturally revealed. The fact that he is the author of grace, or that there is grace, is not a fact of natural reason, or intrinsically evident to natural reason. It, therefore, is not and cannot be a matter of science, but must be a matter of faith. Hence, the Apostle says again, Heb. xi. 6, *Credere enim, oportet accedentem ad Deum quia est, et inquirentibus se remunerator sit:* " He that cometh to God must *believe* that he is, and that he is a rewarder of them that seek him." That he is as author of nature, we *know*, but that he is as author of grace, or that he is a rewarder of them that seek him, we *believe*.

Now, the revelation of Jesus Christ is preëminently the revelation of God as the author and dispenser of grace, and therefore preëminently the revelation of the supernatural. " The law was given by Moses, but grace and truth by Jesus Christ." St. John, i. 17. Hence, to believe the truth and all the truth which Jesus Christ taught is to believe truth pertaining to the supernatural order.

Unitarians, it is true, eliminate from the Gospel a great part of the mysteries, and reduce it, so to speak, to a mere republication of the law of nature; their theology is in the main natural theology; their faith in God is in him as the author of nature, and the immortality they look for is merely a natural immortality; but the sounder part of them, do, nevertheless, to some extent, admit that Jesus Christ revealed truths not naturally intelligible, and which pertain to the supernatural order. They admit that the Gospel is itself, in some sense, a revelation of grace, and therefore a revelation of the supernatural. They also admit the necesssity, in order to be Christian believers, of believing in several particular things which pertain to the supernatural order. Among these we may instance remission of sins, the resurrection of the dead, and final beatitude, or the heavenly reward. We are not aware that they question these; and we are sure no one can question them without losing all right to the Christian name. But these all pertain to the supernatural order.

Remission of sin, whatever else it may mean, means at least, remission of the penalty which God has annexed to transgression. The penalty is annexed by God either as author and sovereign of nature, or as supernatural. If by God as supernatural, the penalty must itself be supernatural; and therefore he who believes in its remission must believe in the supernatural, for no man can believe in the remission of a penalty which he does not believe to have been annexed. If God annexes the penalty as author and sovereign of nature, its *remission* must be supernatural. To assume that the order of nature remits it, is to assume nature to be in contradiction with herself, or to deny the remission by denying the existence of any penalty to remit. Where the remission begins, there ends the penalty. If the remission be in the order of nature, then the order of nature imposes no penalty beyond the point where the remission begins; and then there is no remission, for nothing is remitted. To say that God as author and sovereign of nature remits what in the same character he imposes is to assume that he imposes no penalty that goes farther than the commencement of the remission. Then, in fact, no remission. The penalty, in this case, would be exhausted, not remitted. Remission, then, must be by God as supernatural, not as natural; not as author and sovereign of nature, but as author and dispenser of grace. Remission is necessarily an act of grace, and therefore supernatural. Then, whatever, view be taken of the penalty itself, he who believes in its remission must believe in the supernatural order.

So of the resurrection of the dead. We do not mean to say that by natural reason we cannot demonstrate a future continued existence, but that a fact answering to the term *resurrection* is naturally neither cognoscible nor demonstrable. Resurrection means rising again, and evidently pertains, not to the soul, which never dies, but to the body, and implies that the same body which died is raised; for if not, it would not be a *re*-surrection, but a simple *surrection*, or perhaps new creation. Now, by no natural light we possess can we come to the knowledge of the fact that our bodies shall rise again. Yet we are undeniably taught in the Gospel that such is the fact.

Moreover, the Apostle Paul tells us that the body shall not only be raised, but it shall be raised in a supernatural condition. "It is sown a natural body, it is raised a spiritual body." It is to be made like to our blessed Saviour's glorious body. But a glorified body does not pertain to the order of nature; because the natural body it is said, is to be "*made* like to the body of his glory," which implies that it must be changed from its natural to a supernatural condition, before it is a glorified body. But by what natural powers we possess do we arrive at the fact that there are glorified bodies, much more, that our vile bodies shall be changed into glorified bodies? And by what process of reasoning, not dependent for its *data* on the revelation, can we, now we are told it shall be so, prove that it will be so?

So, again, as to our final destiny. The truth we are to believe pertains to the supernatural order. St. Peter says, "By whom (Jesus Christ) he hath given us very great and precious promises, that by these you may be made partakers of the divine nature,"—*efficiamini diviniæ consortes naturæ*. 2 Pet. i. 4. That this is to partake of the divine nature in a supernatural sense, and not in the sense in which we naturally partake of it, in being made to the image and likeness of God, is evident from the fact that the Apostle calls it a *gift*, and says it is that which is *promised*. What pertains to nature is not a *gift*, and what is already possessed cannot be said to be something *promised*. Therefore the participation of the divine nature in question is not a natural, but a supernatural, participation. The blessed Apostle John tells us, "We are now the sons of God, and it hath not yet appeared what we shall be. We know that when he shall appear we shall be like him, because we shall see him as he is." 1 John iii. 2. Here it is asserted that we are to be something more than sons of God in the sense we now are; for we know not, even being sons of God, what we shall be. But this we do know, that when he shall appear we shall be *like him*. But this likeness is supernatural, not that to which we were created; otherwise it would be a likeness *possessed*, not *to be* possessed. How by the light of nature learn this fact, that we are to become like God, partakers of the divine nature, in a supernatural sense? Again, the blessed Apostle in the same passage says, "We shall be like him, because we shall see him as he is." So St. Paul, 1 Cor. xiii. 12: "Now we see through a glass, darkly, but then face to face; now I know in part, but then I shall know even as I am known." The fact here asserted, to wit, that our future destiny is the beatific vision, that is, to see God as he is, and to know him even as we ourselves are known, is not naturally intelligible, nor demonstrable by natural reason. Moreover, to see God as he is exceeds our nature; for naturally we cannot see God as he is, that is, as he is in himself. The destiny, then, which the Gospel reveals for them that love the Lord is supernatural. For "It is written, The eye hath not seen, ear heard, neither hath it entered into the heart of man, what things God hath prepared for them that love him." 1 Cor. ii. 9. Therefore, to believe the Gospel, or the truth which Jesus Christ taught, it is necessary to believe not only truth supernaturally communicated, but truth pertaining to the supernatural order. But we have already proved that it is necessary to salvation to believe *the* truth and *all* the truth which Jesus taught. Therefore it is necessary to believe truth which pertains to the supernatural order.

The result thus far is, that, in order to be Christians, to be saved, to enter into life, to secure the rewards of heaven, it is necessary to believe the truth which Jesus Christ taught, and that we cannot believe this without believing in that which is supernatural, and supernatural both as to the mode of communication and as to the matter communicated. The truth which Jesus Christ taught is, in general terms, the Gospel, or Christian revelation; and the Christian revelation is a supernatural revelation, and, in part at least, a revelation of the supernatural. This revelation and its contents we must believe, or resign our pretensions to the Christian name. To believe this revelation and its contents is not, we admit, all that is requisite to the Christian character—far from it; for there remain beside, faith, hope and charity, and the greatest is charity. Moreover, faith alone is insufficient to justify us in the sight of God; for faith without works is dead, and therefore inoperative. Nevertheless, faith is indispensable. "For without faith it is impossible to please God," and "He that believeth not shall be condemned." This much we conceive we have established; and this much, we presume, the *Christian Examiner* will concede.

II. Faith or belief, as distinguished from knowledge and science, rests on authority extrinsic both to the believer and the matter believed. In it there is always assent to something proposed *ab extra*. That the sun is now shining, I know by my own senses; it is therefore a fact of knowledge; that the three angles of a triangle are equal to two right angles, which I know not intuitively, but discursively, is a fact of science. The first I know immediately; the second I can demonstrate from what it contains in itself. But in belief the case is different. The matter assented to is neither intuitively certain, nor intrinsically evident. I am told there is such a city as Rome, which I have never seen. Having myself never seen Rome, I have no intuitive evidence that there is such a city. The proposition that there is such a city is not intrinsically evident,—contains nothing in itself from which I can demonstrate its truth. Its truth, then, can be established to me only by evidence extrinsic both to myself and to the proposition, that is, by TESTIMONY. That there is a God is a fact of knowledge; for if it be said that we do not know it intuitively, we know it at least discursively, since from the creation of the world, even the invisible things of God are clearly seen, being understood by the things that are made, as says St. Paul, Rom. i. 20. But that God has destined them that love him to the beatific vision is not a fact of knowledge, or of science; for it is neither intuitively certain, nor internally demonstrable. It may be true; but whether so or not can be determined only by testimony, that is, evidence extrinsic both to the proposition and to myself. Hence St. Paul says, Heb. xi. 1, "Faith is the substance of things hoped for, the evidence of things that appear not;" and St. Augustine, "Faith is to believe what you see not."—Tract 40 in Joan.

There may be matters contained in the Christian revelation which are matters of knowledge or of science, but we are concerned with it now only so far as it is a matter of faith. As a matter of faith, its truth rests solely on extrinsic evidence, or testimony. We cannot, then, as reasonable beings, believe it, unless we have some extrinsic authority competent to vouch for its truth, or some witness whose testimony is credible. But as an object of faith, the Christian revelation, in part at least, is a revelation of the supernatural. Now, this which is supernatural cannot be adequately witnessed to or vouched for by any natural witness or authority. No witness is competent to testify to that which he does not or cannot himself know, either intuitively or discursively. But no natural being, how high so ever in the scale of being he may be exalted, can know either intuitively or discursively the truth of that which, as to its matter, is supernatural. The only adequate authority for the supernatural is the supernatural itself, that is, God. For though angels or divinely inspired men may declare the supernatural to us, yet they themselves are not witnesses to its intrinsic truth, and have no ground for believing its truth but the veracity of God revealing it to them. They may be competent witnesses to the fact of the revelation, but not to the truth of the matter revealed. The authority or ground for believing the supernatural matter revealed is, then, the veracity of God, and we cannot reasonably or prudently believe any proposition involving the supernatural on other authority. We have no sufficient ground for faith in such matters, unless we have the clear, express, testimony of God himself. But the testimony of God is sufficient for any proposition, *in case we have it;* because enough is *clearly seen* of God, from the creation of the world, being understood by the things that are made, to establish on a scientific basis the fact that he can neither deceive or be deceived; for we can demonstrate scientifically, from principles furnished by the light of natural reason, that God is infinitely wise and good, and no being infinitely wise and good can deceive or be deceived. God is the first truth—*prima veritas*—in being, in knowing, and in speaking, and therefore whatever he declares to be true must necessarily and infallibly be true. Nothing, then, is more reasonable than to believe God on his word or simple veracity; for it is no more than to believe that infinite and perfect truth, truth itself, cannot lie. Whatever God has revealed must be true. Even the *Christian Exminer* would admit the doctrine of the Trinity, if it were proved to be a doctrine of Divine revelation. The witness, ground, or authority for believing the supernatural is the veracity of God, and this all will admit to be sufficient, if we have it; and none will admit, if they understand themselves, that a lower authority is sufficient.

But, although the veracity of God is the ground or authority on which we assent to the matter revealed, yet we cannot believe without sufficient evidence of the fact of revelation, or, in other words, without a witness competent to testify to the fact that God has actually revealed the matter in question,—made the particular revelation to which assent is demanded. The *Christian Examiner* is Unitarian, but it will tell us that it ought to believe the doctrine of the Trinity, if God has revealed it. Yet it demands, very properly, evidence of the fact that God has revealed it or declared its truth. Reasonable or a well grounded belief in the supernatural, then, requires two witnesses, two vouchers; one to the truth of the matter revealed, which is the veracity of God revealing it; the other to the fact of the revelation, or that the matter in question has actually been divinely revealed.

The revelation is made to intelligent beings, and must therefore consist in intelligible propositions. We do not mean that the truths revealed should be comprehensible; for every supernatural truth, as to its matter, must be wholly incomprehensible to natural reason; but that the propositions to be believed must be intelligible. What is present to the mind, in believing the revelation, are these propositions, which convey the truth, but in an obscure manner, to the understanding. If we should mistake the propositions actually contained in God's revelation, or substitute others therefor, since it is only through them that we arrive at the matter revealed, we should not believe the revelation which God has actually made, but something else, and something else for which we cannot plead the veracity of God, and therefore something for which we have no solid ground of faith. Suppose you adduce a book which you say contains the revelation God has made, and suppose you bring ample vouchers for the fact that it really does contain such revelation. In this case I should have sufficient ground for believing the book to contain the word of God; but before I should believe the word of God itself, I must believe the contents of the book in their *genuine sense*. I must have, then, some authority, extrinsic or intrinsic, competent to declare what is this genuine sense. What I believe is what is present to my mind when I believe. What is present to my mind is the interpretation or meaning I give to God's word. If this interpretation or meaning be not the *genuine sense*, I do not, as we have said, believe God's word, but something else. Faith in the supernatural requires, then, in addition to the witness that vouches for the fact that God has made the revelation, an interpreter competent to declare the true meaning of the revelation.

The faith we are required to have is equally required of all men. It is said, *qui non credideret*,—that is, any one, without any limitation, who believeth not, shall be condemned. Then there must be no limitation of the essential conditions of faith. Then the witness for the faith, and the interpreter of God's word, must be present in all nations, and subsist through all ages, —Catholic in space and time. We who live in this country at the present day need them just as much and in the same sense as the Jews did in the age of the Apostles.

The witness to the fact of the revelation, and the interpreter of the word, must not only subsist through all ages and nations, but must be *unmistakable;* and unmistakable not only by a few philosophers, scholars, and men of parts and leisure, but by the poor, the busy, the weak, the ignorant, the illiterate; for all these are equally commanded to believe, and have a right to have a solid ground of belief, which they cannot have if they may, with ordinary prudence, mistake the true witnessand interpreter, and call in a false witness and a misinterpreter.

The witness and interpreter must be infallible; for, if fallible, it may call that God's word which is not his word, and assign a meaning to God's word itself which is not the genuine meaning. We may, then, be deceived, and think we are believing God's word when we are not. But where there is a possibility of deception, there is room for doubt, and where there is room for doubt, there is no faith; for the property of faith is to exclude doubt. The Apostle says, "I know in whom I believe, and am certain," and whoever cannot say as much has not yet elicited an act of faith. Faith is a theological virtue, which consists in believing, explicitly or implicitly, all the truths God has revealed, without doubting, on the veracity of God alone. It requires absolute certainty, objective as well as subjective. Where there is belief without sufficient objective, certainly the belief is not faith but mere opinion or persuasion. Mere subjective certainty, that is, an inward persuasion, even though it should exclude all actual doubt, would not be faith, unless warranted by evidence in which reason can detect no deficiency. It is a blind prejudice, and would vanish before the light of intelligence. A man may fancy that his head is set on wrong side before, and be so firmly persuaded of it that no reasoning can convince him to the contrary; but his internal persuasion is not faith. For faith is primarily, though not exclusively, an act of the understanding, and must be reasonable, and he who has it must have a solid reason to assign for it. The man has not faith, if he doubts, or may reasonably doubt; and he may reasonably doubt, if the evidence is not sufficient. He who has for his faith only the testimony of a fallible witness, that may both deceive and be deceived, has always a reasonable ground for doubt, and consequently no solid ground for faith. If he reasons at all on the testimony, if he opens his eyes at all to his liability to be deceived, he cannot, however earnestly he may try to believe, avoid doubting. Therefore, since, with a fallible witness, or fallible interpreter, we can never be sure that we are not mistaken, it necessarily follows, if we are to have faith at all, that we must have a witness and interpreter that cannot err, that is, infallible.

We sum up again by saying, that it is necessary to believe the truth Jesus Christ revealed, or, in other words, the Christian revelation; that to believe this is to believe truths which pertain to the supernatural order; and that, to have a solid ground for believing truths pertaining to the supernatural order, we must have, 1. The word or veracity of God; 2. A witness to the fact of revelation, and an interpreter of the genuine sense of what God has revealed, infallible and subsisting through all ages and nations, and, with ordinary prudence, unmistakable by even the simple and unlearned. The first the *Christian Examiner* will not deny us. We proceed to prove the second.

III. There must be such a witness and interpreter, or, in other words, some infallible means of determining what is the word of God, because God has made belief of his word the essential condition of salvation. We know from natural theology, that is, from what is evident to us of God by natural reason, that he is, that he is just, and that he would not be just, should he make faith the essential condition of salvation, and not provide the necessary conditions of faith. He has made faith the condition of salvation, as we have proved, and as the *Christian Examiner* must admit, unless it chooses to deny the Christian revelation altogether. But the infallible witness and interpreter alleged is a necessary condition of faith, as we have shown from the nature of faith itself. Therefore, God, since he is just and cannot belie himself, *has* provided us with the witness and interpreter required, or, what is the same thing, some infallible means of determining what is the word he commands us to believe.

There is, then, the witness and intepreter of God's word in question. Who or what is it? To this question four answers may be returned:—1. Reason; 2. The Bible; 3. Private Illumination: 4. The Apostolic Ministry, or the Church teaching.

1. Reason may be taken in two senses:—1. The intellective faculty, as distinguished from the sensitive faculty; 2. The discursive or reasoning faculty. In the first sense, it is the faculty of knowing intuitively, and is the principle of *knowledge*, in distinction from what is technically termed *science*. In this sense, reason, in order to answer our purpose, to serve as the witness and interpreter proved to be necessary, must be able either to know God intuitively, or to apprehend intuitively the intrinsic truth of his word. Reason must see God face to face, know intuitively that it is God who speaks; or it cannot testify, on its *own* knowledge, to the fact that the speaker alleged is God. But reason cannot see God thus face to face. We have and can have no intuitive knowledge of God in this sense. Reason cannot be the witness on the ground of its intuitive apprehension of God, nor can it be on the ground of its intuitive perception or apprehension of the intrinsic truth of the matter revealed. Our natural reason or power of knowing cannot extend beyond the bounds of nature. But the matter revealed, or the truths to be believed, are supernatural, and therefore transcend the reach of the natural intellect. If the natural intellect could attain to them, they would be, not supernatural, but natural. Moreover, if the intrinsic truth of the revelation could be apprehended, intuitively known, it would be, not a matter of faith, but of knowledge; for faith is, to believe what is not seen, *argumentum non apparentium*. Heb. xi. 1. But it is a matter of faith, as already proved, and therefore not of knowledge. Therefore reason cannot apprehend the intrinsic truth of the revelation, and from the intrinsic truth know it to have been divinely revealed. Therefore reason, as the simple intellective faculty, or power of intuition, cannot be the witness.

Reason, in the second sense, is discursive, the subjective principle of science, in distinction from intuitive knowledge,—the faculty of deducing conclusions from given premises. If the premises are true, the conclusions are valid. But reason cannot furnish its own premises. They must be *given* it; hence, they are called *data*. These *data* must be furnished either by intuition, or by faith. But in the case before us they can be furnished by neither;—not by intuition, as we have just proved; and not by faith, because faith is the matter to be determined.

Proof by reason, in the sense we now use the term, is called demonstration. The position assumed, when it is alleged that the discursive reason is the witness of the fact of revelation, is, that reason can find in the internal character of the revelation itself, or what purports to be a revelation, the *data* from which it can demonstrate that it is actually the word of God. But this is possible only on condition that reason, independently of all revelation, be in possession of so perfect a knowledge of God as to be able to say *a priori* what a revelation from God will and necessarily must be. But this is inadmissible; 1. Because it would imply that the revelation is intrinsically evident to natural reason, and therefore that it is an object of science and not of faith; and 2. Because the revelation is of God as supernatural, and reason can know God as supernatural, only through the medium of supernatural revelation itself. The knowledge which reason has of God prior to the revelation is simply what is contained in natural theology, that is, knowledge of God simply as author, sustainer, and sovereign of nature. From this it is, indeed, possible to obtain *data* from which we may conclude, within certain limits, what a supernatural revelation cannot be, but not what it must be. God, whether as author of nature, or as author and dispenser of grace, that is, as natural or as supernatural, intelligible or superintelligible, is one and the same being and therefore cannot in the one be in contradiction to what he is in the other. If, in what purports to be a revelation from him, we find that which contradicts what is clearly seen of him, from the creation of the world, through the things that are made, we havé the right to pronounce it, *a priori* not his revelation. But beyond this reason cannot go; for it is not lawful to reason from nature to grace, from the natural to the supernatural, from *data* furnished by natural science to supernatural revelation. Reason, then, has no *data* from which it can conclude what is the revelation. Therefore it cannot be the witness demanded.

Moreover, if reason knew enough of God, independently of the supernatural revelation, to be able, from the intrinsic character of the revelation, to pronounce on its genuineness, not only negatively, but affirmatively, it would know all of God the revelation itself can teach. The revelation would then be superfluous,—in fact, no revelation at all; and the question of its genuineness would be an idle question, not worth considering. To assume the competency of reason, as the witness, would then be to deny the necessity of the revelation and its value, which, in fact, is what all our Rationalists do, and probably wish to do.

But, in denying the competency of reason as the witness to the fact of the revelation, we do not deny the office of reason in determining whether a revelation has been made, nor that the fact of revelation is, can, and should be, made evident to natural reason. We merely deny that it is *intrinsically* evident. It is not *in*trinsically evident, but *ex*trinsically evident; not internally demonstrable, but externally provable. It can be proved not *by* reason, but *to* reason by testimony; and of the credibility of the testimony, reason may, and should judge.

Three things must always be kept distinct in the question of supernatural revelation:—1. The ground of faith in the truths revealed; 2. The authority on which we take the fact of revelation; 3. The credibility of this authority. The first, as we have seen, is the veracity of God, and is sufficient, because God is the ultimate truth in being, in knowing, and in speaking, and therefore can neither deceive nor be deceived. The second we are seeking, and it is not a witness to the truth of the matter revealed, but to the fact that God reveals it, and can be competent only on condition of being itself supernatural or supernaturally enlightened. The third is the crediblity of the witness to the fact of revelation, and must be evidenced to natural reason; or there will be an impassable gulf between reason and faith, and we can have no reason for our faith, and therefore no faith.

The fact of revelation, we shall show in its proper place, may be evidenced to natural reason through the credibility of the witness, and therefore, that faith is possible. But because reason is competent to judge of the credibility of the witness, we must not conclude that it is itself a competent witness to the fact of revelation. This, conceded, the first answer is inadmissible, for the fact of revelation is neither intuitive nor demonstrable.

2. The answer just dismissed is that of the Rationalists, and is, in one of its forms, substantially the one which we ourselves gave in all we preached and wrote on the subject while associated with the Unitarians. The second answer is the Protestant answer, and the one, if we understand him, adopted by the writer in the *Christian Examiner*. This assumes that the Bible is the witness; that is, the Bible interpreted by the private reason of the believer, availing himself of such aids, philological, critical, historical, &c., as may be within his reach. But this answer cannot be accepted, because, without an infallible authority independent of the Bible, it is impossible, 1. To settle the canon; 2. To establish the sufficiency of the Scriptures; 3. To determine their genuine sense.

The Bible can be adduced as the witness only in the character of an authentic record of the revelation actually made; for, according to its own confession, as we may find on examining it, it was not the original medium of the revelation itself. The revelation, according to the Bible itself, in great part at least, was in the first instance made orally, and orally published before it was committed to writing. This is especially true of the Christian revelation, in so far as distinguished from the Jewish. It was communicated orally to the Apostles, by our Lord, and by them orally to the public; and converts were made, and congregations of believers gathered, before one word of it was written. The writing was subsequent to the teaching and believing, and evidently, therefore, the primitive believers either believed without having any authority for believing, or had an authority for believing independent of written documents. To them what we term the Bible was not the witness. It, then, was not the original witness, or, as we have said, the original medium of the revelation. Its value, then, must consist entirely in the fact, that it faithfully records, in an authentic form, what was actually revealed. It is, then, only as a record that it can be adduced as evidence. But a record is no evidence till authenticated. It cannot authenticate itself; for, till authenticated, its testimony is inadmissible. It must be authenticated by some competent authority independent of itself. This authentication of the Bible as a record of the revelation made is what we call settling the canon.

Now, it is obvious, that, till the canon is settled, we have no authentic record, no Bible, to adduce. We may have a number of books bound up together, to which the printer has given the title of *The Bible;* but what we want is not the book called the Bible, but authentic records to which we may appeal as evidence; and if the book we call the Bible contains books which are not authentic records, or does not contain all that are, we cannot appeal to it as evidence; for we may, in the one case, take for revelation what is not revelation, and, in the other, leave out what is revelation. This is evident of itself. We must, then, settle the canon. But where is the authority to settle it?

The authority must be, 1. Independent of the Bible; 2. Infallible. But the advocates of the answer we are considering admit no infallible authority but that of the Bible itself. Therefore they have no authority by which to settle the canon, or to determine what is Bible or what is not Bible.

It will not do to say, the canon is all those books which have been received by the Church as canonical; because the advocates of this answer deny the authority of the Church, and stoutly contend that she may both deceive and be deceived. It will not do to appeal to tradition; for what vouches for the inerrancy of tradition? And what right have Protestants to appeal to tradition, whose authority they do not admit, and which they contend may err and does err on many and the most vital points? Nor will it do to adduce the Fathers; for they only establish what in their time was the tradition or belief of the Church, by no means the intrinsic truth of that tradition or belief. Where, then, is the authority for settling the canon?

There is no authority on Protestant principles, as is evident from the fact that Protestants have no canon. They all exclude from the canon established by the Church several books which the Church holds to be canonical. As to the remaining books, they dispute whether all are canonical or not. Luther rejects the Catholic Epistle of St. James, which he denominates "an epistle of straw," and also doubts the canonicity of several others. Mr. Andrews Norton, a learned and leading Unitarian, formerly a professor in the *Divinity School*, Cambridge, rejects pretty much the whole of the Old Testament; the Epistle to the Hebrews, the Epistles of James and Jude, the second of Peter, and the Apocalypse, in the New Testament; casts suspicion on the canonicity of all the Pauline Epistles, strikes out the first chapters of Matthew and Luke, and such portions of the remaining books as are demanded by the conveniences of his critical canons, or the exigencies of his dogmatic theology. Not a few of our Unitarians restrict the canon to the four Gospels. Several of the Germans strike from these the Gospel according to St. John; while Strauss, Baur, and Theodore Parker, regard the remaining Gospel narratives rather as a collection of anecdotes illustrating the notions of the early Christian believers, than as authentic histories of events which actually transpired; and the great body of Liberal Christians, who are the Protestants of Protestants, agree that the Bible is so loosely written, is so filled with metaphor and Oriental hyperbole, that no argument, especially no doctrine, can be safely built on single words, or even single sentences, however plain, positive, and uncontradicted, or unmodified by other portions of Scripture, their meaning may seem to be. It is evident from this statement of facts, that Protestants have no canon; that each private man is at liberty to settle the canon according to his own judgment or caprice; and therefore that they have no authentic record to adduce as evidence of the fact of revelation. They must agree among themselves what is Bible, what is inspired Scripture, and authenticate the record, before they can legitimately introduce it as an infallible witness.

But pass over the difficulty of settling the canon; suppose the canon to be settled according to the decision of the Church, and that, by an inconsistency which in the present case cannot be avoided, the authority of the Church to settle the canon is conceded; still there remains the question of the *Sufficiency* of the Scriptures. The record, however authentic it may be, can be evidence only for what is contained in it. If it does not contain the whole revelation, it is not evidence for the whole. If not evidence for the whole, it is not sufficient; for it is the *whole* revelation, not merely a part, to which the witness is needed to testify, since it is repugnant to the character of God to suppose that he should reveal any truth but for the purpose of having it believed.

That the Scriptures do contain the whole revelation is not to be presumed prior to proof; because they themselves testify that they are not, at least only in part, the original medium of the revelation. If the revelation had been, in the first instance, made by writing, and by writing only, then, if we had the entire *written* word, we should have the right to conclude that we had the whole *revealed* word. But since a part of the revelation, to say the least, was communicated orally, taught and believed before the writing was commenced, we cannot conclude from the possession of the entire written word the possession of the entire revealed word, unless we have full evidence that the whole revealed word has been written. The fact of the sufficiency of the Scriptures is not, then, to be presumed from the fact of their canonicity. It is a fact to be proved, not taken for granted.

But this fact cannot be proved by tradition, by the authority of the Church, or by the testimony of the Fathers; for these all, on Protestant principles, are fallible, and not to be depended upon; and, moreover, they all testify against the fact in question. It cannot be proved by reason; because reason takes cognizance not of the fact of revelation, but simply of the motives of credibility. It must be proved by an authority above reason, and, as already established, by an authority which cannot err. But the Bible is asserted to be the only inerrable authority. Therefore it must be proved from the Bible itself. But the Bible proves no such thing, for it nowhere professes to contain the whole revelation which has been made, but even indicates to the contrary. Therefore the sufficiency of the Scriptures cannot be proved, for the sufficiency of the Scriptures must mean that they are sufficient to teach not only the whole revelation of God, but the fact that they do teach the whole, since without this no one can know whether he has the faith God commands him to have, or not. But in failing to prove their sufficiency, they fail to prove this fact; therefore prove their own insufficiency.

It may be replied, that, though the Scriptures may not contain a full record of all that was revealed, they nevertheless contain all that is necessary to be believed in order to be saved. We reply, 1. That the command of God to us is not to believe the Bible or the written word, but the revelation which he has made; and therefore we are not to presume that we have the faith required, from the fact that we believe the whole written word, unless we have first established the fact that the written word is commensurate with the revealed word. 2. God, we know by natural reason, cannot reveal what he does not require to be believed; for the truth revealed while unbelieved, is as if unrevealed, and its revelation has no sufficient reason. But God cannot act without a sufficient reason. No sufficient reason for the revelation of truth, but that it should be believed, can be conceived, or possibly exist. God reveals it that it should be believed. Then he requires it to be believed. No one can fail to do what God requires, without sin; because God cannot require what he does not make possible. If we cannot fail to believe what God has revealed, without sin, we cannot be saved without believing it. Therefore, it is necessary to salvation to believe all that God has revealed.

God cannot make a revelation and require us to believe it without making it so evident that we can have no intellectual reason for not believing it. Unbelief, then, must be the result of some perversity of the will, some moral repugnance, which withholds us from the consideration of the truth revealed, and blinds us as to the evidences of the fact of its revelation. But this perversity of will, this moral repugnance, is a sin, and as much so in the case of one truth revealed as in the case of another. Therefore it is necessary to believe all that God has revealed, in order to be saved. Therefore the Scriptures do not contain all that it is necessary to believe for salvation, unless they contain all that God has revealed.

3. But waiving these considerations, it is either a fact that the Scriptures do contain all that is necessary to salvation, or it is not. If it be a fact, it is a fact which must be proved, and proved by a competent authority. The only competent authority, on Protestant principles, is the Bible itself. If the Bible asserts that it contains all that is necessary to be believed in order to be saved, then it may be conceded that it does. If it assert no such thing, then it does not. But the Bible nowhere asserts that it contains all that is necessary to be believed in order to be saved. Therefore, the Bible does not contain all that is necessary to be believed; for this fact itself, of the sufficiency of the faith it does contain, is itself essential to that sufficiency.

Finally, even admitting the Scriptures may contain the whole revelation, it is not possible by private reason alone to be infallibly certain of their genuine sense. To believe that the Scriptures contain the whole word of God is not to believe that word itself. It is merely believing them to be authoritative, which is indeed something, and, in this age of infidelity, rationalism, and transcendentalism, no doubt a great deal; but is not the faith required. The command is not to believe that the Bible is an authentic record of the revelation, but to believe the truths revealed,—not the Bible, but what the Bible, rightly interpreted, teaches. The truths revealed are the object, the material object, of faith; and these evidently are not believed, unless the Bible be believed in its genuine sense, even assuming the Bible to contain them all.

We insist on this point, because it is one on which there are frequent and dangerous mistakes. The matter of faith is these revealed truths, which are fixed and unalterable, universal and permanent, and which must be carefully distinguished from our notions or apprehensions of them, which are dependent on our mental states or conditions, and change and fluctuate as we ourselves change or fluctuate. These notions are not the matter of faith, and to hold fast these is quite another thing from holding fast the truths themselves. If these notions, which are our interpretations or constructions of the truth, were the faith required, the faith would be one thing with one man, another thing with another, and one thing with the same man yesterday, another to-day, and perhaps still another to-morrow. The true faith is an undoubting belief of the TRUTH, not what a man *thinks* to be the truth, but what really is truth; otherwise men could be saved so far as belief is necessary to salvation, under one form of belief as well as another, for there is probably no form of error which its adherents do not think is truth. Sincerity in the belief of error cannot be the substitute for Christian faith; for we have found that the faith which is the condition *sine qua non* of salvation is belief of truth and not falsehood, and of that very truth which Jesus Christ revealed. But this truth we do not believe, unless it lie in our interpretation as it lies in the mind of Jesus Christ himself. If it do not so lie, then we misinterpret it, and the misinterpretation of truth is not truth, and to believe this misinterpretation is to believe not the truth, but something else. If, then, we do not believe the revelation made in the Scriptures, in its genuine sense, in the sense intended by Almighty God, we do not believe the revelation at all.

Now, it is necessary not only that we seize, without any mistake, this genuine sense, but that we be infallibly certain that we have seized it. Even admitting that with nothing but private reason we could hit upon the genuine sense of Scripture, it would avail us nothing, unless we had this infallible certainty; because without this infallible certainty we cannot have faith. Will any man pretend that it is possible by private reason alone to be infallibly certain that we have the genuine sense of the Scriptures? We may, perhaps, *feel* certain; but this *feeling* certain is not faith. Faith is a firm, unwavering, and unwaverable conviction of the understanding, as well as a cheerful assent of the will. The mere feeling is worth nothing. Every enthusiast, every fanatic, has the feeling; but he who has nothing else is a mere reed shaken with the wind, or a wild beast let loose in society, as unacceptable to God as unprofitable to himself or dangerous to his associates. It is not this Almighty God demands of us, and it is not for the want of this that he places us under condemnation and suffers his wrath to abide upon us. No; we must have certainty, an intellectual certainty, certainty which the mind can grasp, and its hold of which all the craftiness of subtle sophists, all the allurements of the world, all the temptations of the flesh, and all the assaults of hell, cannot induce it for one moment to relax. We must have a faith which can be proof against all trials, come they from what quarter they may; for our life is a warfare, an incessant warfare, and there come to all of us moments when nothing but a firm, fixed, and unalterable faith can sustain us,—moments when feeling, when the dearest affections of the heart, when all that can powerfully affect us as creatures of time and sense, conspire against us, and we must stand up against them and even against ourselves. O, in these terrible moments, in the sacred name of

Christian charity, mock us not with a faith that melts away into mere feeling, and vanishes in mere fancy!

Now, it needs no words to prove that a faith which is not grounded on the word of God, who can neither deceive nor be deceived, will not answer our wants, will not be proof against the many "fiery trials" to which it must needs in this world be subjected. But we have no such faith merely because we have the Bible in our possession, nor because the Bible contains the word of God, nor because we read and study it and believe that we believe it. We have such a faith only on condition of knowing infallibly that what we take to be the meaning of the Bible is God's meaning; for the faith is belief of the truth as it is in Jesus, not as it is in us. We ask again, Can private reason give us this certainty?

This is a serious question, and one which the Protestant must answer, before he can have any solid reason for his faith. It will not do to call upon us to prove the negative; even if we could not prove that it is impossible from the Bible and private reason to become infallibly certain of the genuine sense of the word of God, it would not follow that we can from them obtain the infallible certainty without which there is no faith, and, if no faith, no salvation. He who affirms the proposition must prove it, not for the sake of meeting the logical conditions of his opponent's argument, for that is an affair of small moment; but for himself, for his own mind, to have in himself and for himself a well-grounded faith. Now, how will he prove this proposition, that from the Bible and private reason alone he can ascertain the genuine sense of the word of God, and know infallibly that he has that sense?

Will he prove this proposition from the Bible? He is bound by his own principles to do so; for this is his rule of faith, and his rule of faith should rest on Divine authority. But he admits no Divine authority except the Bible. Then he must prove it from the Bible, or admit that he has no sufficient authority for it. Can he prove it from the Bible? Not in express terms, for the Bible in express terms does not assert it, as is well known. It can be proved from the Bible only by means of certain passages which are assumed to imply it. But whether these do imply it or not depends on the interpretation we give them. It can be proved from Scripture, then, only by a resort to interpretation. But the interpretation demands the application, the use of the rule, as the condition of establishing it. But how determine that the interpretation which authorizes the rule is not itself a misinterpretation, especially since it is an interpretation which is disputed? Can the rule be proved from reason? Not from reason, as the faculty of intuition; because the fact, that from the Bible and private reason alone we can infallibly determine what it is that God has actually revealed, is evidently not intuitively certain. From reason, as the principle of reasoning? From what *data* shall we conclude it? It may be said, that God is just, that he has made a revelation, commanded us to believe it, and made our belief of it the condition *sine qua non* of salvation; but he would not be just in so doing, if this revelation were not infallibly ascertainable in its genuine sense by the prudent exercise of natural reason. Ascertainable by natural reason *in some way*, we grant; but by private reason and the Bible alone, we deny; for God may have made the revelation ascertainable only by a divinely commissioned and supernaturally guided and protected body of teachers, and the office of natural reason to be to judge of the credibility of this body of teachers. From the fact that the revelation is addressed to reasonable beings, and is to be believed by such, and therefore must be made intelligible, it does not necessarily follow that it must be intelligible from the Scriptures and private reason alone. For this would imply that the Scriptures were intended to be the medium and the only medium through which God makes his revelation to men; the very question in dispute.

Can it be proved as a matter of fact, from experience? We have before us the history of Protestant sects for the last three hundred years. A three hundred years' experience ought to suffice to demonstrate the possibility of their ascertaining the sense of God's word, if it be thus ascertainable. Yet Protestants during this long period have done little but vary their interpretations, dispute, wrangle, divide, subdivide, and sub-subdivide, on the question of what it is God has revealed. They are now split up into some five or six hundred sects. There is not a single doctrine in which they all agree; not a single doctrine has been asserted by one that has not been denied by another. The writer in the *Christian Examiner* is a conscientious and devout Unitarian, and yet how large a portion of his Protestant brethren will not deem it an excess of courtesy to treat him and his associates as Christian believers? The Gospel according to Dr. Channing has very little affinity with the Gospel according to Dr. Beecher. Now, truth is one, and can admit of but one true interpretation. Of these many hundred Protestant interpretations, only one at most can be the true interpretation; all the rest are false interpretations, and their adherents are no true Christian believers. Can any Protestant say with infallible certainty that his interpretation is the true one? If not, how can he elicit an act of faith, how, if come to the use of reason, can he be a Christian?

The writer in the *Christian Examiner* makes very light of these different interpretations of the word of God, and thinks difference of interpretation can do no great harm, because, in his judgment, over it all "there may prevail a harmony of sentiment and a harmony of life." But he mistakes the end of unity of faith. Unity of faith is essential because truth is one, and there can be but one true faith, and without this true faith salvation is not possible. "Without faith it is impossible to please God." And this must needs be the true faith, not a false faith, which is no faith at all. Our Unitarian friend seems to imagine that what we are required to believe is, not the truth, but what we *think* to be the truth; that is, we are required to believe the truth not as it is in Jesus, but as it is in ourselves! Does he find any proof of this convenient doctrine in the Scripture? Can he adduce a "Thus saith the Lord" for it? If not, according to his own principles, it rests only on human authority, on which he does not allow us to believe; for he makes it the duty of the believer to stand up firm against all human dictation in matters of belief. In this he is right, and we must have higher authority than his, before we can consent to regard any man's constructions of the truth, unless we have infallible authority for believing them the true constructions, as the truth Almighty God commands us to believe, and without believing which, we must lie under his wrath and condemnation.

No argument can be drawn, it is evident, from experience, to prove that from the Bible and private reason alone we can determine with infallible certainty what is the revelation of God. So far as experience throws any light on the subject, it warrants the opposite conclusion, and makes it certain that without something else faith is out of the question. Protestants, in fact, have no faith; nay, so far from having any faith, nearly all of them deny its possibility. They have, as we have seen, no authority from the Bible, from reason, or from experience, for their rule of faith; and they cannot be such poor logicians as to infer that they can have faith by virtue of a rule which is not authorized. This is no doubt, a serious matter for them; for, ever must ring in their ears *sine fide impossibile est placere Deo,—qui non crediderit condemnabitur.* We must, then, either give up the possibility of faith, or seek some other than the Protestant answer to the question, Who or what is the witness to the fact of revelation?

3. The insufficiency of this answer has been felt even by Protestants themselves, and some of them have proposed a *third* answer, which we may denominate Private Illumination, because it is a revelation made for the special benefit of him who receives it, and not a revelation to be communicated by him for the faith or confirmation of the faith of others. It is contended for, under various forms, but the more common form, and the one with which we are principally concerned in this discussion, is the Calvinistic, or what is usually denominated *Christian experience.* This concedes the defectiveness of the logical evidence of the fact of revelation, and pretends that it

is supplied by a certain interior illumination from the Holy Ghost in the fact of regeneration, whereby the believer is enabled to know by his own experience the truth of the docrine he believes or is required to believe. The famous Jonathan Edwards was a great advocate for this, and sets it forth with considerable ability in his *Treatise on the Affections*, and especially in a sermon on *The Reality of the Spiritual Light*, preached at Northampton in 1734. It is insisted on, we believe, by all the Protestant sects that claim to be *Evangelical*. Indeed, this, in their estimation, constitutes the chief mark by which Evangelicals are distinguished from Non-evangelicals.

That there is a Christian sense, so to speak,—internal tradition, as it is sometimes called, to distinguish it from the external,—which belongs to Christians, and which makes them altogether better judges of what is Christian truth than are those who are not Christians, and that the just, those who belong to the soul of the Church, have a clearer perception, a more vivid appreciation, of the truth, beauty, grandeur, and work of Christian faith than have the unregenerate or the unjust, we of course very distinctly and cheerfully admit. We also admit, and contend, that "faith is the gift of God," not merely because it is belief in truth which God has graciously revealed, as our Unitarian friends apparently maintain, but because no man can believe, even now that the truth is revealed, without the aid of divine grace, that is to say, without grace supernaturally bestowed. Faith is a virtue which has merit ; but no virtue possible without the aid of divine grace has merit,—that is, merit in relation to eternal life. The grace of faith is absolutely essential to the eliciting of the act of faith.

But this considers faith in as much as it is divine faith, a gift of God, and lying wholly in the supernatural order, not as simply human faith, in which it depends on extrinsic evidence or testimony, and the obligation of a man under the simple law of nature to believe,—the only sense in which, in this discussion, we consider it. Unbelief, in those to whom the Gospel has been preached is a sin not merely against the revealed law, but also against the natural law, which it could not be, if the Gospel did not come accompanied with sufficient evidence to warrant belief in every reasonable man. No man is to blame for not believing what is not sufficiently evidenced to his understanding, or for not taking, prior to his knowledge of his obligation to do so, the necessary steps to obtain through grace the faith that translates him from the natural order into the supernatural kingdom of God. Sin is predicable of the will, not of the intellect, and if the evidence were not all that can be justly required to convince the intellect, there could be no sin in simple refusal of the will to believe. The sin lies in the refusal to believe what is sufficiently evidenced; for the refusal can then proceed only from some moral repugnance to the truth, or some propensity of the will, which restrains the man from duly considering the truth and weighing its evidence. Undoubtedly, grace, to illustrate the understanding and to incline the will, is necessary to enable a man to elicit the supernatural act of faith, or to be a true Christian believer; but it is not needed to supply the defect of the evidences objectively considered, because simple natural reason itself is bound to assent to the truth of the Gospel. The Gospel is addressed to man as a reasonable being, and therefore must satisfy the reasonable demands of reason, and it is because it does so satisfy them, that not to believe it is a sin under the natural law. Reason itself commands us to believe it. Hence grace cannot be necessary, simply for the purpose of supplying the defect of evidence, considered as all evidence must be, as addressed to natural reason.

But the Calvinistic view is not that the private illumination, or the grace of faith is simply necessary to translate one into the kingdom of grace, and enable him to elicit an act of divine or supernatural faith, but to supply the defect of logical evidence, for it is asserted as the witness to the fact of revelation. The grace is bestowed in the fact of regeneration, and therefore implies that prior to regeneration there is no sufficient evidence for believing revelation. The moral obligation to believe cannot begin till the evidence is complete, so the unregenerate are under no obligation to believe, and in them unbelief is, and can be, no sin! This is not the Christian doctrine, for God commands all men to repent and believe in his Son, under pain of present wrath and eternal condemnation.

But according to the Evangelical doctrine regeneration consists precisely in the gift of faith. There is, according to the same doctrine, no amissibility of grace; once in grace, always in grace; consequently, after regeneration unbelief is impossible, and the regenerate can never contract the sin of unbelief. Before regeneration unbelief is not a sin, consequently, there can never be any sin of unbelief—a most convenient doctrine to all misbelievers and infidels. Yet the New Testament clearly teaches, if it clearly teaches anything, that infidelity is a most grievous sin. This Calvinistic view is therefore clearly inadmissible.

In another form, the doctrine of private illumination is made to mean not merely the confirmation of the believer's faith in a revelation previously made and propounded for his belief, but the medium of the revelation itself. It regards all external revelation, all that may be called historical Christianity, as unnecessary, and teaches that each man has, by grace, the infallible witness in himself, that the Spirit of Truth, promised by Christ to his Apostles to lead them into all truth is, and has been, in every man born into the world, from Adam to the present moment, and is in every man an infallible teacher, revealing and confirming to him all the truth which concerns his spiritual state, relations, and destiny. We say, *by grace;* for we do not here speak of the doctrine of our modern Transcendentalists, which, though often confounded with the view we have given, which is the Quaker view, is yet quite distinguishable from it. The Transcendentalist doctrine excludes all grace, all that is supernatural, and assumes, that man, by virtue of his natural union with the Divinity, is able to apprehend intuitively all spiritual truth. This, with a transcendental felicity of expression, has been denominated "Natural-supernaturalism." But this is only another way of stating the doctrine refuted under the head of the sufficiency of reason as the principle of intuition.

"Natural-supernatural" is a barbarism, and involves a direct contradiction. Either the truths attained lie within the range of our natural powers, or they do not. If not, the Transcendental doctrine is false, for then the knowledge of them would be supernatural. If they do, then they are not supernatural at all. Transcendentalism, in point of fact, admits no supernatural order. Its adherents, following the sublimated nonsense of that profound opium-eater, and literary plagiarist, Coleridge, define supernatural to be *supersensuous;* and because by science we evidently can attain to what is not sensuous, they sagely infer that we are able to know naturally the supernatural! Just as if what is naturally attained could be supernatural, either as the object known, or as the medium by which it is known? Just as if nature could not include the supersensible as well as the sensible, as if the soul were not as natural as the body, an angel as a man! But this "natural-supernaturalism" which makes the fortune of Carlyle, Emerson, Parker, and we know not how many German dreamers, is nothing but a Transcendental way of denying all supernatural revelation, and its refutation does not belong to the present discussion. It is intended to account for the phenomena presented by the religious history of mankind, without the admission of the supernatural or gracious intervention of Almighty God, and would deserve attention if we were defending Christianity against unbelievers. We have no concern with it now, for at present we are defending the Church against heretics, not against infidels.

The Quaker view is theoretically, though perhaps not practically, distinct from this Transcendental natural-supernaturalism. It does not assume that the supernatural is naturally intelligible, nor that the supernatural is merely the supersensible. It admits the supernatural order, and contends that the witness in every man is distinct from human reason, and is in the proper sense of the term supernatural. Now this witness, called "the light within," either enables us to see intuitively the truth, or it merely witnesses to the fact of revelation. If the first, it is too much; for it would imply that the truth is matter of knowledge and not of faith, contrary to what we have proved. Moreover, it would imply that man is blest with the beatific vision in this life, and sees and knows God intuitively, as he is in himself, which is not true. If the second, then, to the fact of *what* revelation does it witness? To the revelation which God has made us through his Son Jesus Christ? Does it witness to this by an inward perception of the truth of the matter revealed? or by simply deposing to the fact that God revealed it? Not the first, because that would make the truth revealed a matter of science. Then the second. But of this we demand proof. Do you say, that the spirit beareth witness to the fact? How will you prove to me, or even to yourself, that it does so witness, and that the spirit witnessing in you is veritably and infallibly the spirit of God? Do you allege, the spirit is in every man testifying to the same fact, and proving itself to each man to be really and truly the infallible spirit of God? I deny it, and millions deny it with me. What have you to oppose to our denial? Do you admit our denial? Then you abandon your doctrine? Do you say our denial is false? Then, also, you abandon your doctrine; for you admit that we err, and therefore cannot have in us an infallible teacher. If I deny, I deny by as high authority as you affirm; and what reason, then can you give why your affirmation must be received rather than my denial?

Again: How do you prove that every man has this infallible witness? From the external revelation, by passages from the Holy Scriptures? Then you reason in a vicious circle; for you take the inward witness to prove the Scriptures and then the Scriptures to prove the witness. From immediate revelation to yourself? Then you must prove that you are the recipient of such revelation, which you can do only by a miracle, for a miracle is the only proper proof of such a fact.

But do you abandon the ground that it is the external revelation to which the witness deposes, and contend that it is rather the medium of a revelation made solely to the individual, than the witness to a revelation made and propounded for the belief of all men in common? Then it is nothing to the purpose. Granting its reality, it can avail only each man separately; nothing to a *common* belief, and be no ground for crediting a common revelation, or for making a public or external profession of faith. But the revelation to which we are seeking a witness is not a new revelation, not a private revelation which Almighty God may see proper to make to individuals, but a revelation already made, and propounded for the belief of all men. This is the revelation to be established; and since your private revelation does not establish this, or, if so, only by superseding it and rendering it of no value (for it can prove it even to the individual only by its being seen to be identical with what the individual receives without it), it evidently cannot be the witness we are in pursuit of. And this is the common answer to the alleged private illumination, whatever its form. It is valid, if valid at all, only within the bosom of the individual, and can be alleged in support of no common or public faith; therefore can be no witness in any disputed case. It may be a private benefit, or may not be. It is a matter not to be spoken of, and a fact never to be used, when the question relates to anything but the individual himself. The faith we are required to have is a faith propounded to all men, a public faith, and must be sustained by public evidence, by arguments which are open to all and common to all. We must, therefore, reject this *third* answer, as inappropiate and insufficient.*

4. From what we have established it follows that the witness to the fact of revelation is not reason, the Bible interpreted by private reason, nor private illumination. No witness, then, remains to be introduced but the Apostolic ministry, or *Ecclesia docens*. We do not deny the possibility on the part of God of adopting some other method; but he manifestly has not adopted any other than one of the four methods we have enumerated. The first three of these four we have proved he cannot have

* This subject the reader will find still further discussed in the articles which follow in reply to the *Episcopal Observer*, and Professor Thornwell.

adopted, because they are inadequate. Then, either the last method is adopted, and the Apostolic ministry is the witness, or we have no witness. But we have a witness, as before proved. Therefore, the Apostolic ministry, or *Ecclesia docens*, is the witness.

This conclusion stands firm without any further proof, but we do not intend to leave it without proving it by plain, positive, and direct evidence. But before proceeding to do this, we must dispose of one or two preliminary difficulties. According to the principles we have laid down, the witness to the supernatural is incompetent unless it be itself supernatural, or, what is the same thing, supernaturally aided. But the Apostolic ministry is composed of men, each of whom, taken singly, is confessedly only human. The whole is only the sum of the parts. Therefore the ministry itself is only human. If human, natural. If natural, incompetent. Therefore the Apostolic ministry cannot be such a witness as is demanded.

This objection is founded on the supposition that the collective body of teachers are assumed to be the witness by virtue of their natural powers or endowments, which is not the fact. Left to their natural powers, the body of teachers, taken either singly or corporately, would be altogether incompetent, however learned, wise, or saintly. The competency of the body of teachers is asserted solely on the ground that Jesus Christ is with it, and supernaturally speaks in and through it; and in and through the body rather than the teachers taken singly, because his promise, on which we rely, is made to the body, and not to the individuals taken singly. The ministry is the organ through which our Lord *supernaturally* bears witness to his own revelation. If this be a fact, if our Lord really, by his supernatural presence, be with the Ministry, if in its authoritative teachings he makes it his organ and speaks in and through it, its competency cannot be questioned; for we then have in it the supernatural witness to the supernatural. Whether this be a fact or not will be soon considered.

But it is still further objected, that, if the witness to the supernatural must be itself supernatural, the supernatural can never be witnessed to natural reason, and therefore man can never have any good grounds for believing the supernatural, unless he be himself supernaturally elevated above his nature. For the competency of the supernatural witness is a supernatural fact which can be proved only by another supernatural witness, which in turn will require still another, and thus on, *in infinitum*, which is impossible. But we must distinguish between the competency of the witness to testify to the fact of revelation and the motives of the credibility of the witness. The competency of the witness depends on its supernatural character; the motives of credibility being needed only by natural reason, are such as natural reason may appreciate. The credibility of the witness is supernaturally established to natural reason by means of miracles. A miracle is a supernatural effect produced in or on natural objects, and therefore connects the natural and supernatural, so that natural reason can, in some sense, pass from the one to the other. Since the miracle is wrought on natural objects, it is cognizable by natural reason, and natural reason is able to determine whether a given fact be or be not a miracle. From the miracle the reason concludes legitimately the supernatural cause, and the Divine commission or authority of him by whom it is wrought. Having established the divine commission or authority of the miracle-worker, we have established his credibility, by having established the fact that God himself vouches for the truth of his testimony. The miracle, therefore, supersedes the necessity of the supposed infinite series of supernatural witnesses, by supernaturally connecting the natural with the supernatural. It is God's own assurance to natural reason, that he speaks in and by or through the person by whom it is performed. Then we have the veracity of God for the truth of what the miracle-worker declares, and therefore infallible certainty; for natural reason knows that God can neither deceive nor be deceived.

The supernatural, it follows, is provable. Consequently the character of the Apostolic ministry, as the supernatural witness to the fact of revelation, is provable, that is, is not intrinsically unprovable. It becomes a simple question of fact, and is to be proved or disproved in like manner as any other question of fact falling under the cognizance of natural reason. The process of proof is simple and easy. The miracles of our blessed Lord were all that was necessary to establish his Divine authority to those who saw them; for it was evident, as Nicodemus said to him, "No man can do these miracles which thou doest, unless God be with him." St. John iii. 2. These accredited him as a teacher from God. Then he was necessarily what he professed to be, and what he declared to be God's word was God's word. This was sufficient for the eyewitness of the miracles.

But we are not eyewitnesses. True; but the fact, whether the miracles were performed or not, is a simple historical question, to which reason is as competent as to any other historical question. If it can be established infallibly to us that the miracles were actually performed, we are virtually and to all intents and purposes in the condition of the eyewitnesses themselves, and they are to us all they were to them. Then they accredit to us, as to them, the Divine commission of Jesus, and authorize the conclusion that whatever he said or promised was infallible truth; for whether you say Jesus was himself truly God as well as truly man, or that he was only divinely commissioned, you have in either case the veracity of God as the ground of faith in what he said or promised.

Now, suppose it be a fact that Jesus appointed a body of teachers, and promised to be always with them, protecting them from error and teaching them all truth; and suppose, farther, that the appointment and promise are ascertainable by natural reason, infallibly ascertainable, we should then have infallible certainty that Jesus Christ does speak in and through this body, that it is infallible in what it teaches, and therefore that what it declares to be the word of God is the word of God; for it is infallibly certain that Jesus Christ will keep his promise, since the promise is made by God himself, either directly, as we hold, or through his accredited agent, as the *Christian Examiner* holds, and it is impossible for God to lie, or to promise and not fulfil. In this case, calling this body of teachers the Catholic Church, we could make our act of faith without the least room for doubt or hesitation. "O my God! I firmly believe all the sacred truths the Catholic Church believes and teaches, because *thou* hast revealed them, who canst neither deceive nor be deceived."

Taking the facts in the case to be as here supposed, the only points in the process to which exceptions can possibly be taken, or which can by any one be alleged to be not infallibly certain, are, 1. The competency of natural reason from historical testimony to establish the fact that the miracles were actually performed; 2. Admitting the facts to be infallibly ascertainable, the competency of reason to determine infallibly whether they are miracles or not; 3. The competency of reason to conclude from the miracle the Divine authority of the miracle-worker; 4. Its competency from historical documents to ascertain infallibly the fact of the appointment of the body of teachers, and the promise made them. These four points, unquestionably essential to the validity of the argument, are to be taken, we admit, on the authority of reason. Can reason determine these with infallible certainty? But, if you say it can, you affirm the infallibility of reason, and then it of itself suffices, without other infallible teacher; if you say it cannot, you deny the possibility of establishing infallibly the infallibility of your body of teachers.

Reason is infallible within its own province, but not in regard to what transcends its reach. To deny the infallibility of reason within its province would be to deny the possibility not only of faith, but of both science and knowledge, and to sink into absolute skepticism,—even to "doubt that doubt itself be doubting,"—which is impossible; for no man doubts that he doubts. Revelation does not deny reason, but presupposes it. The objection to reason is not that it cannot judge infallibly of *some* matters, but that it cannot judge infallibly of *all* matters. But, because it cannot judge infallibly of all matters, to say it can judge infallibly of none is not to reason justly. As well say, I am not infallibly certain that I see the tree before my window, because I cannot see all that may be going on in the moon. It is infallibly certain that the same thing cannot both be and not be at the same time; that two things respectively equal to a third are equal to one another; that the three angles of a triangle are equal to two right angles; that what begins to exist must have a creator; that every effect must have a cause, and that every supernatural effect must have a supernatural cause, and that the change of one natural substance into another natural substance is a supernatural effect; that every voluntary agent acts to some end, and every wise and good agent to a wise and good end. These and the like propositions are all infallibly certain. Reason, within its sphere, is therefore infallible; but out of its sphere it is null.

Human testimony, within its proper limits, backed by circumstances, monuments, institutions which presuppose its truth and are incompatible with its falsehood, is itself infallible. I have never seen London, but I have no occasson to see it in order to be as certain of its existence as I am of my own. History, too, is a science; and although everything narrated in it may not be true or even probable, yet there are historical facts as certain as mathematical certainty itself. It is infallibly certain that there were in the ancient world the republics of Athens, Sparta, and Rome; that there was a peculiar people called the Jews, that this people dwelt in Palestine, that they had a chief city named Jerusalem, in this chief city a superb temple dedicated to the worship of the one God, and that this chief city was taken by the Romans, this temple burnt, and this people, after an immense slaughter, were subdued, and dispersed among the nations, where they remain to this day. Here are historical facts, which can be infallibly proved to be facts.

Now, the miracles, regarded as facts, are simple historical facts, said to have occurred at a particular time and place, and are in their nature as susceptible of historical proof as any other facts whatever. Ordinary historical testimony is as valid in their case as in the case of Cæsar's or Napoleon's battles. Reason, observing the ordinary laws of historical criticism, is competent to decide infallibly on the fact whether they are proved to have actually occurred or not. Reason, then, is competent to the *first* point in the process of proof, namely, the fact of the miracles.

It is equally competent to the *second* point, namely, whether the fact alleged to be a miracle really be a miracle. A miracle is a supernatural effect produced in or on natural objects. The point for reason to make out, after the fact is proved, is whether the effect actually witnessed be a *supernatural* effect. That it can do this in every case, even when the effect is truly miraculous, we do not pretend; but that it can do it in some cases, we affirm, and to be able to do it in one suffices. When I see one natural substance changed into another natural substance, as in the case of converting water into wine, I know the change is a miracle; for nature can no more change herself than she could create herself. So, when I see a man who has been four days dead, and in whose body the process of decomposition has commenced and made considerable progress, restored to life and health, sitting with his friends at table and eating, I know it is a miracle; for to restore life when extinct is no less an act of creative power than to give life. It is giving life to that which before had it not, and is therefore an act which can be performed by no being but God alone. Reason, then, is competent to determine the fact whether the alleged miracle really be a miracle. It is competent, then, to the second point in the process of proof.

No less competent is it to the *third*, namely, the Divine commission of the miracle-worker. In proving the event to be a miracle, I prove it to be wrought by the power of God. Now, I know enough of God, by the natural light of reason, to know that he cannot be the accomplice of an impostor, that he cannot work a miracle by one whose word may not be taken. The miracle, then, establishes the credibility of the miracle-worker.

3

Then, the miracle-worker is what he says he is. If he says he is God, he is God; if he says he speaks by Divine authority, he speaks by Divine authority, and we have God's authority for what he says. The third point, then, comes within the province of natural reason, and may be infallibly settled.

The *fourth* point is a simple historical question; for it concerns what was done and said by our Blessed Lord in regard to the appointment of a body of teachers. It is to be settled historically, by consulting the proper documents and monuments in the case. It is not a question of speculation, of interpretation even, but simply a question of fact, to which reason is fully competent, and can, with proper prudence and documents, settle infallibly.

These remarks accepted, it follows that the infallible certainty we demand is possible, that is, is not *a priori* impossible. In passing from the possible to the actual, it is necessary to establish, by historical testimony, the miracles of our Blessed Lord, from which we conclude his Divinity or Divine commission, and that he did appoint a body of teachers, commission the Church teaching, with the promise of infallibility and indefectibility. The first, the *Christian Examiner* concedes; we proceed, therefore, to the proof of the second.

The question before us, distinctly stated, is, Has Jesus Christ commissioned a body of pastors and teachers, and given this body the promise of infallibility and indefectibility? If not, faith, as we have seen, is impossible, and no man can have a solid reason for the Christion hope he professes to entertain. It is, then, worth inquiring, whether we have not sufficient proof of the fact that he has commissioned such a body.

In settling this question, we shall use the New Testament, but simply as an historical document. We do this because it abridges our labor, and because the New Testament, so far as we shall have occasion to adduce it, is admitted as good authority by those against whom we are reasoning. It is their own witness, and its testimony must be conclusive against them.

Moreover, its general authenticity, as a contemporary historical document, would fully warrant its use, even if not adduced by our adversaries.

It must not be objected to us, that, after what we have said of the necessity of an infallible authority to authenticate the canon, to quote the Bible to establish the commission in question is to reason in a vicious circle. This is the standing Protestant objection. We do not admit it. For, 1. We do not depend on the Bible for the historical facts from which we conclude the commission of the *Ecclesia docens*, or body of pastors and teachers; for these facts we can collect from other sources equally reliable, and do so collect them when we reason with unbelievers; and 2. We do not, in this controversy, quote the Bible as an *inspired* volume, but simply as an *historical* document, and therefore not in that character in which the authority of the Church is necessary to authenticate it.

Nor, again, let it be said, that, since, in quoting the Bible to establish the point before us, we have only our private reason for interpreter, we are precluded by our own principles from quoting it at all; for to be able from the Bible and private reason alone to deduce the faith which is the condition *sine qua non* of salvation is one thing; to be able from the New Testament as an historical document to ascertain a simple matter of fact which it records is another and quite a different thing. Some things are clearly and expressly recorded in the Bible, and some are not. Those which are not clearly and expressly stated are not to be infallibly ascertained without an infallible interpreter. But if we are to deduce our faith from the Bible alone, we must be able by private reason alone to ascertain these as well as the others; for we are not to presume that Almighty God has revealed anything superfluous, or not essential to the faith. That we can so ascertain all that is contained in the Bible we have denied, and still deny; and so must every honest man who has ever seriously attempted the work of interpreting the Sacred Scriptures. But that there are some things in the Bible which may be infallibly ascertained, we have not denied, nor dreamed of denying. What is clearly and expressly taught in the Bible can be as easily and as infallibly ascertained as what is clearly and expressly taught in any other book; and if all in the book, were clear and express, we should no more need any interpreter, but our own reason prudently exercised, than we should for a decree of a council or a brief of the Pope. It is the character of the book itself that renders the interpreter necessary; and the fact, that its character is such as demands an interpreter to make obvious its contents, is, to say the least, a strong presumption that Almighty God never intended it as the fountain from which we are to draw our faith by private reason alone. If he had so intended it, he would have made it so plain, so express, so definite, that no one, with ordinary prudence, could fail to catch its precise meaning. But admitting the obvious insufficiency of private reason to interpret the whole Bible and deduce from it the faith we are required to have, we may still contend that by the reason common to all men we are able to determine even infallibly some of its contents. No objection can, then, be urged against our quoting it in the present controversy, especially since we shall quote only what is clear, distinct, and express, and what all must admit to be so.

In proof of our position, that Jesus Christ has appointed, commissioned, a body of teachers with authority to teach, we quote the well-known passage in St. Matthew's Gospel, xxviii. 18, 19, 20, "All power is given unto me in heaven and in earth. Go ye, therefore, and teach all nations, ... teaching them to observe all things whatsoever I have commanded you; and behold, I am with you all days unto the consummation of the world;" also, St. Mark, xvi. 15, "Go ye into all the earth, and preach the Gospel unto every creature;" and, Eph. iv. 11, "And some indeed he gave to be apostles, and some prophets, and some evangelists, and others pastors and teachers."

These are conclusive as to the fact that Jesus Christ did commission a body of teachers, or institute the *Ecclesia docens*.

The commission is from one who had authority to give it, because from one unto whom was given all power in heaven and in earth; it was a commission to *teach*, to teach all nations, to preach the Gospel to "every creature,"—equivalent, to say the least, to all nations and individuals,—and to teach *all things whatsoever* Jesus Christ himself commanded. The commission is obviously as full, as express, as unequivocal, as language can make it, and was given by our Blessed Lord after his resurrection, immediately before his ascension.

That this was not merely a commission to the Apostles personally is evident from the terms of the commission itself, and the promise with which it closes. It was the institution and commission of a body or corporation of teachers, which beginning with the Apostles and continuing the identical body they were, must subsist unto the consummation of the world. For they who were commissioned were commanded to teach all nations and individuals, and in the order of succession as well as in the order of coexistence; for such is the literal import of the terms. But this command the Apostles personally *did* not fulfil, for all nations and individuals, even using the term *all* to imply a moral and not a metaphysical universality, have not yet been taught; they *could* not fulfil it, for during their personal lifetime all nations and individuals were not even in existence. Then one of three things;—1. The Apostles failed to fulfil the command of their Master; 2. Our Blessed Lord gave an impracticable command; or, 3. The commission was not to the Apostles in their personal character. We can say neither of the first two; therefore we must say the last.

But the commission was to the Apostles, and therefore the body of teachers must, in some way, be identical with them, as is evident from the command, "Go *ye*," indisputably addressed to the Apostles themselves. But they can be identical with the Apostles in but two ways:—1. Personally; 2. Corporately. They are not personally identical, for that would make them the Apostles themselves, as numerical individuals, which we have just seen they are not. Then they must be corporately identical. Then the commission was to a corporation of teachers. The commission gave ample authority to teach. Therefore Jesus Christ did commission a body of teachers with ample authority to teach,—and, since commissioned to teach all nations and individuals in the order of succession as well as of coexistence, a perpetual or always subsisting corporation. Thus the very letter of the commission sustains our position.

The *promise* with which the commission closes does the same. " Behold I am with you all days unto the consummation of the world." They to whom this promise was made, and with whom the Saviour was to be present were identical with the Apostles, for he says to the Apostles, " I am with *you*." They were to be in time, that is, in this life; for he says, I am with you all *days*,—πάσας τὰς ἡμέρας—which cannot apply to eternity, in which the divisions of time do not obtain. They were not the Apostles personally, because our blessed Saviour says again, " I am with you all days unto the *consummation of the world*," which is an event still future, and the Apostles personally have long since ceased to exist as inhabitants of time. But they were identical with the Apostles, and, since not personally, they must be corporately identical. Therefore the promise was to be with the Apostles, as a body or corporation of teachers, all days even unto the consummation of the world. But Jesus Christ cannot be with a body that is not. Therefore the body must remain unto the consummation of the world. Therefore our Blessed Lord has instituted, appointed, commissioned a body or corporation of teachers, identical with the Apostles, continuing their authority, and which must remain unto the consummation of the world.

The same is also established by the blessed Apostle Paul in the passage quoted from Ephesians, iv. 11, " And he indeed gave some to be apostles, and some prophets, and some evangelists, and others to be pastors and teachers," taken in connexion with 1 Cor. xii. 28, " And God indeed hath set some in the Church, first, apostles, secondly, prophets, thirdly, teachers; after that miracles, then the graces of healings, helps, governments, kinds of tongues, interpretations of speeches." These texts, so far as we adduce them, clearly and distinctly assert that God has set in the Church, or congregation of believers, pastors and teachers as a perpetual ordinance. They prove more than this, for which at another time we may contend; but they prove at least this, which is all we are contending for now. "God hath set," "God gave to be." These expressions prove the pastors and teachers to be of Divine appointment, and therefore that they are not created or commissioned by the congregation itself. They are set in the Church, given to be, as a perpetual ordinance; for the rule for understanding any passage of scripture, sacred or profane, is to take it always in a universal sense, unless the assertion of the passage be necessarily restricted in its application by something in the nature of the subject, or in the context, some known fact, or some principle of reason or of faith. But obviously nothing of the kind can be adduced, to restrict the sense of these passages either in regard to time or space. They are, therefore, to be taken in their plain, obvious, unlimited sense. Therefore the institution of pastors and teachers is not only Divine, but universal and perpetual in the Church.

We may obtain the same result from the end for which the pastors and teachers are appointed; for the *argumentum ad quem* is not less conclusive than the *argumentum a quo*. If the end to be attained cannot be attained without assuming the authority and perpetuity of the body of pastors and teachers, we have a right to conclude their authority and perpetuity; since they are appointed by God himself, who cannot fail to adapt his means to his ends. For what end, then, has God instituted this body of pastors and teachers? The Apostle answers, "For the perfection of the saints, for the work of the ministry, unto the edification of the body of Christ, till we all meet in the unity of the faith, and of the knowledge of the Son of God, unto a perfect man, unto the measure of the age of the fulness of Christ; that *we may not now be children tossed to and fro, and carried about with every wind of doctrine, in the wickedness of men, in craftiness by which they lie in wait to deceive;* but, performing the truth in charity, we may in all things grow up in him who is the head, Christ." Eph. iv. 12–15. This needs no comment. The end here proposed, for which the Christian ministry is instituted, is one which always and everywhere subsists, and must so long as the world remains. But this is an end which obviously cannot be secured but by an authoritative and perpetual body of teachers. Therefore the body of teachers is authoritative and perpetual. Therefore, God, or God in Jesus Christ, has appointed, commissioned, a body of teachers, the *Ecclesia docens,* as an authoritative and perpetual corporation, to subsist unto the consummation of the world.

We have now proved the first part of our proposition, namely, the fact of the institution and commission of the *Ecclesia docens* as an authoritative and perpetual corporation of teachers. Its authority is in the commission to teach; its perpetuity, in the fact that it cannot discharge its commission without remaining to the consummation of the world, in the promise of Christ to be with it till then, which necessarily implies its existence unto the consummation of the world, and in the fact that the promise is to it as a corporation identical with the Apostles. The proof of this first part of our proposition necessarily proves the second, namely, the *infallibility* of the corporation. The Divine commission necessarily carries with it the infallibility of the commissioned to the full extent of the commission. It is on this fact that is grounded the evidence of miracles. Miracles do not prove the truth of the doctrine taught; they merely accredit the teacher, and this they do simply by proving that the teacher is Divinely commissioned. The fact to be established is the Divine commission. This once, established, it makes no difference whether established immediately, by a miracle, or mediately, by the declaration of one already proved by miracles, as was our Blessed Lord, to speak by Divine authority. Jesus, it is conceded, spoke by Divine authority, even by those who, with the *Christian Ex-*

aminer, deny his proper Divinity. Then a commission given by him was a Divine commission, and pledged Almighty God in like manner as if given by Almighty God himself directly. The teachers were, then, Divinely commissioned. Then in all matters covered by the commission they are infallible; for God himself vouches for the truth of their testimony, and must take care that they testify the truth and nothing but the truth.

Moreover, the command to teach implies the obligation of obedience. The commission is a command to teach, and to teach all nations and individuals. Then all nations and individuals are bound to believe and obey these teachers; for authority and obedience are correlatives, and where there is no duty to believe and obey, there is no authority to teach. But it is repugnant to reason and the known character of God to say that he makes it the duty of any one to believe and obey a fallible teacher, one who may both deceive and be deceived. Were he to do so, he would participate in the same fallibility, and be the false teacher's accomplice, which is impossible; for he is, as we have said, *prima veritas in essendo, in cognoscendo, et in dicendo*, and therefore can neither deceive nor be deceived. Therefore they whom he has commissioned, must be infallible.

We prove the promise of infallibility also from the express testimony of the New Testament. "I will ask the Father," says the Saviour, addressing the disciples, "and he shall give you another Paraclete, that he may abide with you for ever, the Spirit of Truth, whom the world cannot receive, because it seeth him not, nor knoweth him; but ye shall know him, because he shall abide with you, and be in in you. . . . . He shall teach you all things, and bring all things to your mind whatsoever I shall have said to you. . . . . When he, the Spirit of Truth, shall come, he shall teach you all truth; for he shall not speak of himself, but whatsoever things he shall hear he shall speak. He shall glorify me, for he shall receive of mine and declare it unto you." St. John, xiv. 16, 17, 26 ; xvi. 13, 14.

They to whom is here promised the Spirit of Truth are unquestionably the Apostles, who, we have seen, were commissioned as teachers; but to them nececessarily in their corporate capacity, as the *Ecclesia docens*, not personally, because it is said, the Paraclete shall " abide with you *for ever*." It is not to a body of teachers in general, that is, to any body of teachers which may claim to be Apostolic, that the promise is made, but to that body which is identical with the Apostles, because it is said, " he shall abide with *you*," that is, the Apostles. This identifies the subjects of this promise with the subjects of the commission before ascertained. The promise is express, and unmistakable. The Spirit of Truth was not only to abide with the teachers for ever, but was to teach them all things, and bring to their minds whatever Jesus may have said to them; in a word, to teach them " *all truth*," that is, all truth included in the terms of the commission. If this be not a promise of infallibility, we confess we know not what would be.

The infallibility of the teachers is, then, established. But, for the special benefit of our Protestant readers, who are a little dull of apprehension on this subject, we repeat, that we do not predicate this infallibility of the body of teachers in their natural capacity, nor of their personal endowments. It in no way, manner, or shape depends on their personal qualities or personal characters, however exalted, whether for intelligence, learning, sagacity, or sanctity. It is God speaking in and through them; God, who can choose the foolish things of this world to confound the wise, weak things to bring to naught the mighty, nay, base things, and things that are not, and out of the mouth of babes and sucklings show forth his truth and perfect his praise; who can make the wrath of men praise him, and even the wicked the instruments of his will and the organs of his word; and who does do so at times, that it may be seen that his truth does not stand in human wisdom, nor his Church depend on human virtue.

For the special benefit of the same class of readers, we remark, also, that the infallibility claimed extends only to those matters included in the terms of the commission. These are to "teach all things whatsoever" Jesus commands. In relation to those matters Jesus did not command, or concerning which he gave no commandment, infallibility is not claimed, and could not be established if it were. Nevertheless, from the nature of the case, the Church teaching must be the judge of what things Jesus has commanded her to teach, and therefore unquestionably the interpreter of her own powers. To assume to the contrary would be to deny her authority while seeming to admit it. If she alone has received authority to teach, she alone can say what she has authority to teach.

The *indefectibility* of the *Ecclesia docens* follows as a necessary consequence from what has been already established. The commission is the pledge of its own fulfilment. Whatever commission God gives must be fulfilled. This must be admitted, because the commission pledges God himself. The commission was not of a body of teachers, that is, of some body of teachers who should always be found, but it was solely, exclusively, and expressly to the Apostolic ministry. It was to the identical body to whom Jesus himself spoke. He spoke to the Apostles. It was to them, and to them only, the commission was given. But it was a commission the terms of which imply that the commissioned must remain even unto the consummation of the world. But the Apostles none of them personally did so remain. Therefore, though given to them exclusively, it was not given to them in their personal character, but was given, as we have proved, to them as a corporation or body of teachers, in which sense they may continue unto the consummation of the world; for one of the attributes of a corporation is immortality, and, so long as the terms of its charter are observed, it is perpetuated as the same identical corporation. Now, as the commission was given to the Apostles as a corporation, it was given only to that identical corporation, continued or perpetuated in space and time, which they were. But this commission is a commission to this corporation to teach, and to teach even to the consummation of the world. Then it must exist as the identical corporation to the consummation of the world. Then it can never fail to exist, or lose its identity. The commission is a pledge of infallibility. Then it can never fail, or lose its identity as an infallible body. If it fail in neither of these respects, is is indefectible, so far as we have affirmed its indefectibility; for we have affirmed its indefectibility only as a body of infallible teachers.

If there be any truth in the principles laid down, any reliance to be placed on the promises of Almighty God made through his Son Jesus Christ, it is infallibly certain that God has, through his Son, established an infallible and indefectible ministry, or *Ecclesia docens*, commanded it to teach all nations and individuals "all things whatsoever" he has revealed, and therefore commanded all nations and individuals to submit to it, to believe, observe, obey whatsoever it teaches as the revelation of God. The only remaining question for us is, Which of the pretended Christian ministries now extant is the true Apostolic ministry; that is to say, which is the body of teachers that inherits the promises? For if we find this one, we know then that it has the promise of infallibility, and that whatever it declares to be the word of God is the word of God. We can know then in whom we believe, and be certain. We need spend but a moment in answering this question. The ministry must be the identical Apostolic ministry, the identical corporation to which the promises were made. It is the corporate identity that is to be established. It is known already, that it, at any period we may assume, is in existence; for it is indefectible, and cannot fail. We say, then,

It is the Roman Catholic ministry. It can be no other. It cannot be the Greek Church. The Greek Church was formerly in communion with the Church of Rome, and made one corporation with it. The Church of Rome was then the true Church, *Ecclesia docens*, or it was not. If not, the Greek Church is false, in consequence of having communed with a false Church. If it was, the Greek Church is false, because it separated from it. So, take either horn of the dilemma, the

Greek Church is false, and its ministry not the Apostolic ministry which inherits the promises. The same reasoning will apply with equal force to any one of the Oriental sects not in communion with the See of Rome, and *a fortiori* to all the modern Protestant sects. Therefore the Roman Catholic ministry is the Apostolic corporation, because this corporation can be no other.

You object, in behalf of the Greek Church, that Rome separated from her, not she from Rome. This we deny. It is historically certain that the Greek Church, prior to the final separation, agreed with the Church of Rome on the matters (the Supremacy of the Pope and the Procession of the Holy Ghost) which were made the pretexts for separation. In the separation, the Greek Church denied what she had before asserted, while Rome continued to assert the same doctrine after as before. Therefore the Greek Church was the dissentient party. Prior to the separation, the Greek Church agreed with the Roman in submitting to the papal authority. In the separation, the Greek Church threw off this authority, while the Roman continued to submit to it. Therefore the Greek Church was the separatist.

You insist, that, though the act of separation may, indeed, have been formally the act of the Greek Church, yet the separation was really on the part of Rome, who had corrupted the faith, and rendered separation from her necessary to the purity of the Christian Church. But, if this be so, whatever the corruptions of the faith Rome had been guilty of, the Greek Church participated in them during her communion with Rome. If they vitiated the Latin Church, they equally vitiated the Greek. Then both had failed, and the true Church, which we have seen is indefectible, must have been somewhere else. Then the Greek Church could become a true Church by separating from the communion of the Latin Church only on condition of coming into communion with the true Church. But it came into communion with no Church. Therefore the Greek Church, at any rate, is false.

The same reasoning applies to the before mentioned Oriental sects, and *a fortiori* to Protestants. Protestants were once in communion with Rome. They either were then in communion with the Church of Christ, or they were not. If they were, they are not now, because they have separated from it. If they were not, they could come into communion with the Church of Christ only by joining the true Church. But they joined none. Therefore they are not in communion with the Church of Christ, and their pretended ministries are none of them the Apostolic ministry. Therefore, we say again, it is the Roman Catholic ministry, because it can be no other, and must be some one.

You object, that the true Church always subsists, indeed, but not always as a visible body, and therefore may be neither one nor another of the special church organizations extant, but in point of fact be dispersed through them all. But this objection is not pertinent; for we are not considering the question of the Church in the sense in which it is taken in this objection. The objection takes the word *church* in the sense of the congregation of the just, or persons called and sanctified; we, in the question before us, take it in the sense of the congregation of Christian pastors and teachers, in which sense it can neither be invisible nor dispersed. It is the witness to the fact of revelation, and it is essential that the witness should be visible, that its competency and credibility may be judged of. It is commanded to teach all nations and individuals, and all nations and individuals are therefore commanded to believe and obey whatever it teaches. But, if invisible, this command is impractible; for we could never know where, when, or what it teaches, and therefore whether we believed and obeyed its teachings, or not. It cannot be dispersed through various communions, because it is a corporation, and its dispersion would be its dissolution. It is a corporation of *teachers*. No man has a right to teach, unless commissioned by Jesus Christ. Jesus Christ, as we have seen, commissions individuals only in and through the commission of the body. Then one must be united to the body, as the condition of receiving a commission to teach. Therefore the teachers cannot be dispersed through different corporations. The teaching body is infallible, and, if dispersed through all communions, the truth must be infallibly taught in all communions. But it is so taught only in one communion; because all communions differ among themselves, and could not differ had they no error. As no two can be found that agree, only one can have the truth, the whole truth, and nothing but the truth. Therefore the ministry in question is only one, and not dispersed. It cannot be dispersed; for, if it were, it could not answer the end of its institution, which is to maintain unity of faith, perfect the saints in the knowledge of the Son of God, and prevent us from being children tossed to and fro and carried about with every wind of doctrine; for to secure this end it must be public, recognizable, one, uniform, and authoritative. Nor could the individual teacher ever verify his commission, as a teacher sent from God, unless he can point to the visible body of which he is a member, and which was commissioned by Jesus Christ, and from him inherits the promises. Therefore we dismiss this notion of the invisible Church, and of an invisible body of true Christian teachers dispersed through various and conflicting communions. Such teachers would be as good as none, for no one could distinguish them from false teachers.

We repeat, then, the Roman Catholic ministry is the Apostolic ministry, for this ministry can be no other. This conclusion very few, perhaps none, would deny, if they admitted, what we have proved, that Jesus Christ did institute such a ministry as we contend for. If there be an infallible Church, authorized by the Saviour to teach, all must say, it is indisputably the Roman Catholic Church; for all see it can be no other, and, in fact no other even pretends to be it.

But we may prove our proposition not merely by the removal or destruction of the negative, but by plain, positive, affirmative evidence. The first method of proof is conclusive in itself; the second is also conclusive in itself. All that is to be done to prove the proposition affirmatively is, to identify the Roman Catholic ministry, as a corporation, with the corporation Jesus Christ instituted and commissioned in the persons of the Apostles. The kind of evidence needed is the same as is requisite in any case of the identification of a corporation. The identity is established by showing that the corporation retains its original name, and has regularly succeeded to the original corporators. The *name* is not conclusive evidence, but is a presumption of identity. In the present case, it is easy to prove that the ministry in question retains the Apostolic name. This name is *Catholic*, and the Roman Catholic Church bears it, and always has borne it. It is and always has been known and distinguished by it, and no other corporation is or ever has been known or distinguished by it. The old Donatists claimed it, but could not appropriate it. They are known only as *Donatists*. Some members of the English and American Episcopal Church, now and then, put on airs, and with great emphasis call themselves *Catholics ;* but the bystanders only smile, for they see the long ears peering out from under the lion's skin. While, on the other hand, go into any city in the world and ask the first lad you meet to direct you to the *Catholic* Church, and he will direct you without hesitation to the *Roman* Catholic Church. This shows, that, by the common judgment and consent of mankind, the distinctive appellation of the Church in communion with the See of Rome is *Catholic*.

The regular succession of the Roman Catholic ministry to the Apostolic is easily made out. We can establish the regular succession of pontiffs from St. Peter to Gregory the Sixteenth, the present Pope ; and this establishes the unity of the corporation in time, and therefore its identity. The regular succession and unity of authority of the corporation can also be established in the orders and mission of the pastors ; for the Catholic ministry has never been schismatic. This regular succession and unity of authority establishes, of course, the identity of the corporation. Then the Catholic ministry is identical with the Apostolic ministry. The two points on which this conclusion depends we leave, of course, without adducing in detail the historical proof of them. Established historically, they warrant the conclusion. They can be established by conclusive historical proof. Therefore the conclusion stands firm.

We establish our proposition, then, by showing that the Apostolic ministry *can* be no other than the Roman Catholic, and by showing that it *is* the Roman Catholic. Nothing more conclusive than this double proof can be desired. Then we sum up by repeating, that Jesus Christ has instituted and commissioned an infallible and indefectible body of teachers, and this body is the congregation of the Roman Catholic pastors in communion with their chief. The Catholic Church, then, is the witness to the fact of revelation. What its pastors declare to be the word of God is the word of God; what they enjoin as the faith is the faith without which it is impossible to please God, and without which we are condemned and the wrath of God abideth on us. What they teach is the truth, the whole truth, and nothing but the truth; for God himself has commissioned them, and will not suffer them to fall into error in what concerns the things they have been commissioned to teach.

The question of the Church as the congregation of believers can detain us but a moment. We agree with the *Christian Examiner*, that the Church in this sense embraces "the whole company of believers, the uncounted and wide-spread congregation of all those who receive the Gospel as the law of life; that the Church of Christ comprehends and is composed of all his followers." But who are these? "My sheep," says our blessed Lord, "hear my voice and follow me." We must hear his voice, as the condition of following him, or being his followers. But we cannot hear his voice where it is not, where it speaks not. Where, then, speaks his voice? In the Catholic Church, in and through the Catholic pastors, and nowhere else. Then we hear his voice only as we hear the voice of the Catholic Church, and follow him only as we follow what this Church in his name commands. Only they, then, who hear and obey the Catholic Church are of the Church,—only they who are in the communion of this Church are in the communion of Christ. It is time, then, to abandon No-Churchism, and to return to the one fold of the one Shepherd, and submit ourselves to the guidance of the pastors he has made rulers and teachers of the flock.

We do not suppose this conclusion will be very pleasing to our Protestant readers, and we do not suppose anything we could say, conscientiously, would please them; for we do not see any right they have to be pleased, standing where they do. There is the stubborn fact, that no man has God for his father who has not the Church for his mother, which cannot be got over; and if we have not the true Church for our mother, then "are we bastards and not sons." The presumption, to say the least, is strongly against our Protestant brethren; and they have great reason to fear, that, after all, they are only "children of the bondwoman." They may try to hide this from themselves, and to stifle the voice of conscience by crying out "Popery!" "Papist!" "Romanist!" "Idolatry!" "Superstition!" and the like, but this can avail them little. They may make light of the question, and think themselves excused from considering it. But there comes and must come to the greater part of them an hour when they feel the need of something more substantial than anything they have. They may use swelling words, and speak in a tone of great confidence; but the best of them have their doubts, nay, long periods when they can keep up their courage, and persuade themselves that they hope, only by shutting their eyes, refusing to think, plunging into religious dissipation, or giving way to the wild and destructive bursts of fanaticism and superstition. The great question of the salvation of the soul must at times press heavily upon them, and create no little anxiety. For it is a terrible thing to be forced into the presence of God uncovered by the robe of the Redeemer's righteousness,—a terrible thing to have all the sins of our past life come thronging back on the memory, and to feel that they are registered against us, unrepented of, unforgiven; a terrible thing to feel that the number of these sins is daily and hourly increasing, that we ourselves are continually exposed to the allurements of the world, the seductions of the flesh, and the temptations of the devil, with no weapon but our own puny arm with which to defend ourselves, and no strength but our own infirmity with which to recover and maintain our integrity. Alas! we know what this is. We know what it is to feel oppressed with the heavy load of guilt, to struggle alone in the world, against all manner of enemies, without faith, without hope, without the help of God's sacraments; we know what it is to feel that we must trust in our own arm and heart, stand on the pride of our own intellect and conviction. We know, too, what it is to feel all these defences fail, all this trust give way; for to us have come, as well as to others, those trying moments when the loftiest are laid low, and the proudest, prostrate in the dust, cry out from the depth of their spiritual agony, "Is there no help? O God! why standest thou afar off? Help, help, or I perish!" Alas! there are moments when we cannot trifle, when we cannot lean on a broken reed, when we *must* have something really Divine, something on which we can lay hold that will not break, and leave us to drop into everlasting perdition. It is a terrible question this of the salvation of the soul, and no man can prudently put it off. It must be met and answered, and the sooner the better.

We urge this upon our Protestant brethren. They have no solid ground on which to stand, no sure help on which to rely Their own restlessness proves it; their perpetual variations and shifting of their creeds prove it; the new and strange sects constantly springing up amongst them prove it; their worldly-mindedness, their universal and perpetual striving after what they have not, and find not, prove it; the wide-spread infidelity which prevails among them, and the still more destructive indifferency prove it. Their spiritual strength is the strength of self-confidence or of desperation. They cannot live so. There is no good for them in their present state. Why will they not ask if there be not a better way? If they will but seek, they shall find,—knock, it shall be opened to them. There is that faith which they deny, and that certainty which they ridicule. But they will find it not in their pride. They will find it not, till they learn to look on him they have despised, and to fly for succour to him they have crucified. But we have been betrayed into remarks, which, though true, would come with a better grace from one whose faith is less recent than our own. Yet we have said nothing by way of vain-glory. If we have faith, it is no merit of ours. We have been brought by a way we knew not, and by a Power we dared not resist; and His the praise and the glory, and ours the shame and mortification that for so many years we groped in darkness, boasting that we could see, and holding up our farthing-candle of a misguided reason as a light that was to enlighten the world!

We have been asked, "How in the world have you become a Catholic?" In this essay we have presented an outline, or rather a specimen, of the answer we have to give. It is incomplete; but it will satisfy the attentive reader, that not without some show of reason, at least, have we left our former friends and the endearing associations of our past life, and joined ourselves to a Church which excites only the deadly rage of the great mass of our countrymen. The change with us is a great one, and a greater one than the world dreams of, or will dream of. At any rate, it is a change we would not have made if we could have helped it,—a change against which we struggled long, but for which, though it makes us a pilgrim and a sojourner in life, and permits us no home here below, we can never sufficiently praise and thank our God. It is a great gain to lose even earth for heaven. If, however, we be pressed to give the full reason of our change, we must refer to the grace of God, and the need we felt of saving our own soul.

THE EPISCOPAL OBSERVER versus THE CHURCH.

THE EPISCOPAL OBSERVER, VOL. I., NO. III. BOSTON. MAY, 1845. MONTHLY.*

This periodical, the recently established organ of the Evangelical division of the Protestant Episcopal Church, in its number for May last, contains an attempted refutation of the article headed *The Church against No-Church*, in our last Review. The writer after a preliminary flourish or two, says his "purpose is to have the pleasure of refuting" us. We presume from this that his purpose is to have the pleasure of refuting the main position or leading doctrine of the article. That position or doctrine, as we stated it, is, that, "with this theory alone (the No-Church theory), it is impossible to elicit an act of faith:" or, in other words, that it is not possible to elicit an act of faith, unless we accept the authority of the Roman Catholic Church as the witness and expounder of God's word. Now, to refute this, it is not enough to invalidate our reasoning in this or that particular, but it is necessary to prove positively that an act of faith *can* be elicited by those who reject this authority. But this the writer has not done, and, so far as we can see, has not even attempted to do. He cannot, then, whatever else he may have done, have refuted us. All he has done, admitting him to have done all he has attempted, is, to prove, not that we were wrong in asserting the necessity of the authority of the Church to elicit an act of faith, but that it is impossible for any one to elicit an act of faith at all, as we shall soon have occasion to see.

But, in point of fact, the writer has not done what he attempted; he has not invalidated our reasoning in a single particular; and if he has succeeded in refuting any one, it is himself. He begins by giving, professedly, a synopsis of our argu-

* July, 1845.

ment; but his synopsis is very imperfect. It leaves out several distinct positions we assumed and attempted to establish as essential to the argument we were conducting. If this is by design, it impeaches the fairness and honesty of the writer; if unintentional, it shows that he did not comprehend the article he undertook to refute, and impeaches his capacity.

Our readers will recollect that we begin our argument by assuming, that, in order to be saved, to be acceptable to God, to enter into life, it is necessary to be a Christian. We then proceed to establish, 1. That, in order to be a Christian, it is necessary to be a believer, to believe *somewhat ;* 2. That this somewhat is TRUTH NOT FALSEHOOD; 3. That the truth we are to believe is the truth Jesus Christ taught or revealed; and, 4. That this truth, pertains, in part, at least, to the supernatural order. Now, the second position, namely, that, in order to be a Christian believer, it is necessary to believe TRUTH, NOT FALSEHOOD, the *Observer* entirely omits, and takes no notice of it, in its attempted refutation of us. Why is this? The *Observer* cannot suppose we inserted this proposition without a design, or that it is of no importance to our agument. The position is both positive and negative, and asserts, that, to be a Christian believer, it is necessary not only to believe truth, but truth without mixture of falsehood. A very important position, and one on which much of our subsequent reasoning depended, and designed to meet the very doctrine contended for by the *Observer*,—namely, that we have all the faith required of us, if we believe Christian truth, though we believe it mixed with error, in an exact or in a false sense.

After having established the four positions just enumerated, we proceed, in the second division of our article, to state the necessary conditions of faith in truths pertaining to the supernatural order, or what we need in order to be able to elicit an act of faith in a revelation of supernatural truth. Under this division, we attempt to establish, 1. That faith demands an authority on which to rest, extrinsic both to the believer and the matter believed; 2. That the only, but sufficient, authority for the *intrinsic* truth of the matter of supernatural revelation is the veracity of God; 3. That a witness to the fact that God has actually revealed the matter in question, that is, a witness to the fact of revelation, is also necessary; 4. That this witness must be not merely a witness to the fact that God has made a revelation, or to the fact of revelation in general, but to the precise revelation in each particular case in which there may be a question of what is or is not the revelation of God,—therefore *an interpreter*, as we expressed ourselves, of the genuine sense of the revelation; 5. That this witness must be universal, subsisting through all times and nations; 6. Unmistakable, with ordinary prudence, by the simple and illiterate; and, 7. Infallible.

Now, of these seven positions, the writer in the *Observer* objects expressly to the *fourth*, and, by implication, to the *seventh*. But he takes no notice of our definition of faith, namely, that "*it is a theological virtue, which consists in believing, without doubting, explicitly or implicitly, all the truths Almighty God has revealed, on the veracity of God alone*,"—on which, he must be aware, rests nearly the whole of our argument for the necessity of an infallible witness to the fact of revelation; for, if faith consists in believing *without doubting*, it is obvious that it is impossible to elicit an act of faith on the authority of a fallible witness. It can be possible only where there is no reasonable ground for doubt as to what God has actually revealed; and there always is reasonable ground for doubt, where the reliance is on a fallible witness, that is, a witness that may deceive or be deceived. Our conclusion, then, that the witness must be infallible, or faith is not possible, must be admitted, if our definition of faith is accepted. We were not to be refuted, then, on this point, except by a refutation of our definition of faith. But the writer in the *Observer* does not refute this definition, for he does not even notice it. How, then, can he claim to himself the "pleasure" of having refuted us?

But the writer in the *Observer* objects strongly to the *fourth* position of the second division of our article. He says we affirm that we need "an interpreter of the genuine sense of what God has revealed, because God has made faith the condition *sine qua non* of salvation; and if we should mistake the propositions actually contained in God's revelation, or substitute others therefor, since it is only through the proposition we arrive at the matter revealed, we should not believe the revelation God has actually made, *but something else, and something for which we cannot plead the veracity of God, and therefore something for which we have no solid ground of faith.*" The portion of this sentence in Italics the writer discreetly omits in his quotation. Our doctrine was this:—The ground of faith in the truth or matter revealed is the veracity of God revealing it. But when we believe the matter revealed in a false sense, not in its genuine sense, we do not, in fact, believe what is revealed, but something else, and, therefore, something which God has not revealed, and for the truth of which we have not his veracity. Consequently, we need an interpreter, that is, some means, or, as we say in the article, "*some authority,* extrinsic or intrinsic," to say what is or is not the revelation in its genuine sense; which is only saying, what is or is not the revelation Almighty God has actually made. Is it not so? Are we not right in this? The writer in the *Observer* says no. He objects to this, because we here, he says, assume "three things ..... which need a little looking after: 1. That God's revelation to man is not intelligible. 2. That a human interpreter can make it plain. 3. That, unless the nice theological shades of meaning in God's word are appreciated, one cannot be saved. In general terms, we deny all these propositions." So do we; and, moreover, we deny that we assume, or that our argument implies, either one or another of them.

The *Observer* contends that God's revelation is made to us in terms as express and as intelligible as human language can make it. "Natural reason," it says, "teaches us enough of God to know that he is infinitely wise, benevolent, and good. An infinitely wise, benevolent, and good being, in making a revelation to dependent and erring creatures, could not do otherwise than adapt it, in the most perfect manner, to their condition." Be it so; we said as much, more than once, ourselves. But what is "the most perfect manner?" "A revelation," continues the *Observer*, " coming from such a being, would be conveyed in intelligible propositions, so expressed and arranged as to be least liable to be misunderstood." In propositions intelligible through the ministry of the Church teaching, we grant it; otherwise, we deny it, *because he has not so conveyed, expressed, and arranged it.* "Then, if a revelation have come from God, it must be as clear and intelligible as human language can make it." Through the same ministry, we concede it; otherwise, we deny it, and for the same reason.

There was no occasion to assert the intelligibleness of divine revelation against us, for that we conceded. The real question at issue is not whether the revelation be intelligible, but whether it be intelligible without the aid of the pastors of the Church. The *Observer* was bound to show that no such aid is needed, or else not secure the "pleasure" of refuting us. We knew beforehand the only argument he could adduce, and that argument we ourselves adduced and replied to. The *Observer* has merely brought against us this objection, without *noticing our reply to it.* We stated, " It may be said that God is just, that he has made us a revelation, commanded us to believe it, and made belief of it the condition *sine qua non* of salvation ; but that he would not be just in so doing, if this revelation were not infallibly ascertainable in its genuine sense by the prudent exercise of natural reason." Here is the argument of the *Observer*, taken in connexion with what we had previously said of what natural reason teaches us of God, as clearly and as forcibly put as the *Observer* itself has put it; and here is our reply :—" Ascertainable by natural reason, *in one method or another,* we grant ; by private reason and the Bible alone, we deny ; *for God may have made the revelation ascertainable only by a divinely commissioned and supernaturally guided and protected body of teachers, and the office of natural reason to be to judge of the credibility of this body of teachers.*" This reply is conclusive, at least till shown to be inconclusive; consequently the writer in the *Observer* was precluded, by the most ordinary rules of logic and morals, from insisting on the objection, till he had not only noticed, but refuted, the reply. He has done neither. He has taken an objection which we had anticipated and replied to, urged it against us, without deigning to notice our reply, and this he calls refuting us!

The writer in the *Observer* proceeds in his argument against a position he says we assume but which we do not assume, on the assumption that the revelation Almighty God has made to us is made exclusively in the written word, and is made "in intelligible propositions, so expressed and arranged as to be least liable to be misunderstood," "as clear and as intelligible as language can make it." This assumption we met and refuted, or attempted to refute, in our article; but the *Observer*, according to its custom, takes no notice of our refutation, or attempted refutation. This assumption is provable only in two ways: 1. *A priori*, by reasoning from the known character of God; 2. *A posteriori*, by reasoning from the character of the revelation actually made. The first method can avail it nothing, for the reason we before assigned, and have just now repeated. We adduced, in our article, several arguments and facts to show that the second method can avail it just as little. These facts and arguments it does not set aside, does not attempt to set aside, for it does not even notice them, or make an effort to show that its assumption may be true in spite of them. And yet it purposed to have the "pleasure" of refuting us! and we are gravely assured by another Episcopal organ, *The Christian Advocate and Witness*, that it really has refuted us, and in a masterly manner turned our logic against us. Really, these Episcopalians have queer notions of what constitutes a refutation of an opponent.

But we deny the assumption of the *Episcopal Observer*, and call upon the writer to reply to the facts and arguments we adduced against it. Will he, in open day, maintain that the several articles of Christian faith, even as he holds them, are expressed in the Sacred Scriptures in propositions as clear and intelligible as human language can make them? He is an Episcopalian, and therefore believes, we are bound to presume, in the Nicene creed. Will he tell us where in the Sacred Scriptures the consubstantiality of the Son to the Father, or the procession of the Holy Ghost from the Father and the Son,—*Filioque*,—is expressed in terms as clear, as intelligible, and as unequivocal as in the creed? It will not be enough to adduce passages which teach or imply one or the other of these doctrines, but he must adduce passages which teach them as expressly, in a manner as clear and intelligible, as they are taught in the creed; for his assumption is, that they are expressed in the Sacred Scriptures in a manner as clear and intelligible as they can be in human language. Adduce the passages, if you please. You, as an Episcopalian, are bound to admit infant baptism as an article of the Christian faith. Do you find this expressed in the Bible in a manner " as clear and intelligible as human language can make it?" If so, why have you not been able, long ere this, to settle the dispute with your Baptist brethren, who have as much reverence for the Bible as you have, are as learned, and no doubt as honest? If the articles of Christian faith be expressed in the Sacred Scriptures in propositions as clear and intelligible as language can make them, how happens it that men dispute more about their sense as contained in the Sacred Scriptures than they do about their sense as drawn out and defined in the creed? Is there an article of faith held to be fundamental by the *Episcopal Observer* that has not been disputed on what has been conceived to be the authority of Scripture itself? Yet all is in Scripture as clear and as intelligible as human language can make it! Who is at a loss to know what the Catholic Church means by her decisions? Who questions the sense of the dogma as given in her definition of it? If she can define an article of faith so as to end all dispute concerning its sense, so far as she defines it, it follows that articles of faith can be expressed in language,

—for her definitions are expressed in language,—so as to preclude uncertainty as to their meaning. But this cannot be said of the articles of faith as expressed and arranged in the Sacred Scriptures, because men have doubted and disputed from the first, and do now doubt and dispute, as to what they are, as is proved by the number of ancient sects, and the some five hundred or more Protestant sects still extant; and also by the violent controversy, concerning what the writer in the *Observer* must regard as fundamentals, now raging in his own Church, both in this country and in England. Nay, the Scriptures themselves are express against the rash assumption of the *Observer*. "And account," says St. Peter, "the long-suffering of our Lord is salvation, as also our most dear brother Paul, according to the wisdom given him, hath written to you; as also in all his epistles, speaking in them of these things, in which there are certain things *hard to be understood*, which the *unlearned* and unstable wrest, as they do also the *other Scriptures*, to their own destruction."—2 Pet. iii. 15, 16. This is to the point. The Scriptures, according to their own declaration, do contain things *hard* to be understood, and which the unlearned wrest to their own destruction; aud these are not unessentials, because their misinterpretation involves the destruction of those who misinterpret them. Where is the intelligence, where is the conscience, of this rash writer? Has he no reverence for truth, no fear of God before his eyes, that he hesitates not to give the lie to the Holy Ghost, and to affirm what is so obviously untrue? Let him show as much unanimity among the aforesaid five hundred or more Protestant sects, who all hold the Bible to be the word of God, and profess to take it as their rule of faith and practice, concerning what he himself holds to be fundamentals, as we can show him among Catholics concerning the meaning of the articles of faith the Church has defined, and we will listen to his assertion, that the revelation of God, as contained in the Sacred Scriptures,—for this is his meaning,—is "as clear and intelligible as human language can make it;" but till then, we recommend him to moderate his tone, and meditate daily on the solemn fact that a judgment awaits us, and we must all give an account for all our thoughts, *words*, and deeds. An induction contradicted by glaring and lamentable facts is inadmissible; and such is his, that the revelation of God, as expressed in the Sacred Scriptures, is "as clear and intelligible as human language can make it." We admit the revelation to be perfectly intelligible in the way and manner, and by the means, intended by the Revealer; but in the way and manner asserted by the *Observer*, we deny its intelligibleness, as must every honest man who has seriously undertaken to interpret the Holy Scriptures by the aid of private reason alone.

The writer in the *Observer* asserts that we assume "that a human interpreter can make it (divine revelation) plain." We assume no such thing; and moreover, if he is capable of understanding, in any degree, his mother tongue, and has read our article through, he knows that we not only do not, but, with our general doctrine, that we could not. Does he not know, that, throughout the article, we are attempting, among other things, to establish the utter incompetency of a merely human interpreter? Does he not know that we contend for the competency of the Church to interpret or declare the revelation of God, only on the ground that she has the promise of the superhuman, the supernatural, guidance and assistance of the Holy Ghost? Does he not know, that, according to all Catholics, it is not the Humanity of the Church, but the Divinity, whose Spouse she is, that decides in her decisions, and in her interpretations is the interpreter? Prove us wrong in holding this, if you can; but do not assert that we assume, either consciously or unconsciously, that the revelation of God can be made plain by a mere human interpreter. It was not for a human interpreter we contended, but for a divine interpreter; and our argument was to prove, that, without a divine interpreter of divine revelation, it is impossible to elicit an act of faith. Will the *Episcopal Observer* remember this? The folly and absurdity it ascribes to us, of contending for a human interpreter, we leave to Low-Churchmen and their dearly beloved children and grandchildren, the No-Churchmen.

The *Observer* also charges us with assuming, "that, unless the nice theological shades of meaning in God's word be appreciated, one cannot be saved." There is little pleasure in replying to an opponent who has yet to learn the simplest elements of the matters in debate, and on which he affects to speak as a master. The writer in the *Observer* does not appear to have ever read a single elementary work on theology. He appears to be wholly ignorant of any distinction between faith and theology. We said not one word about "nice theological shades of meaning;" we neither said, nor implied in anything we said, that theology is at all necessary to salvation. We spoke of *faith* as the condition *sine qua non* of salvation, we admit, but not of *theology;* and we contended that the faith must be embraced in its purity and integrity, or one cannot be saved: but not that one cannot be saved unless he appreciates the nice distinctions of theology. Theology and its distinctions belong to science, a science constructed by human reason from principles derived from the light of nature and the supernatural revelation made immediately to faith. It is useful, because, in the ordinary course of divine providence, we cannot have faith, propagate, preserve, and defend faith, without it; for by it, as says St. Augustine, *Fides saluberrima, quæ ad veram beatitudinem ducit, gignitur, defenditur, roboratur.** Theology is necessary or useful only as subservient to faith; but faith is indispensable to salvation, as says the blessed Apostle, "Without faith it is impossible to please God;" and whoso does not please God, we take it, is not in the way of salvation. As to distinctions or nice shades of meaning in faith, we said nothing about them, for we were not aware of their existence. Faith is one, a whole, and must be embraced in its purity and integrity, or it is not embraced at all.

"But it is derogatory to the character of God and the interests of religion," says the writer in the *Observer*, "to say that

---

* Lib. XIV. *De Trin.* Cap. 1

the *exact mind* of the Spirit must in every point in revelation be fully seen and acknowledged, as the condition of being saved." On what authority is this said? Does he deny faith to be the condition *sine qua non* of salvation? Of course not, for we assert it in our article, and he takes no exception to our assertion. Must not this be faith in what the Holy Ghost has revealed, that is, in the revelation Almighty God has made? Has not Almighty God made belief of this revelation a necessary condition of salvation? If so, has he made it necessary to believe the *whole*, or only a *part?* In its *exact* sense, or in an *inexact* sense? If you say a part is not necessary to be believed, will you tell us what part? Will you be so obliging as to favor us with a specification, on divine authority, of the portions of revelation which we have the permission of the Holy Ghost to disbelieve or not believe?

That it is necessary to believe the *whole* revelation, as the condition *sine qua non* of salvation, is evident from the very definition we gave of faith, namely, that it is "a theological virtue, which consists in believing *all* the truths God has revealed, on the veracity of God alone." Does the *Observer* deny this definition of faith? If it does, why has it not said so, and refuted it by refuting the arguments by which we attempted to sustain it? and, since its purpose was to have the *pleasure* of refuting us, why did it not give and sustain a definition in opposition to ours? Was it a sufficient refutation of us for it to pronounce, as it does, that, in that portion of the article in which we give this definition, we "enter into a bog and flounder till we reach the opposite side?" Was it afraid, if it followed us, it would itself sink in the "bog," stick fast in the "morass?" or was it only the *pleasure*, not the *pain*, of refuting us it promised itself? If faith consist in believing all the truths Almighty God has revealed,—and dare the *Observer* assert that it does not?—and if faith be, as the blessed Apostle declares, the condition without which we cannot be saved, it follows necessarily that the whole mind of the Spirit, so far as revealed, must be believed, as the condition of being saved.

Will the writer in the *Observer* deny this? Let him do it, and he may possibly find himself in " a bog " to which there is *no* " other side."

But it may be the writer in the *Observer* does not mean to assert, that "it is derogatory to the character of God and injurious to the interests of religion" to say, that *all* the truths Almighty God has revealed must be explicitly believed, as the condition of being saved, but simply that it is derogatory, &c., to say they must be explicitly believed in their *exact* sense, as they lie in the mind of the Holy Ghost. We say *explicitly believed*, for this is what he must mean by being "fully seen and acknowledged." What he means to object to is the assertion, that the *exact* mind of the Spirit must be believed as the condition *sine qua non* of salvation. "The exact mind of the Spirit" must mean the entire revelation Almighty God has made, in its *exact sense*, or, as we expressed ourselves, in its genuine sense. Then we can understand by the exact mind of the Spirit neither more nor less than "the pure word of God." Then it is derogatory to the character of God and injurious to the interests of religion to say, that the pure word of God—the revelation in its purity and integrity—must be believed as the condition of being saved. Then, in order not to derogate from the character of God, and not to injure the interests of religion, we must say, the impure word of God, that is, the word of God corrupted by a greater or less admixture of falsehood and error, is sufficient, all that it is necessary to believe, in order to be saved, or to have that faith without which "it is impossible to please God!" Is the *Episcopal Observer* prepared to adopt this conclusion? It must adopt it. It will not allow us to insist on the *exact* mind of the Spirit. But if we do not take the exact mind of the Spirit, we must take the *inexact* mind. The inexact mind, so far forth as inexact, is not the mind of the Spirit at all,—is not the word of God,— is not truth, but falsehood, and therefore of the Devil, who is a liar from the beginning, and the father of lies. The inexact mind of the Spirit is the impure or corrupt word of God, the word of God and the words of the Devil combined. If it be derogatory to the character of God and injurious to the interests of religion to insist on the necessity to salvation of faith in the *pure* word of God, it must be honorable to the character of God and advantageous to the interests of religion to contend that belief of the impure word, the corrupt word, the word of God combined with the words of the Devil, is sufficient as the condition of being saved! A very comforting doctrine to all classes of errorists; for they all hold the truth, or some portion of truth, but mixed with error,—that is, in an inexact, a false, or a corrupt sense. The *Observer's* own church defines the visible Church of Christ to be "a congregation of faithful men, in the which the pure word of God is preached." Art. XIX. We suppose they who preach the pure word of God preach it because they hold its belief to be necessary as the condition of being saved. The Church of Christ, then, inasmuch as it preaches, and, we presume, insists on, the *pure* word of God, or the exact mind of the Spirit, as necessary to salvation, does that which is "derogatory to the character of God and injurious to the interests of religion!" Happily, however, for the writer in the *Observer*, his church is not obnoxious to this charge; for it is unquestionably innocent of the sin of preaching the pure word of God.

After all, this is rather a singular doctrine for a Protestant to *avow*, however consistent it may be for him to *entertain* it. The charge against the Church of Rome by the pseudo-reformers was not that it did not hold the word of God, but that it had ceased to hold it in its purity. It had corrupted the word of God, not the written word, not the text, but the sense, the doctrine, that is, "the mind of the Spirit," and therefore had become a corrupt church, in the bosom of which salvation had become impossible, or, at least, exceedingly doubtful. On this ground they pretended to separate from its communion, and on this ground their children have generally attempted to vindicate their separation. But the *Episcopal Observer*, it seems, abandons this ground, and gives the Reformers a very unfilial blow.

According to this modern Protestant, the fact that a church has corrupted the word of God, and preaches not the pure word, but the impure word, is rather to its credit, and should be a motive for seeking or remaining in its communion, instead of a motive for separating from it. The only good ground of separation, if we accept his doctrine, would be the fact that the Church preaches the pure word of God, and commands belief in the exact mind of the Spirit, as the condition of salvation. From such a church it must be one's duty to separate, because such a church derogates from the character of God, and injures the interests of religion. Perhaps it was on this ground, after all, that the Reformers separated from the communion of the Holy See, and on this ground that Protestants generally remain separate from that communion.

But the *Observer* not only protests against the necessity of belief in the exact mind of the Spirit, but it contends that the exact mind of the Spirit cannot possibly be communicated to us. "Thoughts may be communicated," it says, " by a written or spoken language; but *perfectly, entirely, unmistakably*, by neither. To this rule the thoughts of God form no exception. When communicated to erring men, they come clothed under the guise of the erring representative, human language; and of necessity, therefore, are liable, in some of their shades, to be misconceived." So Almighty God himself cannot, if he will, teach us the exact truth, nor make to us a revelation of his will which we may believe without mixture of error! The truth as it is in God cannot be communicated to us; we can never receive what God is pleased to reveal, "*perfectly, entirely, unmistakably;*" but must always misconceive it to a greater or less extent, and substitute, for the mind of the Spirit, our own mind, —for the word of God, our own words, or the words of the Devil! And yet, the *Observer* tells us, the revelation God has made us is so easy of comprehension, "that the wayfaring man, though a fool, *shall not err therein.*" Nevertheless, Almighty God himself cannot make a revelation that can be perfectly received, that can be embraced without mistakes and misconceptions. It is a convenience, sometimes, when we wish to secure the "pleasure" of refuting an opponent, to have short memories and flexible principles.

But, according to the *Observer*, we can never, even by the help of Almighty God, embrace the word of God in its purity and integrity; for, coming to us "clad in the defectible exterior of human language," it must, "by a *law of necessity*, be understood differently by different minds." We can never know precisely what it is God requires us to believe, and we never can believe what he requires us to believe, without mixing with it more or less of error and falsehood. Be it so. Will the *Observer* oblige us, then, by telling us how far we may combine with the word of God, or substitute for it, our own words, or those of the Devil, without danger to the soul? Will he tell us, *on divine authority*, where is the exact boundary, on one side of which mistakes and misconceptions, errors and falsehoods, are harmless, and on the other side of which they are destructive? Will he give us some rule by which we may always know whether we are on the right side or the wrong side? The rule is important, and we pray this Protestant theologian, who proposes to himself the very great pleasure of refuting us, to give us the slight pleasure of furnishing us this rule, so that we may not only know whether he really has refuted us, but also whether we have more or less error than we may with safety entertain.

But if we cannot receive the revelation of God without mistaking or misconceiving it, how is it possible for us to know whether we have the faith Almighty God requires of us or not? If we mistake on one point why may we not on another? And if we are always liable to err, if even Almighty God cannot set us right, because he can speak to us only through human language, which is always and necessarily a distorting medium, where is faith, or even the possibility of faith? Faith is to believe *without doubting*, and is possible only where there is absolute certainty. But where there is a liability to err, nay, a necessity to mistake and misconceive, there is and can be no absolute certainty, but is and necessarily must be doubt, and, therefore, no faith. If the *Observer* is right in its doctrine, faith is impossible. It clearly shows, then, that, on its premises, faith, properly so called, is impossible,—the very conclusion to which, we stated, in advance, we intended to force it and all who reject the authority of the Catholic Church as the witness and expounder of God's word. Yet it claims " the pleasure" of having refuted us!

We can understand now, why, in his synopsis of our argument, the writer in the *Observer* leaves out our definition of faith, and our position that what we are to believe is *truth, not falsehood*. If faith be to believe without doubting, it is not possible without absolute certainty, and absolute certainty is possible only in the case of absolute truth; and absolute truth he foresaw he was not likely to get, without going to Rome; for, without going to Rome, he knew he could, at best, have only truth mixed with falsehood. To controvert our definition of faith, or to refute the arguments by which we sustained our position, that what we are to believe is " truth, not falsehood," was no easy matter, and not safe to be attempted; and yet he must have the pleasure of refuting us.

The whole controversy between Catholics and Protestants turns on the questions here involved. Catholics say that Almighty God has made us a revelation, and commanded us to believe it, without doubting, *in its integrity and genuine sense*, as the condition *sine qua non* of salvation. Protestants also say God has made us a revelation, and commanded us to believe it without doubting, as the condition *sine qua non* of salvation, *but*, virtually, if not expressly, *that he does not command us to believe it in its integrity and genuine sense, but only so much of it as commends itself to our own minds and hearts, and in the sense in which it pleases us to understand it.* They are obliged to say this, or acknowledge the authority of the Catholic Church, and condemn themselves, as not having that faith without which they cannot be saved.

The presumption, to say the least, is in favor of the Catholics·

for we cannot reasonably suppose that the Holy Ghost reveals what he does not require us to believe, nor that he can consent that we should believe his word in any sense but his own. The Protestants are, then, presumptively in the wrong, and consequently, the *onus probandi* rests on them. They can justify themselves only by producing, on divine authority, a specification of the portions of God's word they have the permission of the Holy Ghost to disbelieve or not believe, according to their own caprice; and also the permission of the Holy Ghost to believe his word in their own sense, rather than in his. God has made us a revelation; this they admit, as well as we. He has commanded us to believe it; this they admit as well as we. He has made belief of it a necesssary condition of salvation; this they dare not deny. What, then, is the fair presumption from these premises? Is it not, that God commands belief in his revelation in its purity and integrity as the condition of salvation? Unquestionably. Then, unless you have his authority for saying that he neither requires you to believe all he has revealed, nor to believe what you do believe in its true sense, you are convicted of not having the faith he commands, unless you actually believe his whole revelation, and in its true sense.

Moreover, the ground on which you are to believe this revelation is the veracity of God alone. Now, this ground is sufficient ground of faith in all that God has revealed, and you can with no more propriety refuse to believe one portion of it than another. To refuse to believe this revelation is to make God a liar, and you make him a liar in refusing to believe one article, as much as you would in refusing to believe the whole. You must, then, believe the whole, or you make God, in your own mind, a liar; and are you prepared to maintain that he who charges God with falsehood, which is to blaspheme the Holy Ghost, is in the way of salvation?

So must you also believe the revelation in God's sense; *for it is only in his sense that it is his word.* If you put a meaning upon my words different from the meaning I put upon them, they cease to be my words, and become yours. So, when you put a meaning upon God's word different from the meaning he puts upon it, it ceases to be his word, and becomes your word, and you believe then the truth not as it is in God, but as it is in you. You must, then, believe the revelation in its true sense, or you do not believe the revelation Almighty God has made. Is it not remarkable that Protestants seem never to be aware of this?

Again, God commands *faith* in his revelation. But faith is to believe without doubting, and is, as we have seen, possible only on condition of infallible evidence, which leaves no room for doubt, but gives absolute certainty. The certainty of faith, though different in kind, must be equal in degree to the certainty of knowledge, or it is not faith. But this certainty is not possible in case of error or falsehood. Error or falsehood cannot be infallibly evidenced; for, if it could, it would not be error or falsehood, but truth. It follows, therefore, that the requisite degree of evidence to elicit faith is possible only in the case of absolute truth. But the revelation of God, when misinterpreted, when taken not in its exact sense, is not absolute truth, and therefore cannot be so evidenced to the mind as to elicit faith. But we must have faith, or be eternally damned. Then you must take the revelation in its exact sense, or not be saved.

Do you reply, that faith, in this sense, is impossible, because it is impossible to have infallible certainty of the exact mind of the Spirit? This is a plain begging of the question. Impossible, on your ground, we admit; but not, therefore, necessarily, on every ground. Your objection merely proves that you cannot, as Protestants, elicit an act of faith, which is what we contend; but when you say *therefore* we cannot elicit faith at all, you assume that your ground is the true and only ground, which is what we deny, and what it is your business to prove. Because you cannot elicit faith, it does not follow that faith cannot be elicited. God has commanded it, as you yourselves dare not deny; but God cannot command what is impossible; therefore faith is possible. Then the fact that it is not possible, on your ground, only proves that you are wrong.

One of the objections we brought against the Bible, as the witness to the fact of revelation, was, that, without an infallible authority, distinct from the Bible, it is impossible to prove the *sufficiency* of the Scriptures. We contended, for several reasons, which we gave, that they who take the Bible, as interpreted by private reason alone, for the only and sufficient rule of faith, are bound to prove that their rule is sufficient from the Sacred Scriptures themselves. But this they cannot do, for the Scriptures nowhere assert their own sufficiency. The *Observer* contends that they are not bound to prove the sufficiency of the Scriptures, but that we are bound to prove their *insufficiency!* But it nowhere takes up or replies to our objections, and nowhere shows on what principle we are bound to prove a negative. Doubtless, if we deny a proposition, we are bound to justify our denial by adducing a good reason for it; but in most cases it is sufficient to allege the fact that the affirmative proposition is not proved. Protestants assert the sufficiency of the Scriptures; it is their business to prove that sufficiency, and by divine authority, too,—a thing they never have done, and a thing they know perfectly well, if they know anything of the subject, they never can do. By what right do they assume a position, without offering a single particle of evidence appropriate in the case to prove it, and then call upon us to disprove it? Is rational culture so neglected among Protestants, and even Protestant theologians, that they have no more sense of sound reasoning than this implies?

But we went further, and *disproved* the sufficiency of the Scriptures, which was more than our argument required. Faith is to believe, without doubting, *all* the truths Almighty God has revealed, and, therefore, is possible only on condition that we have absolute certainty that what we receive as the revelation of God is his revelation, and the whole of his revelation, as we proved before and have now proved again. The witness, to be adequate, sufficient, must, then, testify to the fact that the matter believed or to be believed is the revelation, and the whole revelation. Now, to this last fact, namely, that they contain the whole revelation, or the whole word of God, the Scriptures do not testify. Therefore, they are insufficient, for this very reason, if for no other. This is the argument adduced in our article, and, certainly, before the *Observer* can legitimately claim the *pleasure* of having refuted us, and the right to assert the sufficiency of the Scriptures, it is bound to set this argument aside. But it does not even notice it.

The *Observer*, we apprehend, does not understand what a witness to the *fact* of revelation means. He seems to reason on the supposition, that, when we contended for a witness to the fact of revelation, we meant merely that we must have a witness to the fact that God has made a revelation. We assure him this was not our meaning. We mean by the fact of revelation, not simply the fact that God has made a revelation, but that he has revealed this or that is a fact; and we mean by a witness to the fact of revelation, not merely a witness to revelation in general, but to each particular point of the revelation. Assume, for instance, that the mystery of the Trinity is the point in question. The ground of faith in this mystery is the veracity of God revealing it. But before we can know that we have God's veracity for the truth of this adorable mystery, we must know that God has revealed it, that is, the *fact* that he has revealed it. Now, the witness we demand is a witness to this fact, and to the like fact in every other case; and unless we have such a witness—an infallible witness, too—in each particular case, we have and can have no faith. Does the *Observer* understand this? Will it deny that a witness, and an infallible witness, in the sense here defined, is the condition *sine qua non* of faith? Can it say that God has revealed this or that article of faith, if it have no witness to the fact that God has revealed it? Can it say it with absolute certainty without an infallible witness? and if it cannot say with infallible certainty that God has revealed it, can it believe, without doubting, that he has revealed it? No man has faith, till he can say with St. Augustine, "O God, if I am deceived, *Thou* hast deceived me," and this, too, in every single article of faith. Who can say this, unless he has infallible evidence that the particular article, which is in question, is actually God's word?

We must, then, have the witness, or faith is impossible. What is this witness? We stated that it must be, 1. Reason; 2. The Bible; 3. Private illumination; or, 4. The Apostolic ministry, or *Ecclesia docens*. We demonstrated that it could not be the first three, and, therefore, inferred that it must be the fourth, or we have no witness. The *Observer* nowhere meets our arguments; but merely cavils at one or two collateral points. It does not bring out, clearly and distinctly, any doctrine of its own; but, so far as we can understand its loose statements, it assumes that the witness is the Bible, interpreted, not by private reason, but by private illumination, or what he calls " the internal monitor." We prove by historical testimony that the Scriptures contain the revelation of God, and by the internal monitor we ascertain its sense.

But, 1. We cannot, by historical testimony, prove that the Bible contains the *whole* revelation of God; and yet, assuming a revelation to have been made, and belief of it enjoined as the condition of being saved, we can demonstrate, as we have shown, by reason, that it is necessary to believe, and to know that we believe, the whole.

2. There are many false prophets gone out into the world, and we are not to believe every spirit, but to try the spirits if they be of God.—1 St. John, iv. 1. There must, then, be some criterion by which we may distinguish the true from the false. This cannot be the internal monitor, *because that is precisely what we are to try.* What is this criterion? The blessed Apostle tells us. " We are of God. He that knoweth God heareth us. He that is not of God heareth not us. By this we know the spirit of truth from the spirit of error."— *Ib.* 6. If you have the spirit of truth, you hear the Apostles, that is, abide in the Apostolic doctrine and communion. You must, then, prove that you abide in the Apostolic doctrine and

communion, before you have proved your right to follow your "internal monitor."

3. We are commanded to give a reason to them that ask us of the hope that is in us. But, according to the *Observer* itself, this inward witness is authority only for the individual himself, and, therefore, no reason to be assigned to others.

4. All men are required to believe the revelation God has made, on pain of eternal condemnation. To believe the revelation is to believe it in its integrity and genuine sense. But it must be propounded to those who are as yet unbelievers in this sense, as the condition of their believing it. Now, it must be propounded with infallible evidence that it is the revelation of God, or without it. If without it, unbelievers are justifiable in rejecting it, which no Christian can admit. But if the sense is to be ascertained only by the inward monitor of the individual, it cannot be propounded with the infallible evidence required, for this evidence must be evidence to the revelation in its genuine sense, since otherwise that which is evidenced would not be the word of God, but something else,—the words of man, or of the Devil.

5. The internal monitor is the Holy Ghost. Is the Holy Ghost given to unbelievers? If you say yes, we demand the proof, which the *Observer* admits cannot be given. If you say no, then, we ask, where is the sin of unbelievers in that they are unbelievers? The revelation is not *credible*, save in its true sense. They who are not privately illuminated by the Holy Ghost know not and cannot know it in its true sense. Then they cannot believe it. Yet they are, by all Christian theology, declared sinners in consequence of their unbelief. Is a man a sinner for not doing what he has not the ability to do?

6. But lastly, the practical effects of this doctrine prove that it is not of God. It paves the way for lawless enthusiasm, and the introduction of all manner of false doctrines. Every enthusiast may allege that he has the Holy Ghost, and though what he teaches is as false as hell and wicked as the Devil, you have no means of convicting him. He speaks by the Holy

Ghost; would you shut the mouth of the Holy Ghost? He follows the Spirit; would you resist the Spirit? Each man is the *Ecclesia docens*, and professes to speak with infallible authority. What will you do? What will you say? Your mouth is shut. Does not the Spirit witness to itself? What right have you to oppose your Spirit to his? Has he not as high authority as you have? You say, No; he says, Yes; and how are you to prove your *no* is above his *yes*? What is to decide between you? The Bible? Not so fast. Your rule of faith is the Bible interpreted by the internal monitor. He appeals to the Bible, as well as you; and the question is not, whether the Bible be or be not the word of God, but whether he or you have its genuine sense. What does the Bible mean? You, on the authority of what you call the Holy Ghost, say it means this; he, on what he alleges to be the same authority, says it means that. Which of you is right? What is to decide? Nothing. You cannot convict him, nor he you. There you are, eternally at loggerheads, and the most damnable heresies are rife in the land, and ruining the people, both for this world and for that which is to come. This is one of the glorious effects of your " glorious Reformation !" Can a doctrine, leading to such disastrous consequences, be a doctrine from God? And has Almighty God provided no safer rule for the instruction of his children in that faith he requires them to believe as the condition of being saved? Out upon the foul blasphemy! Say it not, but rather go and sit in sackcloth and ashes at the foot of the cross, look on him ye have crucified, and weep in silence over your folly and wickedness.

The *Observer* complains of us, that we assumed, in our argument, that Protestants admit that God has made us a revelation, and that we did not reason with them as if they were Jews, Mahometans, or infidels. Perhaps we were wrong in this, but it will do us, we hope, the justice to acknowledge, that we did not assume them to be *believers* in the revelation of God; we only assumed that they *profess* to believe it, at least, some portions of it. We have known Protestants too long and too intimately to be guilty of the folly of inferring their *belief* from their *profession*. We hope this explanation will satisfy the *Observer*, and induce it to withdraw its complaint. We assumed that Protestants admit that God has made us a revelation, and that the Scriptures, so far as we had in our argument occasion to appeal to that revelation, contain an authentic record of it. This they profess; and in reasoning with them, we supposed it would be more respectful to take them at their profession than it would be to go behind it for their actual belief or want of belief. If, however, they object to this, prefer to have us reason with them as if they were infidels, and really believe that this would be more in accordance with truth, we will hereafter do our best to accommodate them.

On one point the *Observer* seems really to believe that it has caught us in a difficulty, and its antics on the occasion are quite diverting. We contended that we cannot elicit an act of faith without an infallible witness to the fact of revelation, and that this witness cannot be reason, the Bible, nor private illumination, but is and must be the Apostolic ministry. On this, the *Observer* breaks out:—" We have, then, no proof of the fact of revelation, unless we can find it in the testimony of the Apostolic ministry. Very well, Mr. Brownson, as the first important matter is *the fact that we have a revelation*, bring forward the witness. The witness! the witness! we must have the witness!" With all my heart, dear Mr. *Observer;* only contain yourself a moment. You call for a witness to the fact that God has made us a revelation, and to this fact you imply that we have no witness to produce but the Apostolic ministry. With your leave, this is a mistake. There is a wide difference between what we call the fact of revelation, and the fact that God has made us a revelation. To the fact of revelation, that is, to prove what is or is not the revelation Almighty God has made, the Apostolic ministry is *to us* the only competent witness; but to the fact that Almighty God has made a revelation, it is not, nor did we pretend or imply that it is, the only witness. To this fact we adduce as the witness HISTORICAL

TESTIMONY, by which we prove that there was such a person as Jesus Christ, and that he wrought miracles which prove him to have spoken by divine authority. Here is the witness you demand. Do you object to its testimony? Bring forward, then, your objections, and we will reply to them when we come to defend the Church against infidels.

If the *Observer* had read our article from page 45 to page 50, it would, perhaps, have suspected that we could extricate ourselves more easily from the difficulty it has conjured up, than it appears to have imagined. It is often a convenience to understand your opponent, before attempting to refute him,—though sometimes an inconvenience, we admit, if one is resolved beforehand, come what will, to have the "pleasure" of refuting him. The Apostolic ministry, existing, as it has, in uninterrupted succession through eighteen hundred years, is itself, by the very fact of its existence, a proof of the fact that Almighty God has made us a revelation; but we did not adduce it, nor are we obliged, by the logical conditions of our argument, to adduce it, in proof of this fact; for we prove this fact independently of its authority, by the historical testimony by which we establish the authenticity of the Scriptures as historical documents.

The *Observer* accuses us of reasoning in a *vicious* circle, because we assert that the Apostolic ministry is the only competent witness to the fact of revelation, and yet appeal to the Scriptures in proof of the fact that a revelation has been made, and to determine the commission of the ministry. We confess we can detect no *vicious* circle in this. The fact that a revelation has been made was evidenced to those who lived in the age in which it was made by miracles, which accredited those by whom it was made, as we showed in our article. We appeal to the Scriptures, in the first instance, not to ascertain what this revelation is, but as a simple historical record of the miracles and other facts, which prove that a revelation has been made, or that God has really spoken to man. It is perfectly legitimate to say, the Apostolic ministry is the only witness competent to say what it is God has or has not spoken, and yet appeal to the Scriptures as historical doctrines to prove that he has spoken. Here is no *vicious* circle.

Nor do we reason in a *vicious* circle when we assume the Apostolic ministry to be the only witness to the fact of revelation, and yet adduce the Scriptures as historical documents in proof of the commission of the ministry. Because we do not first assume the authority of the ministry as the only proof of the Scriptures as historical documents, and then adduce the Scriptures in proof of the commission which authorizes it to testify to that authenticity. We take the Scriptures, already proved to be authentic historical documents, so far forth as historical in their character, at least, so far forth as we have occasion to use them in the argument, to prove one simple historical fact, namely, the commission which Jesus Christ gave to his Apostles; and then we take the ministry, proved, through the commission of the Apostles, to be Apostolic, as the witness to the fact and the expounder of revelation, whether contained in the Scriptures or deposited elsewhere. Here is no *vicious* circle, and we say so on the authority of the *Observer* itself. We accused the advocates of private illumination with reasoning in a *vicious* circle, when they take the witness to prove the Scriptures, and then the Scriptures to prove the witness. Not at all, says the *Observer:* "For while we take the Scriptures to prove the witness, we do not take the witness to prove the *truth* of the Scriptures, but their *sense*. The establishment of the fact of their existence, as the record of God's revealed will, is antecedent to their use to prove the witness, and independent of his testimony." This, though not a complete reply to us,—because, as a matter of fact, the establishment of the existence of the Scriptures as the record of *God's revealed will* is not antecedent to their use to prove the witness, since the fact that they are the record of the *revealed will* of God in its purity and integrity is one of the facts to which the witness is to testify, —is nevertheless a valid distinction, and a complete refutation of the *Observer's* charge against us. For, while we take the

Scriptures *as historical documents*, to prove the conmmission of the Apostolic ministry, we do not take the Apostolic ministry to prove that the Scriptures are authentic historical documents, but to prove what is or is not the word which Almighty God has spoken. The establishment of the fact of their existence as authentic historical documents is antecedent to their use to prove the commission of the Apostolic ministry, and independent of its testimony. The blunder of the *Observer* comes from confounding the fact of the existence of the Scriptures as authentic historical documents with the fact of their authority as a record of revelation.

The *Observer*, however, is not to be so easily balked of the "pleasure" of refuting us.

"We want no easier task than to establish false religions on the principle here laid down. There would be no difficulty to get the appointment of a body of pastors and teachers, and then to find witnesses to testify to the *fact of the appointment*. And then, if this body of teachers were allowed to say that such and such books contained the record of a revelation from God, we could not only have as many false teachers as we wanted, but a correspondent number of spurious Bibles. If the lying 'witness' swear to a false revelation, the untrue revelation would of course vouch for the appointment of the witness. It is easy enough, then, to bring historical testimony to the appointment of a witness; but the *authority* of the witness—is it from heaven, or of men? If you say, of men, then, why believe the testimony? if from heaven, then it is a *revealed* fact, and on your principles cannot be known but by the testimony of the 'witness.' Bishop Sherlock, in his day, fell in with just such reasoners as Mr. Brownson, and pushed them around the circle after this manner: 'The Scriptures are very intelligent to honest and diligent readers, in all things necessary to salvation; and if they be not, I desire to know how we shall find out the Church; for certainly the Church has no charter but what is in the Scriptures; and then, if we must believe the Church before we can believe or understand the Scriptures, we must believe the Church before we can possibly know whether there be a church or not! If we prove the Church by the Scriptures, we must believe and understand the Scriptures before we can know the Church. If we believe and understand the Scriptures upon the authority and interpretation of the Church, considered as a church, then we must know the Church before the Scriptures. The Scripture cannot be known without the Church, nor the Church without the Scripture, and yet one of them must be known first; yet neither of them can be known first, according to these principles; which is such an absurdity, as all the art of the world can never palliate.'

"That Mr. Brownson may have no ground to say he is treated unfairly in this matter, we give him leave to hang upon just which horn of the dilemma he may choose; but as for hanging upon both, we insist that he shall do no such thing."—pp. 138, 139.

With the *Observer's* permission, we will, at present, hang on neither horn. To the extract from Bishop Sherlock we reply, that the Scriptures, as authentic historical documents, are logically, though not chronologically, in our argument, before the Church as a divinely commissioned body; but the Church, as the divinely commissioned witness and expounder of the word of God, is both logically and chronologically before the Scriptures, for, as a matter of fact, the Church is older than the Scriptures.

The divine *authority* of the commission is inferred from the fact that it was given by Jesus Christ, proved, by the miracles he performed, to speak by divine authority. The fact that he wrought miracles, and the fact that he gave the commission, are both historical facts, and provable by historical testimony, without our being obliged to appeal to the authority of the witness.

But the *authority* of the commission, if of God, is a *revealed* fact. If revealed, it can be proved only by the authority of the Apostolic ministry, because that is the only witness we acknowledge to the fact of revelation. Then we must assume the divine authority of the commission as the condition of proving it, which is absurd; or we must admit some other witness than the Apostolic ministry, and then we contradict ourselves, and our whole reasoning falls to the ground. This objection was urged against us by the *Christian World*, one of the organs of the Unitarians. The reply is simple and easy. The Apostolic ministry is nothing but the continuation of Christ's own ministry while he was on the earth; and the Church teaching, which we have called the Apostolic ministry, was, while he was on earth, in him. But in him its authority to teach is not established by the commission to the Apostles, but by the miracles he wrought. We take the authority of the Church teaching in him while he was on earth, proved by miracles to be of God, to establish the Divine authority of the commission to the Apostles. Consequently, we neither deny the Apostolic ministry to be the only witness, nor do we fall into the absurdity of assuming the divine authority of the witness as the condition of proving its divine authority. Will the *Observer* tell us on which horn of his imagined dilemma we now hang?

The commission to the Apostles created no new ministry, but simply provided for the continuance, unto the consummation of the world, of the visible ministry our blessed Saviour had himself exercised while on the earth. "As my Father hath sent me, so send I you." When he was on earth the witness was visible in him, now it is visible in the body of the pastors and teachers of the Roman Catholic Church, but, though visible under other conditions, it is one and the same; "For, behold," says our blessed Saviour, "I am with you all days unto the consummation of the world." He is the witness, and testifies through them. Does the *Observer* ask a better witness? If it does, it must find him, for we never pledged ourselves to produce a better.

One point more we notice, and then take our leave of this *Episcopal Observer*, till we hear from him again. Our readers will recollect the argument we used to identify the *Ecclesia docens*, or Church teaching, with the Roman Catholic ministry.

"It is the Roman Catholic ministry. It can be no other. It cannot be the Greek Church. The Greek Church was formerly in communion with the Church of Rome, and made one corporation with it. The Church of Rome was then the true church, *Ecclesia docens*, or it was not. If not, the Greek Church is false, in consequence of having communed with a false church. If it was, the Greek Church is false, because it separated from it. So take either horn of the dilemma, the Greek Church is false, and its ministry not the apostolic ministry which inherits the promises. The same reasoning will apply with equal force to any of the Oriental sects not in communion with the see of Rome; and, *a fortiori*, to all the modern Protestant sects. Therefore, the Roman Catholic ministry is the Apostolic corporation, because this corporation can be no other."

Upon this the *Episcopal Observer* remarks:—

" It is one of the easiest things in the world to make out a false conclusion, if one can be allowed to slip a false premise into the process of induction. There are so many violations of the rules of logic in the above paragraph, that the reader would hardly have patience to follow us in their exposure. Precisely the same reasoning, in the same words, with only a slight interchange of terms, will best show its absurdity.

" 'It is the ministry of the Greek Church. It can be no other. It cannot be the Roman Catholic ministry. The Roman Catholic Church was formerly in communion with the Greek Church, and made one corporation with it. The Greek Church was then the true church, *Ecclesia docens*, or it was not. If not, the Church of Rome is false, in consequence of having communed with a false church. If it was, the Church of Rome is false, because it separated from it. So, take either horn of the dilemma, the Church of Rome is false, and its ministry not the Apostolic ministry which inherits the promises,' &c."— p. 141.

Now, will it be credited that we anticipated this retort and replied to it? Yet such is the fact. Here is what we said:—

"You object, in behalf of the Greek Church, that Rome separated from her, not she from Rome. This we deny. It is historically certain, that the Greek Church, prior to the final separation, agreed with the Church of Rome on the matters (the Supremacy of the Pope and the Procession of the Holy Ghost) which were made the pretexts for separation. In the separation, the Greek Church denied what she had before asserted, while Rome continued to assert the same doctrine after as before. Therefore the Greek Church was the dissentient party. Prior to the separation, the Greek Church agreed with the Roman in submitting to the papal authority. In the separation, the Greek Church threw off this authority, while the Roman continued to submit to it. Therefore the Greek Church was the separatist.

"You insist, that, though the act of separation may, indeed, have been formally the act of the Greek Church, yet the separation was really on the part of Rome, who had corrupted the faith, and rendered separation from her necessary to the purity of the Christian Church. But, if this be so, whatever the corruptions of the faith Rome had been guilty of, the Greek Church participated in them during her communion with Rome. If they vitiated the Latin Church, they equally vitiated the Greek. Then both had failed, and the true Church, which we have seen is indefectible, must have been somewhere else. Then the Greek Church could become a true Church by separating from the communion of the Latin Church only on condition of coming into communion with the true Church. But it came into communion with no Church. Therefore, the Greek Church, at any rate, is false."

Yet the *Observer* nowhere notices the fact that we had thus replied in advance, nor even that we were aware of the objection. It has not noticed these replies, express to its objection, and yet it claims to have refuted us! Yes, it has refuted us, by urging the objections we ourselves brought, but without noticing our answers! This may be a refutation in the Protestant sense, but, thank God! it is not in the Catholic sense. The conduct of the *Observer*, in this respect, we shall not trust ourselves to characterize as it deserves, nor shall we suffer it to surprise us. Deprived, as the writer is, by the simple fact that he is a Protestant, of the ordinary means of divine grace, nothing better was to be expected of him. He has a cause to maintain, which does not admit of candor and truthfulness, honesty and fair dealing, and we should be more surprised to find him exercising such virtues than we are by finding him sinning against them.

It is worthy of note that this Episcopal writer has passed over the articles in our Review against his own church, and, churchman as he professes to be, has entered the lists only against an article the main design of which was to defend the Church against No-Church. It is also worthy of note, that the objections he has brought against us were nearly all brought previously in the *Christian Register* and *Christian World*, the two weekly organs of the No-Church Unitarians. What does this indicate? Are Unitarians and Episcopalians acting in concert? or are we to infer that a common dread of Catholicity is combining all the various Protestant sects against the Catholic Church? This last seems to us not improbable. The signs of the times seem to indicate that the several tribes of Goths, Vandals, Huns, and other barbarians, are forming a league for a new invasion of Rome. Well, be it so. "He that dwelleth in heaven shall laugh at them, and the Lord shall deride them." The Episcopalians may read their destiny in that of the old Donatists, whom, in many respects, they resemble; and all the Protestant sects combined are not so formidable to the Church as were, at one period, the old Arians. The Church triumphed over the Arians; she will triumph over the Protestants. A union whose principle is hatred will not long subsist, but will soon break asunder. Protestantism is doomed. The Devil may be very active and full of wrath, and utter great swelling words, for a season, because he knows that his time is short; but Protestantism must go the way of all the earth. The Lord will remember mercy, and will not much longer afflict the nations, but will recall them to the bosom of his Church.

THORNWELL'S ANSWER TO DR. LYNCH.*

APRIL, 1848.

Sometime in 1841, Mr. Thornwell, a Presbyterian minister, and "Professor of Sacred Literature and the Evidences of Christianity in the South-Carolina College," published, anonymously, in a Baltimore journal, a brief essay against the divine inspira-

* The Apocryphal Books of the Old Testament proved to be Corrupt Additions to the Word of God.—The Arguments of Romanists from the Infallibility of the Church and the Testimonies of the Fathers in Behalf of the Apocrypha discussed and refuted. By JAMES H. THORNWELL. New York: Leavitt, Trow, & Co. Boston: Charles Tappan. 1845. 16mo. pp. 417.

tion of those books of the Old Testament which Protestants exclude from the canon of Scripture. To this essay, as subsequently reprinted with the author's name, the Rev. Dr. Lynch, of Charleston, S. C., replied, in a series of letters addressed to Mr. Thornwell, through the columns of *The Catholic Miscellany*. The volume before us is Mr. Thornwell's rejoinder to Dr. Lynch, and contains, in an Appendix, the original essay, and the substance of Dr. Lynch's reply to it. The rejoinder consists of twenty-nine letters, which cover nearly the whole ground of controversy between Catholics and Protestants, and, though written in a Presbyterian spirit, they are respectable for ability and learning. The work, though nothing surprising, is, upon the whole, above the general average of publications of its class.

The purpose of the essay was to "assert and endeavor to prove that *Tobit, Judith, the additions to the Book of Esther, Wisdom, Ecclesiasticus, Baruch, with the Epistle of Jeremiah, the Song of the Three Children, the Story of Susannah, the Story of Bel and the Dragon, and the First and Second Books of Maccabees* are neither sacred nor canonical, and of course of no more authority in the Church of God than Seneca's Letters or Tully's Offices." (pp. 339, 340.) In the present work, the author attempts to maintain the same thesis, and to refute the objections urged by Dr. Lynch against it. He professes on his very title-page to have *proved* the books enumerated "to be corrupt additions to the word of God," and to have discussed and *refuted* "the arguments of Romanists from the infallibility of the Church and the testimonies of the Fathers in their behalf." The question very naturally arises, Has he done this? Has he proved that these books are uninspired, as he must have done, if he has proved them to be corrupt additions to the word of God; and has he refuted the arguments of Catholics, or rather of Dr. Lynch, in their behalf?

The arguments which Dr. Lynch adduces for these books are drawn from the infallibility of the Church and the testimony of the Fathers. If the Church is infallible, the testimony of the Fathers is of subordinate importance, for the infallibility alone suffices for the faithful; if the Church is not infallible, it is of still less consequence what the Fathers testify; for then all faith is out of the question, both for Catholics and all others. We may, therefore, waive all consideration, for the present, of the argument for the deutero-canonical books drawn from the testimony of the Fathers, and confine ourselves to that drawn from the infallibility of the Church. The argument from infallibility must, of course, be refuted, before the author can claim to have refuted Dr. Lynch, or to have proved his general thesis, that the books in question are "corrupt additions to the word of God."

The Catholic Church, undeniably, includes these books in her canon of Scripture, and commands her children to receive them as the word of God. This is certain, and the author concedes it; for he adduces it as a proof of her "intolerable arrogance." If she is infallible in declaring the word of God, as all Catholics hold, these books are certainly inspired Scripture, and rightfully placed in the canon. This is the argument from infallibility; and it is evident to every one who understands what it is to refute an argument that it can be refuted only by disproving the infallibility, or, what is the same thing, proving the fallibility, of the Church. To prove the Church fallible, moreover, it is not enough to refute the arguments by which Catholics are accustomed to prove her infallibility; for a doctrine may be true, and yet the arguments adduced in proof of it be unsound and inconclusive. It will, therefore, avail the author but little to refute our arguments for the infallibility, unless he refutes the infallibility itself; for so long as he is unable to say positively that the Church is fallible, he is unable to refute the argument *from* her infallibility. It may still be true that she is infallible, and if she is, the books are not uninspired compositions, but infallibly the word of God.

Mr. Thornwell, who regards himself as an able and sound logician, appears to have some consciousness of this, and indeed to concede it. Accordingly, he devotes a third of his whole volume to disproving the infallibility of the Church, or rather, to proving her fallibility. "I have insisted," he says in his Preface, "largely on the dogma of infallibility,—more largely, perhaps, than my readers may think consistent with the general design of my performance,—because I regard this as the prop and bulwark of all the abominations of the Papacy." (p. 8.)

But to prove the fallibility of the Church, or to disprove her infallibility, is a grave undertaking, and attended with serious difficulties. The Church cannot be tried except by some standard, and it is idle to attempt to convict her on a fallible authority. If the conviction is obtained on a fallible authority, the conviction itself is fallible, and it, instead of the Church, may be the party in the wrong. The Professor cannot take a single step, cannot even open his case, unless he has an infallible tribunal before which to summon the Church,—some infallible standard by which to test her infallibility or fallibility. But before what infallible tribunal can he cite her? What infallible authority has he on which he can demand her conviction?

The only possible way in which the fallibility of the Church can be proved is by convicting her of having actually erred on some point on which she claims to be infallible. But it is evident, that, in order to be able to convict her of having erred on a given point, we must be able to say infallibly what is truth or error on that point. Clearly, then, the Professor cannot commence his action, much less gain it, unless he has an authority which pronounces infallibly on the points on which he seeks to convict her of having actually erred. But what authority has he? Unhappily, he does not inform us, and does not appear to have recognized the necessity on his part of having any authority. He sets forth, formally, no authority, designates no court, specifies no law, lays down no principles. This is a serious inconvenience, and affects both his legal and his logical attainments. His argument, let him do his best, must be *minus* its major proposition; and from the minor alone we have always understood that it is impossible to conclude any thing.

Mr. Thornwell denies the infallibility of the Church, and he recognizes no infallible authority in any one of the sects, including even his own. He has, then no authority which he can allege, but the authority of reason, and his own private judgment. His own private judgment is of no weight, and cannot be adduced in a public discussion. The authority of reason we acknowledge to be infallible in her own province; but her province is restricted to the natural order, and she has no jurisdiction in the supernatural order, to which the Church professes to belong. The Church has the right to be tried by her peers. Reason is not, and cannot be, the peer of the supernatural, and is totally unable, in so far as the Church lies within the supernatural order, to pronounce any judgment concerning her infallibility one way or the other.

Reason, undoubtedly, knows that God is, and that he can neither deceive nor be deceived. It knows, therefore, if he appoints the Church, commissions her, as his organ, to declare his word, that she must declare it infallibly; for then it is he himself that declares in her declaration, and if she could either deceive or be deceived, he himself could either deceive or be deceived. If, then, reason finds sufficient or satisfactory grounds for believing that God has appointed or instituted the Church to declare his word, to teach all nations to observe all things whatsoever he has revealed, it pronounces her infallible, and acknowledges its obligation to receive, without any questioning, whatever she teaches.

Reason, again, knows that God cannot be in contradiction with himself, and therefore, since both the natural order and the supernatural are from him, that he cannot establish principles in the one repugnant to those established in the other. On the authority of reason, then, we may always assert that he cannot teach one thing in the natural order and its contradictory in the supernatural order. If, then, it be clearly established, that the Church, on matters on which she claims to teach infallibly, teaches what is in contradiction either to the supernatural or the natural order, it is certain that she is fallible. But as reason cannot go out of the order of nature, we can on its authority establish the fallibility of the Church only on the condition of convicting her of having actually contradicted some law or principle of the natural order. If the Church, in other words, contradict reason, reason is competent to conclude against her, but not when she merely transcends reason; for what is *above* reason may be true, but what is *against* reason cannot be.

It follows from this that the authority of reason in the case before us is purely negative, and that the Professor can conclude from it against the Church only on condition that he proves that she actually contradicts it. But it is necessary even here to bear in mind that the natural can no more contradict the supernatural than the supernatural the natural. When the motives of credibility have convinced reason that the Church teaches by supernatural authority, her teaching is as authoritative as any principle of reason itself, and may be cited to prove that what is alleged against her as a principle of reason is not a principle of reason, with no less force than the alleged principle itself can be cited to prove that she contradicts reason. The Professor must, then, in order to prove her fallibility, adduce a case, not of apparent contradiction, but of real contradiction,— a case in which what she teaches must evidently contradict an evident principle of reason,—so evident that it is clear that to deny it would be to deny reason itself.

The position, then, which the Professor must take and maintain, in order to establish his thesis, is, that *the Church, in her teaching on matters on which she claims to teach infallibly, has taught or teaches what contradicts an evident and undeniable principle of reason.* This he must do before he can prove the fallibility of the Church, and he must prove the fallibility of the Church before he can refute the argument drawn from it for the books enumerated. Has he proved this? Unhappily, he does not appear to have understood that this was at all necessary, or to have suspected that it was only by proving the Church to be against reason that he could conclude her fallibility. He does not appear to have known that there are and can be no questions debatable between Catholics and Protestants but such as pertain exclusively to the province of reason. He labors under the hallucination, that he has something besides the reason common to all men which he may oppose to us, that he has the revelation of Almighty God, and that he is at liberty to attempt to convict the Church, not on reason alone, but also on the word of God. This would be ridiculous, if the matter were not so grave as to make it deplorable. He has no word of God to cite against us, and if he cites the Holy Scriptures at all, he must cite them either in the sense of the Church, or as simple historical documents; because it is only in the sense of the Church that we acknowledge them to be inspired. We can cite them as inspired Scripture against him, as an *argumentum ad hominem;* for he holds them to be inspired Scripture as interpreted by private judgment. But he cannot against us; for the argument would not be *ad hominem*, unless cited in the sense of the Church, since it is only in that sense, that, on our own principles, they are the word of God.

The fact is, Mr. Thornwell from first to last forgets in his argument that we are as far from admitting his authority as he is from admitting ours. He writes under the impression, that he has the true Christian doctrine, and is invested with ample authority to define what is, and what is not, the word of God. He assumes his Presbyterianism to be true, and when he has proved that Catholicity contradicts it, he concludes at once that Catholicity is false. But Presbyterianism is only his private judgment, and therefore of no authority. By what right does he erect his private judgment into a criterion of truth and falsehood, assume that it is infallible, and proceed to pronounce *ex cathedra* on the revealed word of God? We cannot recognize his authority as sovereign pontiff, unless he brings us credentials from heaven, duly signed and witnessed. His assumption we cannot admit. He is confessedly fallible, and his decisions we cannot even entertain. He does not come to us duly commissioned by Almighty God to teach us his word; he is simply a man, with no authority in the premises which may not be claimed and exercised by every other man as well as by himself. In an argument with Catholics he can be only a man, and is at liberty to adopt no line of argument that would not be equally proper in the case of a pagan, Mahometan, or any other infidel.

Protestant controversialists are exceedingly prone to forget this. They assume that they have the word of God, that they know and believe what God has revealed, and that they have in their opinions a standard by which to try the Church. Yet they claim to be reasoners, and tell us that we have surrendered our reason! But whether the Church be or be not commissioned to declare the word of God, it is certain that they are not. Certain is it, that, if she is not authorized to declare it, no one else is; and equally certain is it, that no one not so authorized has any right to adduce in an argument any thing he takes to be the word of God, save by the sufferance or consent of his opponents. It is a grave mistake to suppose that there is any other common ground between us and our adversaries than that of reason. It will not do for our adversaries to suppose, that, because we hold to the inspiration of the Scriptures, they may allege them in their own sense against us; for we admit their inspiration only on the authority, and in *the sense*, of the Church. On her authority, and in the sense in which she defines their doctrines, we hold them to be the word of God; but in no other sense, and on no other ground. Independently of her authority and interpretations, there are no inspired Scriptures for us. This fact must never be lost sight of, and it would save Protestants an immense deal of labor, if they would keep it in mind, and govern themselves accordingly. If they cite the Bible against us, on any authority or in any sense but that of the Church, it is not for us the word of God, but simply their private opinion, by which we are not and cannot be bound. Among ourselves, who admit the authority of the Church, and therefore the inspiration of the Scriptures, it is lawful, on a point on which the actual teaching of the Church is matter of inquiry, to appeal to the written word, as also to the Fathers and Doctors of the Church, and also to the analogies of faith; but it is never lawful for those out of the Church, denying her authority, to make a like appeal against us; for the *authority* to which we appeal is resolvable into the authority of the Church, which they deny.

The rule we here insist upon is that of common sense and common justice, and rests for its authority on the principle, that no man has the right to assume in his argument the point that is in question. We ourselves cite the Scriptures against our adversaries, but always either *ad hominem*,—because they, though we do not, admit their inspiration independently of the authority of the Church,—or as simple historical documents, whose authenticity and authority as such documents, but not as inspired writings, reason is competent to determine. But we never assume our Church and her definitions as the authority on which to convict those without of error; for to do so would be a sheer begging of the question. Undoubtedly, if our Church is right, all her adversaries are wrong. It needs no argument to prove that. We, therefore, take our stand in the argument, either on what our adversaries concede, or on the common reason of mankind, and attempt to prove from the one or the other, or both, that every one is bound to believe and obey the Church. Protestants must not expect us to allow them more than we claim for ourselves. They may need more in order to make out their case; but we are not aware that they have any right to special privileges, or to exemption from the common obligations of reason and justice. As there are no concessions of ours which can avail them, they must in their controversies with us take their stand on the reason common to all men, and, since common to all, alike theirs and ours. They must bring their action at common law, not on a special statute. Then they must restrict themselves to those questions which come within the jurisdiction of reason, and which she is competent to decide without appeal. Then they must waive all questions which pertain to the subject-matter of revelation; for these all undeniably lie in the supernatural order, and therefore without the province of reason.

We frankly concede that Mr. Thornwell has proved that Catholicity is not Presbyterianism, and that, if Presbyterianism is the revelation of God, Catholicity is not. But this amounts to nothing; Presbyterianism is neither proved nor conceded to be Christianity. He cannot, therefore, assume it against us. We concede him not one inch of Christian ground on which to set his foot. We demur to every argument he adduces or attempts to adduce from the convictions or prejudices of his sect, or from his own conceptions of the word of God. We listen to no arguments, we entertain no objections, we plead to no charges, not drawn from the common reason of mankind. We must, therefore, beg him to descend from his tripod, and meet us as a man with no authority but that which belongs to the reason of every man.

We must, in view of this state of the case, eliminate from Mr. Thornwell's arguments against infallibility, as not to be entertained, all that he urges on the authority of his own religious convictions or prejudices, and confine ourselves simply to what he adduces on the simple authority of reason. These last, all that is legitimately adduced, consist of an attempted refutation of Dr. Lynch's argument for the infallibility of the Church, and certain philosophical, historical, and moral objections alleged against the Church.

We might well pass over Mr. Thornwell's attempt to refute Dr. Lynch's argument for infallibility, because, if successful, it would accomplish nothing to his purpose. The argument he has to refute is the argument *from* the infallibility of the Church, not the argument *for* it; for the question is not on believing that infallibility, but on denying it. It may, as we have said, be true, and yet the arguments by which we attempt to prove it be unsound and inconclusive. The defect of proof is a good reason for not believing, but it is not always an adequate reason for denying. The thesis the Professor seeks to maintain requires him to deny the infallibility of the Church, or to assert her fallibility, and therefore the burden of proof devolves on him. He asserts that the disputed books are corrupt additions to the word of God, which he cannot possibly prove without disproving the infallibility of the Church, which declares them to be inspired Scripture. But he claims to have won a victory over Dr. Lynch, and his friends have bound the laurel around his brows. We are, therefore, disposed to subject his claim to a slight examination, and to inquire if his shouts have not been a little premature, and if, after all, the victory does not remain with his opponent. If he has succeeded, he has gained nothing for his thesis; but if he has failed, we can conclude against it at once, at least so far as he is concerned.

Mr. Thornwell states Dr. Lynch's general argument for the disputed books to be,—

" Whatever the pastors of the Church of Rome declare to be true must be infallibly certain:

" That the Apocrypha [the books enumerated] were inspired, the pastors of the Church of Rome declare to be true:

" Therefore it must be infallibly certain."

This is stated in Mr. Thornwell's language, not in Dr. Lynch's, and is by no means so well expressed as it might be; but let that pass. Substituting the names of the books alleged by Mr. Thornwell to be corrupt additions to the word of God for the term *Apocrypha*, we are willing to accept it. To this argument, which he has shaped to suit the objections he wishes to bring against it, Mr. Thornwell's first objection is, that it is "vitiated by the ambiguity of the middle." The words "pastors of the Church," may be understood either universally, particularly, or distributively,—to mean the whole body of the pastors, some of them, and every one individually.

Ambiguity of the middle is where the words are taken in one sense in the major, and in another sense in the minor; but where they are taken in the same sense in both the premises, although in themselves susceptible of several meanings, there is no ambiguity of the middle. In the argument as stated, the words, *pastors*, &c., are, in themselves considered, susceptible of the senses alleged, but as used in the argument they are tied down to one sense. The rule of construction is, to understand all words used in a general or universal sense, unless there be some reason, expressed or implied, in the context or the nature of the subject, for not doing so. There is, in the present case, no such reason in either premise, and therefore we must take the words generally, or universally, in both,—for the whole body of pastors. If so, there is no ambiguity of the middle.

But Mr. Thornwell asserts that Dr. Lynch does use the words in the three different senses mentioned. He accuses him of meaning by them, at one time, the whole body of pastors *collected or assembled* in council, at another time, *a part* only, and finally, *every one* individually; and alleges as proof, the fact, that in his Letter he predicates infallibility, 1. of the whole body of pastors in their collective capacity, 2. of the Council of Trent, in which only a part were personally assembled, and 3. of each single teacher or missionary.

1. That Dr. Lynch, when he predicates infallibility of the body of pastors in their collective capacity, means the whole body, takes the words, *pastors*, &c., universally, is conceded, but that he means the whole body *assembled in council* we deny. He speaks of them as a body of individuals in their *collective* capacity, not as a collected or congregated body; and that he does not mean the body of pastors assembled in council is evident from the fact, that he contends that the pastors of the Church had decided the question of the inspiration of the books in dispute long before the Council of Trent, since, to do so, they did not need to assemble in a general council. Thus he says expressly,—"The doctrines of the Catholic Church can be known from the universal and concordant teaching of her pastors, even when her bishops have not assembled in a general council and embodied those doctrines in a list of decrees." (pp. 370, 371.) It is evident, then, that Dr. Lynch holds the pastors of the Church to be a body of individuals, to have a collective capacity, and the faculty of teaching infallibly in that capacity, even when not congregated. If Mr. Thornwell had recognized a difference between *collective* and *collected*, or congregated,

he would easily have surmounted this part of his difficulty, without any foreign aid.

2. The acts of the Holy Council of Trent, touching faith and morals, Dr. Lynch unquestionably holds to be infallible, not because he predicates infallibility of a part of the body of pastors, but because they were the acts of the whole Church represented in it, or at least made so by subsequent adoption, as is evident enough from his language. The proof, therefore, that he takes the words in a partitive sense, is inadequate.

3. That each single pastor teaches infallibly in his *collective capacity*, as "member" of the body of pastors, is conceded, but that he does so individually or in his individual capacity is denied; for in his individual capacity he cannot teach at all. Dr. Lynch speaks of his teaching infallibly only in his capacity as member of the body. As member of the body, the only sense in which he is a teacher at all, he participates of its infallibility, and teaches by its authority, and infallibly, not because he is individually infallible, but because it is infallible. Consequently in representing the single teacher as teaching infallibly, Dr. Lynch does not use the words *pastors*, &c., in a distributive sense.

Mr. Thornwell is unfortunate in his proofs, notwithstanding he had shaped his statement of the argument with special reference to them. He fails to substantiate his objection of "ambiguity of the middle," and consequently all that he says, which is founded on it, falls to the ground. The beautiful argument he had constructed to prove that a Catholic can never know when and where to find the infallible authority on which he had expended so much labor, and lavished so many rare ornaments, falls to pieces through default of a foundation. Decidedly, it is an inconvenience to build without any thing to build with or to build on. It is worse than being compelled to make bricks without straw.

Mr. Thornwell, after his objection to the form of the argument, proceeds to deny and to refute its major, namely, the infallibility of the Church. His first effort is to refute Dr. Lynch's argument for it. Dr. Lynch contends that "we cannot be called on to believe any proposition without adequate proof;" that "when Almighty God designed to inspire the works contained in the Holy Scriptures, he intended they should be believed to be inspired;" and that "therefore there *does* exist some adequate proof." Thus far all is evident enough, and the Professor brings no objection to what is alleged. We may presume it, then, as conceded, that there *does* exist some adequate proof of their inspiration, that is to say, some authority competent to declare the fact. What is it? "It must be," says Dr. Lynch, "a body of individuals to whom, in their collective capacity, God has given authority to make an unerring decision on the subject." It must be such a body, because it can be nothing else. This body is composed of the pastors of the Catholic Church. Therefore the pastors of the Catholic Church have authority to make an unerring decision, that is, have infallible authority to declare the word of God.

Mr. Thornwell does not deny, that, if such a body exists, it is the pastors of the Roman Catholic Church. On this point he raises no question, and we may regard him as conceding it. He denies the necessity of any such body as Dr. Lynch asserts. He objects, first, to the form of the argument by which Dr. Lynch undertakes to prove it. The argument, he says, sins by an imperfect enumeration of particulars. It is a destructive disjunctive conditional, which must contain in the major all the suppositions which can be conceived to be true, and in the minor destroy all but one. But Dr. Lynch has not included all such suppositions in his major, and therefore, conceding that he has destroyed in the minor all he has enumerated save one, he is not entitled to his conclusion. Dr. Lynch has enumerated four methods:—1. Every individual, on the strength of his own private examination, is to decide for himself,—private judgment; 2. Every individual, is to receive books as inspired, or reject them as uninspired, according to the decisions of such persons as he judges qualified by their erudition and sound judgment to determine the question,—the judgment of the learned; 3. We must take the inspiration of Scripture from some individual whom God has commissioned to announce this fact to the world; or 4. From a body of individuals to whom, in their collective capacity, God has given authority to make an unerring decision on the subject. But a *fifth* supposition is possible, says the Professor, namely, " God himself by his Eternal Spirit may condescend to be the teacher of men, and enlighten their understandings to perceive in the Scriptures themselves infallible marks of their inspiration." This supposition Dr. Lynch has " entirely overlooked," "strangely suppressed," and therefore cannot even by destroying the first three suppositions conclude the fourth.

But Dr. Lynch has not "entirely overlooked," "strangely suppressed," this fifth supposition, but expressly mentions it, and gives his reason for not including it in the number of supposable methods. Mr. Thornwell has generously furnished us the evidence of this. After enumerating the four methods stated, Dr. Lynch says (Appendix, p. 359) :—" I might perhaps add a *fifth* method; that each one be informed what books are inspired by his *private spirit*. But I omit it, as, were it true, it would be superfluous, if not a criminal intrusion on the province God would have reserved to himself, to attempt to prove or disprove, when our duty would be simply to await in patience the revelation to each particular individual. You are not a member of the Society of Friends, and your essay is not an *exposé* of the teachings of your private spirit, but an effort to appeal to argument." With this passage before his eyes, we cannot understand how the Presbyterian minister could assert that Dr. Lynch entirely overlooked this fifth method, for undeniably the Catholic Doctor means by the private spririt precisely the same thing the Presbyterian does by God condescending to teach men by his Eternal Spirit. Moreover, the reasons assigned by Dr. Lynch for not including it in the list of supposable methods are conclusive, at least till answered. These reasons are two:—1. That, if assumed, all argument would be forclosed, either as superfluous or as criminal; and 2. Mr. Thornwell evidently rejects it, because he appeals to argument, and therefore against him it cannot be necessary to include it. These are solid reasons, and Mr. Thornwell should have met them before accusing Dr. Lynch of having entirely overlooked the method of interior illumination, and especially before insisting upon its being supposable.

Mr. Thornwell is apparently disposed to maintain that this fifth method is the one actually adopted, but this he is not at liberty to do. The method is private, not public, and cannot be appealed to in a public debate. In a public debate, the appeal must always be to a public authority, that is, to an authority common to both parties. If the authority to which the appeal is to be made is private, there can be no public debate; if private, interior, immediate, as must be the teachings of the spirit, there can be no argument. Argument in such a case would be superfluous and even criminal. When, therefore, a man resorts, on a given question, to argument, and to public argument, he necessarily assumes that the authority which is to determine the question is public, and denies it to be private. Mr. Thornwell in his essay made his appeal to argument, and wrote his essay to prove that the question he raised is to be settled, not by the private spirit, but by public facts, arguments, and authority. He therefore cannot fall back on the private spirit. Having elected public authority, he must abide by it. If he cannot now fall back on the private spirit, he cannot allege it as a supposable method; and if he cannot so allege it, he cannot accuse Dr. Lynch's argument of sinning by an imperfect enumeration of particulars, because it omits it.

Mr. Thornwell, furthermore, is very much affected by Dr. Lynch's supposed temerity in restricting the number of supposable methods to the four enumerated. He grows very eloquent, and manifests no little pious horror at what he calls an effort to set bounds to Omnipotence. All this is very well, but he himself excludes the method of private teaching, by writing his book to prove, on other grounds, that the books in question are uninspired, and he does not even attempt to suggest an additional method. Nobody, unless it be himself, seeks to limit Omnipotence; nobody, to our knowledge, denies that Almighty

God might have adopted the private method, if he had chosen to do so. The question is not, as is evident from the whole train of Dr. Lynch's reasoning, on abstract possibilities, but on what is or is not possible *in hac providentia*. Nobody pretends that the private spirit is not supposable because it is metaphysically impossible, but it is not supposable because incompatible with other things which we know must be supposed, and which Mr. Thornwell undeniably does suppose.

The alleged *fifth* method not being supposable, unless Mr. Thornwell chooses to condemn himself for attempting to argue the question, and to confess that all his arguments are senseless and absurd, nay, profane and criminal, the objection raised to Dr. Lynch's major falls to the ground; and as he does not pretend that the conclusion is not logical, he must grant the conclusion or deny the minor. But he cannot grant the conclusion without conceding the infallibility of the Church, which he seeks to disprove. He therefore asserts that "the minor is lame, and can at best yield only a lame and impotent conclusion." The minor is proved only by removing or destroying the first three suppositions. But this is not done; for the arguments by which Dr. Lynch seeks to do it apply with equal force against the fourth, which he must retain. But the legitimacy of this reply is questionable. One of the four suppositions must be true, for some adequate proof does exist. If the objections adduced are in themselves considered sufficient to remove the three, they cannot be urged against the fourth, for that would prove too much, namely, that there is no adequate proof. If insufficient, they must then be shown to be so on other grounds, or else we can always reply, one supposition is true, and it must be the fourth, because it cannot be one or another of the first three.

We deny the assertion, that the arguments against the three apply with equal force against the fourth. We begin with Dr. Lynch's argument against the first supposition,—that every individual is to decide for himself on the strength of his own examination. This is utterly impossible; for the bulk of mankind want the ability, the leisure, and the opportunity to acquire the amount of science and erudition necessary to enable them to come to an absolutely certain conclusion on the subject of the inspiration of the Scriptures. This is evident to every one who considers,—1. The controversies which have obtained respecting the canon; 2. The nature of the questions to be settled, and what it needs to enable one to decide respecting the fact of the inspiration of ancient books on intrinsic grounds; 3. That every one is required to believe the truth on the subject, not only after a life of inquiry, and historical and scientific investigation, but from the moment of coming to years of discretion; and 4. The actual condition of the generality of mankind in relation to science and erudition. These considerations are amply sufficient to disprove the first supposition; for every one is commanded to believe, and the proof, to be adequate, must be adequate in the case of every one,—of the ignorant slave and rude savage, as well as of the learned and gifted few,—of the boy or girl in whom reason has just dawned, as well as of the scientific veteran or the grey-haired scholar.

The Professor replies: The learning asserted to be necessary, if necessary at all, must be so because the fact of inspiration in general is not determinable without it, and therefore must be as necessary in the body supposed as in the individual deciding for himself. But the body must acquire it either by investigation or by inspiration. If by investigation it has no advantage over the individual, and whatever proves his inability applies with equal force against its ability. If by inspiration, then it must have the same learning to be able to determine the fact of its own inspiration, and the people who are to receive its decision must also have it in order to be able to judge of its inspiration. Hence the Professor sums up triumphantly,—" When you shall condescend to inform me how the Fathers of Trent could decide with infallible certainty upon the Scriptures, without the learning which is necessary, in your view, to understand the evidence, if they themselves were uninspired; or how, if inspired, they could without this learning, either be certain themselves of the fact, or establish it with infallible certainty to the people, who, without your learning, must judge of the inspiration of the Holy Council,—when, consistently with your principles, you resolve these difficulties, one of the objections to your argument will cease." (p. 51.)

This is the argument in all its force. Its substance is, whatever difficulties there may be in the way of the method of private judgment, precisely the same difficulties are in the way of the body of individuals supposed, and can no more easily be overcome by it than by the individual himself. This is the common Protestant reply to our objections against the method of private judgment, and is tantamount to saying, that a man has just the same difficulties to overcome in simply declaring what he believes and always has believed as in determining by personal inquiry and examination what he ought to believe; or that it is as easy to ascertain and verify the truth we are ignorant of as it is merely to express with precision the truth we already possess and always have possessed from the first moment of our existence!

But let us examine this famous argument, which, in one form or other, is the great, and virtually the only, argument by which Protestants seek to evade the force of the objections of Catholics to their scheme of proof. Dr. Lynch asserts that a certain amount of science and erudition is necessary to enable an individual, on the strength of his own examination, to come to an absolutely certain decision on the fact of the inspiration of an ancient writing, whose inspiration is determinable, not on extrinsic, but mainly on intrinsic grounds. Then, says the Professor, the same amount is necessary to enable an inspired individual to judge of the evideuce of his own inspiration. But this conclusion can follow only from the assumption, that the evidence of inspiration must be the same for the inspired and the uninspired. If you make the evidence mediate in the uninspired, you must also make it mediate in the inspired; and if immediate in the inspired, then also immediate in the uninspired. But it is not mediate in the inspired; for, unquestionably, he who inspires immediately evidences the fact to the one he inspires. How, then, contend for mediate evidence in the uninspired? Grant this reasoning, and the author condemns himself. The evidence is immediate, and yet he has written a book to settle the question by argument and erudition, both of which are mediate. He has, on this hypothesis, evidently proved nothing; for he has offered inappropriate evidence, and must be mistaken when he says that he has proved the books enumerated to be "corrupt additions to the word of God."

Again; the Professor asserts, that, if the learning alleged be necessary in the particular case, it is so because the fact of inspiration is determinable in no case without it, that is, that a thing cannot be true in the particular unless it be true in the universal,—as if one should say, some men cannot be black, because all men are not black; or, some are black, therefore all men are black! We presume Mr. Thornwell's servant is a black man; therefore, he himself is a black man. The principle the Professor adopts is, not only that what is true of the *genus* must be true of the *species*, but, also, that what is true of the *species* must be true of the *genus*. Thus, man is an animal; but a goose is an animal; therefore, man is a goose;— or, a goose is an animal; but man is an animal; therefore, a goose is a man. But the principle, if adopted, carries us farther yet. It is the denial of all *differentia*,—the fundamental error of Spinozism or pantheism. Thus, under the *genus* substance, God is substance; but a moss is substance; therefore, God is a moss, or reverse it, and a moss is God! Is this a principle to be adopted by a Professor of "the Evidences of Christianity" in so respectable an institution as the South Carolina College? Has the Professor yet to make his philosophy, as well as his theology?

But, evidently, there is a difference of species; for the Professor would take it as unkind, nay, uncivil, in us, if, because he comes under the genus animal, as does every man, we should insist on including him in the species *goose*. It cannot therefore, follow, that, because a thing is true in the particular, it must be true in the universal. Consequently, Dr. Lynch may assert that a certain amount of science and erudition is necessary to decide on a particular fact by a particular agent, on particular grounds, and yet not be obliged to concede that the same amount is necessary in every case, whoever the agent, and whatever the grounds on which he is to decide. The amount alleged to be necessary may not be necessary in the case of the inspired themselves to determine the fact of their own inspiration; it may not be necessary in the case of the eyewitnesses of the miracles by which the inspired evidence the fact that God speaks to and by them; it may not be necessary to those who receive the fact immediately from the inspired themselves, or on the authority God himself has commissioned to declare it; and yet be indispensable in the case of a single individual who has, on the strength of his own examination, to decide whether a book written some two or three thousand years ago is or is not an inspired composition; as it needs no argument to prove.

The knowledge, be it more or be it less, necessary in the case, to determine what books are and what are not inspired, must be possessed by the body supposed, as well as by the individual, we concede; and if that body is destitute of it and has it to learn, it must learn it either from investigation or inspiration, we also concede; otherwise we deny it. But the body asserted in the hypothesis is, by the very terms of the supposition, already in possession of the truth, and of all the knowledge necessary to declare it, and, in deciding the question, has only to declare solemnly what it already holds and has held from the moment of its institution. Therefore, it has to acquire the knowledge neither by investigation nor by inspiration; for it has not to acquire it at all. Unless, then, the Professor chooses to maintain that to declare what one already holds directly from our Lord or his Apostles is the same thing as for an individual ignorant of it to learn it by the examination of historical documents and scientific investigation, he must concede that the parity he seeks to establish between every individual deciding the fact of inspiration on the strength of his own examination, and the Church, or body of teachers supposed, doing it on the authority of our Lord and his Apostles, from whom it received it immediately, has no foundation except in his own fancy, and that the conclusions which depend upon it fall to the ground.

The Professor's reasoning is vitiated by his supposing a *body* of individuals totally different from that supposed in the hypothesis he is arguing against. The body he supposes is no body or corporation at all; but a simple aggregation of individuals who at any given time compose it. Between such a body and the Apostles there must needs be all the distance of time and space, that there is between the Apostles and the individuals themselves. It would and it could possess only what the individuals composing it should bring to it, and they could bring to it only what they acquire in their individual capacity. "The mere fact of human congregation," as the Professor rightly contends, could confer no power, beyond the aggregate power of the individuals congregated. Hence the aggregate body, or collection of individuals, as well as the single individual, would need to obtain, either by investigation or inspiration, the knowledge necessary to come to an infallible decision. It needed no learned professor to tell us all this, which is by no means beyond the reach of any man of ordinary sense. Indeed, we feel humbled when we find learned men bringing such objections to us,—humbled for ourselves, that they can think so meanly of our understandings as to suppose us capable of holding any thing against which objections so obvious even to a child may be urged, and humbled for them, that they should imagine, that, in bringing such objections, they are telling something recondite, or that it is possible that such objections can have any power to demolish that lofty and spacious edifice, the Church, founded upon the rock, firmly built and cemented, which has withstood all the assaults of wicked men and devils for eighteen hundred years, and against which the gates of hell shall never prevail, not even to loosen a single stone or to detach a single tile.

But *this* body, this aggregate of individuals, is not *the* body supposed by Dr. Lynch, and to prove that this has no advantage over the individual is nothing to the purpose, for nobody certainly no Catholic, denies it. The Professor's argument is a sheer paralogism, of that species which consists in proving what is not supposed in the question, and which is not denied by the adversary,—a sophism for which the learned Professor has a peculiar fondness, and into which he falls with remarkable facility. The body supposed by Dr. Lynch is the Church teaching; for he says, " the pastors of the Catholic Church claim to compose it." But the Catholic Church, as a body or corporation, the only sense in which it is alleged to have any teaching faculty at all, is not an aggregation of individuals who at any given time compose it,— a body born and dying with them; but the contemporary of our Lord and his Apostles, in immediate communion with them, and thus annihilating all distance of time and place between them and us. She is, in the sense supposed, a corporation, and, like every corporation, a collective individual possessing the attribute of immortality. She knows no interruption, no succession of moments, no lapse of years. Like the eternal God, who is ever with her, and whose organ she is, she has duration, but no succession. She can never grow old, can never fall into the past. The individuals who compose the body may change, but she changes not; one by one they may pass off, and one by one be renewed, while she continues ever the same; as in our own bodies, old particles constantly escape, and new ones are assimilated, so that the whole matter of which they are composed is changed once in every six or seven years, and yet they remain always identically the same bodies. These changes as to individuals change nothing as to the body. The Church to-day is identically that very body which saw our Lord when he tabernacled in the flesh. She who is our dear Mother, and on whose words we hang with so much delight, beheld with her own eyes the stupendous miracles which were performed in Judea eighteen hundred years ago; she assisted at the preaching of the Apostles on the day of Pentecost, when the Holy Ghost descended upon them in cloven tongues of fire; she heard St. Peter, the prince of the

Apostles, relate how the Spirit descended upon Cornelius and his household, and declare how God had chosen that by his mouth the Gentiles should hear the word of God and believe; she listtened with charmed ear and ravished heart to the last admonition of "the disciple whom Jesus loved,"—"My dear children, love one another;" she saw the old Temple razed to the ground, the legal rites of the old covenant abolished, and the once chosen people driven out from the Holy Land, and scattered over all the earth; she beheld pagan Rome in the pride and pomp of power, bled under her persecuting emperors, and finally planted the cross in triumph on her ruins. She has been the contemporary of eighteen hundred years, which she has arrested in their flight and made present to us, and will make present to all generations as they rise. With one hand she receives the *depositum* of faith from the Lord and his commissioned Apostles, with the other she imparts it to us. Such is the body supposed, between which and the individual Mr. Thornwell must establish the parity he contends for, or not establish it at all. What has this body to do, in order to decide what books are, and what are not, inspired? Merely to declare a simple fact which she has received on competent authority,—merely what our Lord or his Apostles have told her. What needs she, in order to do it with infallible certainty? Simply protection against forgetting, misunderstanding, and misstating; and this she has, because she has, according to the hypothesis, our Lord always abiding with her, and the Paraclete, who leads her into all truth, and "brings to her remembrance" all the words spoken to her by our Lord himself personally, or by his inspired Apostles,—keeping her memory always fresh, rendering her infallible assistance rightly to understand and accurately to express what she remembers to have been taught. Here are all the conditions requisite for an infallible decision; and all these must be supposed, because they are all asserted in the hypothesis.

Now we demand what parity there is between such a body, which has only to state what it believes and always has believed on the inspiration of Scripture, and which has the supernatural assistance of the Holy Ghost to state it infallibly, and an individual who has nothing but certain writings before him, and who has to determine, by the examination of documents and scientific investigation of the intrinsic evidences, whether they are inspired or not,—a fact which, since it is supernatural, lies out of the order of nature, and is therefore only extrinsically provable. Who so blinded by passion, by pride, by prejudice, or ignorance, as to pretend, that such a body, supposing it to exist, can no more come to a certain conclusion, is in no better condition for coming to a certain conclusion, on the fact of the inspiration of the Holy Scriptures, than an ignorant slave on our plantations, or a rude savage of our forests? Who is he? Indeed, it is the learned Presbyterian minister, the "Professor of Sacred Literature and the Evidences of Christianity in the South Carolina College!" It is evident to any man of ordinary sense, that such a body can decide the question infallibly, and equally evident that the ignorant slave or the rude savage cannot.

To the dilemma, therefore, in which the Professor affects to have placed his Catholic opponent, we reply:—The Council of Trent could, uninspired, but simply assisted by the Holy Ghost, decide with infallible certainty upon the inspiration of the Scriptures, without the learning necessary in the case of the individual deciding for himself on the strength of his own examination, *because it had only to give an authoritative expression to the actual faith of the body of pastors it represented,*—and it could establish the infallibility of its expression to the people who were to receive it, because, to do so, it had only to establish that it did express the universal faith of that body, easily collected from its being received by the whole body as soon as made known. The other part of the dilemma falls of itself. We do not assume, nor are we obliged to assume, that the Fathers of Trent were inspired. Inspiration is needed only where the truth to be promulgated is unknown and has to be revealed: where nothing is to be done but infallibly state the truth already revealed and believed, the infallible assistance of the Holy Ghost, without inspiration, suffices.

We have here shown that the difficulties suggested are resolvable on Catholic principles; the Professor must therefore concede, according, to his promise, that one objection to Dr. Lynch's argument ceases. But this one objection is his only objection to that argument, so far as it bears against the first-named method; and since this is removed, the argument, thus far, is not refuted. If not refuted, it, at least against the Professor, is sound, and, then, the first method is destroyed, and Dr. Lynch is entitled to his conclusion against it.

There remain to be considered the second and third suppositions. The second, that of relying on the judgment of the learned, the Professor passes over in profound silence, and therefore yields it up as indefensible. It is remarkable, however, that Mr. Thornwell should do so; for it is really the method actually adopted by the majority of Protestants, and abandoning it is virtually abandoning Protestantism itself. Undoubtedly, Protestants assert private judgment; but the private judgment on which they actually rely is not the private judgment of each individual, but the private judgment of those assumed to be learned and wise and prudent. Protestantism must never be taken at its word; for one of its essential properties is, to profess one thing and to do another, or to give us the name without the thing,—the sign without the thing signified. Whoever knows Protestants at all knows that they take their opinions, not on their own private judgment, but on the authority of their masters. Whenever they do not do so, we find them becoming downright Rationalists, or absolute apostates from Christianity; and it is never, only as grouped around some leader, swearing by the words of some master, that we see them retain anything of the form of religion, or present any compact appearance. The people are aware of their own inability to decide for themselves what they ought to believe, and they only decide what heresiarch they will follow,—what master they will have. Thus they say,—" So said Martin Luther, so said John Calvin, or George Fox; so teach Edwards and Dwight, Owen and Gill, Wesley and Swedenborg, Murray and

Ballou, Channing and Fourier, Emerson and Parker." It is not in himself the poor Protestant confides, but in some leader who seems to him, for his learning, wisdom, and sound judgment, worthy of confidence. If here and there a bold, energetic individual starts up with perfect confidence in his own judgment, and has the courage or the audacity to proclaim, as the truth of God, his own personal conceits or convictions, he either founds a new sect, or a new party or faction in the sect, to which he pertains; as we see in the instance of Muncer and George Fox, Brown and Sandeman, Wesley and Whitefield, Erskine and Irving, Southcote and Pusey, Campbell and Bushnell, Channing and Parker. If each judged for himself, we should see no sects, parties, or groups; each would stand alone, on his own two feet, acknowledging no master, and no fellow, saying always *I*, never able to say *we*.

This must needs be. How, except by relying on such men as Mr. Thornwell, could the great body of Presbyterians, for instance, come to any conclusion on the question discussed in the volume before us? In fact, they do not attempt to obtain a conclusion by any other means. "Mr. Thornwell is a godly man; he is a great and learned man; he has investigated the subject; he wont deceive us; and we will believe what he says." Here is the fact, disguise it as you will, and Mr. Thornwell knows it as well as we do. We must, therefore, regard his passing this method over in silence as a tacit confession that in his judgment Protestantism is not defensible.

Nevertheless, we cannot be much surprised that Mr. Thornwell passes this method over in silence. It is not a method to be avowed. Protestant ministers would have a short lease of their power, if they were to avow it. They would be pressed with a multitude of questions, which it would be very inconvenient to answer. "After all,"—the justly indignant people whom they have led might say,—"this private judgment you preached was only a pretext, a bait to catch gudgeons. You never meant it; you only meant that we must submit our judgments to yours! Is it true that you monopolize all the learning, all the wisdom, all the judgment, in the world? What guaranty can you give us, fallible men as you confess yourselves, that you yourselves are not deceived,—nay, that you are incapable of deceiving us? You deceived us, when you promised us the right of private judgment. What reason have we to suppose you do not deceive us in other things also?" Such questions might be put, and, if put, it is obvious that it would be very inconvenient to answer them.

The first method is disproved; the second is abandoned; only the third remains. This, that of a single individual duly commissioned by Almighty God to announce the fact of inspiration to the world, the Professor does not attempt to defend as true, or as one which he does or can hold; but he maintains, that, on Catholic principles, it is probable, and therefore Dr. Lynch is entitled only to a probable conclusion,—not sufficient for his purpose, because he must conclude with absolute certainty. The Professor concludes, that, on Catholic principles, this hypothesis is probable, from the fact, that, on Catholic principles, it is a probable opinion that the Pope is infallible. But his argument involves a transition from one *genus* to another, and therefore concludes nothing. The single individual asserted in the hypothesis is commissioned in his individual capacity to announce the fact, and it is in this capacity that he is to do it. But such a commissioned individual is not the Pope, or Sovereign Pontiff. No Catholic holds the Pope in his individual capacity to be infallible. He is infallible, as we hold, and as we presume Dr. Lynch also holds; but only in his capacity of Supreme Head of the Church, in which sense he is included in the fourth hypothesis, as joined to the body of individuals asserted, inseparable from it, and essential to it. Concede, then, the infallibility of the Sovereign Pontiff, nothing is conceded in favor of the third method; for in the sense in which he is infallible he is the Church, or essentially included in the fourth method; since the head is not without the body, nor the body without the head.

The third method, then, is not the method. Then no one

of the first three. Then the fourth is; because some method of proof does exist, and it can be no other. Mr. Thornwell, therefore, has not refuted Dr. Lynch's argument. If he has not refuted it, against him, it stands good. Then the method of proof is the body supposed. But this body has authority to make an unerring decision on the subject of inspiration, that is, to declare unerringly what is or is not the word of God, therefore infallible in declaring the word of God. But this body is composed of the pastors of the Catholic Church. Therefore the pastors of the Church are infallible in declaring the word of God, the proposition Dr. Lynch undertook to prove. It would seem from this, that the learned and logical Professor's shouts of victory were decidedly premature. It is clear, also, since we are not considering what is or is not possible in the abstract, but *in hac providentia*, that the whole controversy turns between the first method and the fourth; for the private spirit is not admissible, and the Professor does not defend the second, and cannot, and would not if he could, defend the third. It is, then, either private judgment or the Catholic Church. So the Professor virtually concedes or maintains. What, therefore, he further adduces in his Fourth Letter, namely, that it is as easy to prove the inspiration of the Scriptures as the infallibility of the Church, cannot be entertained. There does exist some adequate proof; this is conceded. It evidently cannot be the method of private judgment; for it is absolutely impossible for a field slave, for instance, ignorant of letters, and with no time or ability to learn, to be able to decide for himself, on his own examination, whether *Tobias* or *Ecclesiasticus* is or is not an inspired composition. But, if not private judgment, it must be the infallible Church, and therefore the Church and its infallibility follow from the necessity of the case. This necessity overrides every possible objection. Bring as many objections as you please, and we dismiss them, as proving, if any thing, too much, and therefore nothing. *Quod nimis probat, nihil probat.*

Thus far we have confined ourselves, after stating the question, to showing that the Professor has not refuted Dr. Lynch's argument for the infallibility of the Church. This has been perfectly gratuitous on our part, for the burden of proof is on the Professor. But having vindicated Dr. Lynch's argument for the infallibility of the Church, we are now able to conclude it against Mr. Thornwell from the necessity of the case, the strongest argument that it is possible to use. Infallibility overrides all objections; and consequently, the Professor, let him do his best, cannot prove the fallibility of the Church. Here, then, we well might rest; but we find our author rather an amusing companion, and we should be sorry to part company with him so soon. We hope, therefore, to be able, in an early number, to consider the direct proofs of the fallibility of the Church, which he has attempted to bring. In the meantime, we recommend him, since he must hold his logical reputation dear, to make himself acquainted with Catholicity, before attempting again to write against it, and review also his logic, before he again asks his opponent to reason in syllogisms.

THORNWELL'S ANSWER TO DR. LYNCH.*

JULY, 1848.

MR. THORNWELL begins his argument against the Church (Letter IV.) by asserting, in substance, that we are unable to prove her infallibility, or if able, only by a process which supersedes the necessity of an infallible church to determine what is or is not the word of God. "It is just as easy," he says, "to prove the inspiration of the Scriptures as the infallibility of

* The Apocryphal Books of the Old Testament proved to be Corrupt Additions to the Word of God.—The Arguments of Romanists from the Infallibility of the Church and the Testimony of the Fathers in Behalf of the Apocrypha discussed and refuted. By JAMES H. THORNWELL. New York: Leavitt, Trow, & Co. Boston: Charles Tappan. 1845. 16mo. pp. 417.

any church." The evidence for both "is of precisely the same nature." The infallibility of the Church—"the inspiration of Rome," as he improperly expresses it—" turns upon a promise which is said to have been made nearly two thousand years ago; the inspiration of the New Testament turns upon facts which are said to have transpired at the same time. Both the promise and the facts are to be found, if found at all, in this very New Testament." You must prove its credibility, or you cannot prove the promise; and if you prove its credibility, you prove the facts. Therefore "you cannot make out the historical proofs of Papal infallibility without making out at the same time the historical proofs of Scriptural inspiration." Consequently, if you contend that the proofs are insufficient for the inspiration, you deny their sufficiency for the infallibility, and then cannot assert your infallible Church; if you say they are sufficient for the infallibility, you concede their sufficiency for the inspiration, and then do not need your infallible Church to determine what is or is not the word of God. (pp. 57–65.)

But Dr. Lynch proves, as we have seen in our former article, and as is sufficiently evident without proof to every one of ordinary reflection, that it is morally impossible to determine, with absolute certainty, what Scriptures are or are not inspired, except by the infallible Church. To assert, after this, that the infallible Church itself is provable only by proving Scriptural inspiration, is only asserting, in other words, that no adequate proof of what is or is not inspired Scripture exists. But some adequate method *does* exist, as Dr. Lynch proves, and Mr. Thornwell concedes. This method, if not private judgment, is the infallible Church, as he also virtually concedes; for private illumination is not a method of proof, since, if a fact, it is not a fact that can be adduced in evidence; and the other two methods supposed, namely, the judgment of the learned, and the single individual commissioned by Almighty God to announce the fact of inspiration to the world, he either abandons or cannot assert. The method, then, is either the infallible Church, or private judgment. It cannot be private judgment, if the objections urged against it be conceded. To attempt, without answering these objections, to show that equal objections bear against the Church, is, for the purposes of the argument at least, to concede them, and therefore to prove, if any thing, that no adequate method of proof exists, which is not allowable. As long, then, as private judgment remains unrelieved of the objections which declare it an impossible and therefore an unsupposable method, the argument proves too much for the Professor as well as for us, and consequently nothing.

This answers sufficiently Mr. Thornwell's reasoning, as far as it is intended to bear against Dr. Lynch's argument for infallibility from the necessity of the case. But we have a higher purpose in view than the simple vindication of Dr. Lynch, or the formal refutation of Professor Thornwell, and will therefore waive this reply and meet the reasoning on its intrinsic merits. Mr. Thornwell's conclusion rests on two assumptions:—1. That in order to establish the infallibility of the Church, Catholics are obliged to establish the credibility of the New Testament; and 2. That the credibility of the New Testament, when established, is all that is needed to establish Scriptural inspiration,—that is, to settle the question what Scriptures are and what are not inspired. Both of these assumptions we deny.

1. In order to establish the infallibility of the Church, it is not necessary to establish the credibility of the New Testament. All that is needed to establish the infallibility is the miraculous origin of the Church. If she had a miraculous origin, she was founded by Almighty God; for none but God can work a miracle. If founded by Almighty God, she is his Church and speaks by his authority; therefore infallibly; for God can authorize only infallible truth. In order to make out the miraculous origin of the Church, we are not obliged to recur to the New Testament at all; we can do it, and are accustomed to do it, when arguing with avowed unbelievers, without any reference to the authority of the Scriptures, either as inspired or as simple historical documents. We do it by taking the Church as we find her to-day, existing as an historical fact, and tracing her up,

step by step, through the succession of ages, till we ascend to her original Founder. The extraordinary nature of her claims, uniformly put forth, and steadily acted upon from the first; her various institutions, professing to embody facts, which could not in the nature of things have sprung from no facts, or from facts pertaining exclusively to the natural order; the external history which runs parallel to hers; the relation held to her from the beginning by the Jewish and pagan worlds, and by the various heresies in each succeeding age from the Gnostics down to the followers of the Mormon prophet;—all these combined prove in the most incontestable manner her supernatural character, and triumphantly establish the fact that her Founder must have had miraculous powers, and she a miraculous origin.

Undoubtedly, the infallibility of the Church turns, in the argument, upon a promise made nearly two thousand years ago; but it is not true that the promise must necessarily be found only in the New Testament. A promise may be expressed in acts as well as in words, in the fact as well as in its record. The promise we rely upon is expressed in the miraculous origin of the Church, and is concluded from it on the principle, that the effect may be concluded from the cause, if the cause be known. In the natural order, God, in giving to a being a certain nature, promises that being all that it needs to attain the end of that nature. So in the supernatural order, in creating a supernatural being, he promises it all the powers, assistance, means, and conditions necessary to enable it to discharge its supernatural functions, or to gain the supernatural end to which he appoints it. In supernaturally founding the Church to teach his word, he therefore promises her infallibility in teaching it: because the function of teaching the word of God cannot be discharged without it.

2. But even if we were obliged—as we are not and cannot be—to assert the credibility of the New Testament in order to make out our historical proofs, it would not be that credibility which would suffice to establish Scriptural inspiration, nor should we be obliged to make out any facts from which Scriptural inspir-

ation could be immediately concluded. As all we have to make out is the miraculous origin of the Church, and as this is made out, if the fact of the miracles of our Lord is established, all that, in any case, we could need to do, in regard to the credibility of the New Testament, would be to make out its credibility so far as requisite to establish this fact. We do not want the New Testament to prove the miraculousness of the facts, for that follows from the facts themselves; nor to accredit as teachers or witnesses those by or in favor of whom Almighty God performs the miracles, for that follows from the miraculousness; we can, at most, need it only for the purpose of proving that the miracles, in their quality of simple historical facts, actually occurred. For this simple historical testimony is sufficient, and consequently the simple *historical* credibility of the New Testament, as far as needed to authorize us to assert that the miracles actually took place, is all that it can even be pretended that we must make out. The New Testament is not one book, but a collection of books by different authors, each resting on its own independent merits, and the proof of the credibility of one does by no means establish the credibility of the rest. The most we can need for our purpose is the historical credibility of one of the Four Gospels, say the Gospel according to St. Matthew; for that Gospel records all the facts necessary to establish the miraculous origin of the Church. Consequently, all the credibility of the New Testament we can, in any case, be required to establish, is the *historical* credibility of St. Matthew's Gospel.

This Gospel may be perfectly credible as an historical document, without being inspired. The facts to be taken on its authority, though supernatural as to their cause, are within the natural order as to their evidence, and as easily proved as any other class of historical facts. They fall under the senses, and require in their witnesses only ordinary sense and ordinary honesty. To the trustworthiness of their historian, who, in recording them, has only to give a faithful narrative of what has transpired before his eyes, or what he has collected from the testimony of eyewitnesses, nothing beyond the ordinary human faculties can be requisite. Hence, many Protestants maintain the credibility of the Evangelical History, and yet deny the inspiration of the Gospels. We have by us a learned and elaborate work, in which the author, who, for learning and ability, ranks second to no Protestant theologian in the country, maintains, on the authority of the Pentateuch, the inspiration of Moses, and the divine origin of the Mosaic law, and yet denies the inspiration of the Pentateuch itself. Indeed, if none but inspired documents could be cited as credible authority for historical facts, human history would need to be closed at once, and Mr. Thornwell would find himself shut out from all means of establishing the *historical* objections he urges with so much zest, in the volume before us, against the Church; for undeniably, he can cite no inspired Scripture for them. It is not prudent for an author to take a ground which must prove more fatal to himself than to his opponent.

This fact, namely, that we need only the historical credibility of the New Testament at most, seems not to have sufficiently arrested Mr. Thornwell's attention; or if it has, he must have too hastily concluded that the same order of credibility which is sufficient for the miracles is also sufficient for the inspiration. He proceeds, apparently, on the assumption, either that simple historical credibility is sufficient to establish the inspiration of the Scriptures, or that we need supernatural credibility to establish the miracles. Thus, he asks:—

"If the books of the New Testament are to be received as credible testimony to the miracles of Christ, why not on the subject of their own inspiration? Are you not aware that the great historical argument on which Protestants rely in proving the inspiration of the Scriptures presupposes only the *genuineness* of the books and the *credibility* of their authors?..... They assert it [their own inspiration], and [if credible] are to be believed...... I had thought that the only difficulty in making out the external proofs of inspiration was in establishing the credibility of the books which profess to be inspired. It had struck me, that, if it were once settled that their own testimony was to be received, the matter was at an end. But it seems now that.....it is still doubtful whether, in the way of private judgment, a man could ever be assured that *credible* books are to be believed on the subject of their origin :"—pp. 62, 63.

This reasoning involves a transition *a specie ad speciem*. Credible books are certainly to be believed within the order of credibility which they are proved or conceded to possess, but not within an order which transcends or rises above it; for nothing can transcend itself, and the conclusion must be in the order of the premises, or the argument is a fallacy. The credibility of the New Testament which we assert, or which it is contended we are obliged to assert, is simply historical credibility, or credibility in the natural order; but the credibility the Professor needs, to establish the *inspiration*, is credibility in the supernatural order; for inspiration pertains, undeniably, to the supernatural order, both as to its cause and as to the medium of its proof. Therefore we may receive the books as credible testimony to the miracles, and not on the subject of their own inspiration.

Mr. Thornwell evidently reasons on the assumption, that we cannot assert the credibility of the New Testament in relation to the miracles without asserting it in relation to the inspiration. That is, a witness cannot be credible at all, unless he is universally credible, and he who receives his testimony in one order binds himself to receive it in every order; if he receives it in one respect, he must in every respect; in matters of fact, then also in matters of opinion! But this is too extravagant for any man in his sober senses seriously to maintain. If this were once admitted, there would speedily be an end to human testimony, and our Presbyterian friend would find himself in a sad plight; for his sole dependence is on private judgment, and he can pretend to nothing better than human testimony for his religious belief. No witness, unless absolutely omniscient, is or can be universally credible; and as no man is absolutely omniscient, it follows, if no one can be credible under one relation without being credible under every relation, that no one can in any respect be credible at all. But we cannot concede this. Every day, in every court of law, in all the practical affairs of life in which there is an appeal to human testimony, we act, and are obliged to act, on the supposition, that a man may be credible in relation to some things without being credible in relation to all things.

Every body knows that a witness may be perfectly credible in testifying to facts which fall under the observation of his senses, and yet be deserving of no credit in relation to his opinions, his judgments, his views, or his explanations of the causes of the facts to which he testifies. Nothing hinders, then, a man from being a credible witness to the facts recorded in the New Testament, even though he should assert and believe himself inspired when in point of fact he was not; for in testifying to the facts he testifies to what has come under his senses, while in asserting his inspiration he is merely giving an opinion, or offering an explanation of certain facts or phenomena of his own internal experience. The erroneous opinion or explanation does not impair his credibility as a witness to the facts, if his error is one which he may innocently entertain. That a man can innocently believe himself divinely inspired when he is not can hardly admit of a doubt. A man so believing is, by the very terms of the supposition, uninspired. He is then, since inspiration is a supernatural fact, necessarily ignorant of inspiration, unacquainted with its phenomena, and destitute of the necessary criterion for determining what it is or what it is not. What more natural, then, than that he should mistake certain phenomena of his own experience, otherwise inexplicable to him, for those of inspiration, and thus honestly believe himself inspired, when in reality he is uninspired?

The Professor argues on the assumption, common to all enthusiasts, that no man can honestly mistake the origin or cause of the phenomena of his own internal experience, and therefore, that, when one says he is inspired, we must believe either that he actually is inspired or that he is a liar, a *wilful* deceiver, whose word is to be received on no subject whatever. There is no reason for this assumption. He who is inspired, undoubtedly, knows the fact, and is as incapable of being deceived in relation to it as he is of deceiving others; but from this it by no means follows that a man who is not inspired must always know that he is not. Inspiration is, sometimes, at least, necessary to enable us to determine what is *not* inspiration, as well as to determine what is. He is little versed in the natural history of enthusiasm, who has yet to learn that honest men, men of rare gifts and inflexible principles, whose word on any subject within the range of sensible observation we would not hesitate a moment to take, not unfrequently labor under the impression that they hold immediate intercourse with the Almighty, are inspired, or divinely illuminated, when such is far from being the fact. Witness, for instance, Jacob Boehmen, George Fox, and Emanuel Swedenborg. These men are not inspired, nor are they liars. They do not *intend* to deceive, and are not even deceived themselves as to the facts of their internal experience, from which they infer their inspiration; they are deceived only in their opinions, their judgments of those facts, the explanations of them which they adopt, or the origin and cause which they assign them. Who dare pretend that this destroys their credibility in relation to simple matters of fact, evident to their senses? They do not mistake, they only misinterpret, the facts of their own consciousness; and who may not do as much? All men, however trustworthy they may be as witnesses to sensible facts, unless supernaturally protected from error, are liable, as is well known, to err in their judgments, in their explanations of phenomena,—in relation to the origin and causes of things, and in relation to the origin and causes of their own internal experience as well as of other things.

The Professor falls into the common mistake of Protestants; that the inspiration of a genuine book, by an author proved to be historically credible, may be concluded from its own declaration. We say he falls into this mistake; for we cannot suppose that he falls into the still grosser one of supposing that we can prove the miracles only by a supernaturally credible witness, since that would deny that Christianity itself can be proved,—nay, that any thing supernatural is or can be provable, and therefore that man is or can be the subject of a supernatural revelation. If the miracles cannot be proved without a supernaturally credible witness, the supernatural credibility of the witness will in turn demand another supernaturally credible witness to establish it, and this another, and thus on *ad infinitum.* We should need an infinite series of supernatural witnesses in order to establish the supernatural. But an infinite series is an infinite absurdity.

As we cannot suppose the Professor ignorant of the absurdity into which he would fall, if he contended for the necessity of any thing more than ordinary historical credibility to establish the miracles, we must suppose him to hold that ordinary historical credibility is sufficient to establish the inspiration of the Scriptures, in case they declare their own inspiration. But the inspiration of a genuine book, historically credible, cannot be concluded from its own declaration; because inspiration, being a supernatural fact, falling in no sense, as do the miracles, within the natural order, can be proved only by a supernaturally credible witness, which a merely historically credible witness is not. Before, from the declaration of the book, the Professor can conclude its inspiration, he must prove its author a credible witness to the supernatural. But no witness is a credible witness to the supernatural, unless he is himself inspired or divinely commissioned. The witness is not credible, unless competent. In ordinary cases, a witness may be competent, and not credible; but in no case can he be credible, if incompetent. No witness, unless inspired or divinely commissioned, is competent to testify to the supernatural. The witness is not competent, unless he can intellectually attain to or take cognizance of that to which he is to testify. But no witness can intellectually attain to or take cognizance of the supernatural,—which, by the fact that it is supernatural, transcends all natural intellect,—without something more than natural intellect; that is, without supernatural illumination or assistance,—precisely what is meant by being inspired or divinely commissioned. Therefore the Professor cannot conclude the inspiration from the mere historical credibility of the witness, and must prove the author to be inspired, or divinely commissioned, before, from its own declaration, he can conclude a given book is inspired Scripture.

Now, since in making out our historical proofs the most which it can be pretended that we must do is to make out the historical credibility of the books of the New Testament, or the credibility of their authors, in their quality of author, merely in relation to the natural order, it is not true, even in case we must appeal for our facts to the New Testament, that we cannot make out the historical proofs of the infallibility of the Church, without making out at the same time the historical proofs of the inspiration of the Scriptures; for we are not obliged to assert the credibility of the New Testament in relation to the supernatural, the sense in which it must be asserted in order to be credible authority for its own inspiration.

Nor, waiving this, do we, in making out the credibility which we are supposed to be under the necessity of making out, establish any facts from which the inspiration of the New Testament can be immediately concluded. The Professor himself says the Protestant argument "presupposes the *genuineness* of the books and the *credibility* of their authors." In addition, then, to the credibility of the authors, it is necessary, in order to establish the inspiration, to establish the genuineness of the books; that is, that they were actually written by the persons whose names they bear, and have come down to us in their purity and integrity. Now this, even if we must make out the credibility of the New Testament, we are not obliged to make out. An historical document may be authoritative without being genuine. If it contains a faithful narrative of facts as they occured, it is sufficient for the ordinary purposes of history. That the Gospel according to St. Matthew, for instance, does contain such a narrative, is provable, without proving its inspiration, in the usual way of authenticating historical documents, by the nature of the narrative itself, the quality of the facts recorded, the circumstances under which it was published or first cited, the estimate in which it was held by those best qualified to judge of its authority, the manner in which it was treated by those who had an interest in discrediting it, and by reference to various contemporary or subsequently existing monuments, especially public institutions implying, founded upon, or growing out of, the facts which it professes to record. In this way we could accredit this Gospel as an historical document, even if it had come down to us without the author's name. Indeed, ancient historical works in general derive but little authority from the *names* of their authors, and, other things being equal, the works of Herodotus, Livy, and Tacitus would have no less authority than they now have, even if they had been anonymous productions. As the genuineness of the book is an essential element in any method of proof of its inspiration, except that by the infallible Church, and as we are under no necessity, prior to the Church, of proving it in the case of a single one of the books of the New Testament, it follows that we are not obliged, in making out the historical proofs of the infallibility of the Church, to make out at the same time the historical proofs of the inspiration of the Scriptures.

We can now easily expose the fallacy of Mr. Thornwell's pretended dilemma. Assuming what we have just disproved, he says to Dr. Lynch, in his peculiarly sweet and delicate manner :—

"Now, Sir, one of two things must be true; either the credibility of the Scriptures can be substantiated to a plain, unlettered man, or it cannot. If it can be, there is no need of your infallible body to authenticate their inspiration, since that matter can be easily gathered from their own pages. If it cannot, then your argument from the Scriptures to an Indian or negro in favor of an infallible body is inadmissable, since he is incapable of apprehending the premises from which your conclusion is drawn. You have taken both horns of this dilemma, pushing Protestants with one. and upholding Popery with the other, and both are *fatal* to you. Now, as it is rather difficult to be on both sides of the same question at the same time, you must adhere to one or the other. If you adhere to your first position, that all human learning is necessary to settle the *credibility* of the Scriptures, then you must seek other proofs of an infallible body than those which you think you have gathered from the Apostles. . . . . . A circulating syllogism proves nothing; and if he who establishes the credibility of the Scriptures by an infallible body, and then establishes the infallibility of the body from the credibility of the Scriptures, does not reason in a circle, I am at a loss to apprehend the nature of that sophism. If you adhere to your other position, that the *accuracy of the Evangelists* can be easily substantiated, then your objections to private judgment are fairly given up, and you surrender the point, that a man can decide for himself, with absolute certainty, concerning the inspiration of the Bible. Take which horn you please, your cause is ruined; and as you have successively chosen both, you have made yourself as ridiculous as your reasoning is contemptible."—pp. 64, 65.

This argument evidently involves a transition from one genus to another. The Professor confounds in the first part of his fancied dilemma the historical *credibility*, and in the second the *accuracy* of the Evangelists in their account of the miracles, with the *inspiration* of the Scriptures, and then concludes as if they were all facts of the same order; which is a sad blunder, and little creditable to the "Professor of Sacred Literature and the Evidences of Christianity in the South Carolina College." Dr. Lynch does not say that it requires "all human learning to settle the *credibility* of the Scripturers" in any sense in which he can need their credibility prior to the Church; he simply maintains that all human learning, and perhaps more too, is necessary to settle, with absolute certainty, by private judgment, on intrinsic grounds, the *inspiration* of ancient writings,—which is a generically distinct proposition. The "accuracy of the Evangelists," which he asserts can be substantiated to the Indian or negro, is not the *inspiration* or the *supernatural* credibility of the Scriptures; but their accuracy as historians of the miracles, or that the miracles which they record actually transpired. As this accuracy does not presuppose or necessarily imply the inspiration or the supernatural credibility of the Scriptures, nothing hinders Dr. Lynch from adhering to both of the positions he has assumed, "pushing Protestants with one, and upholding Popery with the other," however inconvenient it may be to his Presbyterian adversary.

"He who establishes the credibility of the Scriptures by an infallible body, and then establishes the infallibility of the body from the credibility of the Scriptures, reasons in a circle," *if the credibility in both cases be taken in the same sense,* we concede; if in *different* senses, we deny. But Dr. Lynch does not establish the infallibility of the Church from the credibility of the Scriptures at all; or if he does, it is not from their credibility in that sense in which he contends that their credibility can be proved only by the infallible body. The only sense in which he can be said to establish the infallible body from the credibility of the Scriptures is their simple historical credibility; the sense in which he asserts the infallible body as necessary to prove their credibility is their credibility as inspired writings. As they can have the former without having the latter, we may, without any *vicious* circle, take the facts we need to prove the infallible body from their historical credibility, and then take the infallible body to prove their inspiration, or supernatural credibility, although we are, as we have shown, under no necessity of doing so. Does the Professor deny that we can do so? Does he contend that this would be to reason in a *vicious* circle? What, then, shall we say of his own reasoning for the inspiration of the New Testament? If he denies the distinction we have made, the historical credibility of the New Testament and its inspiration are one and the same thing,—convertible terms. Then we retort his argument. He says the infallibility of the Church "turns upon a promise which is said to have been made nearly two thousand years ago,—the inspiration of the New Testament turns upon facts which are said to have transpired at the same time. *Both the promise and the facts are to be found, if found at all, in this very New Testament.*" Here it is positively asserted that the facts which prove the inspiration can nowhere be found but in the New Testament itself. Then they must be taken on its credibility. But credibility and inspiration, according to him, are one and the same thing, convertible terms.

Then he must take the inspiration of the New Testament to prove the facts, and then the facts to prove the inspiration. If this be not to reason in a circle, we are " at a loss to apprehend the nature of that sophism."

Now one of two things must be true ; either this reasoning is valid, or it is not. If it is, Mr. Thornwell cannot make out the inspiration of the Scriptures ; for " a circulating syllogism proves nothing." If it is not, he fails to refute Dr Lynch, and then is refuted by him, as we proved in our former article. In either case, he is refuted. " Take which horn you please, your cause is ruined." Although the Professor says " it is rather difficult to be on both sides of the same question at the same time," yet he contrives to surmount the difficulty. He assumes that this reasoning is not valid, by urging, in spite of it, his own argument for Scriptural inspiration, and that it is valid, by urging it against Dr. Lynch. We may, then, reply to him in his own choice language :—" Take which horn you please, your cause is ruined; and as you have successively chosen both, you have made yourself as ridiculous as your reasoning is contemptible."

But even this is not the worst. Mr. Thornwell's conclusion rests on the assumption that the Scriptures declare their own inspiration, that their inspiration " is a matter" which " may be easily gathered from their own pages." " They assert," he maintains, " their own inspiration, and, if credible, are to be believed." But, granting that they declare their own inspiration, we have shown that it does not necessarily follow that they are inspired, because, to render their own testimony sufficient for that, they must be proved to be supernaturally credible, since inspiration is a supernatural fact, provable only by a supernaturally credible witness, and the only credibility, if any, which the Professor can claim for them is simple historical credibility. He binds himself to reason from our premises, because he says we cannot make out the historical proofs of the Church without making out at the same time the historical proofs of inspiration. Consequently, since the *historical* credibility of the Scriptures is all that we, at most, can be obliged to make out, it is all the

Professor can have as the principle from which to reason against us. This is conclusive against him. But waiving this, waiving the objection to the order of credibility, and giving—what we do not concede—that we must make out the genuineness of the books it is pretended we must cite, still he cannot conclude Scriptural inspiration, *because no one of the books whose historical credibility we need or can need declares its own inspiration.* We have shown, that for our purpose it suffices, in any case, to establish the credibility of one of the Four Gospels as an historical document. But no one of the Four Gospels declares or intimates that it is inspired Scripture, or even asserts the inspiration of any other of the Scriptural books. Consequently, the Professor has not even its own declaration for the inspiration of Scripture, and must be mistaken in saying that Scriptural inspiration is a matter which "may be easily gathered from" the pages of the Scriptures themselves.

But, adds the Professor, "you [Dr. Lynch] have yourself admitted that the teaching of the Apostles was supernaturally protected from error, and if their oral instructions were dictated by the Holy Ghost, why should that august and glorious Visitant desert them when they took the *pen* to accomplish the same object when absent, which, when present, they accomplished by the *tongue?*" (p. 62.) The question is irreverent and impertinent. We have no right to demand of the Holy Ghost the reasons of what he does or does not do. It is competent for him, if such be his pleasure, to inspire men for one thing and not for another, to inspire them to teach and not to write, to enable them to accomplish a given object by one method and not by another method; and the Professor cannot say that he does not, because he sees no reason why he should. The Holy Ghost may have reasons not known to the learned Professor of Sacred Literature, &c., in the South Carolina College.

Dr Lynch admits that the teaching of the Apostles was supernaturally protected from error, and we must prove that it was, or not prove the infallibility of the Church; but that it therefore necessarily follows that they were *inspired* as authors, or even as teachers, we neither admit nor are bound to admit. To be inspired, is, undoubtedly, to be supernaturally protected from error, but to be supernaturally protected from error is not necessarily to be inspired. Every Catholic believes his Church supernaturally protected from error; but no one believes her to be inspired. As all Catholics make this distinction, Dr. Lynch's admission is no admission of inspiration even in the teaching of the Apostles. Inspiration is necessary only when the mission is to reveal truth; when the mission is simply to teach a revelation already consummated, supernatural assistance, without inspiration, is all that is needed. If the mission of the Apostles was simply to teach a revelation which they had received through their personal intercourse with their Master, while he was yet with them in the flesh,—and prior to the Church, this certainly is all that we can be required to establish,—they had no need of inspiration, either as teachers or as writers, in order to be supernaturally protected from error. To concede or to assert such protection, then, is not to concede or assert their inspiration. We certainly cannot be required to make out for the Apostles any thing more than we claim for the Church, and since all we claim for her is supernatural protection from error in teaching a revelation already consummated, this is all that we can be obliged to make out for them.

Nor does the inspiration of the Apostles or of their writings follow immediately from the facts on which we must rely in order to prove the infallibility of the Apostles, or their supernatural protection from error. The facts on which we do and must rely are the miracles. These do not of themselves prove the inspiration, but simply the divine commission of him by or in favor of whom Almighty God works them, on the principle asserted by St. Nicodemus :—" Rabbi, we know thou art come a teacher from God ; for no man can do the miracles which thou doest, unless God be with him." The divine commission follows necessarily from the miracles, and the supernatural protection from error, or the infallibility, follows necessarily from the divine commission. But the inspiration does not, because the teacher may be commissioned to teach, and may teach infallibly, without being inspired. Even Apostolic inspiration, then, cannot be immediately concluded from the facts on which we must rely; then *a fortiori*, not the writings of the Apostles. We say *immediately*, for to say it can be mediately is nothing to the purpose. We ourselves hold that the inspiration both of the Old Testament and the New can be mediately proved, that is, through the teaching of the Church, proved by the miracles to be supernaturally protected from error.

But the Professor continues,—" The Apostles themselves declare their writings possessed the same authority with their oral instructions. Peter ranks the Epistles of Paul with the Scriptures of the Old Testament, which were confessed to be inspired; and Paul exhorts the Thessalonians to hold fast the traditions they had received from him, either by word or epistle." (p. 62.) That the Apostles anywhere declare their writings possess the same authority with their oral instructions, we have not found in any of the writings attributed to them with which we are acquainted; and if they did, it would not be sufficient, for the question at this moment relates, not to the authority, but to the inspiration, of the Scriptures, and it is not yet proved that even the *oral* instructions of the Apostles were inspired.

The Epistles of St. Peter and of St. Paul are not admissible testimony, because they are not included in that portion of the New Testament whose credibility we can, in any case, be obliged to make out. We can have no occasion for their testimony, prior to the Church; and as the Professor binds himself to the testimony we must use, or to what necessarily follows immediately from it, he cannot use it. The question now before us is, not whether he can or cannot, without the Church, prove the inspiration of the Scriptures, but whether he can prove it from the facts which we must prove in order to prove the infallibility of the Church.

St. Paul was not one of the twelve; his vocation was subsequent to the establishment of the Church; and in no case can it be necessary for us even to establish his divine commission in order to establish the miraculous origin of the Church, from which her infallibility immediately follows. But even if the Professor could cite the authority of St. Paul, he would be obliged to make out, before his citation would avail him any thing,—1. That St. Paul's oral instruction was inspired; 2. That the Epistle to the Thessalonians is genuine; 3. That the Epistle to which he refers in it was *the* Epistles which we now have under his name; and, 4. That these Epistles are possessed by us precisely as he wrote them. Here are four facts not easy to make out, and which the Professor must make out for himself; for we are under no obligation to make them out for him, and they do not follow necessarily from any thing we are bound to make out.

The divine commission of St. Peter as one of the Apostles, we, of course, are obliged to make out; but *ubi Petrus, ibi Ecclesia*—when we have done that, we have, in fact, made out our infallible Church. Let this, however, pass for the present. Though we are obliged to make out the divine commission of St. Peter as one of the twelve, we are not obliged to make out his inspiration, or the authenticity or genuineness of the Epistles attributed to him. The Epistle the Professor cites is no authority till its authenticity and genuineness are proved, and it happens to be precisely one of those books of the New Testament whose authenticity and genuineness Protestant theologians, at least many of them, call in question. But granting its genuineness, it avails nothing till the Professor proves that the Epistles of St. Paul to which it refers are those we now have, and that we have them as St. Paul wrote them; for the Professor is not merely to prove that there were inspired writings, but he is to prove what writings now possessed by us are or are not to be received as inspired Scripture. But even suppose this done, it does not follow that these Epistles are inspired. St. Peter does not, as the Professor asserts, "rank them with the Scriptures of the Old Testament, which were confessed to be inspired," but simply with "the other Scriptures." What Scriptures these were, whether inspired or uninspired, the Professor may or may not have some means of knowing, but St. Peter, in the writings attributed to him, nowhere informs him. That the Scriptures of the Old Testament were confessed to be inspired, we know from tradition and the Church, but not from the New Testament. From the New Testament alone we can prove neither that the books of the Old Testament were inspired, nor of what books the Old Testament consisted. St. Paul tells us, indeed, that "all Scripture divinely inspired is profitable," &c., but he nowhere tells us what books or portions of books are divinely inspired Scripture. It is not true, then, that the inspiration of the Scriptures can "be easily collected from their own pages." Then the whole argument of the Professor falls to the ground; for even if their own testimony were to be received, it would still be necessary to have the infallible body to prove their inspiration, since they themselves do not assert it.

We are not surprised that Mr. Thornwell should strive earnestly to convict his Catholic opponent of reasoning in a vicious circle. He must, as a Protestant, do so. Protestantism would abnegate herself, should she once concede that it is possible for us to prove the infallibility of the Church, without having recourse to the supernatural authority of the Scriptures. It is with the Protestant, therefore, a matter of life and death. If he fails, it is all over with his cherished Protestantism. Her friends must follow her in long and sad procession to her final resting-place, howl their wild requiem, and leave the night-shade to grow over her grave, and return to their desolate hearths, with none to comfort them. What, indeed, is the essential principle of Protestantism, in so far as she pretends to be distinguished from the open and total rejection of all supernatural religion? What is it, but the assertion that the Bible is the original and only source or authority from which Christianity is to be taken? Every body knows that this is her essential, her fundamental principle, in every sense in which she can even pretend to be a religion. To admit it to be possible for us to establish the infallibility of the Church without the Scriptures, or without their supernatural authority, would be to surrender this principle, and with it Protestantism herself, as far as she can claim to be distinguishable from infidelity.

All Protestants know this, and hence they always assert that we do and must reason in a vicious circle. It would be so convenient, it is so necessary, for them, that we should, they have for so long a time so uniformly and so confidently asserted that we do, that it is hard for them now to admit, or even to believe, that we do not and need not. Like inveterate story-tellers, they appear to have come at last, by dint of long and continued repetition, to believe their own falsehoods,—the last infirmity of the credulous and the untruthful. Indeed, we can hardly doubt that the great body of Protestants really do labor under the hallucination, that we must, in order to establish the Church, first establish, in the usual Protestant way, the authority of the Scriptures as inspired documents; and as we contend that the infallibility of the Church is necessary to prove their inspiration, that we must prove the inspiration by the Church, and the Church by the inspiration,—a manifest vicious circle. But as a circle proves nothing, they think they may well say, that in proving the Christian religion we have and can have no advantage over them. Grant, say they, we must prove the credibility of the Scriptures before we can conclude their inspiration, from which we take our faith, you must prove the same credibility before you can conclude the infallibility of the Church, from which you are to take yours, and you have and can have, prior to the Church, no means of proving that credibility which we have not.

When the credibility is once established, our difficulties are ended, for the inspiration is easily collected from the express declaration of the Scriptures themselves; but the infallibility of the Church is not. We have the express authority of the divinely accredited witness, but you have only your own interpretations or constructions of certain texts, in which you may err; and if you do not, you cannot assert that yours is the church intended, without making a full course of universal history for eighteen hundred years. How much simpler is our method than yours! With how many difficulties you encumber yourselves from which we are free! You have to make out all that we must make out, and in addition the fact of an infallible church, and the further fact that yours is it.

You may tell us that we may mistake the sense of Scripture, that our method is encumbered with difficulties, that it does not give us absolute certainty, and that something easier and surer is desirable. Be it so, what then? You have nothing to say, for you have nothing better to offer us. Suppose the Church; what do you gain? You must take it from the Scriptures, and the Scriptures themselves from the same authority that we do, that is, private judgment. You must take it also from the Scriptures by your private interpretation of them; and you must take the fact that yours is the Church from your private interpretations of history. Every step in your process of proof must be taken by private judgment, and we should like to know how private judgment is more certain in your case than in ours, —why it is to be condemned in us, and commended in you. Be it that it does not yield absolute certainty; what then? Absolute certainty,—who can have it? What presumption for such frail and erring mortals as we are to pretend to it! We do not need it. It is not in accordance with the intentions of Providence, nor compatible with our moral interest, that we should have it. "The true evidence of the Gospel is a *growing* evidence, sufficient always to create obligation and assurance, but *effectual* only as the heart expands in fellowship with God, and becomes assimilated to the spirits of the just. . . . . . Our real condition *requires* the possibility of error, and God has made no arrangements for absolutely terminating controversies and settling questions of faith, without regard to the moral sympathies of men." (pp. 74, 75.) With such certainty as we have we study to be satisfied. It is not the characteristic of wisdom to aim at impossibilities, or of honesty to profess to have what it has not.

Thus they reason, and must reason, wise and honest souls! who assert that the Bible is the original and only source of

Christian doctrine, and who define faith, with Professor Stuart of Andover, to be a species of probability, more certain, perhaps, than mere opinion, but less certain than knowledge, or ring the death-knell of their own system. If it be possible in the nature of things or the providence of God to bring an unbeliever to Catholicity without first converting him to Protestantism, they must for ever shut their mouths, or open them only to give vent to their mortification and despair. But, happily for us, the reasonings which demand the principle of universal skepticism for their postulate are not apt to convince, and the assertions of men who deny all infallible authority, and confess to their own fallibility and want of certainty, are not absolutely conclusive. It is possible, after all, that these learned Protestants are mistaken, nay, laboring under "strong delusions," and that we poor benighted Papists have the truth. At worst, the authority on which we rely can be no more than fallible, while that on which they rely must be fallible at best. At worst, then, we are as well off as they can be at best.

But are these Protestants, who would have us regard them as full-grown men, strong men, the lights and support of the age, aware, that, in all this argumentation on which they pride themselves, and which they hold to be our complete refutation, they are merely reasoning against us from their own principles, and not from any principles common to them and us? Their reasoning, undeniably, rests on the assumption of the Bible as the original and only source, under God, of Christian doctrine,—a fundamental principle of Protestantism, and which we no more admit than we do the other fundamental principle of Protestantism, namely, private judgment. They are very much mistaken, if they suppose that we merely object to their rule of private judgment, if they suppose that they and we occupy common ground till we reach the limits to which the Bible extends, and that our only controversy with them, as far as the Bible goes, is one of simple exegesis, and after that merely a controversy in relation to certain points of belief not to be found in the Bible. Our main controversy with them is prior to the Bible, and relates to the origin or fountain and authority from which the faith is to be drawn.

Protestantism, taking it according to the professions of its most distinguished doctors, is resolvable into two principles, if principles they can be called, namely,—1. The Bible is the original and only source of Christian faith; and, 2. The Bible is to be taken on and interpreted by private judgment. These are its two rules. It is nothing to us whether these two rules are or are not compatible one with the other, and we do not inquire now whether the latter does or does not necessarily and in fact absorb the former, and reduce Protestantism to sheer Transcendentalism in principle, for that is a matter which we have already sufficiently discussed elsewhere; but we say, what every body knows, that Protestantism professes these two rules as fundamental, and that they are essential to its very existence, and one of them as much as the other. Now we, as Catholics, reject and anathematize both of these rules, as Protestants ought to know. Consequently, for them to urge an argument against us which assumes either as its principle is a sheer begging of the question, or an assumption of Protestantism as the principle from which to conclude against Catholicity. Yet this is precisely the method of argument adopted in the brief summary of their reasoning which we have given.

This is not lightly said. Mr. Thornwell's whole reply to Dr. Lynch is a striking illustration and proof of it. Dr. Lynch states certain objections to private judgment; Mr. Thornwell replies, You cannot urge those objections, because, whatever their weight, they bear as hard against the Church as against us. What is the proof of this? You must take the Church from the Scriptures, or not take it at all; and if you take it from them, you must do so by private judgment, for you cannot use your Church before you get it; and as you can get your Church only subsequently to the Scriptures, you must take the Scriptures themselves on private judgment, or use a circulating syllogism, which proves nothing. But the proof that we must take the Church from the Scriptures? Why you must take it from the

Scriptures—because you have nothing else to take it from. But the proof that we have nothing else to take it from? The Professor has no possible answer, but the assumption of the Bible as the original and only source of Christian faith. Consequently, at bottom, whether he knows it or not, he simply assumes one principle of Protestantism as the principle of his answers to objections urged against the other. That is, if we consider Protestantism in its unity, he attempts to prove the same by the same; if in its diversity, he reasons in a vicious circle,—proving private judgment by his Bible rule, and his Bible rule by private judgment! And yet Mr. Thornwell has the simplicity to accuse Dr. Lynch of using a circulating syllogism.

Undoutedly, it is very convenient for Protestants, when hard pressed as to one of their principles, to resort to the other; but as both rules are denied, and are both directly or indirectly called in question in every controversy they have or can have with us, they would do well to bear in mind that the arguments they thus adduce are as illegitimate and worthless as if drawn from the very principle they are brought to defend. We really wish that our Protestant friends would study a little logic, at least make themselves acquainted with the more ordinary rules of reasoning and principles of evidence. It would save us some trouble, and themselves from the ridicule to which they expose themselves, whenever they undertake to reason. It is idle to attempt to convince a man by arguments drawn from the principle or system he is opposing, or to pretend to have refuted him by reasons which derive all their force from principles which he neither admits nor is obliged to admit. In reasoning, each party must reason from principles admitted by the other, or from principles proved by arguments drawn from principles which the other does not or cannot deny. Our Protestant friends ought to know this; for Mr. Thornwell very considerately informs us (p. 72) that they are not "prattling babes and silly women," but "bearded men."

Protestants seem to have inquired how it would be convenient for them that we should reason, and to have concluded, because, if we should reason in a given manner, it would be just the thing for them, that we of course do and must reason in that manner. If we admitted their doctrine as to the Bible, we undoubtedly should be obliged to reason in the manner they allege. If the road from unbelief to Catholicity lay through Protestant territory, if we could convert the unbeliever to the Church only by first converting him to Protestantism, as Mr. Thornwell virtually contends, we should, of course, be obliged to make out the divine authority of the Scriptures, if at all, in the way in which Protestants attempt to do it, and then many of the objections we now urge and insist upon against private judgment we should be obliged to meet as well as they; but, surely, some other proof that such is the fact should be brought forward than this, that, if it be not so, then Protestantism must be false; for the conclusion is not one which we are not able to concede. In reasoning with Protestants, we are generally civil enough to take them at their word; and as we find them professing to hold the divine authority of the Scriptures, we draw our arguments against them from the Scriptures, because it is always lawful to reason against a man from his own principles; but in reasoning against unbelievers, we make no appeal to the Scriptures, unless it be sometimes as simple historical documents, proved to be such by general historical criticism, in which character we can legitimately appeal to them. The assertion, that we are obliged, by the nature of the case, to take the Church from the Scriptures, is altogether gratuitous, and even preposterous. It rests, as we have seen, on the assumption, that the Bible is the original and sole authority for Christian faith. This is what Mr. Thornwell holds, what as a Protestant he must hold. The Bible, then, occupies the same place in his system that the Church does in ours; for this is precisely what we say of the Church. The Bible is for him the original and sole depositary of the faith,—its keeper, witness, teacher, and interpreter. He must, then, establish the divine authority of the Scriptures, as we the divine authority of the Church; for only a divine authority is sufficient for Christian faith. To do this, as we have already established, he must have a supernaturally credible witness. Prior to and independently of the supernatural authority of the Scriptures, then, he must obtain such witness. This he can do, or he cannot. If he cannot, he cannot establish the divine authority of the Scriptures. If he can, then we also can; for prior to the Scriptures, we stand, at least, on as good ground as he. But such a witness is all we need for the divine authority of the Church. Then either the Professor cannot establish the divine authority of the Scriptures, or we can establish the divine authority of the Church without the Scriptures. Where now are the Professor's assumption, and his triumph about reasoning in a circle?

Again. The divine authority of the Scriptures is itself an article of faith, because a supernatural fact, and a revealed fact, if a fact at all. This can be proved without the Scriptures, or it cannot. If it cannot, then it cannot be proved at all, for the Scriptures can authorize no article of faith till their own divine authority is established. If it can, it is false to say the Scriptures are the original and only authority for faith, for here is an article of faith not taken from them, but from some other source and authority. Or in another form: Either the supernatural witness supposed can be obtained, or cannot. If the Professor says the latter, he abandons his Protestantism, by confessing to his inability to establish the divine authority of the Scriptures, from which alone he is to take it. If he says the former, he also abandons his Protestantism; for then he concedes the possibility of another authority for faith than the Scriptures, which Protestantism does and must deny, or deny itself. The Professor may take which alternative he pleases; in either case, he must surrender his Protestantism, as far as at all distinguishable from sheer infidelity.

Thus easy is it to overthrow the strongest positions of Protestants, and we confess that our only practical difficulty in refuting Protestantism lies precisely in its weakness, nay, its glaring absurdity. Our arguments against it fail to convince, because too easily obtained, and because they are too obviously conclusive. People doubt their senses, and refuse to trust their reason.

They think it impossible that Protestantism, which makes such lofty pretensions, should be so untenable, so utterly indefensible, as it must be, if our arguments against it are sound. We succeed too well to be successful, and fail because we make out too strong a case. Indeed, Protestantism owes its existence and influence, after its wickedness, to its absurdity. If it had been less glaringly absurd, it would long since have been numbered with the things that were. *Fuit ilium.* But many people find it difficult to believe it to be what it appears; they think it must contain something which is concealed from them, some hidden wisdom, some profound truth, or else the *enlightened* men among Protestants would not and could not have manifested so much zeal in its behalf,—forgetting that Socrates ordered just before his death a cock to be sacrificed to Æsculapius, that Plato advocated promiscuous concubinage, and that Satan, notwithstanding his great intellectual power, is the greatest fool in the universe,—a fool whom a simple child saying *credo* outwits and turns into ridicule. But they may be assured that it is not one whit more solid than it appears, and that the deeper they probe it, the more unsound and rotten they will find it.

Protestants would do well to study the Categories, or Prædicaments, and learn not to contemn proper and necessary distinctions. They should know that they cannot conclude the supernatural from the natural; and that the historical credibility of the Scriptures does not, of itself, establish their divine authority in relation to the supernatural order. Historical credibility suffices for the miracles; and miracles accredit the teachers, but not immediately the teaching, whether oral or written. The teaching is taken on the authority of the accredited teacher. Consequently, between the miracles and the divine authority of the Scriptures the authority or testimony of the teacher must intervene, and whether it does intervene in favor of the Scriptures or not is a question of fact, not of reason.

Hence it is easy to detect the falsity of Mr. Thornwell's general thesis, that " it is just as easy to prove the inspiration of the Scriptures as the infallibility of any church." The inspiration of the Scriptures and the divine authority or infallibility of the Church are both supernatural facts, and therefore provable only by evidence valid in relation to the supernatural. In order to prove the inspiration of the Scriptures, the Professor must prove their divine authority; for he is to take their inspiration from their own testimony, which is not adequate, unless supernaturally credible. But to prove the divine authority of the Scriptures, he must prove the divine commission of the Apostles. The supernatural is provable in two ways,—by miracles, and by divinely accredited or commissioned teachers. The miracles accredit or prove the divine commission of the teachers, but, as we have just seen, not the divine authority of the writings. This must be taken on the authority of the teachers themselves, and the Apostles are the only teachers supposable in the case; because all, whether Church or Scriptures as a matter of fact, comes to us from God through them. Consequently, the Professor must establish, in some way, their divine commission, or not establish the divine authority of the Scriptures, and therefore the supernatural credibility of their testimony to their own inspiration.

This we also must do, or not be able to assert the infallibility of the Church. The divine commission is a point common to us both; both must make it out,—he without the authority of Scripture, and we without the authority of the Church. If he can make it out, we can, and if we can make it out, he can; for we both, in relation to it, stand on the same ground, have the same difficulties, and the same, and only the same, means with which to overcome them.

The divine commission of the Apostles is made out, if at all by the miracles historically proved to have actually occurred. These, thus proved, accredit the teachers, that is, the Apostles, as teachers come from God, therefore commissioned by him; and if commissioned by him, what they teach, as from him, must be infallibly true, because he cannot authorize the teaching of what is not infallibly true. Thus history proves the miracles, the miracles prove the divine commission, and the divine commission proves the infallibility. Thus far, we and the Professor travel together. But—and this is the point he overlooks—when we have gone thus far, and obtained the divinely commissioned Apostles, we have got the infallible Church; for they are it, in all its plenitude and in all its integrity. Has the Professor got his inspired Scriptures? No. He has not yet got even their divine authority, and does not as yet even know that there are any Scriptures at all, much less what and which they are; and he can know only as these divinely commissioned Apostles inform him, that is, as taught by the infallible Church,—precisely what we have always told him, and what he ought to have known in the outset.

Does the Professor answer, that we have not yet proved the present existence of the infallible Church, and that ours is it? Be it so. We must, of course, establish the fact of communion between us and the Church of the Apostles, or not be able to assert the infallibility of our Church. But the Professor has also to establish the fact of his communion with the same Church, before he can assert the divine authority of the Scriptures; for he is to assert it on her authority, and this he cannot do until he proves that he has her authority. The simple question, then, between us is, whether it is as easy for him to establish the fact of the communion in his case, as it is for us to establish it in ours. He must prove, not only that it is *possible* in his case, but that it is as *easy* in his as in ours, or abandon his thesis.

As yet, the Professor has only the point in common with us of the divine commission, or infallible Church, of the Apostles. The authority of this Church he must bring home to the sacred books with absolute certainty, and with so much exactness as to include no uninspired and to exclude no inspired Scripture. He must bring it home, not merely to some books, but to all whose inspiration is to be asserted; and this not in general only, but also in particular,—to each particular book, chapter, verse, and sentence. This, in the nature of the case, he can do only by proving the genuineness of the Apostolic writings, and the identity, purity, and integrity of all those books which, though not written by the Apostles themselves, are to be received as inspired on their authority. This he must do before he can establish the divine authority of the Scriptures, and be able to conclude their inspiration from their own testimony, in case he has it.

This is what the Professor has to do, in order to make out the fact of Apostolic communion in his case; but all we have to do, in order to establish it in ours, is to prove historically the continuance in space and time of the Church of the Apostles, and its external identity, or its identity as a visible corporation or kingdom, with our Church. Now which is the easiest? Is it as easy to prove the authenticity, purity, and integrity of some sixty or seventy ancient books, written in different languages, and transcribed perhaps a thousand times, subject to a thousand accidents, as to establish the external identity of a visible corporation or kingdom, extending over all nations, the common centre around which, in one form or another, revolve all the significant events of the world for eighteen hundred years, and no more to be mistaken than the sun in the cloudless heavens at noonday? We are to prove, we grant, the external identity of our Church with the Church in the days of the Apostles,—a thing, in its very nature, as easy to be done as to establish the continuance and identity of any civil corporation, state, or empire, ancient or modern. But the Professor has to do as much as this, and more too, in the case of the Bible, and of each separate book, chapter, and sentence in the Bible,—a thing morally impossible to be done, as all the attempts of Protestants to establish the divine authority of the Scriptures sufficiently prove.

But even if this were done, the Professor would not have established the inspiration of a single sentence of Scripture, as Scripture. The divine authority of the Scriptures does not prove their inspiration, unless they themselves declare it; for the Professor must gather their inspiration from their own pages. He can assert no book to be inspired, unless, if it be a genuine Apostolic writing, it clearly and unequivocally asserts its own inspiration, and if it be not an Apostolic writing, unless it is clearly and unequivocally declared to be inspired by some book whose divine authority is established. And even this would not be enough for his purpose; for he must not only make out the inspiration of certain books, but he must establish by divine authority what books are, and what are not, to be received as inspired Scripture. He must bring divine authority to say, These, and these only, are to be so received. This last is impossible, for it is well known that Scripture nowhere draws or professes to draw up a list of the inspired books. This of itself is conclusive against the Professor. The former, also, is impossible, for none of the Apostolic writings, unless it be the Apocalypse, whose authenticity many Protestants deny, assert their own inspiration, and, with this exception, and some portion of the prophetic books, what is received as Scripture is nowhere in Scripture asserted to be inspired. Hence there are amongst us Protestant Doctors of Divinity, who, while professing to acknowledge the authority of our Lord and his Apostles, and the general historical fidelity and authority of the Bible, deny entirely its inspiration.

The Professor, therefore, must be decidedly mistaken in saying that, "it is just as easy to prove the inspiration of the Scriptures as the infallibility of any church." His meaning is, that, in the nature of the case, it must be as easy to prove the inspiration as the infallibility, which we see is by no means the fact; because, on no hypothesis, can he prove the inspiration of the Scriptures without first proving the infallible Church, and the historical identification of the Church in space and time is a thing infinitely easier to make out than the authenticity, identity, purity, and integrity of ancient writings. The latter can be done, if at all without a continued infallible authority, only with extreme difficulty, and by a few gifted individuals, who have ample opportunities and learned leisure for the purpose. The other is a thing easily done. It is, making allowance for the greater lapse of time between the two extremes, as easy to prove that Pius IX. is the successor of St. Peter in the goverment of the Church, as that James K. Polk is the successor of George Wash ington in the Presidency of the United States; and the fact of the succession in the former case as much proves that the Church of which Pius IX. is Pope is the Church of St. Peter, that is, of the Apostles, as the succession in the latter case proves that the United States of which Mr. Polk is President are the same political body over which George Washington presided. Even the allowance to be made for lapse of time dwindles into insignificance, the moment we consider the more important part in the affairs of the world performed by the Church than by the United States, or by any temporal state or kingdom of ancient or modern times.

To identify and to establish the purity and integrity of an ancient book, which has been subject to all the accidents of two or three thousand years, is by no means an easy task; but the identity in space and time of an outward visibly body, " a city set on a hill," the common centre of nations, and spreading itself over all lands and conducting the most sublime and the most intimate affairs of mankind, everywhere with us, at birth, baptism, confirmation, marriage, in sickness and health, in joy and sorrow, in prosperity and adversity, in life and death,—taking us from our mother's womb, and accompanying us as our guardian angel through life, and never leaving us for one moment till we arrive at home, and behold our Father's face in the eternal habitations of the just,—is the easiest thing in the world to establish through any supposable series of ages. You may speak of its liability to corruption; but far less liable must it be, even humanly speaking, to corruption than the Scriptures, and indeed, after all, it is only from its incorruptness and its guardian care, that even you, who blaspheme the Spouse of God, conclude the purity and integrity of the Scriptures. Far easier would it be to interpolate or mutilate the Scriptures, without detection, than for the Church to corrupt or alter her teachings, always diffused far more generally, and far better known than their pages. If publicity, extent, and integrity of the Christian people are to be pleaded for the purity and integrity of the sacred text, as they must be, then *a fortiori* for the purity and integrity of the Church's teaching.

But passing over all this, supposing, but not conceding, that the Professor could make out the inspiration of Scripture, it would amount to just nothing at all; for the real matter to be determined is, what is or is not to be received as the word of God, and till this is determined, or an unerring rule for determining it is obtained, nothing is done of any practical moment. To prove that the Scriptures are inspired, and therefore contain the word of God, is only to prove *where* the word, or some portion of the word, of God is, not *what* it is. Between *where* and *what* there is a distance, and, unless some means are provided for bridging it over, an impassable gulf. We are not told *what* the word of God is, till we are told it in the exact sense intended by the Holy Ghost, and this is not told us by being told that the word of God or some portion of it, is contained in a certain book. How will the Professor tell us this?

The controversy turns on the means of evidencing the word of God to the Indian or negro. Suppose the Professor goes to the Indian or negro, with his copy of the Holy Scriptures; suppose, *per impossible*, that he succeeds in proving to him that the several books were dictated by the Holy Ghost, and in the exact state in which he presents them. What is this to him? He cannot read, and the book is to him a sealed book, as good as no book at all. What shall be done? Shall the Indian or negro wait till he has learned to read, and to read well enough to read, understandingly, the Bible,—which is out of his power,—and also till he has read it through several times, and some five or six huge folios besides, to explain its unusual locutions, and its references to strange manners and customs, and to natural and civil history, before hearing or knowing what is the message sent him by his Heavenly Father? What, in the mean time, is he to do? Is he to remain a heathen, an infidel, an alien from the commonwealth of our Lord? If he needs the Gospel as the medium of salvation, how can he wait, as he must, on the lowest calculation, more than half the ordinary life of man, without peril to his soul? If he does not need it, what do you make the Gospel but a solemn farce? Suppose he does wait, suppose he does get the requisite amount of learning; what surety have you, even then, that he will not deduce error instead of truth from the book, and instead of the word of God embrace the words of men or of devils?

The pretence of Protestants, that they derive their belief, such as it is, from the Bible, is nothing but a pretence. If not, how happens it that, as a general rule, children grow up in the persuasion of their parents,—that the children of Episcopalians find the Bible teaching Episcopalianism, Presbyterian children find it teaching Presbyterianism, Baptist children Baptist doctrine, Methodist children Methodism, Unitarian children Unitarianism, Universalist children Universalism? Why is this? The Professor knows why it is, as well as we do. He knows it is so, because their notions of religion are not derived from the Bible, but from the instructions of their parents, their nurses, their Sunday-school teachers, their pastors, and the society in the bosom of which they are born and brought up, and that, too, long before they read or are able to read the Bible so as to learn any thing from its sacred pages for themselves. He knows, too, that, when they do come to read the Bible,—which may happen with some of them,—they read it, not to learn what they are to believe, not to find what it teaches, but to find in it what they have already been taught, have imbibed, or imagined. All Protestants know this, and it is difficult to restrain the expression of honest indignation at their hypocrisy and cant about the Bible, and taking their belief from the Bible,—the Bible, the precious word of God. The most they do, as a general rule, is to go to the Bible to find in it what they have already found elsewhere, and it rarely happens that they find any thing in it except what they project into its sacred pages from their own minds.

To hear Protestants talk, one would think they were the greatest Bible-readers in the world, and that they believed every thing in the Bible, and nothing except what they learn from it. It is no such thing. Who among them trusts to the Bible alone?

Where is the Protestant parent, pretending to any decent respect for religion, who leaves his children to grow up without any religious instruction till they are able to read and understand the Bible for themselves? Has not every sect its catechism? A catechism? What means this? With "the Bible, the whole Bible, and nothing but the Bible" on their lips, have they the audacity and the inconsistency to draw up a catechism and teach it to their children? Why do they not follow out their principle, and leave their children to "the Bible, the whole Bible, and nothing but the Bible?" Do you shrink, Protestant parents, as well you may, from the fearful responsibility of suffering your children to grow up without any religious instruction? Why not shrink also from the still more fearful responsibility of teaching them your words for the word of God? You tell us the Bible is your sole rule of faith, that there are no divinely appointed teachers of the word of God, and you sneer at the very idea that Almighty God has provided for its infallible teaching; and yet you, without authority, fallible by your own confession, draw up a catechism, take upon yourselves the office of religious teachers, and do not hesitate to teach your own crude notions, your own fallible, and, it may be, blasphemous opinions, training up your children, it may be, in the synagogue of Satan, keeping them aliens from the communion of saints, and under the eternal wrath of God! How is it that you reflect not on what you are doing, and for your children's sake, if not for your own, you do not tremble at your madness and folly? Who gave you authority to teach these dear children? Who is responsible to their young minds and candid souls for the truth of the doctrines you instil into them? O Protestant father, thou art mad? Thou lovest thy child, art ready to compass sea and land for him, and yet, for aught thou knowest, thou art doing all in thy power to train him to be the eternal enemy of God, and to suffer for ever the flames of divine vengeance!

But the catechism.—Who gave to you authority to draw up a catechism? Would you teach your children damnable heresies? Would you poison their minds with error and their hearts with lies? What it is you do when you draw up and teach a catechism? You deny the authority of the Church to teach, yet here you are, Episcopalians, Presbyterians, Baptists, Methodists, Ranters, Jumpers, Dunkers, Socinians, Unitarians, Universalists, all of you, doing what you make it a crime in her to do,—drawing up and teaching a catechism, the most solemn and responsible act of teaching that can be performed; for in it you demand of confiding childhood simple and unwavering belief in what you teach! But the catechisms, you say, are for the most part drawn up in the language of the Holy Scriptures. Be it so. Who gave you authority to teach the Holy Scriptures? What infallible assurance have you, that, in teaching the words of Scripture, you are teaching the sense of Scripture? Is it a difficult thing either to lie or to blaspheme in the words of Scripture?

We confess that we can hardly observe any measure in our feelings or in our language, when we regard the profession and the practice of Protestants, when we consider how they lie unto the world and unto themselves, and how many precious souls, for whom our God has died, they shut out from salvation. One must speak in strong language, or the very stones would cry out against him. The Professor, whom we have supposed going with his Bible in his hands, and holding it out to the rude savage or poor slave, ignorant of letters, saying, "Read this, my son, and it shall make you wise unto salvation,"—would he wait, think ye, till his tawny son or black brother had learned to read and become able to draw his faith from the Bible for himself, before instructing him? Be assured, not. He would hasten to instruct him without delay in his Presbyterian Catechism, the Westminster Confession of Faith, the Five Points of the Synod of Dort, or some modification of them. Never would he trust him to the Bible alone. So it is with all Protestant missionaries, and so must it be. No matter what they profess, in practice none of the sects place or can place their dependence on the written word to teach the faith without the aid of the living preacher. They all know, or might know, that they use the Bible, not as the source from which the simple believer is to draw his faith, but as a shield to protect the teachers of one sect from those of another; and that they assert its authority only as enabling each preacher to find some plausible pretext for preaching whatever comes into his own head. They place their dependence, not on a dead book, which when interrogated can answer never a word, which lies at the mercy of every interpreter, but, *nolens volens*, on the living teacher, and do without authority, and against their avowed principles, what they condemn us for doing, and what we do at least consistently, and in obedience to our principles.

There is no use in multiplying words or making wry faces about the matter. Whatever men may pretend, if they have any form of belief or of unbelief, their reliance is on the living teacher to preserve and promulgate it. The thing is inevitable. And since it is so, it is absolutely necessary, if we are to know and believe the word of God, that we have teachers duly authorized, divinely appointed to teach that word, so that we may not believe for the word of God the words of fallible men or of devils. Therefore, even if we could establish the inspiration of the Scriptures, as we cannot without the Church, the Church would still be indispensable, for without her we should still have no infallible means of knowing what is the word of God.

We have here refuted the Professor's thesis in all its parts. We have shown him that he has no logical right to urge it; that if he is allowed to urge it, he cannot prove it, but that we can easily prove the contrary; and, finally, that if he could prove it, it would avail him nothing. We hope this will be satisfactory to him and his friends. He has been, even his friends must confess, singularly unsuccessful; but the fault has not been altogether his own. He has done as well as any Protestant could do. But it is an old and expressive proverb, if a homely one, that "nobody can make a silk purse out of a sow's ear." Nobody can make any thing out of Protestantism, and her defence must needs baffle the finest intellects. She is utterly indefensible. No man can construct an argument in her favor, or against the Church, that is not at bottom a mere fallacy. Logic as well as salvation is on the side of the Church, not with her enemies, and Protestantism is as repugnant to sound reason as she is to the best interests of man. Whoever espouses her must needs render himself an object of pity to all good men and good angels. Mr. Thornwell has naturally respectable abilities, even considerable logical powers, and some vigor of intellect. He wants refinement, grace, unction, but he has a sort of savage earnestness which we do not wholly dislike, and manifests a zeal and energy, which, if directed according to knowledge, would be truly commendable. But all these qualities can avail him nothing, for Protestantism at best is only a bundle of contradictions, absurdities, and puerilities. How a man of an ordinary stomach could undertake its defence would be to us unaccountable, did we not know to what mortifications and humiliations pride compels its subjects to submit. Pride cast the angels, which kept not their first estate, down from heaven to hell, and perhaps we ought not to be surprised that it degrades mortal men to the ignoble task of writing in defence of Protestantism.

The refutation of the Professor's thesis gives us the full right to conclude the infallibility of the Church with Dr. Lynch from the necessity of the case, and therefore to assert it, whatever objections men may fancy against it; because the argument for it rests on as high authority as it is possible in the nature of things to have for any objection against it. Nevertheless, we will examine in our next Review the Professor's moral and historical objections to the Church, and dispose of them as well as we can,—we hope to his satisfaction.

THORNWELL'S ANSWER TO DR. LYNCH.*

OCTOBER, 1848.

In the articles already devoted to Mr. Thornwell's book, we have vindicated Dr. Lynch's argument drawn from the necessity of the case for the infallibility of the Church, and proved, unanswerably, if any thing can be so proved, that without the infallible Church, the Protestant is utterly unable to prove the inspiration of the Scriptures. Since he concedes, that, if the infallible Church exists at all, it is the Catholic Church, Mr. Thornwell must then, either acknowledge its infallibility, or give up the Christian religion itself. Having done this, which has been wholly gratuitous on our part, we proceed to the consideration of the Professor's direct arguments for the fallibility of the Church, or his direct attempts to prove that she is not infallible.

We have shown in our first essay, that the nature of the argument the Professor is conducting does not permit him, even in case we should fail to prove the infallibility, to conclude the fallibility of the Church. He denies that she is infallible, that is, asserts that she is fallible, and it is only by proving her fallible that he can maintain his thesis, that the books which he calls apocryphal are "corrupt additions to the word of God." The question is not now on admitting, but on rejecting, the infallibility of the Church, and the *onus probandi*, as a matter of course, rests on him. He is the plaintiff in action, and must make out his case by proving the guilt, not by any failure on our own part, if fail we do, to prove the innocence, of the accused; for every one is to be presumed innocent till proved guilty.

---

* The Apocryphal Books of the Old Testament proved to be Corrupt Additions to the Word of God.—The Arguments of Romanists from the Infallibility of the Church and the Testimony of the Fathers in Behalf of the Apocrypha discussed and refuted. By JAMES H. THORNWELL. New York: Leavitt, Trow, & Co. Boston: Charles Tappan. 1845. 16mo. pp. 417.

We have also shown, that in attempting to prove the fallibility of the Church, Mr. Thornwell must confine himself to such arguments as an infidel may consistently urge. We have already disloged him from every position he might be disposed to occupy on Christian ground. He has no magazine from which he can draw proofs against the Church, but the reason common to all men. He can prove the Church fallible only by proving that she has actually erred; and he can prove that she has actually erred only by proving that she has actually contradicted some principle of reason. It will avail him nothing to prove by reason that she teaches things the truth of which reason cannot affirm; for reason does not know all things, and things may be *above* reason, and yet not *against* reason. Nor will it avail him to prove that she contradicts his private convictions, or the teachings of his sect; for neither he nor his sect is infallible. Nothing will avail him but to prove some instance of her contradiction of a truth of reason, infallibly known to be such truth. The simple question for us to determine, then, in regard to what he alleges, is, Has he adduced an instance of such contradiction? If he has, he has succeeded; if he has not, he has failed, and we, since the presumption, as we say in law, is in our favor, may conclude the infallibility of the Church against him.

1. Mr. Thornwell's first alleged proof that the Church is not infallible is, that Catholics differ among themselves as to the seat of infallibility. It is uncertain where the infallibility is lodged. Then it is not apparent; and if not apparent, it does not exist; for *de non apparentibus et non existentibus eadem est ratio.* But this, supposing it to be true, though a good reason why we cannot assert the infallibility as a fact proved, is not a good reason for asserting that it does not exist. A thing may exist and yet not appear to us. Otherwise the stars would not exist when the sun shines, nor gems in the mine before being discovered. The point to be established is not the *non-appearance* of the infallibility, but its *non-existence;* and if the Professor does not show that non-existence, he fails, for his own maxim then bears against him,—*de non apparentibus et non existentibus eadem est ratio.*

8

But what is alleged is not true. Catholics do not disagree as to the seat of infallibility. Mr. Thornwell is mistaken, when he says (p. 76),—" There are no less than three different opinions entertained in your Church as to the organ through which its infallibility is exercised or manifested." He confounds the three different modes in which Catholics hold that the infallibility is exercised with three different opinions as to its organ, evidently supposing that they who assert one of them must needs deny the other two. All Catholics agree, and must agree, for it is *de fide*, that the pastors of the Church, that is, the bishops in union with the Pope, their visible head, are infallible in what they teach, both when congregated in general council and when dispersed, each bishop in his own diocese; and the great majority hold that the Pope alone, when deciding a question of faith or morals for the whole Church, is also infallible. The only difference of opinion amongst us is as to the fact, whether the Pope is or is not infallible, when so deciding. But as there is no difference of opinion as to the other two modes, whatever difference there may be as to this, it is not true that there are " three different opinions in our Church as to the organ through which its infallibility is exercised or manifested."

2. The Church cannot be infallible, because she requires a slavish submission of all her members, bishops, priests, and laity, to the Pope. "The system of absolute submission runs unchecked until it terminates in the Sovereign Pontiff at Rome, whose edicts and decrees none can question, and who is therefore absolute lord of the Papal faith," (p. 77.) We can see nothing unreasonable in making the Pope, under God, the "absolute lord of the *Papal* faith." As to the submission, if the Pope has authority from God as the supreme visible head of the Church, it cannot be a *slavish* submission; for slavery is not in submission, but in submission to an authority which has no right to exact it. Reason teaches that we are bound to obey God, and to obey him equally through whatever organ it may please him to command us, or to promulgate his will. If he has commissioned the Pope as his vicar in the government of the

Church, there is nothing repugnant to reason in submission or obedience to the Pope. The Professor must prove that the Pope is not divinely commissioned, before, from the fact that the Church obliges us to obey him, he can conclude that she errs or is liable to err. But this he has not proved.

3. The Church makes the Pope greater than God,—*Il papa è più che Dio per noi altri*.—and cannot assert his supremacy without asserting his infallibility. But if she asserts the infallibility of the Pope, she denies that she is an infallible Church; for, during the first six centuries, there was no Pope. (p. 78.) Where the Professor picked up his scrap of Italian, he does not inform us; but if any one has made him believe that Catholics hold the Pope to be greater than God, he may be sure he has been imposed upon. How can we hold the Pope to be greater than God, when we believe him to be simply the *vicar* of Jesus Christ, receiving all that he is and has from God? Grant that Papal supremacy necessarily carries with it Papal infallibility,— a doctrine we by no means dispute,—the conclusion is not sustained; for it is not proved that during the first six centuries there was no Pope. What the Professor alleges as proof is not conclusive. His statements are either false or irrelevant. What he says that is true is not to his purpose; what he says that is to his purpose is not true. He alleges,—1. Till the seventh century, at least, the bishops of the Church, not excepting the bishops of Rome, were regarded as officially equal; 2. According to St. Jerome, wherever there is a bishop, he is of the same merit and the same priesthood, and, according to St. Cyprian, the episcopate is one, and every bishop has an undivided portion of it; 3. St. Cyprian says to the African bishops in the great council at Carthage, that none of them makes himself a bishop of bishops, and that it belongs solely to our Lord Jesus Christ to invest them with authority in the government of his Church, and to judge them; and, 4. St. Gregory the Great disclaimed the title of "Universal Bishop." (pp. 78, 79.)

To the first we reply, that, not only as late as the seventh century were all the bishops of the Church, not excepting the bishops of Rome, regarded as officially equal, but they are, as bishops, so regarded even now; and as the fact that they are now so regarded does not prove that there is now no Pope, the fact that they were so regarded during the first six centuries cannot prove that there was no Pope then. The equality of all bishops is a doctrine of the Church. The Pope, as simple bishop, is only the equal of his brethren; he is superior only as bishop of Rome, of which see the primacy is an adjunct, or prerogative. "Thus, a Roman council, in 378, says of Pope Damasus, that he is *equal in office* to the other bishops, and surpasses them in the prerogative of his see."*

To the second we give a similar reply. The unity of the episcopate, and that each bishop possesses an undivided portion of it, that is, that the bishops possess or hold it *in solido*, according to the felicitious expression of St. Cyprian, is held by the Church now, and believed as firmly by all Catholics as ever it was. As the belief of this doctrine is not now disconnected with the belief in the Papacy, it cannot follow, from its having been entertained in the time of St. Cyprian, that there was then no Pope. This reply disposes of the citation from St. Jerome, as well as of that from St. Cyprian. But the Professor argues, that, if the episcopate be one, and the bishops possess it *in solido*, there can be no Pope. We do not see that this follows. Unity is inconceivable without a centre of unity, and how conceive the bishops united in one and the same episcopate without the Pope as their centre of union?

To the third we reply, that, according to the fair interpretation of the language of St. Cyprian, in reference to its occasion and purpose, it has nothing to do with the subject. But let it be that St. Cyprian intended to deny, and actually does deny, the Papal authority, what then? Before the Professor can conclude that there was no Pope down to St. Cyprian's time, he must prove either that St. Cyprian is a witness whose testimony we as Catholics, are bound to receive, or that he is one who could

---

* Ep. v. Apud Constant, T. I. col. 528, cited by Kenrick, *Primacy of the Apostolic See,* p. 106, 3d edition.

not err. As Catholics, we are bound to receive the testimony of single fathers or doctors only so far as their teaching is coincident with that of the Church. The infallibility attaches to the Church, and to single doctors only in so far as they teach her doctrine. Never, then, can we be bound to receive the testimony of any father or doctor which conflicts with her teaching. The Testimony of St. Cyprian does thus conflict, if what it is alleged to be. Therefore we are not bound to receive it, and it cannot be urged against us, as an *argumentum ad hominem.* Then the Professor must prove that St. Cyprian did not err. But, from the nature of the case, this he can do only by proving that he could not err. This he does not do, and cannot pretend; for he admits no infallible authority but that of the written word. (p. 84.) Consequently, let the testimony of St. Cyprian be what it may, it is not sufficient to prove that there was no Pope down to his time.

Moreover, if the alleged testimony of St. Cyprian refers to the Papal authority at all, it refers to it only inasmuch as it denies the right of St. Stephen, his contemporary, whom Mr. Thornwell himself calls the Pope, to excercise that authority. If St. Cyprian's language does not express *resistance* to the Papal authority, it contains no reference to it. But resistance to an authority proves its existence. There was, then, in the time of St. Cyprian, an actual Pope, that is, a Pope claiming the right to exercise the Papal authority; and the position of the Professor, that there was no Pope, is contradicted by his own witness. "But not according to the constitution of the Church." That is a question, not of reason, but of authority, and therefore not debatable. The simple question, stated in the terms most favorable to the Professor, resolves itself into this,—whether St. Cyprian is to be believed against St. Stephen, who claimed to be Pope, and the Church, who admitted his claim. To assume that he is, is to beg the question. The Professor must, then, give us a valid reason for believing St. Cyprian rather than St. Stephen and the Church, or he proves nothing by St. Cyprian's testimony, be it what it may. But he has given us no such reason. St. Cyprian was fallible, and fallibility is not sufficient to set aside the claim of infallibility.

To the fourth we answer, that St. Gregory the Great disclaimed through humility, as savoring of pride, the title of "Universal Bishop," we grant, but this is nothing to the purpose. The Professor must prove that he disclaimed the Papacy and the Papal authority, or he does not prove his position. But this he does not and cannot do; for St. Gregory the Great, as is well known, on numerous occasions, asserted and exercised that authority; nay, it was in the exercise of it that he rebuked John Jejunator, Patriarch of Constantinople, for arrogating to himself the title of "Œcumenical Patriarch," a *title* which even the Bishop of Rome, though Sovereign Pontiff, forbore to assume.

The Professor, it is evident from these replies, fails to prove that during the first six centuries there was no Pope. His objection, founded on the assumption that there was none, falls, therefore, to the ground; and if it were required by our present argument, we could and would, prove an uninterrupted succession of Popes from St. Peter to Pius the Ninth.

4. The Professor, taking it for granted that he had proved that the infallibility of the Church, if lodged with the Pope, could not be asserted, proceeds to show that it cannot be maintained, if lodged either with general councils or with the *Ecclesia dispersa*. But these three ways are all the possible suppositions, and if in no one of these the Church can be infallible, she cannot be infallible at all. But he has not, as we have seen, disproved her infallibility through the Pope, and, for aught he proves, she may be infallible through her Sovereign Pontiffs. Consequently, as far as the argument to disprove her infallibility is concerned, it is no matter whether she is infallible in either of the other two modes or not.

But she cannot be infallible, if the infallibility be lodged with the general councils; for full two hundred years elapsed from the death of the last of the Apostles before such a council was assembled. (p. 79.) If her infallibility is expressed *only* through general councils, we concede it; but this is no Catholic doctrine; for we all, while we hold the general councils to be infallible, hold also that the bishops of the Church in union with their chief, the Pope, teach infallibly when dispersed, each in his own diocese, as well as when congregated in council.

But the councils cannot be infallible, because the early councils attributed the authority of the canons they settled to the sanction of the Emperor. (p. 80.) As this is asserted without any proof, it is sufficient for us simply to deny it. That the *civil* effect of the canons, or their authority as *civil* laws, depended on the sanction of the Emperor, we concede,—for the Church never assumes to enact civil laws; but that they depended on that sanction for their spiritual effect, or their authority in the spiritual order, we deny, and some better authority than that of one Barrow, an Anglican minister, which is no authority at all, will be needed to prove it.

The infallibility of the Church, continues the Professor, cannot be maintained, if lodged with the pastors of the Church dispersed each in his own diocese; because it would then depend on unanimous consent, and the unanimous consent of all can never be ascertained. (p. 81.) This unanimous consent could not be ascertained, if the pastors of the Church were so many independent and unrelated individuals, like Protestant ministers, we concede; but, whether congregated or dispersed, Catholic pastors are ONE BODY, hold the episcopate *in solido*, and through the Pope, the centre of unity and communion, they all commune with each, and each with all. Each is bound for all, and all for each, and each by virtue of this communion can give the unanimous faith of all. All that we need know is that the particular pastor to whom we are subjected is in communion with the Pope; for if he is, we know he is in communion with the head, then with the body, and then with the members. If thus in communion with the head, with the body, and with the members, what he gives as the unanimous faith of the whole must be the unanimous faith of the whole, or that which has the unanimous consent of all.

5. But the Church cannot be infallible, because she has contradicted herself. "Popes have contradicted Popes, councils have contradicted councils, pastors have contradicted pastors, &c." (p. 83.) This argument is good, if the fact be as alleged. But the fact of contradiction must be proved, not taken for granted. Does the Professor prove it? Let us see. The first proof he offers is, that "the Council of Constantinople decreed the removal of images, and the abolition of image-worship, and the Council of Nice, twenty-three years after, re-established both." (p. 84.) But, unhappily for the Professor, no Council of Constantinople, or of any other place, recognized or received by the Church as a council, ever decreed any such thing. There may have been, for aught we care, an assembly of Iconoclasts at Constantinople, collected by an Iconoclastic emperor, which made some such decree; but that no more implicates the Church than a decree of a college of dervishes or of a synod of Presbyterian ministers.

"The second Council of Ephesus approved and sanctioned the impiety of Eutyches, and the Council of Chalcedon condemned it." (*ib.*) But there was only *one* Council of Ephesus, and that was held before the rise of the Eutychian heresy! There was an Ephesian Latrocinium which approved the heresy of Eutyches, but it was no council, and its doings were condemned, instantly, by the Church.

"The fourth Council of Lateran asserted the doctrine of a physical change in the Eucharistic elements, in express contradiction to the teachings of the primitive Church, and the evident declarations of the Apostles of the Lord." (*ib.*) The Professor is not the authority for determining what was the doctrine of the Apostles or of the primitive Church, and cannot urge his notions of either as a standard by which to try the Church. He must adduce, on the authority of the Church herself, the teachings of the primitive Church contradicted by the decree of the fourth Council of Lateran, before he can allege that decree or assertion as a proof of her having contradicted herself. This he has not done.

"The second Council of Orange gave its sanction to some of the leading doctrines of the school of Augustine, and the Council of Trent threw the Church into the arms of Pelagius." (*ib.*) Here no instance of contradiction is expressed. But it is not true, and the Professor offers no proof, that the Council of Trent threw the Church into the arms of Pelagius; and as a matter of fact, that council defines the doctrines of grace, which condemn the Pelâgian heresy, in the very words of St. Augustine. The Professor would do well to set about the study of ecclesiastical history

" Thus, at different periods, every type of doctrine has prevailed in the bosom of an unchangeable Church." (*ib.*) Not proved, and would not be, even if the foregoing charges were sustained. False inferences and unsupported assertions are not precisely the arguments to disprove the infallibility of the Church. We beg the Professor to review his logic.

" The Church has been distracted by every variety of sect, tormented by every kind of controversy, convulsed by every species of heresy." If this means that she has *sanctioned* every variety of sect and every species of heresy, we simply reply, that the Professor has not proved it; if it means, that, first and last, she has had to *combat* every variety of sect and species of heresy, we concede it. But to adduce this as a proof of her having contradicted herself is ridiculous in logic, and monstrous in morals. You might as well argue that the Church was once Lutheran, because she condemned Lutheranism, Calvinistic, because she condemned Calvinism, that St. John was a Gnostic, because he wrote his Gospel to condemn Gnosticism, or that Mr. Thornwell himself is a Catholic, because he anathematizes Catholicity; nay, that the judge, who, in the discharge of his judicial functions, condemns the crime of murder, must needs be the murderer, and that the eleven were guilty of the treachery of Judas, for they no doubt condemned it. Is this Protestant logic, and Protestant morality?

The Church " at last has settled down on a platform which annihilates the word of God, denounces the doctrines of Christ and his Apostles, and bars the gates of salvation against men." (*ib.*) Indeed! How did the Professor learn all that?

Here is all the Professor adduces to prove the fact of the Church having contradicted herself, and it evidently does not prove it. Then the argument founded on it against the infallibility of the Church must go for nothing. For aught that yet appears, the Church may be infallible. It is certainly a great inconvenience not to know ecclesiastical history when one wishes to reason from it.

From these objections, which the Professor calls "historical difficulties in the doctrine of Papal infallibility," we proceed to consider another class, in his Sixth Letter, which we may term philosophical difficulties. The charge under this head is, that the doctrine of the infallibility of the Church—Papal infallibility, as the Professor improperly expresses it—leads to skepticism. (p. 89.) The proofs assigned, as nearly as we can get at them, amidst a mass of speculations sometimes correct enough, but illustrating, when considered in relation to the argument, only the *ignorantia elenchi*,—a favorite figure of logic with the author,—are two, namely, the Church enjoins dogmas which contradict reason, and holds that doctrines may be philosophically true, and yet theologically false.

1. The instance adduced to prove that the Church requires us to believe what contradicts reason is the doctrine of Transubstantiation. It is a principle of reason that we believe our senses. But this doctrine denies the testimony of our senses, and therefore contradicts reason. "Upon the authority of Rome we are required to believe that what our senses pronounce to be bread, that what the minutest analysis which chemistry can institute is able to resolve into nothing but bread, what every sense pronounces to be material, is yet the Incarnate Son of God, soul, and body, and Divinity, full and entire, perfect and complete. Here Rome and the senses are evidently at war; and here the infallible Church is made to despise one of the original principles of belief which God has impressed upon the constitution of the

mind." (p. 93.) What is here said about the minutest analysis chemistry can institute, &c., amounts to nothing, makes the case neither stronger nor weaker; for chemical analysis, however minute or successful, can give us only sensible phenomena. It never attains to substance itself. The simple assertion is, that the doctrine of Transubstantiation contradicts reason, because it contradicts the senses. But is this true?

There is no contradiction of the senses, unless the doctrine requires us to believe that what is attested by the senses is false. What is it the senses attest? Simply the presence in the Sacred Host of the species, accidents, or *sensible phenomena* of bread. This is all; for it is well settled in philosophy, that the senses attain only to the phenomena, and never to the substance or subject of the phenomena. Does the doctrine of Transubstantiation deny this? Not at all. It asserts precisely what the senses assert, namely, the presence in the Sacred Host of the species, accidents, or sensible phenomena of bread. Then it does not contradict the senses.

"But it is a principle of human nature to believe, that, where we find the phenomena, there is also their subject; that, if in the Sacred Host all the sensible phenomena of bread are present, the substance of bread is also present." Undoubtedly, if reason has no authority, *satisfactory to herself*, for believing the contrary. In ordinary cases, reason has no such authority, and we are to believe that the sensible phenomena and their subject do go together. But reason cannot deny that God, if he chooses, can, by a miraculous exertion of his power, change the subject without changing the phenomena, and if in any particular case it be certified infallibly to her that he actually does so, she herself requires us to believe it. In the Most Holy Eucharist, it is so certified to reason, if the Church be infallible, and therefore, in believing that the sensible phenomena of bread are there without their natural subject, we are simply obeying reason, and of course, then, do not contradict it. It is no contradiction of reason to believe on a higher reason what we should not and could not on a lower reason. In this doctrine, we are simply required to suspend the ordinary reason at the bidding of an extraordinary reason, which is not, and never can be, unreasonable. Consequently, there is in the doctrine nothing *contrary* to reason, and the Church, in enjoining it, does not enjoin a dogma which contradicts either reason or the senses, though she unquestionably does enjoin a dogma which is *above* reason. The first proof, therefore, that the doctrine of infallibility "leads to skepticism," must be abandoned, as having no foundation for itself.

2. The second proof is no better. That certain infidel or paganizing philosophers, in the latter part of the fifteenth and early part of the sixteenth century, maintained that propositions may be philosophically true, yet theologically false, we concede; that this was the doctrine of the Schoolmen, or that it was ever for a moment countenanced by the Church, we deny. Indeed, Leo X., *in Concilii Lateranensis Sess.* 8, 1513, condemns it, by declaring every assertion contrary to revealed faith to be false, and decreeing that all persons adhering to such erroneous assertions be avoided and punished as heretics,—*tanquam hæreticos.* It would not be amiss, if the Professor would bear in mind that proofs which are themselves either false or in want of proof prove nothing, however pertinent they may be.

We cannot follow the Professor in his declamatory speculations in support of his charge. His reasoning is all fallacious. He starts with the assumption, that the Church is fallible, has no authority from God to teach, and then charges her with consequences which would follow, no doubt, if she were fallible, if she had no divine commission; for they are the precise consequences which do follow from the teaching, or rather action, of the Protestant sects. If the Church were fallible, a mere human authority, arrogantly claiming to teach infallibly, we certainly should not defend her, or dispute that her influence would be as bad as Mr. Thornwell falsely alleges; but we do not recognize his right to assume the fallibility of the Church as the basis of his proofs that she is not infallible ; and we cannot accept as facts mere consequences deduced from an hypothesis which we deny, and which is not yet proved, far less receive them as proofs of the hypothesis.

There are in Catholic countries, no doubt, many unbelievers; but before this can be adduced as evidence that the Church, by claiming to be infallible, leads them into unbelief, it is necessary to prove that she is not infallible. If infallible, she cannot have a skeptical tendency; because what she enjoins must be infallible truth, and skepticism, when it does not proceed from malice, results always, not from truth being present to the mind, but from its *not* being present. But it is worthy of remark, that the objections to Christianity on which unbelievers chiefly rely are not drawn from the distinctive teachings of the Catholic Church, nor from the Scriptures as she interprets them. They are nearly all drawn from the Scriptures as interpreted by private judgment, and hence, as we should expect, infidelity abounds chiefly in Protestant countries. Protestant Germany, England, the United States, are, any one of them, far more infidel than even France; and our own city cannot, in religious belief, compare favorably with Paris, infidel as Paris unhappily is. Modern infidelity is of Protestant origin; Giordano Bruno sojourned in Protestant England; Bayle was a Protestant, and resided in Holland; Voltaire, the father of French infidelity, did but transport to France the philosophy of the Englishman Locke, and the doctrines and objections of the English deists, Herbert of Cherbury, Tindal, Toland, Chubb, Morgan, Woolston, and others. Indeed, to England especially belongs the chief glory, such as it is, of infidelizing modern society. France and Germany are nothing but her pupils. Rightly do Protestants regard her as the bulwark of their religion; for in the war against the Church, against the revelation of Almighty God, she, with her sanctimonious face and corrupt heart, has the chief command. It were easy to show, that, aside from the internal malice of unbelievers, the chief cause of infidelity in modern society is Protestantism, which asserts the divine authority of the Scriptures, and then leaves them to be interpreted by private judgment; but it is unnecessary. It is becoming every day more and more obvious, that, the more Protestants circulate the Bible, the more do they multiply scoffers and unbelievers.

In Letter VII. we come to another class of objections, which we may term *moral* objections. These are summed up in the assertion, The Church cannot be infallible, because her "infallibility is conducive to licentiousness and immorality." (p. 105.) The proof of this is, first, the unproved assertion, that the doctrine of the infallibility of the Church leads to skepticism; and, second, the allegation that Catholicity and Jesuitism are one and the same thing. The first assertion we dismiss, for we have just shown that the Professor does not sustain it. As to Jesuitism, we hardly know what to say; for we do not know, and the author does not inform us, what is meant by Jesuitism. For aught that appears, the identity asserted may be conceded without prejudice to the Church. The Society of Jesus is composed of Catholic priests, and we are not aware that these have any peculiar doctrines, either of faith or morals. Indeed, they could not have; for if they were to have any, they would be obliged to leave the Order and the Church. The notion among some Protestants, that the Jesuits are a *sect* in the bosom of the Church, professing certain dogmas of faith or certain principles of morals different from those professed by other Catholics, is a ridiculous blunder. The Church enjoins the same faith and the same principles of morals upon all her children, and no person, or class of persons, would be suffered to teach in her communion, who should add to or take from them. The Jesuits are Catholics, neither more nor less, and it is fair to presume that in faith and principles of morals they agree with all Catholics, and profess what the Church teaches.

But that the Jesuits teach, or ever have taught, doctrines favorable to licentiousness or immorality is a matter to be proved, not taken for granted. What is the proof the Professor offers? Here is all we can find:—" These three cardinal principles—of intention, mental reservation, and probability—cover the whole ground of Jesuitical atrocity." (p. 115.) The Professor labors long and hard to identify Catholicity and Jesuitism. He must, therefore, concede that these three principles cover the whole of what he holds to be atrocious in Catholicity. Catholicity, then, is "conducive to licentiousness and immorality," because it contains the three principles of "intention, mental reservation, and probability." But what is the meaning the Professor attaches to these principles? Unhappily, he gives us no clear and explicit answer; for he writes with his head full of false assumptions.

"The detestable principles," he says, "of the graceless order [the Jesuits] . . . . . may be found embodied in the recorded canons of general councils. That the end justifies the means, that the interests of the priesthood are superior to the claims of truth, justice, and humanity, is necessarily implied in the decree of the Council of Lateran, that no oaths are binding—that to keep them is perjury rather than fidelity—which conflict with the advantage of the Church. What fraud have the Jesuits ever recommended or committed, that can exceed in iniquity the bloody proceedings of the Council of Constance in reference to Huss? What spirit have they ever breathed more deeply imbued with cruelty and slaughter, than the edict of Lateran to kings and magistrates, to extirpate heretics from the face of the earth? The principle on which the sixteenth canon of the third Council of Lateran proceeds covers the doctrine of *mental reservations*. If the end justifies the means, if we can be perjured with impunity to protect the authority of the priesthood, a *good intention* will certainly sanctify any other lie, and a man may always be sure that he is free from sin, if he can only be sure of his allegiance to Rome and his antipathy to heretics. The doctrine of *probability* is in full accordance with the spirit of the Papacy, in substituting authority for evidence, and making the opinions of men the arbiters of faith. And yet these three cardinal principles of intention, mental reservation, and probability, which are so thoroughly Papal, cover the whole ground of Jesuitical atrocity."—pp. 114, 115.

It would seem from this, that the Professor understands by the principle of intention, that the moral character of the actor is determined by the intention with which he acts; by that of mental reservation, that no one can bind himself by oath to do that which conflicts with the advantage of the Church; and by that of probability, the substituting of authority for evidence, and making the opinions of men the arbiters of faith. If this is not his meaning, we are unable to divine what it is.

That Catholicity teaches that the moral character of the actor is determined by his intention, or, in other words, that a man is to be judged according to his intention, may be true· but this must be morally wrong, or it cannot be adduced as a proof that the teaching of the Church is "conducive to licentiousness and immorality." That this is morally wrong, the Professor does not prove, or even attempt to prove. For ourselves, we are not now called upon to prove that it is right. It is for the Professor to prove that it is wrong. But we own, that, from our boyhood, we have always supposed it a dictate of reason that the man is to be praised or blamed according to his intention. If I really intend to do a man evil, my unintentional failure to do him evil does not exonerate me from guilt; if I really intend to do him good, but, in attempting to do him good, unintentionally do him evil, I am not guilty. If I have killed a man in self-defence, the law excuses or justifies me; and it does not hold me guilty of murder, unless the killing has been done with a felonious intent. He who takes the life of a fellow-being through private revenge is a murderer; the public officer who does it in pursuance of a judicial sentence is no murderer, and does but a justifiable act. Whence the difference, if not in the difference of intention? That no act, in relation to the actor, is blameworthy unless done from a malicious intention, or praiseworthy unless done from a virtuous intention, we have always supposed to be the teaching of reason, and we must have high authority to convince us that we have been wrong.

"But on this ground the Church erects her doctrine, that the end justifies the means." We cannot concede this; first, *because the Church has no such doctrine;* and second, because the principle does not imply it. The assertion, that the Church teaches, that any Catholic doctor teaches, or ever did teach, that the end justifies the means, is made without the faintest shadow of a reason, and the reverse is what she does teach, as every man knows who knows anything of her teaching. The doctrine of intention objected to implies nothing of the sort. The Church teaches, indeed, that the act for which we are accountable is the act of the will; but she teaches that no act is done with a good intention that is not referred to God as the ultimate end, and that *every one* of our acts is to be so referred. Now, in choosing the means, we as much *act* as we do in the choice of the end, and therefore must be, as to the means, bound by the same law which binds us as to the end; and then we can no more choose unjust means than we can unjust ends, and therefore can be allowed to seek even just ends only by just means.

The Professor says that "the Jesuit Casnedi maintains in a published work, that at the day of judgment God will say to many, 'Come, my beloved, you who have committed murder, blasphemed, &c., because you believed that in so doing you were right.'" But he takes good care not to give us a reference to the work itself, and we hazard nothing in saying that no Jesuit ever published such a sentence, unless it was to condemn it, as containing a Protestant heresy. That invincible ignorance, if really invincible, excuses from sin, is, no doubt, a doctrine of the Church; for she teaches that no one can sin in not doing that which he has no power to do. No doubt, involuntary mistakes, if unavoidable, springing from no malice in the will, from no culpable neglect of ours, are excusable; but no Catholic divine ever taught that invincible ignorance can extend to the great precepts of the natural law, to such as forbid murder, blasphemy, &c.; for they are engraven on the heart of every man, and are evident to every man by the light of natural reason. The Professor has been misled, by relying on the authority of Pascal, and other writers of his stamp. He refers us to Pascal's *Provincial Letters* "for a popular exposition of the morality of the Jesuits." He might as well refer us to Voltaire's *Philosophical Dictionary* for a popular exposition of the morality of the Gospel. Pascal was a Jansenist, and Jansenists are heretics, not Catholics. The *Provincial Letters* are witty, but wicked,—a tissue of lies, forgeries, and misrepresentations, from beginning to end, as has been amply proved over and over again. If Mr. Thornwell is ignorant of this fact, he will have to search long before he will find a Catholic or a Jesuit doctor that will permit him to hold that his ignorance is excusable.*

* In ordinary times, what we have said in the text is all that would need to be said in reference to the Society of Jesus; but now, when the Society is suffering a severe persecution, even in Catholic countries, we are unwilling to pass the subject over without bearing our testimony, feeble as it is, in favor of the children of St. Ignatius. We do this the more willingly, because we are conscious that we have ourselves frequently done them injustice, both in our thoughts and in our words. It is hard, when we hear a body of men widely and constantly decried, not to be more or less prejudiced against them; and nothing is more natural than, when under the influence of this prejudice, to exaggerate beyond all reasonable bounds the slight imperfections we may observe in here and there an individual member, and to generalize them into characteristics of the body itself. Few persons have been more prejudiced against the Society of Jesus than we ourselves. But having taken some pains to find a basis for the unfavorable judgment we had formed, we hardly know when or how, we confess that we have been entirely unsuccessful. There may have been individual Jesuits whose conduct we could not approve, but we are satisfied, after studying the history of the Order, that it needs no other defence than a simple statement of facts, and no other eulogium than the recital of its deeds.

Every body knows the popular meaning attached to *Jesuitical*. Taking the word in this meaning, there are no men so little *Jesuitical* as the Jesuits. Their whole history proves them to be remarkable for their simplicity of heart, singleness of purpose, and straightforwardness of conduct. No man can take up a work in defence of the Order, written by a member, without being fully convinced that the Jesuit is the antithesis of the character commonly ascribed to him. We have heard many charges, and grave charges, against him; but we have not heard one that we have not seen refuted. Jesuits are men, and, of course, suffer more or less the infirmities common to all men; but we should like to be shown a body of men, of equal numbers, placed in the trying circumstances in which they have been, who have shown less of human infirmity, or been more true to the motto, *Ad majorem Dei Gloriam*. There is no field of science or art which they have not cultivated with success; no department of literature which they have not enriched with their contributions; scarcely a nation to which they have not preached the cross; and hardly a land which they have not consecrated with the blood of their martyrs.

1. The principle of mental reservation happens to be no Catholic doctrine. Protestants would, no doubt, be pleased to find that the Church teaches that lying is sometimes justifiable, for such a doctrine is one they stand very much in need of; but

Even the present persecution of the Society is to its glory. If the Jesuits had been political demagogues,—if they had been violent radicals, ready to sacrifice liberty to license, order to anarchy, religion to politics, heaven to earth,—our ears would not have been stunned with maddened outcries against them; the world would have owned them as her children, and the age would have delighted to honor them. We know it is pretended that they are the enemies of liberty and the friends of despotism, but it needs only a slight knowledge of facts to know that this is mere pretence. Liberty has more than once found her noblest champion in the Jesuits, and the hostility a year or two since manifested to them in France was because they demanded the freedom of education, a right guaranteed by the Charter itself. They may not be, in these days, foremost among those who stir up rebellions and revolutions; they may not regard the fearful events which have recently taken place in Europe, as sure to bring back the golden age of the poets; they may hold their mission to be spiritual, rather than political, and believe it more important to convert individuals and nations to God than to one political creed or another; but if so, it does not follow that they are wrong, or that for this very reason they are not all the more worthy of our respect and confidence.

The Society of Jesus was instituted, not for political, but for religious purposes, and its members, by their profession, are devoted to preaching the Gospel, hearing confessions, and educating youth, and that not for one country only, but for all countries. These ends are the same and of equal importance everywhere and under all forms of government. If the Jesuits were to adopt a political creed, and become its propagandists, how could they devote themselves to the ends of their institute, alike under the monarchy of Europe and the democracy of America? What course would or could be proper for them, but to abstain from declaring themselves in favor of any particular form of government, and to content themselves with simply inculcating upon all citizens to obey the legitimate government of their country, whatever its form or constitution?

The charge against the Jesuits of being in favor of this or that form of government arises from their refusal to declare themselves in favor of one or another, from the fact that they have no political creed, and make it a point of duty to stand aloof from politics, and to confine themselves to the discharge of their spiritual functions. They obey the she teaches nothing of the sort. She does not command her children at all times and on all occasions to speak *all* the truth they may happen to know, but she does command them never to speak any thing but the truth ; and she teaches them, that,

powers that be, and comport themselves as loyal subjects to the authority of the country, whether it be autocracy, as in Russia, constitutionalism, as in France and Great Britain, or republicanism, as in America. What more could we ask of them ? If tyrants denounce them because they will not turn defenders of tyranny, if revolutionists denounce them because they will not join in the war against legitimate authority, whose fault is it ? Are we to condemn the Jesuits because tyrants and revolutionists wrong them ?

Wherever the Jesuits are permitted to establish themselves, they are a blessing. It is not easy to estimate the value to this country of their services as instructors of our youth. It would be difficult to find a substitute for them as educators. In every part of the country, they are, for the pure love of God, founding colleges, and training up our children in the way they should go. Is this nothing ? These colleges are but of yesterday, yet have they already done great service,—as we ourselves can personally testify, and who have peculiar reason to thank Almighty God for raising up and moving the good fathers to devote themselves to the important work of education. But as yet they have really done nothing, in comparison with what they will do. They now rank among the best in the country, and in a few years they will place education with us at least on a level with what it is in the most favored countries of the Old World. And can we count this small service ?

Worldings may despise the Jesuits, infidels and heretics may calumniate them ; misguided Catholics, whose faith is but a dead faith, may distrust them ; but the world needs them, our own country needs them, and though the Church is dependent on no religious order, they are not the least efficient of her servants. Protestants, in their estimation of the Jesuit, betray only their ignorance or their malice, or both. The character they ascribe to the Jesuit they will find in its perfection in their own ministers, and the best definition of *Jesuitical*, in the popular acceptation of the term, is *a Presbyterian minister*, the antithesis of a Jesuit. Mr. Thornwell illustrates and accepts, in the book before us, every element of what he calls Jesuitism. No man can have been brought up among Presbyterians without knowing that the principle, the end justifies the means, is the one on which they generally act, whether they avow it or not. No one can read one of their books against the Church without perceiving that the principle of mental when they use words which by their natural force convey a false sense, they speak falsehood, whatever may have been their secret meaning, and that knowingly and intentionally to use language which is naturally calculated to deceive the hearer, to convey to him a false meaning, or a meaning different from that in the mind of him that uses it, is to lie, to sin against God. All who are acquainted with Catholic morality know that this is her teaching, and whoever asserts the contrary is guilty of the very offence he would fasten upon her, and has no excuse for his conduct. For if he is ignorant of her doctrine, he speaks rashly; if he is not ignorant, he is guilty of a wilful falsehood.

2. The facts which the Professor alleges, granting them to be facts, do not prove the principle of *mental reservation*. We presume the Professor wishes to maintain that the Church teaches that it is lawful for her children to take oaths which conflict with her advantage, but that they must take them with the mental reservation, not to keep them; and that if so taken, it is no sin to break them. This is what he needs in order to make out his case. But this he does not prove. Granting that reservation, or, in plain terms, the right to lie for the purpose of advancing Protestantism, is a principle which they practically adopt, and hold in constant requisition; and whoever will read a Presbyterian dogmatical work will see that to higher certainty than probability its author does not aspire, and that to substitute authority for evidence, and to make the opinions of men the the arbiters of faith, is his boast. Nothing is more ridiculous than for a Presbyterian minister to accuse Jesuits of a want of principle, of candor, of honesty, or to charge them with fraud and cruelty. Who ever heard of a Presbyterian minister that was not, officially, the very impersonation of pride, cant, hypocrisy, bigotry, and cruelty? If such a one there ever was, we may be sure that he did not live and die a Presbyterian. We know something of Presbyterianism; it was our misfortune to have been brought up a Presbyterian. We know what are its secret covenants, the pledges it exacts of its adherents, and the measures it takes to prevent the least ray of light from penetrating their darkness. Take a Protestant's account of Catholicity or Jesuitism, change the name, and it is a faithful picture as far as it goes, of proud, arrogant, bigoted, cruel, and persecuting Presbyterianism. There is not a charge brought against us by Presbyterians that is not substantially true of them.

he has rightly stated the doctrine of the Council of Lateran,—he does not tell us which council,—all he proves is, that the Church teaches that no oath taken to her prejudice is binding; but he does not prove that she teaches that the reason why it is not binding is because it was taken with a mental reservation not to keep it in case it conflicted with her advantage. For aught that appears, the reason why the Church declares that such oaths do not bind is because she holds them to be unlawful oaths,—oaths which no man has a right to take, and which therefore are void *ab initio.* The Professor will hardly maintain the morality of robbers and cutthroats, that a man who has taken an unlawful oath is bound to keep it. He will hardly pretend that he who should swear to assist in a plot for blowing up the Presbyterian Assembly when in session, for instance, would be bound to keep his oath, or to refrain from revealing the plot, simply because he had sworn not to do so. The whole sum and substance of the charge, then, is, that the Jesuits and the Church teach that unlawful oaths do not bind. Does this conflict with reason? Is this "conducive to licentiousness and immorality?" Is it immoral to teach that no man can bind himself to do wrong?

But in this the Church teaches that "the interests of the priesthood are superior to the claims of truth, justice, and humanity; for she holds that all oaths which conflict with her advantage are unlawful." The conclusion is not necessary, for it may be that her interests, her advantage, are identical with the claims of truth, justice, and humanity; or that it is only by promoting her interests and seeking her advantage that it is possible to vindicate the claims of truth, justice and humanity. If she be what she professes to be, this must be so; and that she is what she professes to be the Professor must presume till he has proved the contrary. If she be the Church of God, any oath to her prejudice is an oath against God, and no man can be mad enough to say that an oath against God can bind, or that the claims of truth, justice, or humanity can be prejudiced by not keeping it. But the Professor cannot assume that she is not the Church of God, for that she is not, is the very point he is to prove, and he cannot prove this by assuming it, and making the assumption the principle of his arguments to prove it. Such a procedure would simply beg the question. Granting, then, that the Church does teach that oaths to her prejudice are unlawful, and therefore do not bind, nothing proves that she is not right in so doing, and therefore nothing proves that in doing so she favors " licentiousness and immorality." To condemn the Church, on the ground the Professor assumes, would be to assert the doctrine opposite to hers; namely, unlawful oaths are to be kept,—that, if I have been foolish or wicked enough to swear to do wrong, I am bound in conscience to keep my oath and do the wrong,—a monstrous doctrine, which strikes at the foundation of all morals. It is strange what blunders Protestants commit, in trying to get an argument against the Church. It would seem as if it never occurred to them to examine the principle of the objections they urge. They seem to say, if the Church should favor licentiousness and immorality, then she would not be the Church of God; therefore she does favor licentiousness and immorality. The Church forbids unlawful oathes.

3. The Professor, evidently, is ignorant of the principle of *probability*, or probabilism, as understood by Catholic theologians. That principle, if he did but know it, is very nearly the contrary of what he supposes, and is little else than the well-known maxim of the Common Law, that, if there is a reasonable doubt, the accused is entitled to its benefit. But the principle, as the Professor defines it, is not embraced by the Church, nor defended by a single Catholic divine. He says, the Church substitutes "authority for evidence, and makes the opinions of men the arbiters of faith;" but this, in principle, at least, is a mistake; for the Church teaches that God alone is the arbiter of faith, and that nothing but his word, declared to be his word, by himself through his divinely appointed organ, can be of faith. His word divinely declared to be his word is the highest evidence reason can demand or receive; and if the Church is proved to reason to be his organ for declaring his word, reason has the highest evidence possible for believing that whatever

she teaches as the word of God is infallibly true. She asserts that reason has the right to demand this evidence, and has no right to dispense with it. In principle, then, she denies the principle of probability as set forth by the Professor. If she is what she claims to be, she denies it in her practice, and cannot possibly do as alleged. That she is what she professes to be the Professor is bound, as we have already shown, to presume till he makes the contrary appear; which he does not do.

The Professor identifies Jesuitism with Catholicity, and resolves all that is atrocious in Jesuitism into the three principles enumerated, and therefore all that is atrocious in Catholicity. But the first of these principles is a simple dictate of reason, and contains nothing atrocious. Then all that is atrocious in Catholicity, or all the atrocity that can be charged upon Catholicity, is resolvable into the other two principles, namely, mental reservation and probability. But these are not Catholic principles, and, however atrocious they may be, their atrocity cannot be charged to her. Therefore no atrocity can be charged to her, even according to the Professor's own argument. But to be "conducive to licentiousness and immorality" is undeniably atrocious. Therefore the Church is not conducive to them. So the Professor does not sustain his assertion, that "Papal infallibility is conducive to licentiousness and immorality." Assuredly, the Professor is ignorant of the laws of evidence.

The next proof offered against the infallibility of the Church is, that "it is the patron of superstition and will-worship." (p. 116.) This is a singular objection. How *infallibility* can patronize superstition and will-worship, that is, *well*-worship, or the worship of wells, conceding them to be wrong, is more than we are able to conceive. Infallibility can be the patron of nothing wrong, and the Professor, if he should prove his thesis, would prove that superstition and will-worship are right, not that the Church is fallible. Can he mean that the assertion of her infallibility is the patron of superstition and will-worship? But this he would be troubled to prove, even if he should prove the existence of superstition and will-worship in the Church; for they undeniably exist out of the Church, in communities which lay no claim to infallibility. Does he mean that the Church is not infallible, because she is the patron of superstition, &c.? Why, then, did he not say so? If this is his meaning, his argument is valid, if the fact be as alleged. But, unhappily for his cause, the fact is not as alleged.* Catholics pay divine honors to God alone, as every one knows who knows any thing of Catholic worship. That we keep relics, pictures, and images, and pay them a relative honor as memorials of departed sanctity, we admit; that we venerate the Saints, especially the Ever-blessed Virgin, the Most Holy Mother of God, we also admit; but that this is superstition or will-worship we deny, and the Professor must prove, or not assert it.

The last proof of the fallibility of the Church which the Professor attempts to offer is, that she is not infallible, for "she is hostile to civil government." (p. 143.) His argument is, when reduced to form,—the church that claims and exercises temporal authority is hostile to civil government; but the Roman Catholic Church claims and exercises temporal authority; therefore she is hostile to civil government. The church that is hostile to civil government is fallible; but the Roman Catholic Church is hostile to civil government; therefore, the Roman Catholic Church is fallible, that is, not infallible.

The church that claims and exercises supreme temporal authority is hostile to civil government, if she has received from Almighty God no grant of that temporal authority, we concede; if she has received the grant, we deny. No church which possesses, by the Divine grant, temporal authority, can be hostile to civil government by claiming and exercising it, because she is herself, under God, the civil government. But the Roman Catholic Church, if she has received the grant, does thus possess the temporal authority. Therefore, if she claims and exercises that authority, she is not hostile to civil goverment.

* The reader will find this objection replied to at length in Brownson's Quarterly Review for January, 1848, pp. 101-116.

The church that is hostile to all government in civil affairs is fallible, we concede; for the necessity of government in civil affairs is clearly evinced from reason; the church that is hostile only to distinct and independent civil government is fallible, we deny, for it may be that God has vested the government of civil as well as spiritual affairs in the same hands. The denial of civil government distinct from and independent of the Church is a proof of fallibility only on the supposition that such civil government exists by divine right. But if all government, civil as well as spiritual, is vested in the Church, it does not so exist. Therefore its denial is no proof of fallibility. Moreover, the Roman Catholic Church, as we have seen, cannot be hostile to civil government, even if she claim and exercise the supreme temporal authority, if she has received it as a grant from God, the Supreme Ruler. But it is not proved that she claims or exercises it without such grant. Therefore it is not proved that she is hostile to civil government; and therefore, again, it is not proved that she is fallible. The Professor labors to prove, that, according to Catholicity, "the Pope is the vicar of the Omnipotent God, invested alike with temporal power and ecclesiastical authority." (p. 147.) If so, the Pope is the vicar of God in both orders, and is invested with the supreme authority in both. Then he is by divine appointment the temporal sovereign. But for the temporal sovereign to claim and exercise temporal authority is not to be hostile to the civil government, but to assert and maintain it.

But the claim of the Church to "secular authority merges the state in the Church. Kings and emperors, nations and communities, become merely the instruments and pliant tools of spiritual dominion." (page. 153.) What if the spiritual dominion be legimate? All power is of God, and there is no legitimate authority not from him. Kings, emperors, nations, communities, have no right to exercise temporal authority, save as vicars of the Omnipotent God, and it is only for the reason that they are such that we are under any obligation to obey them. If Almighty God has made the Pope his sole vicar in both orders, obedience is due to him by all both in church and state, and then it is no objection to the Church that she exacts the submission of kings, emperors, nations, communities, for they can, in such case, have no authority not derived from God through the Pope. The Professor, if he grant that the Pope is the vicar of Almighty God in the temporal and in the spiritual order, cannot urge his objection, because in doing so he would resist the authority of the vicar of God, and therefore of God himself.

Again, if the Pope be the vicar of God in both orders, the claim and exercise of the supreme temporal dominion do not merge the state in the church, for then the Church is both church and state. The Church could merge the state in herself by claiming and exercising temporal power, only on condition that she had received no special grant of temporal power, and claimed to exercise it solely by virtue of her grant of spiritual authority. But if she teaches, as the Professor contends, that in the Pope she has been invested with temporal *as well as with spiritual authority*, she does not do this, that is, does not claim the temporal as incidental to the spiritual. Therefore, even granting that she claims the supreme temporal authority, she does not and cannot merge the state in the Church as a spiritual authority, which is the sense intended. This is evinced from the instance of the Papal states. The Pope in regard to them is supreme in both temporals and spirituals, but they exist as a state, as a civil government, as much so as Tuscany or Sardinia.

The Professor does not appear to understand the question he wishes to discuss. The spiritual order is undeniably superior to the temporal, and nothing can be legitimately concluded from the temporal to the prejudice of the spiritual. No man who has any knowledge of even natural morality can pretend that it is the prerogative of the temporal order to define or give law to the spiritual. It is not according to reason that the lower should rule the higher, the body the soul, for instance, or the state the Church. To object to the Church that she subjects the whole temporal order to the spiritual order, or that she makes the spiritual dominion supreme, is to make an objection which reason disavows, because it would be in principle the same as to deny the right of reason to rule the flesh, nay, the same as to deny reason itself. The Church, if she is God's Church, if she has received plenary spiritual authority as the vicar of the Omnipotent God, must needs be superior to the state, and the state can have no authority to do aught she declares to be sinful or morally wrong, and must be bound to do whatever she declares to be required by the law of God. To allege that she subjects kings, emperors, &c., to her dominion is, then, to allege nothing against her.

The Professor does not state the question properly. He begins with an assumption which he has no right to make. He assumes, that, if the Church claims any authority in the temporal order, she is a usurper, and therefore cannot be infallible. He takes it for granted, then, that, if he proves that she has claimed such authority, he has disproved her infallibility. But we demand the proof from reason, that she has no authority in temporals. Till he proves this, he cannot conclude, from the fact that she claims it, that she is a usurper, and therefore failible. It is certain from reason, since all power is of God, and there is and can be no rightful authority to govern in any order not derived mediately or immediately from him, that he *can* make the Pope his sole vicar on earth in both orders, if such be his will and pleasure. If he does so, then it is also certain that the Pope has the right to exercise the supreme authority in both orders, and then that, so far from his temporal authority being usurped, all authority not derived from God through him is usurpation. What the Professor has to prove, then, in case he contends that the Church claims the supreme temporal authority, is, not that she claims it, but that she claims it without having received it from God. If she asserts that she has received it,—since the legal presumption is in her favor, and the argument is not to prove, but to disprove, her infallibility,—he can prove that she has not received it only by proving that she has in the exercise of it violated some principle of natural justice.

We are far from conceding that the Church has ever claimed or exercised temporal authority in the sense intended; but pass over that. Let it be supposed for the present that she has. What is the evidence that she has ever violated any principle of natural justice? You can arraign her only on the law of nature, before the bar of natural reason. Produce, then, the precept of the law of nature which she has violated or contradicted. We have looked carefully through all that the Professor has urged, and we can find nothing that is immoral or unjust. All his proofs are reduced to this, that she claims and exercises temporal authority. Grant all this, what then? Where is your evidence that she has not rightfully claimed and exercised it? You offer none, and only work yourself up into a violent passion against her, because she has claimed and exercised it. Where is your evidence that the exercise you fancy you have proved has been contrary to the law of nature? You offer only two things; first, what you call the Jesuit's oath, and, second, the prohibition of duelling by the Council of Trent. The oath ascribed to the Jesuits is a forgery. The Jesuits have no such oath, for as Jesuits they take no oath at all. The Council of Trent condemns duelling, we grant; but is it the condemnation of duelling, or duelling itself, that is contrary to the precepts of justice? Which is easier to defend,—duelling, or the Church in condemning it? And who is in the wrong,—the Church in condemning, or you in defending, the base, cowardly, and detestable practice of single combat?

But the Church does more than condemn it. According to the statute of the Council of Trent, in its twenty-fifth session, "the temporal sovereign who permits a duel to take place in his dominions is punished not only with excommunication, but with the loss of the place in which the combat occurred. The duellists and their seconds are condemned in the same statute to perpetual infamy, the loss of their goods and deprived, if they should fall, of Christian burial, while those who are merely spectators of the scene are sentenced to eternal malediction." (p. 152.) Well, what then? *What then?* Why, this proves that the

Church claims the right to exercise civil authority, nay, to inflict civil punishments; for such are the forfeiture of goods, and the loss of the place where the combat occurs. Yes, as you cite the statute, but not as it was passed by the Council of Trent.* But let that pass. If so, it is nothing to your purpose, unless the punishment prescribed is in itself unjust. Will you maintain that?

"In a conflict of power between princes and Popes, the first and highest duty of all the vassals of Rome is to maintain her honor and support her claims." (p. 153.) Suppose a conflict of power between the General Assembly of the Presbyterian Church in the United States and the civil authorities of the country, which party would the Professor, as a Presbyterian minister and member of that church, support? The civil authorities? Then he either condemns his church, or raises the temporal order above the spiritual, which he expressly repudiates. Would he side with his church, and maintain the independence of the spiritual order? Then he would recognize and act on the principle he objects to us, and we retort his objection. Suppose a conflict between an infallible church and a fallible civil government, we demand which of the two ought to yield. "But the Church is not infallible." That is for you to prove. If she is infallible, she must be in the right, and then we are bound in reason to support her; if she is not infallible, we deny that we are bound to support her at all, for then she is not God's Church.

"Hence the Jesuit in his secret oath renounces all allegiance to all earthly powers which have not been confirmed by the Holy See." (*ib.*) The Jesuit has no secret oath, and renounces no allegiance to the civil government. The charge is false.

"The Romish Church, too, sets her face like a flint against the subjection of her spiritual officers to the legal tribunals of the state." (*ib.*) Well, what if she does? Where is the proof that in this she is wrong? She "has positively prohibited the intolerable presumption of laymen, though kings and magistrates, of demanding oaths of allegiance from the lofty members

* Vide Conc. Trident. Sess. 25, cap. xix.

of her hierarchy." (*ib.*) *In case they hold nothing temporal of them*, conceded; but what then? Will the Professor be good enough to demonstrate the right of the temporal authority to demand from a minister of religion an oath of allegiance in spirituals?

La Fayette is reported to have said, that, "if ever the liberties of this country should be destroyed, it would be by the machinations of the Romish priests." (p. 154.) *Therefore* the Church is fallible! La Fayette is *reported*, by whom? When? Where? What if he did say so? Was La Fayette infallible? And does it follow that the thing must be so, because La Fayette thought so? If he did once think so, it is possible that he changed his mind, for it is *reported* that he became reconciled to the Church and died a Catholic, and it is well known that he was, when dying, exceedingly anxious for the services of a "Romish priest." He had probably had enough of French philosophism during his lifetime, without wishing to carry any with him into eternity.

"They are all of them [Catholic priests] sworn subjects of a *foreign* potentate." (*ib.*) Not true. The authority of the Church is Catholic, not national, and can be no more *foreign* here than at Rome.

"There are peculiar principles in the constitution and polity of Rome which render it an engine of tremendous power." (p. 159.) Who has more power than God? Because, if we admit the existence of God, we must admit his omnipotence, are we to be atheists? If the Church be not God's Church, she cannot possess the authority we claim for her, without danger, we concede; if she is his Church, and the Pope is his vicar, what have we to fear from her power more than we should have, if it were exerted immediately by God himself? We defend the Church as God's Church, and attempt no defence of her on the supposition that she is not his Church. Prove to us that he has not instituted her, and we will abandon her; but remember that proving that she has a tremendous power is no proof to us that he has not instituted her; for it belongs not to us to say how much or how little power it is proper for him to delegate to her. The claim of similar power for a human or man-made church, like the Presbyterian, would unquestionably be dangerous, and has proved itself so in the whole history of Protestantism. But that it is dangerous in a divinely commissioned church, we know, and so does every man of common sense, is not and cannot be true; for God himself becomes our surety for the right exercise of the power, and that is sufficient.

"The doctrine of auricular confession establishes a system of espionage which is absolutely fatal to personal independence, and from the intimate connection between priests and bishops, and bishops and the Pope, all the important secrets of the earth can be easily transmitted to the Vatican." This is ridiculously absurd. No priest can communicate to any person living the secrets of the confessional, and he can no more do it to his bishop or to the Pope than he can to James H. Thornwell. He cannot speak, out of the confessional, of what has been told him in the confessional, even to the penitent himself. No instance of the secrets of the confessional having been betrayed has ever occurred. Even the vilest apostates have never been known to disclose what they had received under the seal of the confessional. The Catholic clergy do not record the confessions of their penitents in a book, making them a part of the records of the Church, as did the former Puritan ministers of New England, as we had occasion ourselves to know from the inspection of the records of some of their churches, over which it was our misfortune to be settled as pastor.

As to the system of espionage, we all know that it was carried on to its perfection in the Congregational churches of New England; and it still existed in full vigor a few years ago in the Presbyterian churches in the Middle States, as we had personal means of knowing. In most Calvinistic churches, especially the Congregational, the Presbyterian, and the Methodist, the members are bound by a solemn covenant, a covenant frequently renewed, to *watch* over one another, which means, practically, that they shall be spies one upon another; and who that has had the misfortune to be brought up a Presbyterian has not felt that he was under perpetual surveillance, that every member, it might be, of the particular church to which he belonged was on the look-out to catch him tripping? We have ourselves had ample opportunities of learning the degree of personal independence allowed by Presbyterianism, and we never knew the meaning of personal independence till we became a Catholic. There is no comparison, in this matter of personal independence, between Catholicity and any form of Protestantism we are acquainted with, and that is saying much, if what is alleged concerning our frequent changes be not altogether untrue. Catholicity provides us all the helps we need in order to attain to Christian perfection; she exhorts, she entreats us to avail ourselves of them, and to attain to that perfection; but she throws the responsibility on our own individual consciences. Catholics, also, usually mind their own business, and attend rather to their own consciences than to those of their neighbors. Hence, you find among them very little hypocrisy. Their conduct is free, frank, natural, and, as far as we have had opportunities of observing, they generally wear their worst side outward. It needs a close and intimate acquaintance with them to know, or even to suspect their real piety and worth. This indicates any thing but the want of personal independence, and the presence of the system of espionage alleged. Indeed, the Professor in bringing this charge must have argued against us from what he knows to be true of his own sect; but this is to pass from one genus to another,—not allowable in logic. Servility, slavishness, the want of personal independence, the fear to say that our souls are our own, though unquestionably characteristics of the Presbyterian, are no characteristics of the Catholic. There is a total difference between the mild and parental authority exercised by our clergy over us, and the harsh and severe tyranny notoriously exercised by Presbyterian ministers over their flocks; and it would take much to make Catholics believe it possible for a people to stand in such awe and dread of a minister of religion as Presbyterians do of their ministers. Our children are delighted to see a priest come into the house; we, when a boy, if we saw a minister coming, used to run and hide in the barn.

The Professor has mentioned several other points, but they involve no principle not already met and disposed of. The great question of the mutual relation of the temporal and spiritual powers we have not discussed, for it has not lain in our way. In these essays we have not been laboring to establish the claims of the Church, but to test the validity of the objections urged by the Professor. We have shown that he has offered nothing that disproves, or tends to disprove, her infallibility. This is all that was required of us. That the Church is hostile to civil government we deny, and could easily prove, if it were necessary. But the burden of proof is on the Professor, and we are not disposed to assume it for ourselves. The Church represents the spiritual order, and has exclusive jurisdiction under God, for her own children, of all questions which pertain to that order; but as the Church, she has never enacted, or attempted to enact, civil laws. She asserts, undoubtedly, the independence, and if the independence, the supremacy of the spiritual order, because the spiritual order embraces every moral question, and the state is as much bound to obey the moral law as the individual; but as long as the civil government seeks the public good without violating any precept of that law, she leaves it, within its own province, free to adopt and carry out the economical or prudential policy it judges proper or expedient.

The Professor alludes to the struggles which have at times occurred between the civil and ecclesiastical powers, and takes it for granted that in these struggles the civil power was always in the right, and the Church in the wrong. It is singular how readily Protestants, when they wish to deny the infallibility of the Church, assume it for individuals and for civil government. But civil government is confessedly fallible. The simple fact of a conflict between the two powers is, therefore, no evidence that the right is against the Church. Indeed, the conflict itself is a presumption that the state is in the wrong; because the presumption is always in favor of the superior order. Do our Protestant friends ever reflect on the distrust which they manifest of their own pretended churches, when they assume that right must needs be, in every contest, on the side of the temporal authority? Do they remark that they prove themselves thus to be either courtiers or infidels? Even if the Church were only a human institution, it would not follow that she would not be in the right in warring against political tyrants. We certainly have no respect for Presbyterianism, and yet, if we should find the state, by virtue of its own authority, attempting to suppress it, we should side with Presbyterianism against the state; for we hold the utter incompetency of the state in spirituals, and we no more concede its right to sit in judgment on Presbyterianism than we do its right to sit in judgment on Catholicity. The question is one which belongs to the spiritual authority, and the state, in its own right, has and can have nothing to do with it.

It perhaps has never occurred to the Professor that it might be profitable to investigate those struggles which afford him so much matter of virulent but foolish declamation against the Church. In fact, the Popes, in their contests with the civil powers, need no apology. Judged even as a human power, they were always in the right, on the side of justice and humanity, defending the cause of the oppressed, and putting forth their power only to vindicate the rights of conscience, to succor the weak, to console the afflicted, and to protect the friendless. We said all this, and even more, while yet in the ranks of Protestants and far from dreaming that we should one day be a Catholic. We grant that the Pope has excommunicated princes and nobles, deposed kings and emperors, and absolved their subjects from their allegiance; but in this he has only done his duty as the Spiritual Father of Christendom, and what was required by humanity as well as religion. These princes were his spiritual subjects, amenable to his authority by the law of the Church which they acknowledged, and by the constitution of their own states. He was their legal judge, had the right to summon them before him, and to cut them off, if he saw proper, from the communion of the faithful, and excommunication of itself worked virtual deposition. In absolving subjects from their allegiance, he usurped no authority, for he was the legal judge in the case; for whether the allegiance continued or had ceased presented a case of conscience, of which, as Sovereign Pontiff, he had supreme jurisdiction, and because he was by all parties the acknowledged umpire between princes and their subjects. But he never absolved from their allegiance the subjects of infidel princes, or of any princes not Catholic, or bound to be Catholic by the constitution of their states, as the kings and queens of Great Britain are bound, since 1688, to be Protestant.

But what, in fact, was the absolution granted, and in what cases has the Pope exercised, or claimed, the right to grant it? Has the Pope ever claimed the right to absolve from their allegiance the subjects of a legitimate prince, who reigns justly, according to the laws and constitution of his state? Never. In every such case he impresses upon his spiritual children the duty of obedience. But the obligation between prince and subject is reciprocal. If the subject is bound to obey the prince, the prince is bound to protect the subject. This is implied in the very nature of the social compact. The people are not for the prince, but the prince is for the people. The authority of the prince is not a personal franchise or right, but a trust, and he is bound to exercise it according to the conditions on which it is committed to him. Government exists, nor for the good of the governors, but for the good of the governed. The true prince is the servant of his subjects. Government is instituted for the common good, and the moment it ceases to consult the common good, or the public good, it forfeits its rights. The tyrant, the oppressor, has and can have no right to reign, and therefore no right to exact obedience. His subjects cease to be subjects to him, and are free—in a lawful manner—to resist, and even depose him; for resistance to tyrants, if the manner of the resistance be just, is obedience to God. When a prince becomes a tyrant, when he oppresses his subjects, and tramples on the rights of our common humanity, he breaks the compact between him and his subjects, and by so doing releases them from their allegiance. Hence our Congress of 1776 after having alleged George the Third to be a tyrant, conclude,—" Therefore . . . . . these United Colonies are, and of right ought to be, free and independent states; and they *are absolved from all allegiance* to the British crown." Now suppose the subjects of a prince, feeling themselves aggrieved, oppressed, complain to the Holy Father, the judge recognized by both parties in the case, that their prince has broken the compact, violated his oath of office, and become a tyrant; suppose the Holy Father entertains the complaint, and summons both parties to plead before him, and, after a patient hearing of the cause, gives judgment against the prince, declares him to have forfeited his rights, and that his subjects are absolved from their allegiance, what would there be in all this to which reason could object? Well, this is precisely the kind of absolution the Popes have granted, and never have they deposed a prince or absolved his subjects, except in cases precisely similar to the one here supposed. He merely declares the law, and applies it to the facts of the case presented. The absolution itself simply gives a legal character to a fact which already exists. The necessity of some such authority as that which Protestants complain of in the Popes is widely and deeply felt in modern society, and various substitutes for it, such as a congress of nations, have been suggested or attempted, but without any favorable results. Having rejected the Pope as the natural and legal umpire between the prince and his subjects, we find ourselves reduced to the dilemma, either of passive obedience and non-resistance to tyrants, or of revolution, which denies the right of government, renders order impracticable, and resolves society into primitive chaos. To deny the right to resist the tyrant is to doom the people to hopeless slavery; to assert it, and yet leave to each individual the right to judge of the time, the means, and the mode of resistance, is disorder, no-governmentism, the worst form of despotism. In the "dark ages," men were able to avoid either alternative. By recognizing the Pope as umpire, who, by his character and position, as head of the Church which embraced all nations, was naturally, not to say divinely, fitted to be impartial and just, they practically secured the right of resistance to tyranny, without undermining legitimate authority. It will be long before modern nations will be wise enough to recognize how much they have lost by what they call their progress.

For ourselves, we thank God that there was formerly a power on earth that was able to depose tyrants, and to step in between the people and their oppressors. We are not among those who are afraid to glory in the boldness and energy of those great Popes who made crowned heads shake, and princes hold their breath. Our heart leaps with joy when we see St. Peter smite the oppressor of the Church or of his people to the earth, and if we have ever felt any regret, it has been at the slowness of the Holy Father to smite, or at his want of power to smite with more instant effect. Even when a Protestant, we learned to revere the calumniated Hildebrands, Innocents, and Bonifaces, those noble and saintly defenders of innocence, protectors of the helpless, and humblers of crowned tyrants and ruthless nobles. O, how slow even we Catholics are to do them justice! How little do we reflect on the deep debt of gratitude we owe them! O, dumb be the tongue that would rail against the Popes or apologize for their firm resistance to the usurpation of the temporal authorities! Alas! how often in the history of modern Europe have we seen them, under God, the last hope of the world, the only solace of the afflicted, the sole resource of the wronged and downtrodden! Alas! it is precisely because of their noble defence of religion and freedom, of their fidelity to God and to man, that they have been calumniated, and the world has been filled with the outcries of tyrants, and their minions and dupes, against them.

That the interposition of the Sovereign Pontiffs in temporal affairs often occasioned much disturbance, and even civil wars, we are not disposed to deny; but on them who made the interposition necessary must rest the responsibility. In this world, it often happens that right cannot be peacefully asserted and maintained, and tyranny proves a curse, not only while it is unresisted, but even when resisted, and successfully resisted. We cannot permit a band of depredators to go unresisted, because we must disturb them by resisting them. Injustice, iniquity, can never be redressed, the tyrant can never be deposed and the legitimate sovereign restored, without a combat, and often a long and bloody one. Even our Lord himself told us to think not that he had come to send peace on the earth, but a sword rather. But shall we, therefore, make no efforts to right the wronged, to save justice and humanity from utter shipwreck? Let no man who glories in the revolutionary principle, who boasts of being a lover of freedom and the progress of mankind, pretend it. We are no revolutionists; we hold ourselves bound in conscience to obey the legal authority; but we acknowledge no obligation to obey the oppressor, and let the competent authority but declare him an oppressor and summon us to the battlefield, and we are ready to obey, to bind on our armor, rush in where blows fall thickest and fall heaviest, let the disturbance be what it may. We are, thank God, Roman Catholics, and therefore love freedom and justice, and dare not, when called upon, to shrink from defending them against any and every enemy, at any and every sacrifice.

The Professor contends that the Church is hostile to civil government; we would respectfully ask him if he has reflected, that, without her, civil government becomes impracticable. How, without her as umpire between government and government, and between prince and subject, and without her as a spiritual authority to command the obedience of the subject and the justice of the prince, will he be able to secure the independence of nations, and wise and just government? Will he learn from experience? Let him, then, read modern history. The age in politics discards the Church. Protestantism for three hundred years has been the religion of nearly a third, and, in politics, of the whole of Europe. Three hundred years is a fair time for an experiment. Well, what is the result? DESPOTISM on the one hand, and ANARCHY on the other. There is not, at this moment, a single well-organized civil government on the whole Eastern continent, and only our own on the Western. The government of Great Britain may seem to be an exception for the Old World, but it is a perfect oligarchy; it fails to secure the common weal; enriches the few and impoverishes the many; and its very existence is threatened by a mob which the ever-increasing poverty of the industrial classes hourly augments, and grim want is rendering desperate. Our own government is sustained solely by the accidental advantages of the country, consisting chiefly in our vast quantities of unoccupied fertile lands, which absorb our rapidly increasing population, and form a sort of safety-valve for its superfluous energy. Strip us of these lands, or let them be filled up so that our expanding population should find its limit, and be compelled to recoil upon itself, our institutions would not stand a week.

Here in the present state of the world, hardly to be paralleled in universal history,—when old governments are either all fallen or tottering ready to fall; when all authority is cast off, and law is despised; when the streets of the most civilized cities run with the blood of citizens shed by citizens, and the lurid light of burning cottage and castle gleams on the midnight sky; when saintly prelates bearing the olive-branch of peace are shot down by infuriated ruffians; when murder and rapine hardly seek concealment, and all civilization seems to be thrown back into the savagism of the forest,—here we may read the wisdom of those who discard the Church, and denounce her as hostile to civil government,—the wisdom of the doctrine which a scoffing and unbelieving age opposes to the truth which Almighty God has revealed, and to the lessons of universal experience. Alas! how true it is, that God permits strong delusions to blind the impious and the licentious, that they may bring swift destruction upon themselves!

But it is time to bring our remarks to a close. We have examined the principal arguments which Mr. Thornwell has brought forward to prove the fallibility of the Church, and we leave our readers to judge for themselves whether we have not proved, that, in every instance, they are either unsound in principle or irrelevant, proving nothing but the Professor's own malice or ignorance. The Professor has made numerous assumptions, numerous bold assertions, but in no instance has he done better than simply to assume the point he was to prove. He has declaimed loudly against the Church, he has said many hard things against her, but he has harmed only himself and his brethren. We now take our leave of him. We have done all we proposed. We have vindicated the Catholic argument for the disputed books drawn from the infallibility of the Church, which is enough, without the testimonies of the Fathers, although we have even these. We regret that the task of answering the Professor had not been assumed by Dr. Lynch himself, who would have accomplished it so much better than we have done. Yet it was hardly fitting that he should have assumed it. He could not, with a proper respect for himself and his profession, have replied to such a vituperative performance as Mr. Thornwell's book. We were brought up a Presbyterian, and have been accustomed from our youth to the sort of stuff we have had to deal with, and therefore have been able to reply without feeling the degradation we should have felt, had we all our lifetime been accustomed to the courtesy and candor of Catholic controversialists.

PROTESTANTISM ENDS IN TRANSCENDENTALISM.*

JULY, 1846.

WE have no intention of reviewing at length the book the title of which we have just quoted. Indeed, we have read it only by proxy. We have heard it spoken of in certain literary

---

* Margaret, a Tale of the Real and Ideal, Blight and Bloom, including Sketches of a Place not before described, called Mons Christi. Boston: Jordan & Wiley. 1846. 12mo. pp. 460.

circles as a remarkable production, almost as one of the wonders of the age. The Protestant lady who read it for us tells us that it is a weak and silly book, unnatural in its scenes and characters, coarse and vulgar in its language and details, wild and visionary in its speculations; and, judging from the portions here and there which we actually have read, and from the source whence it emanates, we can hardly run any risk in indorsing our Protestant friend's criticism. The author is a man not deficient in natural gifts; he has respectable attainments; and makes, we believe, a tolerably successful minister of the latest form of Protestantism with which we chance to be acquainted; though, since we have not been introduced to any new form for several months, it must not be inferred from the fact that we are acquainted with no later form, that none later exists.

So far as we have ascertained the character of this book, it is intended to be the vehicle of certain crude speculations on religion, theology, philosophy, morals, society, education, and matters and things in general. The *Mons Christi* stands for the human heart, and Christ himself is our higher or instinctive nature, and if we but listen to our own natures, we shall at once learn, love, and obey all that our Blessed Redeemer teaches. Hence, Margaret, a poor, neglected child, who has received no instruction, who knows not even the name of her Maker, nor that of her Saviour, who, in fact, has grown up in the most brutish ignorance, is represented as possessing in herself all the elements of the most perfect Christian character, and as knowing by heart all the essential principles of Christian faith and morals. The author seems also to have written his work, in part at least, for the purpose of instructing our instructors as to the true method of education. He appears to adopt a very simple and a very pleasant theory on the subject,—one which cannot fail to commend itself to our young folks. Love is the great teacher; and the true method of education is for the pupil to fall in love with the tutor, or the tutor with the pupil, and it is perfected when the falling in love is mutual. Whence it follows, that it is a great mistake to suppose it desirable or even proper that tutor and pupil should both be of the same sex. This would be to reverse the natural order, since the sexes were evidently intended for each other. This method, we suppose, should be called "LEARNING MADE EASY, OR NATURE DISPLAYED," since it would enable us to dispense with school-rooms, prefects, text-books, study, and the birch, and to fall back on our natural instincts. These two points of doctrine indicate the genus, if not the species, of the book, and show that it must be classed under the general head of Transcendentalism. If we could allow ourselves to go deeper into the work and to dwell longer on its licentiousness and blasphemy, we probably might determine its species as well as its genus. But this must suffice; and when we add that the author seems to comprise in himself several species at once, besides the whole genus humbuggery, we may dismiss the book, with sincere pity for him who wrote it, and a real prayer for his speedy restoration to the simple genus humanity, and for his conversion, through grace, to that Christianity which was given to man from above, and not, spider-like, spun out of his own bowels.

Yet, bad and disgusting, false and blasphemous, as this book really is, bating a few of its details, it is a book which no Protestant, as a Protestant, has a right to censure. Many Protestants affect great contempt of Transcendentalism, and horror at its extravagance and blasphemy; but they have no right to do so. Transcendentalism is a much more serious affair than they would have us believe. It is not a simple "Yankee notion," confined to a few isolated individuals in a little corner of New England, as some of our Southern friends imagine, but is in fact the dominant error of our times, is as rife in one section of our common country as in another; and, in principle, at least, is to be met with in every popular Anti-Catholic writer of the day, whether German, French, English, or American. It is, and has been from the first, the fundamental heresy of the whole Protestant world; for, at bottom, it is nothing but the fundamental principle of the Protestant Reformation itself, and without assuming it, there is no conceivable principle on which it is possible to justify the Reformers in their separation from the Catholic

Church. The Protestant who refuses to accept it, with all its legitimate consequences, however frightful or absurd they may be, condemns himself and his whole party.

We are far from denying that many Protestants, and, indeed, the larger part of them, as a matter of fact, profess to hold many doctrines which are incompatible with Transcendentalism; but this avails them nothing, for they hold them, not as Protestants, but in despite of their Protestantism, and therefore have no right to hold them at all. In taking an account of Protestantism, we have the right, and, indeed, are bound, to exclude them from its definition. Every man is bound, as the condition of being ranked among rational beings, to be logically consistent with himself; and no one can claim as his own any doctrine which does not flow from, or which is not logically consistent with, his own first principles. This follows necessarily from the principle, that of contradictories one must be false, since one necessarily excludes the other. If, then, the doctrines incompatible with Transcendentalism, which Protestants profess to hold, do not flow from their own first principles, or if they are not logically compatible with them, they cannot claim them as Protestants, and we have the right, and are bound to exclude them from the definition of Protestantism. The man cannot be scientifically included in the definition of the horse, because both chance to be lodged in the same stable, or to be otherwise found in juxtaposition.

The essential mark or characteristic of Protestantism is, unquestionably, *dissent* from the authority of the Catholic Church, in subjection to which the first Protestants were spiritually born and reared. This is evident from the whole history of its origin, and from the well known fact, that opposition to Catholicity is the only point on which all who are called Protestants can agree among themselves. On every other question which comes up, they differ widely one from another, and not unfrequently some take views directly opposed to those taken by others; but when it concerns opposing the Church, however dissimilar their doctrines and tempers, they all unite, and are ready to march as one man to the attack. As dissent, Protestantism is negative, denies the authority of the Catholic Church, and can include within its definition nothing which, even in the remotest sense, concedes or implies that authority. But no man, sect, or party can rest on a mere negation, for no mere negation is or can be an ultimate principle. Every negation implies an affirmation, and therefore an affirmative principle which authorizes it. He who dissents does so in obedience to some authority or principle which commands or requires him to dissent, and this principle, not the negation, is his fundamental principle. The essential or fundamental principle of Protestantism is, then, not dissent from the authority of the Catholic Church, but the affirmative principle on which it relies for the justification of its dissent.

What, then, is this affirmative principle? Whatever it be, it must be either out of the individual dissenting, or in him; that is, some external authority, or some internal authority. The first supposition is not admissible; for Protestants really allege no authority for dissent, external to the individual dissenting,— have never defined any such authority, never hinted that such authority exists or is needed; and there obviously is no such authority which can be adduced. In point of fact, so far from dissenting from the Church on the ground that they are commanded to do so by an external authority paramount to the Church, they deny the existence of all external authority in matters of faith, and defend their dissent on the ground that there is no such authority, never was, and never can be.

But some may contend, judging from the practice of Protestants, and what we know of the actual facts of the original establishment of Protestantism in all those countries in which it has become predominant, that it does recognize an external authority, which it holds paramount to the Church, and on which it relies for its justification. Protestantism, as a matter of fact, owes its establishment to the authority of the lay lords and temporal princes, or, in a general sense, to the civil authority. It was, originally, much more of a political revolt than of a strictly religious dissent, and its external causes must be sought in the ambition of princes, dating back from Louis of Bavaria, and including Louis the Twelfth of France, rather than in any real change of faith operated in the masses; and its way was prepared by the temper of mind which the temporal princes created in their subjects by the wars they undertook and carried on ostensibly against the popes as political sovereigns, but really for the purpose of possessing the patrimony of the Church, and of subjecting the Church, in their respective dominions, to the control of the secular power. The Reformers would have accomplished little or nothing, if politics had not come to their aid. Luther would have bellowed in vain, had he not been backed by the powerful Elector of Saxony, and immediately aided by the Landgrave Philip; Zwingle, and Œcolampadius, and Calvin would have accomplished nothing in Switzerland, if they had not secured the aid of the secular arm, and followed its wishes; the powerful Huguenot party in France was more of a political than of a religious party, and it dwindled into insignificance as soon as it lost the support of great lords, distinguished statesmen and lawyers, and provincial parliaments. In Denmark, Sweden, and Norway, the Reform was purely the act of the civil power; in the United Provinces, it was embraced as the principle of revolt, or of national independence; in England, it was the work, confessedly, of the secular government and was carried by court and parliament against the wishes of the immense majority of the nation; in Scotland, it was effected by the great lords, who wished to usurp to themselves the authority of the crown; in this country, it came in with the civil government, and was maintained by civil enactments, pains, and penalties. We might, therefore, be led, at first sight, to assert the fundamental principle of Protestantism to be the supremacy in spirituals of the civil power. But this would be a mistake, because it did not recognize this supremacy unless the civil power was Anti-Catholic, and because the assertion of this supremacy of the civil power in spirituals was itself a denial of the authority of the Church, and therefore could not be made without making the act of dissent. There is no question but the Protestants did, whenever it suited their purpose, assert the supremacy of the state in spiritual matters; and it must be conceded that it is very agreeable to its nature to do so, as is evident from the fact, that even now, and in this country, it opposes the Catholic Church chiefly, and with the most success, on the ground that Catholicity asserts the freedom of religion, or, what is the same thing, the independence of the spiritual authority. Still this cannot be its ultimate principle. The Church taught and teaches, that, though the independence of the civil power in matters purely temporal is asserted, its authority in spirituals is null. To deny this is to deny the Church, and as much to dissent from her authority as to deny her infallibility, her divine authority, or any article of the creed she teaches; and this must be denied before the supremacy of the civil power in spirituals can be asserted. Therefore, if Protestantism did openly, avowedly, assert the Erastian heresy of the supremacy of the civil power in spirituals, it would not justify her dissent by an external authority, unless she could make this assertion itself on some external authority acknowledged to be paramount to the Church. But for this she has no external authority, since the Church denies it, and the authority of the state is the matter in question. She can, then, assert the supremacy of the state only on the authority of some principle in the individual dissenting, and therefore only on some internal authority. Whatever authority, then, Protestentism may ascribe to the civil power, it is not an external authority, because the authority asserted is always of the same order as that on which it is asserted, and can never transcend it.

Others, again, may think, since Protestants, and especially those among them denominated Anglicans and Episcopalians, occasionally appeal to Christian antiquity and talk of the Fathers, and sometimes even profess to quote them, that they have, or think they have, in Christian antiquity an authority for dissent, virtually, at least external to the individual dissenting. But Christian antiquity, unless read with a presumption in favor of the Church, save on a few general and public facts manifestly against Protestants, decides nothing. Understood as the Church understands it, and it evidently *may*, without violence to its letter or spirit, be so understood, it condemns Protestantism without mercy. To make it favor Protestantism even negatively, it is necessary to resort to a principle of interpretation which the Church does not concede, and the adoption of which would, therefore, involve the dissent in question. If we take with us the canon, that all the Christian Fathers are to be understood in accordance with the Church when not manifestly against her, Christian antiquity will be all on the side of the Roman Catholic Church; if we take the canon, that all in the Christian Fathers is to be understood in a sense against the Church, when not manifestly in her favor, Christian antiquity may, on some important dogmas, leave the question doubtful; though even then it would, in fact, be decisive for the *authority* of the Church, and therefore implicitly for all special dogmas. But, be this as it may, it is undeniable that it is only by adopting this latter canon that Protestantism can derive any countenance from Christian antiquity. But on what authority do they, or can they, adopt such a canon? Protestants call themselves reformers; they are accusers, dissenters, and therefore all the presumptions in the case are manifestly against them, as they are against all who accuse, bring an action or a charge against others; and they must make out a strong *prima facie* case, before they can turn the presumptions in their favor. This is law, and it is justice. Till they do this, the presumption is in favor of the Church; and then it is enough for her to show that the testimony of antiquity *may*, without violence, be so understood as not to impeach her claims. Till then, nothing will make for Protestants which is not manifestly against her, so clear and express as by no allowable latitude of interpretation to be reconcilable with her pretentions. That is to say, the Protestant must impeach the Church on *prima facie* evidence, before he can have the right to adopt that canon of interpretation without which it is manifestly suicidal for him to appeal to Christian antiquity. Take, as an illustration of what we mean, the testimony of St. Justin Martyr to the Catholic doctrine of the Real Presence. It is clear to any one who reads the passage, that the words in a plain and easy sense confirm the Catholic doctrine ; and yet, if there were an urgent necessity for interpreting them otherwise, we are not certain but, without greater deviation from the literal sense than is sometimes allowed, they *might* be so understood as not to be inconsistent with the views of the Blessed Eucharist which some Protestant sects profess to entertain. But by what authority, because they *may* be so interpreted, are we to say they *must* be ? In truth, it is nothing to the Protestant's purpose to say they *may* be, till he establishes by positive authority they *must* be, for it is obvious they also *may* not be. Now, what and where is this positive authority ? Manifestly not in Christian antiquity itself; and yet it must be had, before Christian antiquity can be adduced as authorizing dissent from the Catholic Church. This authority, as we said before, must be either external to the dissenter or internal in the dissenter himself. It cannot be external; for, after the Church, there is no conceivable external authority applicable in the case. It must, then, be internal. Then the authority of Christian antiquity, as alleged against the Church, is only the authority there is in the dissenter himself, according to the principle already established, that the authority asserted is necessarily of the same order as that on which it is asserted.

Finally, it will, perhaps, be alleged, inasmuch as all Protestants did at first, and some of them do now, appeal to the written word, or the Holy Scriptures, in justification of their dissent, that they have in these a real or a pretended authority, external to and independent of the dissenter, distinct from and paramount to that of the Church. But a moment's reflection will show, even if the Scriptures were not in favor of the Church, that this is a mistake. The Holy Scriptures proposed, and their sense declared, by the Church, we hold with a firm faith to be the word of God, and therefore of the highest authority; but, if not so proposed and interpreted, though in many respects important and authentic historical documents, and valuable for their excellent didactic teachings, they would not and could not be for us the inspired, and, in a supernatural sense, the authoritative, word of God. To the Protestant they are not and cannot be an authority external to the dissenter; because, denying the unwritten word, the Church, and all authoritative tradition, he has no external authority to vouch for the fact that they are the inspired word of God, or to declare their genuine sense. If there be no external authority to decide that the Bible is the word of God, and to declare its true sense, the authority ascribed to it in the last analysis, according to the principle we have established, is only the authority of some internal principle in the individual dissenting; for, in that case, the individual, by virtue of this internal principle, decides, with the Bible as without it, what is and what is not God's word, what God has and has not revealed; and therefore what he is and what he is not bound to believe, what he is and what he is not bound to do.

It is, moreover, notorious that Protestants do really deny all external authority in matters of faith, and hold that any external authority to determine for the individual what he must believe would be manifest usurpation, intolerable tyranny, to be resisted by every one who has any sense of Christian freedom, or of his rights and dignity as a man. Even the Anglican Church, which claims to herself authority in controversies of faith, acknowledges that she has no right to ordain any thing as of necessity to salvation, which may not be proved from God's word written; and by implication at least, if she means any thing, leaves it to the individual to determine for himself whether what she ordains is provable from the written word or not; and, therefore, abandons her own authority, by making the individual the judge of its legality. No one will, furthermore, pretend that Protestants even affect to have dissented from the Catholic Church, in which they were spiritually born and reared, in obedience to an external authority; that is to say, another Church, which they held to be paramount to the Roman Catholic Church. If they had admitted that there was anywhere an authoritative Church, they would have agreed that it was this Church, and could have been no other. In denying the authority of the Roman Catholic

Church, they denied, and intended to deny, in principle, all external authority in matters of faith; and the chief count in the indictment of the Church, which they have drawn up, and on which they have been for these three hundred years demanding conviction, is, that she claims to be such authority, when no such authority was instituted, or intended to be instituted. We may, then, safely conclude that the affirmative principle on which Protestantism relies for the justification of its denial of Catholic authority is not some authority external to the individual dissenting, and held to be paramount to that from which he dissents.

Then the principle must be internal in the individual himself and this is precisely what Protestantism teaches; for by her own confession, nay, by her own boast, her fundamental principle is, PRIVATE JUDGMENT. This was the only principle which, in the nature of the case, she could set up as the antagonist of Catholic authority; and it is notorious the world over, that it is in the name of this principle that she arraigns the Church, and commands her to give an account of herself. We see, even to-day, emblazoned on the banners borne by the motley hosts of the so-called "Christian Alliance," this glorious device,—THE RIGHT OF PRIVATE JUDGMENT. This is their battle-cry, as *Deus Vult* was that of the Crusaders. It is their *In hoc signo vince.* "We want no infallible pope, bishops, or church, to propound and explain to us God's word, to lord it over God's heritage, and make slaves of our very consciences. No! we are freemen, and we strike for freedom, the glorious birthright of every Christian to judge for himself what is or what is not the word of God; that is, what he is or is not to believe." There is no mistake in this. If there is any thing essential, any thing fundamental, in Protestantism, any thing which makes it the subject of a predicate at all it is this far-famed and loud-boasted principle of PRIVATE JUDGMENT.

In saying this, we of course are not to be understood as asserting that Protestants always, or even commonly, respect, in their practice, this right of private judgment. Practically, every

Protestant says, "*I* have the right to think as I please, and *you* have the right to think as I do; and if you do not, I will, if I have the power, compel you to do so, or confiscate your goods, deprive you of citizenship, outlaw you, behead, hang, or burn you; at least, imprison you, flog you, or bore your ears and tongue." In point of fact, Protestants, we grant, have very generally violated the principle of private judgment, and have practised, in the name of religious liberty, the most unjust, tyranny over conscience,—unjust, because, on their own principles, they have received from Almighty God no authority to dictate to conscience, and because they also concede, what is unquestionably true, that conscience is accountable to God alone. Every attempt of any man, set, or class of men, not expressly commissioned by Almighty God,—so expressly that the authority exercised shall be really and truly his,—to exert the least control over conscience is a manifest usurpation, an outrageous tyranny, which every man, having a just reverence for his Maker, will resist even unto death. The Catholic Church, indeed, claims plenary authority over conscience; but only on the ground, that she is divinely commissioned, and that the authority which speaks in her is literally and as truly the authority of God, as that of the representative is that of his sovereign. If *per impossibile*, she could suppose herself not to be so commissioned, and therefore not having the pledge of the divine supervision, protection, and aid which such commission necessarily implies, she would concede that she has no authority, and should attempt to exercise none. We cheerfully obey her, because in obeying her we are obeying not a human authority, but God himself. In submitting to her we are free, because we are submitting to God, who is our rightful sovereign, to whom we belong, all that we have, and all that we are. Freedom is not in being held to no obedience, but in being held to obey only the legal sovereign; and the more unqualified this obedience, the freer we are. Perfect freedom is in having no will of our own, in willing only what our sovereign wills, and because he wills it. If the Church, as we cannot doubt, be really commissioned by God, the more absolute her authority, the more unqualified our submission, the more perfect is our liberty, as every man knows, who knows any thing at all of that freedom wherewith the Son makes us free. But in yielding obedience to a Protestant sect, it is not the same. When any one of our sects undertakes to dictate to conscience, it is tyranny; because, by its own confession, it has received no authority from God. It is tyranny, even though what it attempts to enforce be really God's word; for it attempts to enforce it by a *human*, and not by a *divine* authority. It would still tyrannize, because it has no right to enforce any thing at all. It may say, as our sects do say, it has the Bible, that the Bible is God's word, and that it only exacts the obedience to God's commands which no man has the right to withhold. Be it so. But who has made it the keeper and executor of God's laws? Where is its commission under the hand and seal of the Almighty? It is, doubtless, right that the civil law should be executed,— that the murderer, for instance, should be punished; but it does not *therefore* follow that I, as a simple citizen, have the right to execute them, and to inflict the punishment. That may be done only by the constituted authorities, and is not my business; and it is a sound as well as a homely adage, Let every one mind his own business. Protestants, on this point, fall into grievous errors. The simple possession of the Holy Scriptures does not constitute them *keepers* of the word,—even supposing the Scriptures to contain the *whole* word,—and give them the right to dictate to conscience, as they imagine, any more than the fact of my having in my possession the statute-book constitutes me the guardian and administrator of the laws of the commonwealth. Protestants, whenever they interfere with the right of private judgment, convict themselves, on their own principles, of practising on what, in these days, is called "Lynch law;" and Lynch law is to the state precisely what Protestantism, in practice, is to the Church.—This is a fact which deserves the grave consideration of those sects which contend for creeds and confessions, and claim the right to try and punish as heretics such as in their judgment do not conform to them. Even Dr. Beecher himself came very near, a few years since, being *lynched* by his Presbyterian associates; and if it had not been for an extraordinary suppleness and marvellous skill in parrying blows, hardly to have been expected in one of his age, it might have been all up with him. Our Presbyterian, Dutch Reformed, Puritan, and Anglican friends should lay this to heart, and never suffer themselves to complain of the practice of "Lynch law," or to find the least fault with the commission of Judge Lynch himself,—for it emanates from the same authority as their own, and is as regularly made out and authenticated. But this is foreign from our present purpose. It is enough for our present purpose, that Protestants assert, in theory, as they unquestionably do, the right of private judgment, and make it the principle of their dissent from the authority of the Catholic Church.

But all men, at least as to their inherent rights, are equal. The right of private judgment, then, cannot be asserted for one man, without being at the same time, and by the same authority, asserted for all men. Then Protestants cannot assert private judgment as their authority for dissenting from the Catholic Church, without erecting it into a universal principle. We may assume, then, that Protestantism begins by laying down as its principle the right of *all men* to private judgment.

But the right of all men to private judgment is in effect the *unrestricted* or universal right to private judgment. This may not have been clearly seen in the beginning, and there is no question but Protestants intended in the commencement to restrict the right of private judgment to the simple interpretation of the written word. But every one, whatever may be his intentions, must be held answerable for the strict logical consequences of the principles he deliberately adopts; for if he does not foresee these consequences, he ought not to take upon himself the responsibility of adopting the principles. The right of private judgment, once admitted, can no longer be restricted. If restricted at all, it must be by some authority, and this authority must be either external or internal. If internal, it is private judgment itself, and then it cannot restrict, for it would be absurd to say that private judgment can restrict private judgment. It cannot be an external authority, because Protestants admit no external authority, and because we cannot assert an external authority to restrict private judgment, without denying private judgment itself. Either the authority must prescribe the limits of private judgment, or private judgment must prescribe the limits of the restriction; if the first, it is tantamount to the denial of private judgement itself, for private judgment would then subsist only at the mercy of authority, by sufferance, and not by right; if the latter, the *authority* is null; for private judgment may enlarge or contract the restriction as it pleases, and that is evidently no restriction which is only what that which is restricted chooses to make it. It is impossible, then, to erect private judgment into a principle for all men, and afterwards to restrict it to the simple interpretation of the Holy Scriptures.

If we assert the right of private judgment to interpret the Holy Scriptures, we must assert its right in all cases whatsoever; for the principle on which private judgment can be defended in one case is equally applicable in every case. Will it be said that private judgment must yield to God's word? Granted. But what is God's word? The Bible. How know you that? Do you determine that the Bible is the word of God by some external authority, or by private judgment? Not by some external authority, because you have none, and admit none. By private judgment? Then the authority of the Bible is *for you* only private judgment. The Bible does not propose itself, and therefore can have no authority higher than the authority which proposes it. Here is a serious difficulty for those Protestants who set up such a clamor about the Bible, and which shows them, or ought to show them, that, whatever the Bible may be for a Catholic, for them it can, in no conceivable contingency, be any thing but a human authority. *The authority of that which is proposed is of the same order as that which proposes, and cannot transcend it.* This is a Protestant argument, and is substantially the great argument of Chillingworth against

Catholicity. Nothing proposes the Bible to Protestants but private judgment, as is evident from their denial of all other authority; and therefore in the Bible they—not we, thank God! —have only the authority of private judgment, and therefore only the word of man, and not the word of God. If the authority on which Protestants receive the word of God is only that of private judgement, then there is for them in the Bible only private judgment; and then nothing to restrict private judgment, for private judgment can itself be no restriction on private judgment.

Moreover, if we take the Bible to be the word of God on the authority of private judgment, and its sense on the same authority, as Protestants do and must, then we assume private judgment to be competent to decide of itself what is and what is not the word of God, what God has revealed and what he has not revealed, has commanded and has not commanded,—and therefore competent to decide what we are to believe and what we are not to believe, and what we are to do and what we are not to do. But this is to assume the whole for private judgment, and therefore to assume its unrestricted right. We, may, then, assume, in the second place, that Protestantism not only lays down the principle of the right of all men to private judgment, but the right of all men to the universal or unrestricted right of private judgment.

But private judgment itself is not, strictly speaking, ultimate, and therefore, though it be the principle of Protestantism, is not its ultimate principle. The ultimate principle of Protestantism lies a little farther back. Rights are never in themselves ultimate, but must always, to be rights, rest on some foundation or authority. The right of private judgment necessarily implies some principle on which it is founded. Every judgment is by some standard or measure; for when we judge it is always *by* something, and this, whatever it is, is the principle, law, rule, criterion, standard, or measure of the judgment. In every act of private judgment this standard or measure is the individual judging. The individual judges by himself, and to judge by one's self is precisely what is meant by private judgment. In it the individual is both measurer and measure,—in a word, his own yard-stick of truth and goodness. But rights, to be rights, must not only be founded on some principle, but on a *true* principle ; for to say they are founded on a false principle is only saying in other words, that they have no foundation at all. The right of all men to unrestricted private judgment, then, necessarily implies that each and every man is in himself the exact measure of truth and goodness. In laying down the principle of private judgment as the principle of its dissent from the Catholic Church, Protestantism, then, necessarily lays down the principle, that each and every man is in himself the exact measure of truth and goodness,—the very fundamental proposition of Transcendentalism. The identity in principle is, then, perfect; and no Protestant, as we began by saying, can refuse to accept Transcendentalism, with all its legitimate consequences, without condemning himself and his whole party

This conclusion is undeniable, for the acutest dialectician will find no break or flaw in the chain of reasoning by which it is obtained. We, then, may assume this very important position, that Transcendentalism is the strict logical termination of Protestantism ; and if some Protestants, as is the case, refuse to admit it, it is at the expense of their dialectics ; because they cannot, or dare not, say, Two and two make four, but judge it more prudent to say, Two and two make five, or to compromise the matter and say, Two and two make three. There are few things which are more disgusting than the cowardice which shrinks from avowing the legitimate consequences of one's own principles. The sin of inconsequence is, as the celebrated Dr. Evariste de Gypendole justly remarks, a mortal sin,—at least, in the eyes of humanity ; for it is high treason against the rational nature itself ; and he who deliberately commits it voluntarily abdicates reason, and takes his place among inferior and irrational natures. If your principles are sound, you cannot push them to a dangerous extreme ; and if they will not bear pushing to their extreme consequences, you should know that they are unsound, and not fit to be entertained; for it is always lawful to conclude the unsoundness of the principle from the unsoundness of the consequences.

Taking this view of the case, we confess the Transcendentalists appear to us the more respectable, and indeed the only respectable because the only consistent, class of Protestants. Consistent as Protestants, we mean, not as men; for Transcendentalism is the *ne plus ultra* of inconsistency and absurdity; but as Protestants they are consistent in so far as they carry out with an iron logic the Protestant principle to its legitimate results; and in doing this, in the providence of God, they are rendering no mean service to the cause of truth. They are a living and practical *reductio ad absurdum* of Protestantism. They strip it of its disguises, expose it in its nakedness, and subserve the cause of truth as the drunken Helotæ subserved the cause of temperance in the Spartan youth by exposing to them the disgusting effects of drunkenness.

It is of great practical importance that Protestantism should be exhibited by its followers in its true light as it really is in itself. Thus far Protestants have owned their success and influence, in the main, to the fact, that the mass of them have never seen and comprehended Protestantism in its simple, unadulterated elements. It has always been presented to them in a livery stolen from Catholicity. The great mass of the Protestant people, seeing it only in this livery, have supposed that it appertained to the household of faith, and that they had in it all that is essential to the Christian religion. Unable to penetrate its disguises, unable to distinguish between what was genuinely Protestant and what was surreptitiously taken from the Church, they could not understand the force or truth of the Catholic accusations against them. It seemed to them utterly false to say that they had no faith, no church, no religion, and that their Protestantism necessarily involved the denial of the whole scheme of revealed religion, and left them in reality nothing but mere Naturalism. Had they not something they called a church?

Had they not places of worship modelled after Christian temples? Had they not the Holy Scriptures, pastors and teachers, hymns, prayers,—all the exterior forms of worship? Did they not profess to believe in God, the Holy Trinity, the Incarnation, the Atonement, the necessity of Grace, the endless punishment of the wicked, and the eternal beatitude of the just,—all that even Catholic doctors have ever taught that it is necessary *ex necessitate medii ad salutem* to be explicitly believed? Did they not try to lead holy and devout lives, spend much time in prayer and praise, seek earnestly to know and do the will of God, and actually, in many instances, attain to a moral elevation which would more than compare favorably with that of many Catholics? How say, then, that we have no religion, that our principles are at war with Christianity, and lead necessarily to the destruction of all faith, of all Christian morality? Have we not in our Protestantism, as we hold it, a living lie to your unjust charge, your foul aspersion? It must be confessed, that appearances to the Protestant, were much against the Catholic, and it required considerable insight and firmness of logic to establish the charges which the Catholic, from the principles of an infallible faith, was fully warranted in preferring. But time and events have now made clear and certain to all who can see and reason, what then seemed so doubtful, not to say, so unfounded. In Transcendentalism, which is both the logical and historical development of Protestantism, it may now be seen that the Protestant, not the Catholic, was deceived; that not the Catholic was unjust in his charges, but the Protestant was carried away by his delusions. This is an immense gain, and by showing this, by stripping Protestantism of its disguises, by compelling it to abandon what it had attempted to retain of Catholicity, and to restrict it to its own principles, Trancendentalism is subserving in no ordinary degree the cause of religion and morality. Three hundred years of controversy have resulted in simplifying the question, and in making up the true and proper issue. If the true and proper issue could have been made in the beginning, Protestantism would have died in its birth. The mass of those who have followed the Protestant standard have done so because they supposed *they* had in the Holy Scriptures a divine authority for their belief. Here was their mother delusion. Catholics have really in the Holy Scriptures a divine authority, because they receive them on the proposition of the Church expressly commissioned by Almighty God to propose the truth revealed; but Protestants, as we have seen, since they take the Holy Scriptures only on the authority of private reason, have in them only the authority of private reason,— a merely human authority. It is now seen and understood that the Scriptures, if taken on human authority, have only a human authority; and therefore, as Catholics always alleged, Protestants, with all their pretensions, have only a human authority for the dogmas they profess to derive from them, and therefore are not, and never have been, able to make that act of divine faith without which, if they have come to years of discretion, they possess no *Christian* virtue, and do nothing meritorious for eternal life. If Christianity be a supernatural life, the life which begins in supernatural faith and contemplates a supernatural destiny, it is now clear that Protestants cannot and never could claim to be truly within the pale of the Christian family, but do reject and always have virtually rejected the Christian religion itself.

This being so, it becomes necessary now either to deny the supernatural character of the Christian life, and therefore the necessity of divine or supernatural faith, or to give up Protestantism as having no claim to be called Christian. This is becoming a general conviction among Protestants themselves, and therefore the tendency to reject Christianity, as a supernatural religion, is manifesting itself all over the Protestant world. Even Bishop Butler, the great Anglican light of the last century, declares the Gospel to be only "a republication of the law of nature;" and we have rarely met with a Protestant, whatever might be his unintelligible jargon about the New Birth, that did not hold, substantially, that the Christian life is merely the **continuation and development of our natural life.** The old modes of speech, adopted when Christianity was held to be a supernatural religion, are, we admit, in some instances, retained and insisted upon; but they have lost their former significance. *Supernatural* is defined to be *supersensuous*, as if spiritual existences could not be natural as well as material existences. It is thus Coleridge defines supernatural; it is thus, also, the *Supernaturalists* of Germany, of the school of Schleiermacher and De Wette, understand it, while the Rationalists deny it in name as well as in reality. In no higher sense do we find the word recognized by the mass of Swiss and French Protestants. "What did Almighty God make us for?" said we, the other day, to a worthy Protestant preacher, not without note in this community and the councils of his country. "To develope and perfect our spiritual natures," was the ready reply; that is, to finish the work which Almighty God began, but left incomplete; and this is the reply which, in substance, is almost universally given by those Protestants who plume themselves on having pure and ennobling spiritual views of religion. Thus it is, men everywhere lose sight of their supernatural destiny, and then deny the necessity of a supernatural life, and then the necessity of grace. Thus, in substance, if not in name, they reject the doctrines of the Trinity, the Incarnation, the Miraculous Conception and Birth of our Saviour, Original Sin, the Atonement, Remission of Sins, the Plenary Inspiration of the Scriptures, and, finally, all that is incompatible with the principle of man's sufficiency for himself, as so many reminiscences of Popery, or traditions of the Dark Ages, and as interposing between the human soul and its Creator, and hindering its freedom and growth. It is idle to deny, that all over the Protestant world, the tendency to this result is strong and irresistible, and that it is already reached by the more thinking and enlightened portion of Protestants. The true and proper issue, then, cannot be really any longer evaded. Protestants must meet the simple questions of Naturalism or Supernaturalism, of Transcendentalism or Catholicity, of man or God.

No doubt, a certain class of Protestant doctors do, and will, for some little time to come, struggle to stave off this issue, but in vain. Matters have proceeded too far. It is too late. The internal developments of Protestantism are too far completed, the spirit at work in the Protestant ranks is too powerful, to prevent the direct issue from being made. Transcendentalism, under one form or another, has struck its roots so deep, has spread out its branches so far, and finds so rich a soil, that it must ere long cause all the other forms of Protestantism, as the underbrush in a thick forest, to die out and disappear. The spirit of inquiry which Protestantism boasts of having quickened, the disposition to bring every question, the most intricate and the most sacred, to the test of private judgment, which she fosters, and which it would be suicidal in her to discountenance, will compel these doctors themselves either to give up their vocations, or to fall into the current and suffer themselves to be borne on to its termination. Resistance is madness. The movement party advances with a steady step, and will drive all before it. Whatever Evangelical doctor throws himself in its path to stay its onward march is a dead man and ground to powder. There is no alternative; you must follow Schlegel, Hurter, Newman, Faber, back into the bosom of Catholic unity, or go on with Emerson, Parker, and Carlyle. Not to-day only have we seen this. Think you that we, who, according to your own story, have tried every form of Protestantism, and disputed every inch of Protestant ground, would ever have left the ranks of Protestantism in which we were born, and under whose banner we had fought so long and suffered so much, if there had been any other alternative for us?

The "No Popery" cry which our *Evangelicals* are raising, and which rings in our ears from every quarter, does not in the least discompose us. In this very cry we hear an additional proof of what we are maintaining. We understand the full significance of this cry. The Protestant masses are escaping from their leaders. The sectarian ministers, especially of the species *Evangelical*, are losing their hold on their flocks, and finding that their old petrified forms, retained from Luther, or Calvin, or Knox, will no longer satisfy them,—have no longer vitality for them. Their craft is in danger; their power and influence are departing, and *Ichabod* is beginning to be written on their foreheads. They see the handwriting on the wall, and feel that something must be done to avert the terrible doom that awaits them. Fearfulness and trembling seize them, and, like the drowning man, they catch at the first straw, and hope, and yet with the mere hope of despair, that it will prove a plank of safety. They have no resource in their old, dried-up, dead forms. They must look abroad, call in some extrinsic aid, and, by means of some foreign power, delay the execution of the judgment they feel in their hearts has already been pronounced against them. They must get up some excitement which will captivate the people and blind their reason. No excitement seems to them more likely to answer their purpose than a "No Popery" excitement, which they fancy will find a firm support in the hereditary passions and prejudices of their flocks. Here is the significance of this "No Popery" excitement.

But this excitement will prove suicidal. Times have changed, and matters do not stand as they did in the days of Luther, and Zwingle, and Henry, and Calvin, and Knox. The temper of men's minds is different, and there is a new order of questions up for solution. The old watchwords no longer answer the purpose. What avails it to prove the Pope to be Antichrist, to populations that do not even believe in Christ? What avails it to thunder at Catholicity with texts which are no longer believed to have a divine authority? Protestantism must now fall back on her own principles, and fight her battles with her own weapons. She must throw out her own banner to the breeze, and call upon men to gather and arm and fight for progress, for liberty, for the unrestricted right of private judgment, or she will not rally a corporal's guard against Catholity. But the moment she does this, she is, as the French say, *enfoncée;* for she has subsisted and can subsist only by professing one thing and doing another. Let our Evangelical doctors, in their madness, rally, in the name of progress, of liberty, of private judgment, an army to put down the Pope, and the matter will not end there.

Their forces, furnished with arms against Catholicity, will turn upon themselves, and in a hoarse voice, and if need be, from brazen throats and tongues of flame, exclaim, "No more sham, gentlemen. We go for principle. We do not unpope the Pope to find a new pope in each petty presbyter, and a spy and informer in each brother or sister communicant. You are nothing to us. Freedom, gentlemen; doff your gowns, abrogate all your creeds and confessions, break up all your religious organizations, abolish all forms of worship except such as each individual may choose and exercise for himself, and acknowledge in fact, as well as in name, that every man is free to worship one God or twenty Gods, or no God at all, as seems to him good, unlicensed, unquestioned, or take the consequences. We will no more submit to your authority than you will to that of the Pope."

This is the tone and these the terms in which these "No Popery" doctors will find, one of these days, their flocks addressing them; for we have only given words to what they know as well as we is the predominant feeling of the great majority of the Protestant people. The very means, in the present temper of the Protestant public, they must use to insure their success, cannot fail to prove their ruin. They will only hasten the issue they would evade. Deprived, as they now are, for the most part, of all *direct* aid from the civil power, the force of things is against them, and it matters little whether they attempt to move or sit still. They were mad enough in the beginning to take their stand on a movable foundation, and they must move on with it, or be left to balance themselves in vacuity; and if they do move on with it, they will simply arrive—nowhither. They are doomed, and they cannot escape. Hence it is all their motions affect us only as the writhings and death-throes of the serpent whose head is crushed.

Regarding it of the greatest importance that the whole matter should be brought to its true and proper issue, and believing firmly, that when the real alternatives are distinctly apprehended and admitted, that many Protestants will choose "the better part," we are not displeased to witness the very decided tendency to Transcendentalism now manifesting itself throughout the Protestant world. It is a proof to us that the internal developments of Protestantism are not only bringing it to its strictly logical termination, but, what is more important still, to the *term of its existence*. The nations which became Protestant rebelled against the God of their fathers, the God who had brought them up out of the bondage of ignorance, barbarism, idolatry, and superstition, and said they would not have him to reign over them, but they would henceforth be their own masters, and rule themselves. He, for wise and merciful but inscrutable purposes, gave them up to their reprobate sense, left them to themselves, to follow their own wills, till bitter experience should teach them their wickedness, their impiety, their folly and madness, and bring them in shame and confusion to pray, "O Lord, in thy wrath remember mercy; save us from ourselves, or we perish!" To this desirable result it was not to be expected they would come till Protestantism had run its natural course, and reached its legitimate termination. They would not abandon it till they had exhausted all its possibilities, and till it could no longer present a new face to charm or delude them. In this Transcendental tendency, we see the evidence that it has run or very nearly run its natural course, and in Transcendentalism reaches its termination, exhausts itself, and can go no farther; for there is no farther. Beyond Transcendentalism, in the same direction, there is no place. Transcendentalism is the last stage this side of NOWHERE; and when reached, we must hold up, or fly off into boundless vacuity. In its prevalence, then, we may trust we see the signs of a change near at hand; and any change must certainly be in a better direction.

PROTESTANTISM IN A NUTSHELL.*

OCTOBER, 1849.

We have seen few works written with a more just appreciation of our age than the one before us, or so well adapted to the present state of the controversy which we are always obliged to carry on with the enemies of the Church. Its author understands well the essential nature of Protestantism, and clearly and distinctly points out the proper method of meeting it under the various forms it at present assumes, and of imposing silence on its arrogant and noisy pretensions. He does not confine himself to the field of theological controversy, properly so called, but he meets Protestants on their own chosen ground, on the broad field of European civilization, and shows them that, under the point of view of civilization, of liberty, order, and social well-being, Protestantism has been a total failure, and that, even in reference to this world, Catholicity has found itself as superior to it as it claims to be in regard to the world to come. He does not merely vindicate Catholicity, in relation to civilization, from the charges preferred against it by the modern advocates of liberalism and Progressism, but by a calm appeal to history and philosophy, he shows that the opposing system has interrupted the work of civilization which the Church was prosecuting with vigor and success, and has operated solely in the interest of barbarism. In doing this, he has done a real service to the cause of truth, and we learn with pleasure that one of our friends in England has translated his work, originally written Spanish, and rendered it accessible to the great body of English and American readers.

Such a work as this was much needed in our language. We have, indeed, many able controversial works,—works admirable

---

* Le Protestantisme comparé au Catholicisme dans ses Rapports avec la Civilisation Européenne. Par M. L'Abbe Jacques Balmes. Paris: Debrécourt. 1842-44. 3 tomes 8vo.

for the learning, ability, and skill of their authors; but we have comparatively few which are adapted to the present state of the controversy with Protestants. The greater part of those accessible to the mere English reader are well adapted only to the few individuals whose hearts the grace of God has already touched, and whose faces are already set towards the Church. Truth is one and invariable, but error is variable and manifold. It is always the same truth that we must oppose to error, but it is seldom the same error for two successive moments to which we must oppose it. We must shoot error, as well as folly, " as it flies." and we must be able to shoot it under ever-varying and varied disguises. The works we have, excellent as they are in their way, and admirably fitted to guard the faithful against many of the devices of the enemy to detach them from the Church, and to aid and instruct persons in heretical communions who are virtually prepared to return to the Church, do not hit the reigning form of Protestantism; they do not reach the seat of the disease, and are apparently written on the supposition of soundness, where there is, in fact, only rottenness. The principles they assume as the basis of their refutation of Protestantism, though nominally professed or conceded by the majority of Protestants, are not held with sufficient firmness to be used as the foundation of an argument that is to have any practical efficacy in their conversion. They all appear to assume that Protestants as a body really mean to be Christians, and err only in regard to some of the dogmas of Christianity and the method of determining the faith; that Protestantism is a specific heresy, a distinct and positive form of error, like Arianism or Pelagianism; and that its adherents would regard themselves as bound to reject it, if proved to be repugnant to Christianity, or contrary to the Holy Scriptures. This is a natural and a charitable supposition; but we are sorry to say, that, if it was ever warrantable, it is not by any means warrantable in our times, except as to the small number of individuals in the several sects who are mere exceptions to the rule. Protestantism is no specific heresy, is no distinct or positive form of error, but error in general, indifferent to forms, and receptible of any form or of all forms, as suits the convenience or the exigency of its friends. It is a veritable Proteus, and takes any and every shape judged to be proper to deceive the eyes or to elude the blows of the champions of truth. It is Lutheran, Calvinistic, Arminian, Unitarian, Pantheistic, Atheistic, Pyrrhonistic, each by turns or all at once, as is necessary to its purpose. The Protestant as such has, in the ordinary sense, no principles to maintain, no character to support, no consistency to preserve; and we are aware of no authority, no law, no usage, by which he will consent to be bound. Convict him from tradition, and he appeals to the Bible; convict him from the Bible, and he appeals to reason; convict him from reason, and he appeals to private sentiment; convict him from private sentiment, and he appeals to skepticism, or flies back to reason, to Scripture, or tradition, and alternately from one to the other,—never scrupling to affirm, one moment, what he denied the moment before, nor blushing to be found maintaining, that, of contradictories, both may be true. He is indifferent as to what he asserts or denies, if able for the moment to obtain an apparent covert from his pursuers.

Protestants do not study for the truth, and are never to be presumed willing to accept it, unless it chances to be where and what they wish it. They occasionally read our books and listen to our arguments, but rarely to ascertain our doctrines, or to learn what we are able to say against them or for ourselves. The thought, that we may possibly be right, seldom occurs to them; and when it does, it is instantly suppressed as an evil thought, as a temptation from the Devil. They take it for granted, that, against us, they are right, and cannot be wrong. This is with them a "fixed fact," admitting no question. They condescend to consult our writings, or to listen to our arguments, only to ascertain what doctrines they can profess, or what modifications they can introduce into those which they have professed, that will best enable them to elude our attacks, or give them the appearance of escaping conviction by the authorities from tradition, Scripture, reason, and sentiment which we array against them.

Candor or ingenuousness towards themselves even is a thing wholly foreign to their Protestant nature, and they are instinctively and habitually cavillers and sophisticators. They disdain to argue a question on its merits, and always, if they argue at all, argue it on some unimportant collateral. They never recognize—unless it is for their interest to do so—any distinction between a *transeat* and a *concedo*, and rarely fail to insist that the concession of an irrelevant point is a concession of the main issue. They have no sense of responsibleness, no loyalty to truth, no mental chastity, no intellectual sincerity. What is for them is authority which no body must question; what is against them is no authority at all. Their own word if not in their favor, they refuse to accept; and the authority to which they professedly appeal they repudiate the moment it is seen not to sustain them. To reason with them as if they would stand by their own professions, or could or would acknowledge any authority but their own ever-varying opinions, is entirely to mistake them, and to betray our own simplicity.

Undoubtedly, many of our friends, who have not, like ourselves, been brought up Protestants, and have not to blush at the knowledge their Protestant experience has given them, may feel that in this judgment we are rash and uncharitable. Would that we were so. We take no pleasure in thinking ill of any portion of our fellow-men, and would always rather find ourselves wrong in our unfavorable judgments of them than right. But in this matter the evidence is too clear and conclusive to allow us even to hope that we are wrong. There is not a single Protestant doctrine opposed to Catholicity that even Protestants themselves have not over and over again completely refuted; there is not a single charge brought by Protestants against the Church that some of them, as well as we, have not fully exploded; and no more conclusive vindication of the claims of Catholicity can be desired than may be—nay, than in fact has been—collected from distinguished Protestant writers themselves. This is a fact which no Protestant, certainly no Catholic, can deny. How happens it, then, that the Protestant world still subsists, and that, for the last hundred and fifty years, we have made comparatively little progress in regaining Protestants to the Church?

We may, it is true, be referred to the obstinacy in error characteristic of all heretics; but, in the present case,—unless what is meant is obstinacy in error in general, and not in error in particular,—this will not suffice as an answer; because, during this period, there has been no one particular form of error to which Protestants have uniformly adhered. No class of Protestants adheres to-day to the opinions it originally avowed. In this respect, there is a marked difference between the Protestant sects of modern times and the early Oriental sects. The Jacobite holds to-day the same specific heresy which he held a thousand years ago; and the Nestorian of the nineteenth is substantially the Nestorian of the fourth century. But nothing analogous is true of any of the modern Protestant sects. Protestants boast, indeed, their glorious Reformation, but they no longer hold the views of its authors. Luther, were he to ascend to the scenes of his earthly labors, would be utterly unable to recognize his teachings in the doctrines of the modern Lutherans; the Calvinist remains a Calvinist only in name; the Baptist disclaims his Anabaptist original; the Unitarian points out the errors he detects in his Socinian ancestors; and the Transcendentalist looks down with pity on his Unitarian parents, while he considers it a cruel persecution to be excluded from the Unitarian family. No sect retains, unmodified, unchanged, the precise form of error with which it set out. All the forms Protestants have from time to time assumed have been developed, modified, altered, almost as soon as assumed,—always as internal or external controversy made it necessary or expedient. Here is a fact nobody can deny, and it proves conclusively that the Protestant world does not subsist solely by virtue of its obstinate attachment to the views or opinions to which it has once committed itself, or in consequence of its aversion to change the doctrines it has once professed.

This fact proves even more than this. Bossuet very justly concludes from the *variations* of Protestantism its *objective* falsity, because the characteristic of truth is invariability; but we may go farther, and from the same variations conclude the *subjective* falsity of Protestantism, or that Protestants have no real belief in, or attachment to, the particular doctrines they profess,—not only that Protestants profess a false doctrine, but that they are insecere, and destitute, as a body, of real honesty in their professions. If they believed their doctrines, they could never tolerate the changes they undergo. New sects might, indeed, arise among them, but no sect would suffer its original doctrines to be in the least altered or modified. The members of every sect, if they believed its creed, would, so long as they adhered to it, be struck with horror at the bare idea of altering or modifying it; for it would seem to them to be altering or modifying the revealed Word of God. This is a point of no slight importance in judging the Protestant world, and seems to us to deserve more attention than the great body of Catholics even are disposed to give it. These variations prove, at least, that Protestantism is something distinct from the formal teachings of Protestants, and something that can and does survive them.

That we are neither rash nor uncharitable in our judgment of Protestants, severe as it unquestionably is, may be collected from facts of daily occurrence. The great body of Protestants, it is well known, labor unceasingly to detach Catholics from the Church, and to this end use all the means the age and country will tolerate. It was to combine their forces against Catholicity, that, a few years since, under the pontificate of Gregory XVI., the Protestant ministers held their World's Convention in London; that they formed Protestant alliances in England, Germany, France, Switzerland, and this country, devised a plan in concert with the Italian refugees in these several countries for effecting a civil revolution in every Catholic state, especially in the Papal States, and called upon the Protestant people everywhere to contribute funds for carrying it out,—a plan, even to minute particulars, which the well-known ministers, Bacon, Coxe, Beecher, Kirk, and others, forewarned us of in a meeting of the Protestant Alliance in this city in 1845, and which we have seen to a great extent realized during the last two years, much to the joy of thousands of nominal Catholics, who little suspected themselves to be the dupes of miserable demagogues on the one hand, and of hypocritical Protestant ministers on the other. But while Protestants, in season and out of season, by means fair and by means foul, by means open and by means secret and tortuous, seek to detach Catholics from the Church, they appear quite indifferent as to which of the thousand and one Protestant formulas they are led to embrace, or whether, indeed, they are led to embrace any one of them. Excepting, as we always do, here and there an individual, they are satisfied with the simple fact, that those drawn off from the Church are no longer Catholics. Whatever we lose, they count their gain, and although they are well aware that the majority of those they gain from us turn out rank apostates, infidels, and blasphemers, they nevertheless rejoice over them, and claim them as so many accessions to their ranks. If Protestants had any sincerity in their professions, if they had any sense of religion, how could they regard themselves as triumphing in proportion as they succeed in detaching miserable wretches from us, and sinking them in religion even below the ancient heathen,—especially since none of them dare pretend that we do not embrace all the essentials of the Christian religion, or that salvation is not attainable in our Church? They profess to be Christians, but they would rather make us infidels, apostates, atheists, blasphemers, than suffer us to remain Catholics. What more conclusive proof can you ask of their insincerity,—of the fact that their professions afford no clew to the real state of their minds, and ought to count for nothing?

Doubtless, we are not to be understood to imply that Protestants are always distinctly conscious of their own want of strict honesty and sincerity. No man knoweth whether he deserveth love or hatred. Knowledge of one's self is hard to acquire; self deception is one of the easiest things in the world, and few there are who are certain that they have a *good* conscience, or are sure of the motives which govern them. No doubt, Protestants gloss over their conduct, and have some method of justifying it in their own eyes; no doubt, they persuade themselves that they are sincere,—at least as sincere as they can afford to be, as honest in their belief as people generally are; but they know not what manner of spirit they are of, and as that spirit is inherently a lying spirit, as Catholics well know, it must needs lie unto themselves as well as unto others. Probably every heresiarch dupes himself before he dupes others, and holds the post of leader only because a greater dupe than his followers. That kind of honesty and sincerity compatible with a false spirit and gross delusion, we are not disposed to deny to Protestants; but we should remember that no really sincere and truthful mind ever is or ever can be deluded. No man ever is or ever was strictly honest and sincere in the profession of a false doctrine,—for no false doctrine can ever, in the nature of things, be so evidenced as to exclude doubt; and he who professes to believe what he doubts professes what he knows he does not believe, and therefore professes what he knows is not true. A man may be honestly in doubt as to what is or is not the truth on certain points; but no man can honestly *profess* faith in a false doctrine,—for in a false doctrine no man can have faith.

A sort of honesty and sincerity we certainly concede to the generality of Protestants; but as to the end for which they profess their doctrines, rather than as to the doctrines themselves. The principle common to them, and the only one we can always be sure they will practically adhere to, is, that the end justifies the means. The end they propose is, neither to save their souls nor to discover and obey the truth, but to destroy or elude Catholicity. The spirit which possesses them maddens them against the Church, and gives them an inward repugnance to everything not opposed to her. To overthrow her, to blot out her existence, or to prevent her from crushing them with the weight of her truth, is to them a praiseworthy end, at least a great and most desirable end; directly or indirectly, consciously or unconsciously, it becomes the ruling passion—after money-getting —of their lives,—a passion in which they are confirmed and strengthened by all the blandishments of the world, and all the seductions of the flesh. Any means which tend to gratify this passion, to realize this end, they hold to be lawful, and they can adopt them, however base, detestable, or shocking in themselves, with a quiet conscience and admirable self-complacency.

That the ruling motive or dominant instinct of Protestants, in their character of Protestants, is, at least under a negative point of view to destroy or elude Catholicity, is evident from the character of the variations which their Protestantism has undergone, and is daily and hourly undergoing. Examine these variations, and you will find that they each and all tend to remove Protestantism farther and farther from the Catholic standard, and to shelter it from the blows of Catholic assailants. Each successive reformer eliminates from his sect some Catholic doctrine which it may have retained, or modifies some element of which he sees the Catholic controversialist can take advantage. The tendency of the Protestant world, collectively and in each of its divisions and subdivisions, has been steadily in the direction from the Church against which it protests, and the progress which Protestants so loudly boast, has consisted, and still consists, in getting rid of what they originally retained in common with Catholics. The Protestant vanguard, which announces that the main body is at hand, has advanced very far, and retains less of Christian principle than was retained by the old heathen world in the times of the Apostles. Take your fully developed Transcendentalist, the last word of Protestantism, and you will find him divested of every Catholic principle, and, under the point of view of religion, reduced, not only to nudity, but to nihility. The poor man retains nothing, not even so much as a shadow. He is a Peter Schlemil, and has sold his shadow to the man in black. What can have reduced him to such straits,—driven him to such extremes? Love of truth, force of conviction? Nothing of the sort. Be not so simple as to pretend it. He assigns, and attempts to assign, no authority, no reason, for his nihilism. He even acknowledges that he has no reason to assign, and tells you that he only throws out what he thinks, without pretending to prove it. He is a seer, and utters what he sees, and you must take him at his word, or not at all. Why, then, does he rush into nihilism? Simply, because he is seer enough to see, that, if he admits that anything exist, he will be driven ultimately to acknowledge the truth of Catholicity. Rather than do that, he will sell his soul, as well as his shadow, to the man in black, and consent to deny his own existence. Almost every day, we meet intelligent Protestant gentlemen who frankly acknowledge that there is no alternative but Catholicity or no-religion, and yet who just as frankly tell us that they will not be Catholics. Not long since, a Protestant minister of respectable standing in this city assured us, in all seriousness, that he "would rather be damned than become a Catholic." We of course informed him that he could have his choice, for Almighty God forces no one to accept the gift of eternal life. This worthy minister is, no doubt, very ready to embrace the truth that does not convict him of error, if such truth there be; but if we may take him at his word, he is prepared to resist, at all hazards, the truth that would indict him. Is it truth, or his own opinion that he loves?

The mistake of our popular controversialists seems to arise from their supposition, that Protestantism can be learned from the symbolical books and theological writings of Protestants. Undoubtedly we can thus learn that Protestantism which is put forth to elude Catholicity, or to lure Catholics from their Church, and therefore a Protestantism highly important, for the sake of Catholics, to be studied and refuted; but not thus can we learn the Protestantism which lies in the Protestant mind and heart, and which it is necessary to refute for the sake of Protestants themselves. This Protestantism is not learned from symbolical books or theological writings, and but comparatively few Protestants themselves can give us a clear and distinct statement, much less a just account of it. We can seize it only in the historical developments and manifest tendencies of the Protestant movement, and explain it only by means of a thorough knowledge of human nature on the one hand, and of Catholic faith and theology on the other.

It appears to us, that our controversialists are mistaken, also, in regarding the more reputable sects—that is, the sects which, in their symbols and professions, have departed the least from the Catholic standard—as better exponents of the Protestant mind than the less reputable, and as those whose views it is the most important to study and refute. Nearly all the controversial works we have, originally written in the English language, are directed against the Anglican and Protestant Episcopal sects. We are not aware of a single Catholic work, written expressly against the so-called Evangelical sects, Presbyterians, Baptists, Methodists, or what we may call Pietism. And, with the exception of the profound and scientific work of Father Kollmann, against Unitarians,—too profound and scientific to be intelligible to those for whom it was written,—we have in English not a single work against Rationalism, which, in reality, has a larger number of adherents, in both England and this country, than either Anglicanism or Evangelicalism. This indicates a serious defect in our controversial literature, and seems to us to be owing to a false estimate of the relative importance of the several Protestant sects. There are, no doubt, many individuals included in the more reputable sects, who, if compelled to choose, would sooner return to the Church than follow the Protestant movement to its natural terminus; but they are only a small minority, and would hardly be missed in the sects to which they respectively belong. All the sects are on the move, tending somewhither. Not one of them is stationary. This they make their boast; and one of the most frequent and most effective charges they bring against the Church is, that she is not progressive, but remains immovable, insisting that we shall believe to-day the very doctrines which she taught and believed in the Dark Ages. The dominant tendency of any given sect is the tendency which the great majority of its members obey. Ascertain, then, the dominant tendency of each sect, and you have ascertained the direction in which the great majority of its members are moving, and will continue to move, if diverted or arrested by no foreign influence. But what, in fact, is the dominant tendency of each and every Protestant sect? Is there a single one whose successive developments, modifications, and changes tend to bring it nearer and nearer to the Catholic standard, and to prepare it for communion with the Church? Nobody can pretend it. Everybody knows that every sect is moving in the opposite direction, and that the dominant tendency of the Protestant world, a few individuals excepted, is towards Rationalism, Transcendentalism, and therefore towards pantheism, atheism, nihilism. This is decisive, and proves that those sects which have departed farthest from Catholicity are the truest reprentatives of the Protestant spirit, and the best exponents of genuine Protestantism, as the fully developed man is a better exponent of humanity than the new-born infant. What it is most important, then, to study and refute, must be the principles of these more advanced sects, not those of the sects who remain behind, or are still rocking in their cradle, and therefore Transcendentalism, rather than Anglicanism.

Undoubtedly we see, from time to time, a conservative, perhaps a retrograde, movement in the bosom of the several sects. But this movement is the result, in most cases, of alarm for the credit or prosperity of the sect, rather than of any deep or sincere attachment to the principles or doctrines the sect threatens to leave behind. Besides, the movement is ever but a mere eddy in the stream, or a slight ripple on its surface. It reaches never to the bottom of the sect, and arrests or diverts never its main current. This is evident from the late Oxford movement, one of the most important movements of the kind which has recently been witnessed. There was a time when timid Protestants feared, and many good Catholics hoped, that it would restore England to Catholic faith and unity; but no sooner did it become manifest to all the world that its tendency was to communion with Rome, than it was arrested. A few individuals became reconciled to the Church, but the majority of those at first favorably disposed towards it avowedly or tacitly abandoned it, lapsed into the ordinary channel of their sect, and suffered themselves to be borne onward with it towards its natural term, —no-religion, or nihilism. So it is in every sect in which a similar movement takes place. As soon as it is clear that its tendency is anti-Protestant, that is, towards Rome, it is arrested, and only here and there an individual dares henceforth avow his adherence to it.

It may be thought by some, that the more reputable sects are the real bulwarks of Protestantism, and that, if we refute them, the less reputable sects will fall of themselves. Doubtless this is one reason why our English and American Catholic controversialists direct their attacks so exclusively against Anglicanism and Protestant Episcopalianism. But we are disposed to believe that the real supporters of Protestantism, if not in themselves, at least in their views and influence, are the sects which are farthest removed from Catholicity. If there was nothing below Anglicanism to which Anglicans could descend, we should have short work with it, and the Anglican and Episcopal sects would soon disappear. The more reputable sects, comparing themselves with the immense Protestant world below them, look upon themselves as substantially orthodox, and are more disposed to dwell on what they retain that others have given up, than on what they themselves lack which we have. They form, too, a sort of aristocracy, a *haute noblesse*, in the sectarian world, and are pleased with their rank, and unwilling to forego the importance it gives them in their own eyes. Moreover, the sects below them, all Protestant, and of their own race, smooth the descent for them in proportion as they are driven from their more elevated position, and enable them to descend by an easy gradation, by almost imperceptible steps, to the lowest depths of error. If the High-churchman is defeated, he can descend to Low-churchism; if the Low-churchman is defeated, he can descend to Evangelicalism; if the Evangelical is defeated, he can descend either, on the one hand, to Rationalism, or, on the other, to Transcendentalism,—for, in point of fact, Evangelicalism is nothing but a loose combination of Rationalism and Transcendentalism. It is far easier for a High-churchman to become a Low-churchman than it is for him to become a Catholic, and always is the next step in the descending scale far easier to take than the next step in the ascending scale.

> "Facilis descensus Averno:
> Noctes atque dies patet atri janua Ditis;
> Sed revocare gradum superasque evadere ad auras,
> Hoc opus, hic labor est."

As long as there is a lower step that can be taken without abandoning the essential element of Protestantism, the defeat of the more reputable sects, on the ground they profess to occupy, will do little for their conversion; for they will never acknowledge, even to themselves, that they are defeated, so long as there is any conceivable Protestant ground from which they are not actually driven. It is owing to the fact that Protestants now claim as Protestant all the territory between the ground occupied by Dr. Pusey and that occupied by M. Proudhon, and thus have a larger field for advance or retreat, that we find their conversion in our times so much more difficult than it was formerly. St. Francis of Sales, Bishop of Geneva, himself alone regained seventy-two thousand Protestants to the Church; we are aware of no bishop in the present age, however zealous, learned, able, or saintly, who has the consolation of recovering anything approaching a like number. We cannot, therefore, but regard the views and tendencies of the more advanced sects as those which it is now altogether the most important to study and refute.

Not only does Protestantism, as our divines have from the first maintained, logically lead to the denial of all religion, to atheism, and therefore to nihilism,—for to deny that God exists is to deny that anything is,—but it is now clear to all who have examined the subject, that the great body of Protestants are really prepared, as occasion may require, to follow it thus far. The majority of the Protestant world are really, if not avowedly, Transcendentalists to-day, as every one knows who is acquainted with recent Protestant literature; and Strauss, Feuerbach, Bauer, Parker, Emerson, Michelet, Quinet, and Proudhon have more sympathizers than Hengstenberg, Pusey, Seabury, Nevin, Alexander, Beecher, and Kirk. Proudhon is nothing but a consistent Red Republican; and where is the Protestant, in case he is not restrained by his temporal interest, who does not sympathize with Red Republicanism? Have not Protestants very generally, in England and this country, sympathized with Mazzini and his Roman Republic? Nay, was it not in concert with, and by aid even of, the more reputable Protestant sects, that he expelled the Sovereign Pontiff, and established his Reign of Terror? Is not Protestant sympathy very generally enlisted in favor of the infidel and socialistic revolutions in Europe, all of which have been stirred up and helped on by Protestants, under the lead of their ministers, in the name of liberty, but really for the purpose of overthrowing and annihilating the Church? Evident is it, then, that they will go, as a body, to all lengths which they find necessary to accomplish their purpose of hostility to Catholicity; and as they never can even logically overthrow the Church, so long as the existence of anything is admitted, they must deny everything, and rush into nihilism.

It is necessary, then, if we wish to arrest the Protestant movement, and do what in us lies to save the souls of Protestants, that we reason with them, not as if it were a sufficient refutation of them to prove that they are tending to atheism, but as men who believe nothing, and build up our argument against them from the very foundation. Prove to them that their doctrines are anti-Christian, and they will only beg you to inform them wherefore that is a reason for not believing them; prove Christianity to be true, and they will merely beg you to prove your proofs, and thus demand of you an infinite series of proofs. They are, under the point of view of religion and philosophy, wholly rotten, and from the sole of the foot to the crown of the head there is no soundness in them. Nothing will answer for them that does not descend as low as the last denial that it is possible for the human mind to conceive, and drive them from position to position, till there is no position remaining outside of the Church which they can even affect to take.

Protestantism as we now find it, and even as it was, virtually, in the sixteenth century, is not merely the denial of certain Catholic dogmas, is not merely the denial of the Christian revelation itself, but really the denial of all religion and morality, natural and revealed. It denies reason itself, as far as it is in the power of man to deny it, and is no less unsound as philosophy than it is as faith. It extinguishes the light of nature no less than the light of revelation, and is as false in relation to the natural order as to the supernatural. Even when Protestants make a profession of believing in revelation, they discredit reason. In regard to reason, they are, even when professing to believe, very generally Pyrrhonists. The Evangelical sects, for instance, do not merely deny the sufficiency of reason as our only guide, but they deny its trustworthiness altogether, and assert that we must take for our guide the Scriptures, not as interpreted by an authority accredited to reason, nor as interpreted by reason itself, but as interpreted by the private illuminations of the spirit. They thus supersede, as it were, annihilate, reason, and reduce themselves to the condition of irrational beings, virtually declare man incapable of receiving a supernatural revelation, and then call upon him to believe the Bible, and to walk by the supernatural light of faith. As long as their enthusiasm lasts, as long as they can keep up a sort of unnatural excitement, they may half persuade themselves that they are supernaturally illuminated; but as soon as their fever abates, and they sink to their ordinary level, they experience the most painful misgivings, the supposed supernatural light fades away, and, having no reason on which to fall back, they can believe nothing, and either openly avow themselves infidels, or, merely keep up a show of piety, seek relief by devoting all their energies to worldly distinctions or pleasures. They begin by proposing revelation, not as the complement, but as the substitute, of reason; and when revelation fails, as fail it must if not supported by motives of credibility addressed to reason, and satisfactory to it, nothing remains for them but universal skepticism.

The formalistic sects, as the Anglican and Episcopalian, reach the same result though by a different process. Building on sham, taking the shadow for the substance, and denying both the substance and the light the shadow necessarily implies,—or, in other words, refusing to draw from their premises their logical consequences, afraid to make a complete proposition, to say two and two make four, and stopping short with saying two and two, lest they lose the *via media*, and roll over to Rome, or fall off into Dissent,—they destroy reason by mutilating and enslaving it, and find themselves without anything by or to which a supernatural revelation can be accredited. The Rationalistic sects, seeing the errors of Evangelicals and formalists, think to save reason by resolving the supernatural into the natural; but in doing this they lose revelation, and therefore reason,—because no man can deny revelation without denying reason, and because reason without revelation is insufficient for herself, inadequate to the solution of the great problems of life which she herself raises. Beginning by asking of reason more than she can give, they end by discarding her and falling into universal skepticism, the ultimate term of all Protestantism.

Protestants, it is well known, are able to keep up the self-delusion that they are believers only by obstinately refusing to push their principles to their legitimate consequences, and by shutting their eyes to the objections which may be suggested or urged against them. The condition of a Protestant wishing to retain his Protestantism, and yet keep up the appearance of being a believer, is most pitiable. The poor man has no mental freedom, no intellectual courage, but is a cowardly slave, with all the weakness and meanness characteristic of slaves in general. He never dares trust himself to his principles, and follow them out to their remotest logical consequences, and is doomed, turn which way he will, to be inconsequent, and to submit to a most tyrannical and capricious master; for otherwise he would find himself, on the one hand, approaching too near Catholicity to remain a Protestant, or, on the other, too near to nihilism to even pretend to be a believer. Alas for the poor man! He hugs his chains, and, by the strangest infatuation imaginable, fancies his slavery is freedom. All who have studied the subject know well that Protestants are Protestants, not by virtue of reason, but in spite of reason,—not because they reason, but solely because they do not, will not, and dare not reason. The rejection of reason is their fundamental vice. Reason is our natural light, and, though of no value out of its sphere, in its sphere is inerrable. It does not suffice of itself for all the wants of the human soul, but its annihilation reduces us below the condition of men, and renders us incapable of receiving even a supernatural revelation. Revelation does not abrogate or supersede reason; it restores it and supplies its deficiencies. Grace supposes nature. Christianity is a system of pure grace,—is, in fact, a supernatural creation, but a supernatural creation *for* the natural, designed to repair the damage nature has incurred by guilt, and to enable man to attain the end to which his Creator originally appointed him. Man is not for the Sacraments, but the Sacraments are for man. The first office of grace is to restore nature, or to heal its wounds; having restored it to health, it elevates it, indeed, but always retains it, and uses it. Here is the grand fact that Protestant theologians always overlook. They, in reality, always present nature and grace as two antagonistic powers, and suppose the presence of the one must be the physical destruction of the other. Luther and Calvin, weary of the good works, and shrinking from the efforts to acquire the personal virtues enjoined by Catholicity, began their so-called reform by asserting the total depravity of human nature, and maintaining that original sin involved the loss of reason and freewill, reducing man physically to the condition of irrational animals, and superadding the penalty of guilt. Here, in the very outset, they denied natural reason, all natural religion, and all natural morality, and consequently asserted for man in the natural order, left to his natural powers and faculties, universal skepticism and moral indifference; for without reason there can be no belief, and without free-will no moral obligation, no moral difference of actions.

The Arminians, indeed, saw this, and sought to remedy it by reasserting the natural law; but as they still held to total depravity, the reassertion amounted to nothing; or, if they sometimes abandoned total depravity, they rushed to the opposite extreme, and reasserted Pelagianism or semi-Pelagianism, and restricted the office of grace to enabling us to do more easily what, nevertheless, we are able to do without it. If they succeeded in escaping the peculiar error of Luther and Calvin, they fell into Rationalism. As Luther and Calvin annihilated reason and free-will, the whole spiritual nature of man, and made man purely passive in the work of regeneration and Christian perfection, the Arminians, become Rationalists, disregarding the necessity of grace, made the natural law sufficient, and asserted only a natural morality. But experience proving the inadequacy of the natural law, when taken without its revealed complement and sanction,—of natural morality, when not elevated by supernatural Christian virtue,—they, like the others, lapsed, of necessity, into the same skepticism.

The error of each class is avoidable only by understanding that grace always supposes nature, and that grace without nature would be as a telescope to a man without eyes. Revelation supposes reason, and we as effectually deny Christianity when we deny reason as when we deny revelation; both must be asserted with equal firmness and emphasis, each in its own sphere, in relation to its appropriate office, or nothing is asserted. To deny reason is, *a fortiori*, to deny revelation, and to deny revelation is virtually to deny reason; because the evidences of the fact of revelation are amply sufficient to satisfy reason, and because reason, without revelation, being undeniably insufficient to solve the problems which torture the mind without faith, and to satisfy the craving of our nature for something above itself, cannot maintain itself practically in credit, and necessarily loses its authority. Philosophy, undoubtedly, rests for its basis on natural reason, otherwise we should be unable to distinguish it from Catholic theology, or to draw any intelligible distinction between the natural and supernatural; but without the light of revelation, we shall never be able, in our fallen condition, to construct a sound and adequate philosophy. So, on the other hand, without a sound and adequate philosophy, we can never possess a true and adequate theology; for as revelation is necessary as an instrument in the construction of philosophy, so is philosophy necessary as an instrument in the construction of theology,—that is, theology as a science, and as distinguishable from faith. Hence, in all courses of Catholic instruction, the student makes his philosophy before he proceeds to his theology.

It is clear enough, from what we have said, that the most pressing want of Protestants, under the intellectual point of view, is a sound philosophy, which, so to speak, shall rehabilitate reason, and restore them to natural religion and morality. They have lost reason, and have fallen below the religion or morality which lies in the natural order, and which all revealed religion and morality presuppose. The philosophy needed is nowhere to be found in the Protestant world, and cannot possibly be created by Protestants, for the reason that the revelation which must serve as its instrument they have not, or at best only some detached fragments of it. The only respectable school of philosophy to be found amongst Protestants is the Scottish School of Reid and Stewart; but this school dogmatizes rather than philosophizes. It very justly assumes that all philosophy must proceed from certain indemonstrable principles, and it does not err essentially in its inventory of these principles; but it fails to establish them, or to show us that they have scientific validity. It calls them the constituent principles of human belief, and says, very truly, that they must be admitted, or all science, all philosophy, is out of the question. But this is no more than Hume, whom it aims to refute, himself said. Is science or philosophy possible? is the precise question to be answered. Without the conditions you assert, we grant it is not possible; but what then? Therefore your alleged principles are sound? Why not: Therefore all science, all philosophy, is impossible?

No doubt, the Scottish School has protested vehemently against the skepticism of Hume, but its refutation of that skepticism is a mere paralogism, a simple begging of the question, and therefore, scientifically considered, worthless.

But, after all, we cannot place our chief reliance on philosophy as an instrument in the conversion of Protestants. Philosophy is too indirect and too slow in its operations to meet their wants. They are too far gone, too restless, too impatient, too averse to calm reflection and continuous thought, to listen to us while we set the true philosophy before them, or to submit to the labor absolutely requisite to comprehend and appreciate profound philosophical science. An age of balloons, steam-cars, and lightning telegraphs is not exactly the age for philosophers. Moreover, Protestant perversity would find in the necessity of the long and patient thought, and close and subtile reasoning, demanded by philosophy, an objection to our religion itself. Your religion, they would say, if true, is intended for all mankind, and therefore should be within the reach of every capacity. The thought and reasoning necessary to create or understand the philosophy you insist upon, transcend the capacity of all but the gifted few, and therefore, if necessary to establish your religion, prove that your religion is not true. We might, indeed, reply, that the thought and reasoning objected to are necessary to refute the errors of Protestants, not simply to establish our religion; but that would amount to nothing in practice. The nature of the Protestant is to devise the most subtile errors in his power, and to find an objection to our religion in the very labor he makes necessary for their refutation. When he objects, he may be as subtile and as abstruse as he pleases; but when we reply, he insists that we shall be popular, and never go beyond the depth of the most ordinary capacity,— that we shall answer the objection not only to the mind that raises it, but to the minds of all men. Only the candid among Protestants would acknowledge the justness of our reply, and these would fail to comprehend it; for if you find a candid Protestant, you may safely conclude that he lacks intelligence, as when you find an intelligent Protestant you may be sure that he lacks candor. There must, then, be some briefer and more expeditious way of dealing with Protestants than that of philosophy, if we wish to affect them favorably.

We have defined Protestantism to be hostility to the Church, and virtually nihilism, because Protestants in general, sooner than return to the Church will push their hostility to its last consequence, which is the denial of God, therefore of all existence and existences. But this is not all that we have to say of the matter. No man loves error for its own sake, or wills what does not appear to him to be good. The natural heart of every man recoils instinctively from atheism; and it is seldom, if ever, that one without a fearful and even a protracted struggle abandons all faith and piety, resigns all hope of an hereafter, and consents to place himself in the category of the beasts that perish. Hatred, no doubt, will carry a man to great lengths; but even hatred must have its cause, real or imaginary. Hatred is love reversed, and intense hatred of one thing is the reverse action of intense love of something else. Protestants hate the Church. Wherefore? Because they love truth? Nonsense. Because they believe her false, and destructive to the souls of men? Nonsense again. We hope there is no Catholic so stupid as to believe it. Their hatred of the Church has nothing to do with concern for truth or for salvation. A large portion of them believe in no truth, in no salvation; a larger portion still are of opinion that all men will be saved, and that truth is whatever seems to a man to be true; and the remainder hold that the Church is substantially orthodox, and that salvation is attainable in her communion, as well as in their own. Whatever, then, the cause of their hatred of the Church, it is a cause unconnected with considerations of another world, or with truth as such.

We need not look far for this something which Protestants love and the Church condemns, and for condemning which they are full of wrath against her. It is nothing very recondite, or very difficult to seize. We make quite too much of Protestantism, which is, in reality, a very vulgar thing, and lies altogether on the surface of life. Protestantism is nothing more or less than that spirit of lawlessness which leads every one to wish to have his own way,—very common in women and children, and perhaps not less common in men, only they have, generally, a better faculty of concealing it. Objectively defined, it is expressed in the common saying, "Forbidden fruit is sweetest;" and subjectively, it is a craving for what is prohibited, because prohibited. It imagines that the sovereign good is in what the law forbids, and opposes the Church because she upholds the law, —hates the law because the law restrains it, duty because duty obliges it; and since, as long as it admits the existence of God, it must admit duty, it denies God; and since, as long as it admits the existence of anything, it must admit the existence of God, it denies everything, and lapses into nihilism. Here is the whole mystery of the matter,—Protestantism in a nutshell.

The source of this impatience of restraint, and this desire to have one's own way, is the pride natural to the human heart, the root of every vice and of every sin. "Your eyes shall be opened, and ye shall be as gods, knowing good and evil," said the serpent to Eve; and she reached forth her hand, plucked the forbidden fruit, ate, and sin and death were in the world. Pride is, on the one hand, a denial of our dependence, and, on the other, the assertion of our own sufficiency. Here you may see the origin and the essential characteristic of Protestantism, which is as old as the first motion of pride or of resistance to the will of God. Protestantism, after all, is more ancient than we commonly concede. Dr. Johnson, in his Dictionary, would have been as correct if he had said the Devil was the first Protestant, as he was in saying that he was "the first Whig." It offends pride to be compelled to acknowledge our own insufficiency, to admit that we cannot be trusted to follow our own inclinations, that we must be subjected to metes and bounds, and placed under tutors and masters, who say, Do this, Do that; and we are galled, and we resolve we will not endure it; we will break the withes that bind us; we will stand up on our own two feet, and assert our freedom in face of heaven, earth and hell. Hence we see Protestants, in every age, mounting the tallest pair of stilts they can find or construct, and with more or less vehemence, with more or less eclat, according to the circumstances of time and place, magniloquently asserting the "inborn" rights of man, proudly swearing to be free, to stand up in their native dignity, in the full and resplendent majesty of their own manhood, and making such appeals and forming such alliances as they fancy will best secure their independence, relieve them from all restraints, and give them the opportunity to live as they list.

Such is the general and essential characteristic of Protestantism; its particular character or form is determined by, and varies with, the circumstances of time and place. In itself, as Balmes well shows, it is a phenomenon peculiar to no period of history, but whatever it has that is peculiar it borrows from the character of the epoch in which it appears. It is always essentially the spirit that works in the children of disobedience, but the form under which the disobedience manifests itself depends on exterior and accidental causes. What it resists is what it finds offensive to human pride, to pure, unmitigated egotism, and what it asserts is always asserted as the means of securing free scope to its independent action. In the sixteenth century, pride found itself galled by submission to the Church, for the Church could not tolerate its wild speculations and its theological errors. It then denied the authority of the Church; and in order to make a show of justifying its denial, it asserted the supremacy of the Scriptures, interpreted by private reason, or by the private Spirit. Soon it found that the assertion of the supremacy of the Scriptures, so interpreted, limited its sovereignty, and that it was as galling to its sense of independence to submit to a dead book as to a living Church, and then it denied the Scriptures, and, to justify its denial, asserted the supremacy of reason. But reason, again, galled it, reminded it of its dependence, and would not suffer it to live as it listed. Then it cried out, Down with reason, and up with sentiment!— a Transcendental element paramount to reason,—and thus reached the jumping-off place. In order to resist effectually the Pope, it at one time, as in England, proclaims the divine right of kings; and then, in order to get rid of the divine right of kings, it proclaims the divine right of the people, or, to speak more accurately, of the mob; and finally, in order to get rid of the authority of the mob, it proclaims the divine right of each and every individual, and declares that each and every individual is God, the only God,—thus resolving God into men, and all men into one man, which implies the right of every man to take the entire universe to himself, and possess it as his own property. You laugh at its absurdity? Upon our conscience, we invent nothing, we exaggerate nothing, and say nothing more than is asserted, in sober earnest, by men whom the Protestant world delights to honor.

Turn Protestantism over as you will, analyze it to your heart's content, you can make nothing more or less of it than mere vulgar pride, and the various efforts pride makes from time to time and place to place to secure its own gratification, to realize the assertion of the serpent, "Ye shall be as gods knowing good and evil,"—that is, ye shall know good and evil of yourselves, as God knows them of himself, and shall be independent, and act as seemeth to you good, even as God is independent and doth according to his will, not as subject to a power above himself, and in obedience to another will than his own. Just see the proof of this, in the sympathy now universally given to every revolt against established authority. All your modern literature is Satanic, and approves, and teaches us to approve, every rebel, whether against parental, popular, royal, or Divine authority. The Protestant readers of *Paradise Lost* sympathize with Lucifer, in his war against the Almighty, and if they had been in heaven, as one of our friends suggests, would have sided with him. Our friend, J. D. Nourse,* defending himself against our strictures on his book, boldly asserts that God is a despot, and his government a despotism,—nay, that all authority is despotic.

* See below. *Authority and Liberty.*

Finding the essence of Protestantism to be mere vulgar pride, that it is a moral disease rather than an intellectual aberration, it is evident that we are to treat it as a vice rather than as an error, and Protestants as sinners rather than as simply unbelievers or misbelievers. This may not be very flattering to their pride; nevertheless, it is the only way they deserve to be treated, and the only way in which they can be treated for their good. We honor them quite too much when we treat them as men whose heads are wrong, but whose hearts are sound. The wrongness of the head is the consequence of the rottenness of the heart. The remedy must be applied to the seat of the disease, or it will be wholly ineffectual; and as the disease is in the will rather than in the intellect, we must, as we do with sinners in general, avail ourselves of motives that tend to persuade the will, rather than of those which tend primarily to convince the understanding. Get the heart right, and the intellect will soon rectify itself.

Now it is certain, that, so far as the great body of Protestants are concerned, it is of no use to appeal to any love of truth or regard for salvation they may be supposed to have. They are very generally prepared, with Macbeth, "to jump the world to come," and think only how they shall manage matters for this world. They are worldly, and their wisdom is earthly, sensual, devilish; even their virtues, their honesty, their uprightness of conduct, have reference, not to God, but to their justification, either in the eyes of the world, or in the eyes of their own pride. They are too proud or too vain to do this or that act which is contrary to good manners. We must therefore approach them as men who are wedded to this world, who are Protestants for the sake of living for this world alone, and refuse to be Catholics because Catholicity enjoins humility, detachment from the world, and a life of self-denial and mortification, lived for God alone. As long as it is conceded, or as long as they believe it true, that their Protestantism is more favorable to man, regarded solely as an inhabitant of this world, than Catholicity, we cannot get them to listen to what we have to say for our religion. If they hear, it will be as if they heard not.

But it is a fact, as clearly demonstrable, in its way, as any mathematical problem, that Catholicity enjoins the only normal life for man, even in this world, letting alone what it secures us in another. Human pride just now takes the form of Socialism, and Socialism is *the* Protestantism of our times. It is human pride under this form that we must address, and show to the Socialists, not—as some silly and misguided creatures calling themselves Catholics, and sometimes occupying editorial chairs, are accustomed to do—that Catholicity favors them by accepting their Socialism, but that it favors the object they profess to have at heart,—that it is the true and only genuine Socialism, the basis of all veritable society, and the only known instrument of well-being, either for the individual or for the race. We must show, that, under the social point of view, under the various relations of civilization, Protestantism is an egregious blunder, and precipitates its adherents into the precise evils they really wish to avoid. That it does so is evident enough to all who have eyes to see, and is proved by the very complaints Protestants make of their own movements. Their own complaints of themselves show, to use a vulgar proverb, that they always "jump from the frying-pan into the fire," in attempting to better their condition. They could not endure the authority of the Church; they resisted it, and fell under the tyranny of the sect, even in their own view of the case, a thousand times less tolerable. They rebelled, in the name of liberty, against the Pope, and fell under the iron rule of the civil despot; in England, they could not endure the Lord's bishops, and they fell under the Lord's presbyters, and from Lord's presbyters under the Lord's brethren, and from Lord's brethren under the capricious tyranny of their own fancies and passions. In political and social reforms it has fared no better with them. In France, the *Constituante* were more oppressive than the old monarchy, the *Gironde* than the *Constituante*, the *Mountain* than the *Gironde*; and the present French government, in order to save society from complete destruction, is obliged to adopt measures more stringent than ever Charles the Tenth or Louis Philippe dared venture upon. The overthrow of one tyranny leads to another of necessity more heartless and oppressive, because weaker and possessing a less firm hold on the affections of the people. A strong government can afford to be lenient. A weak government must be stringent. Yet the wise men of the age rush on in their wild-goose chase after worldly felicity, while it flies ever the faster before them. Like the gambler, who has played away his patrimony, his wife's jewels, and pawned his hat and coat, but keeps playing on, they insist on another throw,—though losing all, fancy they are just agoing to recover all, and make a fortune equal to their boundless wishes. If they could but see themselves as the unexcited bystanders see them, they would throw away the dice, and rush with self-loathing from the *hell* in which they find only their own ruin.

The principle on which Protestants seek even worldly felicity is false, and we can say nothing better of them, than that they prove themselves what the sacred Scriptures would term fools in following it. When was it ever known that pride, following itself, did not meet mortification, or that any worldly distinction, or good, sought for its own sake, did not either baffle pursuit, or prove a canker to the heart? Did you ever see a man running after fame that ever overtook it, or a man always nursing his health that was ever other than sickly? Have you no eyes, no ears, no understanding? Fame comes, if at all, unsought, greatness follows in the train of humility, and happiness, coy to the importunate wooer throws herself into the arms of him who treats her with indifference. All experience proves the truth of the principle, "Seek first the kingdom of God, and his justice, and all these things shall be superadded unto you." Take it as inspiration, as the word of God, or as a maxim of human prudence, it is equally true, and he who runs against it only proves his own folly. "Live while you live," says the Protestant Epicurean. Be it so; live while you live, but live you cannot, unless you live to God, according to the principles of the

Catholic religion. Live now you do not, and you know you do not; you are only *just agoing*, and not a few of you fear that you are never even agoing to live, as all your poetry, with its deep pathos and melodious wail, too amply proves.

Here comes in to our aid the excellent work before us. It exactly meets the present state of the Protestant world, and makes the only kind of appeal to which, in their present mood, they will listen. Its author makes no apology for Catholicity, he offers no direct argument for its truth; he simply comes forward and compares the respective influences of Protestantism and Catholicity on European civilization, and shows, that, while Catholicity tends unceasingly to advance civilization, Protestantism as unceasingly tends to savagism, and that it is to its hostile influences we owe the slow progress of European civilization during the last three centuries. He shows that Protestantism is hostile to liberty, to philosophy, to the higher mental culture, to art, to equality, to political and social well-being. He shows it, we say; not merely asserts, but proves it, by unanswerable arguments and undeniable facts. If any one doubts our judgment, we refer him to the work itself, and beg him to gainsay its facts, or answer its reasoning, if he can. The Protestant who reads it will hardly boast of his Protestantism again.

AUTHORITY AND LIBERTY.

APRIL, 1849.

A CRITIC in this city expresses surprise that this book could have been written by a young man born and brought up in Kentucky; but we see no reason why it could not have been written by a young man as well as by an old man, and in Kentucky as well as in any other part of the Union. We suppose

---

* Remarks on the Past, and its Legacies to American Society. By J. D. NOURSE. Louisville (Ky.): Morton & Griswold. 1847. 16mo. pp. 223.

they read and think in Kentucky as well as in Massachusetts; and it is not more strange that a young Kentuckian than that a Bostonian should expend a good deal of thought in elaborating a system compounded of truth and falsehood, common-place and crude speculation. The book certainly indicates some natural and acquired ability, but no ability peculiar to either side of the Alleghanies. The substance of it may be read any day in Schlegel, Carlyle, Macaulay, Guizot, Bancroft, and *The Boston Quarterly Review*. We have discovered nothing new or striking in the views it sets forth, or if now and then something we never met with before, it is usually something we have no desire to meet with again.

The author tells us, in his brief *advertisement*, "that it may seem presumptuous for a young backwoodsman ...... to enter the lists with Schlegel, Guizot, and Macaulay." We think it not only may *seem* so, but that it actually *is* so; for Schlegel and Guizot—to say nothing of Macaulay—are at least men of varied and profound erudition. They are scholars, and have not derived their learning at second or third hand. Mr. Nourse may rival, nay, surpass them, in his ambition and self-confidence; but he must live long, and enjoy advantages of study which neither Kentucky nor Massachusetts affords, before he rivals them in any thing else, or can do much else than travesty them. Not that we ragard either of them as a safe guide. Guizot is eclectic and humanitarian; and Schlegel is too mystical, and too ambitious, to reduce within a theory matters which by their very nature transcend any theory the human mind can form or comprehend. Mr. Nourse has, if you will, extraordinary natural abilities, an honest and ingenuous disposition; but he has not yet begun to master the present, far less the whole past. He has a vague recognition of religion, concedes some influence to Christianity in civilizing the world; but he is without faith, and has yet to learn the very rudiments of the Christian creed. We doubt, also, whether he is able to give even the outlines of a single historical period, or of a single people or institution, with sufficient accuracy to enable them to serve as the basis of a single sound induction. One should know the *facts* of history before proceeding to construct its *philosophy*. He will forgive us, therefore, if we tell him that we do regard him as not a little presumptuous in attempting a work for which he has in reality not a single qualification. He writes, indeed, with earnestness; his style, though somewhat cramped, and deficient in freedom and ease, is dignified, simple, clear, and terse, occasionally rich and beautiful; but this cannot atone for the general incorrectness of his statements, or the crudeness and unsoundness of his speculations.

With sound premises and freed from the prejudices of his education, we doubt not, Mr. Nourse might arrive at passable conclusions; but he is ruined by his love of theorizing, his false philosophy, and his unsound theology. He may have philanthropic impulses and generous sentiments; he may mean to be a Christian, and actually believe that he is a Christian believer; but, whether he knows it or not, the order of thought which he seeks to develop and propagate is neither more nor less than the old Alexandrian Syncretism, as obtained through German Mysticism, French Eclecticism, and Boston Transcendentalism. Radically considered, his system, if system it can be called, is the old Alexandrian system, which sprang up in the third century of our era, as the rival of the Christian Church, ascended the throne of the Cæsars with Julian the Apostate, and fled to Persia in the sixth century, when Justinian closed the last schools of philosophy at Athens. This system was an attempted fusion of all the particular forms of Gentilism, moulded into a shape as nearly like Christianity as it might be, and intended to dispute with it the empire of the world. It borrowed largely from Christianity,—copied the forms of its hierarchy, and many of its dogmas; which has led some in more recent times, who never consult chronology, to charge the Church with having herself copied her hierarchy, her ritual, and her principle doctrines from it. It made no direct war on the Christian Symbol; it simply denied or derided the sources whence it was obtained, and the authority which Christian faith always presupposes. It called itself *Philosophy*, and its pretension was to raise philosophy to the dignity of religion, and to do by it what Christianity professes to do by faith and an external and supernaturally accredited revelation. It was, therefore, Gentile Rationalism, and, in fact, Gentile Rationalism carried to its last degree of perfection. It is this Rationalism, met and refuted by the great Fathers of the third, fourth, and fifth centuries, that lies at the bottom of our author's thought, and which he labors to reproduce with a zeal—we cannot say ability—not unworthy of a disciple of Plotinus, Proclus, and Porphyrius.

This should not surprise us. There is nothing new under the sun. The old Gentile world exhausted human reason ; and it is not possible, even with a full knowledge of all the Church teaches, taking human reason alone as the basis of our system, to surpass the old Alexandrian Syncretism, or Neoplatonism, as it is sometimes called. In constructing it, the human mind had present to it, as materials, all the labors and traditions of Gentilism in all ages and nations, and also all the teachings and traditions of Jews and Christians, as well as of the Jewish and early Christian sects ; and it was, from the point of view of Rationalism, the *resumé* of the whole. It was the last word of heathendom. In it Gentilism, collecting and combining all that was not the Christian Church, exerted all her forces and all her energies for a last desperate battle against the Nazarene, against the triumph of the Cross. Catholicity or Rationalism is, as every one knows or may know, the only alternative that remains to us since the preaching of the Gospel. Impossible, then, is it to depart from Catholicity without falling back on Rationalism, and, if a little profound and consistent, upon Neoplatonism, as Rationalism in its fulness and integrity. All heresies are simply attempts to return to this Rationalism, and in it they find their complement, as may be historically as well as logically established. All your modern philosophies are regarded as profound and complete only as they approach it. Kant, Schelling, Hegel, Cousin, Leroux, De Lamennais, Hermes, Schleiermacher, Carlyle, Emerson, Parker, all belong to the Alexandrian school, and only reproduce, more or less successfully, its teachings, and to the best of their ability renew the war it waged against the Christian Church.

It is no objection to what we assert, that the sects and many of the modern philosophies retain some or even the greater part of the Christian dogmas. Neoplatonism did as much. We must not forget that Neoplatonism is subsequent to the Christian Church; that it took its rise in the school of Ammonius Saccas, in the beginning of the third century of our era; that it received its form and development from Plotinus, who flourished about the year of our Lord 260; and that it proposed itself as the rival rather than the antagonist of Christianity. Its aim was to satisfy the ever-recurring and indestructible religious wants of the human soul, without recognizing the Christian Church, or bowing to the authority of the Nazarene. It was not the Christian doctrines, abstracted from the Christian Church, and received as philosopy on the authority of reason or even private inspirations, instead of the authority of our Lord and his supernaturally commissioned teachers, that it opposed. It was willing to accept Christianity as a philosophy, or a part of philosophy; but not as a religion, far less as a religion complete in itself and excluding all others. Hence, it, as well as the Church, taught one Supreme God existing as a Trinity in Unity, the immortality of the soul, the fall of man and the corruption of human nature, the necessity of redemption, self-denial and the practice of austere virtue; that we are bound to worship God, must live for him, and can attain to supreme felicity only in attaining to an ineffable union with him. In the simple province of philosophy it was often profound and just. In many things it and Christianity ran parallel one with the other. Not unfrequently do the Alexandrian philosophers talk like Christian Fathers, and Christian Fathers talk like Alexandrian philosophers. There is Neoplatonism in St. Gregory Nazianzen, in St. Basil, and St. Augustine. The most renowned of the Fathers studied in its schools, as distinguished Doctors now study in the schools of the philosophers of France and Germany. But Neoplatonism was at bottom a philosophy, and whatever it held from Christianity, it held as philosophy, as resting on a human, not a Divine basis. The philosophers transformed Christianity, so far as they accepted it, into a philosophy; while the Fathers made Neoplatonism, so far as they did not reject it, subservient to Christianity, to the statement and explication of Christian theology to the human understanding, keeping it always within the province of reason, and never allowing it to become the arbiter of the dogmas of faith, or to supersede or interfere with the Divine authority on which alone they were to be meekly and submissively received. The Fathers, therefore, were not less Christian for the philosophy they did not reject, nor the Alexandrians the less Gentile Rationalists for the Christian doctrines they borrowed. One may embrace, avowedly, all Christian doctrine, without approaching the Christian order, if, as Hermes proposed, he embraces it as philosophy, or on the authority of reason; for the Christian, to be a Christian believer, must believe God, and therefore Christianity, because it is his supernatural word, not because it is the word of human reason or human sentiment, as contend our modern Liberal Christians.

It, would be interesting to show historically the resemblance of the whole modern un-Catholic world to the old Alexandrian world represented by Plotinus, Jamblicus, Porphyrius, Proclus, and Julian the Apostate;—how each heresiarch and each modern philosopher only reproduces what the old Christian Fathers fought against and defeated,—how every progress in this boasted age of progress only tends to bring us back to the system which the Gregories, the Basils, and their associates combated from the Christian pulpit and the Episcopal chair; but we have neither the space nor the learning to do it as it should be done. Yet no one who has studied with tolerable care the learned Gentilism of the third, fourth, and fifth centuries of our era, and is passably well acquainted with the modern Rationalism of France and Germany, and the movements of the various heretical sects in our day, can doubt that our own nineteenth century is distinguished for its return to Gentilism, and has nearly reproduced it under its most perfect form. The separate forms of heathenism had become effete; no one of them any longer satisfied the minds or the hearts of its adherents. An age of skepticism and indifference had intervened, attended by a licentiousness of manners and public and private corruption which threatened the universal dissolution of society. Individuals rose who saw it, and felt the necessity of a general reform, and that a general reform was impossible without religion. But they would not, on the one hand, accept the Church, and could not, on the other, hope any thing from any of the old forms of heathenism. The world must have a religion, and could not get on without it. But how get a religion, when all religions were discarded, when all forms of religion were treated with general neglect or contempt?

The Reformers saw that they must have a religion, and, since, none existed which was satisfactory, none which was powerful enough to meet the exigency of the times, they must make one for themselves;—that is, form one to their purpose out of the old particular religions no longer heeded. Alexandria was their proper workshop, for there were collected or lying about in glorious confusion all the necessary materials. They began with the assumption, that all religions are at a bottom equally true, and that the error of each is in its exclusiveness, in its claiming to be the whole of religion, and the only true religion. Take, then, the elements of each, mould them together into a complete and harmonious whole, and you will have the true religion, a religion which will meet the wants of all minds and hearts, rally the human race around it, and be "The Church of the Future." Hence arose the Alexandrian Syncretism, combining in one systematic whole, as far as reason could combine them, all the known religions of the world, which, under the name of philosophy, but which became a veritable superstition, disputed the empire of the world with Christianity for full three hundred years.

What is the movement of our day, but an attempt of the same sort? By the beginning of the eighteenth century, the various forms of heresy, in which the Protestant spirit had developed itself, and which had attempted to reproduce Gentilism without forfeiting their title to Christianity, had exhausted their moral force, and the age began to lapse again into the old license and corruption. Never in its worst days was there grosser immorality and corruption in the Roman Empire than prevailed in England during the earlier half of the last century, under the reigns of George the First and George the Second. Deism was rife in the court, in the schools, in the Church, among the nobility and the people. Germany was hardly better, if so good; and of France under the regency of the profligate Duke of Orleans, or under Louis the Fifteenth with his *parc au cerfs*, we need not speak. Literature was infidel throughout, and atheism became fashionable. To the rabid infidel propagandism, begun by the English deists, and carried on by Voltaire and his associates, under the motto *Ecrasez l'infame*, soon succeeded, as of old, profound skepticism and indifference. Neither false religion nor no religion could rouse the mind from the torpidity into which it sank. Exclusive heresy, or, as we may say, sectarianism, born from the Protestant Reformation, though producing its effects far beyond the limits of the so-called Protestant world, had caused all forms of religion, about the beginning of this century, to be treated as equally false and contemptible.

But, once more, individuals started up frightened at the prospect they beheld. They felt and owned the eternal truth, *Man cannot be an atheist*. They saw the necessity of a general reform, and that a general reform could be effected only by religion. But, disdaining the Church as did the old Alexandrians, and seeing clearly that all the particular forms of Protestantism were worn out, they felt that they must have a new religion, and to have it they must either make it for themselves, or reconstruct it out of such materials as the old religions supplied. The principle on which they proceed is precisely the Alexandrian. To them all religions are equally true or equally false,—true as parts of a whole, false when regarded each as a whole in itself. Take, then, the several religions which have been and are, mould them into a complete, uniform, and systematic whole, and you will have what the Editor of *The Boston Quarterly Review*, and Chevalier Bunsen after him, call "The Church of the Future," and Dr. Bushnell and his friends call "Comprehensive Christianity,"—what Saint-Simon denominated *Nouveau Christianisme*, and M. Victor Cousin brilliantly advocates under the name of Eclecticism, borrowed avowedly from the Neoplatonists.

In perfect harmony with this, you see everywhere attempts to amalgamate sects, to form the un-Catholic world into one body, with a common creed, a common worship, and a common purpose. While the philosophers elaborate the bases of the union, statesmen and ministers attempt its practical realization. This is what we see in "Evangelical Alliances" and "World's Conventions," in the formation of "The Evangelical Church" in Prussia, and the union of Prussia and England in establishing the bishopric of Jerusalem. The aim is everywhere the same that it was with the Alexandrians, the principles of proceeding are the same, and the result, if obtained, must be similar. The movement of the un-Catholic world now, how much soever it may borrow from Christianity, however near it may approach the Catholic model, can be regarded, by those who understand it, only as a conscious or unconscious effort to reproduce the Gentile Rationalism of the old Alexandrian school.

The identity of the two movements might be established even down to minute details. The most fanciful dreams of our Transcendentalists may be found among the Alexandrians,—either with those who disavowed Christianity, or the sects, professing to retain it, allied to them. The very principle of Transcendentalism, namely, an element or activity in the human soul above reason, by which man is placed in immediate communion with the Divine mind, is nothing but the *Ecstasy* or *Trance* of the Neoplatonists, or their *fifth* source of science; and the Alexandrian theurgy and magic are reproduced in your Swedenborgianism and Mesmerism. Moreover, the Protestant Reformation itself not only involved as its legitimate consequence a return to the Alexandrian Rationalism, but was in some measure the effect of such return. To be satisfied of this, we need but study the history of the Revival of Letters and the controversies of the schools in the fifteenth century. We say nothing of the Revival in so far as it was simply a revival of classical antiquity under the relation of art, or beauty of form,—under which relation it was not censurable, but relatively, perhaps a progress. Christian piety and learning can coexist with barbarism in taste, and want of elegance and polish in manners, but do not demand them. The Revival, however, was, in fact, something more than this, and something far different from it. Those Greek scholars who escaped from Constantinople when it was taken by the Turks, and who spread themselves over Western Europe, did not bring with them merely the poets, orators, and historians of ancient Greece, nor merely more complete editions of Plato and Aristotle; they brought with them Proclus and Plotinus, and the old Alexandrian Rationalism, with its Oriental comprehensiveness and its Greek subtlety. They made no attacks on the Church,—they professed profound respect for Catholicity, and with Eastern suppleness readily submitted to her authority; but they deposited in the minds and hearts of their disciples the germs of a system the rival of hers, which weakened their attachment to her doctrines, disgusted them with the barbarous Latin and *un-Greek* taste of her Monks, and the rigid, sometimes frigid, Scholasticism of her Doctors. These germs were not slow in developing, and very soon gave us the Neoplatonists in philosophy, and the Humanists in literature, of the fifteenth and sixteenth centuries. The former destroyed the authority of the Schoolmen; the latter, at the head of whom stood Erasmus, the Voltaire of his time, covered the clergy, especially the Monks, with ridicule, and sowed the seeds of practical, as the others had of speculative infidelity. Combined or operating to the same end, they prepared, and, favored by the politics of the period, produced the Protestant Reformation. Not accidentally, then, has Protestantism from its birth manifested a Gentile spirit, misrepresented and ridiculed every thing distinctively Christian, or that it is now undeniably developing in pure Alexandrian Syncretism, gathering itself up as a grand and well-organized superstition to wage war once more on the old Alexandrian battleground, with the old Alexandrian forces and arms, against the Nazarene, as Julian the Apostate always terms our Lord. Was it by accident that Protestantism, wherever permitted to follow its instincts, began by pulling down, breaking, or defacing the Cross, the sacred symbol of Christianity?

The identity of the modern movement with that which resulted in Alexandrian Syncretism may be traced also in the pantheistic tendencies of the day. The Alexandrian school rejected none of the popular gods; it placed Apis and Jove, Isis and Hercules, and sometimes even Christ himself, in the same temple; but all under the shadow of the god Serapis, the symbol of unity, or rather of THE WHOLE, THE ALL, that is, of pure pantheism, in which all pure Rationalism is sure to end. To what does all modern philosophy tend, but to pantheism? Have we not seen Spinoza in our own day rehabilitated, and commented upon as the greatest of modern philosophers? Cousin's Eclecticism is undeniably pantheistic, and less cannot be said of Schellingism or Hegelism. Socialism, now so rife, is simply pantheism adapted to the apprehensions of the vulgar,—refined and voluptuous with the Fourierists and Saint-Simonians, coarse and revolting with the Chartists and Red Republicans.

But we are pursuing this line of remark beyond our original purpose. We may return to it hereafter. In the meantime we invite those who have the requisite leisure and learning to take up the subject, and consider the relation of all the ancient and modern sects to Gentilism, the persistence of Gentilism in Christian nations down to our own times, in spite of the anathemas of the Church and the unwearied efforts of the Catholic clergy to exterminate it, and its all but avowed revival in our own day under the most comprehensive, scientific, erudite, subtle, and dangerous form it has ever assumed. In doing this, great attention should be paid to chronology; for *the* Gentilism with which it is the fashion among Protestants and unbelievers to compare Christianity, and from which it is pretended the Church has largely borrowed, will be found to have been formed two centuries and a half after the birth of our Lord. That stupendous fabric, that systematic organization of Gentilism, which we find in the time of Julian the Apostate, and which fell with him, was not the model copied by the Church, but was itself modelled after the Christian hierarchy, and it is heathenism that has *Christianized*, not the Church that has *heathenized*. The Platonism of modern times, whether on the Continent or in England, is not the Platonism of Plato, but of the Alexandrians, as every one knows who has studied Plato himself in his own inimitable Dialogues, not merely in the speculations of Plotinus, or the commentaries of Proclus.

That our author, born and brought up in the Protestant world, and formed by its Gentile spirit and tendencies, should even unconciously fall into the Alexandrian order of thought, and labor to reconstruct a system intended to rival the Christian, is nothing strange. In doing so, he only yields to the spirit of the age, and follows the lead of those whom the age owns and reverences as its chiefs. That his system is not Christian, although he would have us receive it as Christian, is evident enough from his *dictum* with regard to miracles. "The miracles ascribed to Christ and his Apostles," he says (p. 61,) "however conclusive to those who witnessed them, are no evidence to us, until *by other means* we have established the truth of the writings which record them,—that is to say, *until we have proved all that we wish to prove.*" There is a sophism in this, which, probably, the author does not perceive. If the writings are the *only* authority for the miracles as historical facts, that we must establish their historical *authenticity* before the miracles can be evidence to us, we concede; but not their *truth*, that is, the truth of the mysteries they teach, the material object of faith,— therefore the matter we want proved. The miracles are not proofs of the mysteries, but simply motives of credibility. "Rabbi, we know that thou art come a teacher from God; for no man could do these miracles which thou doest, unless God were with him." Ordinary historical testimony, though wholly inadequate to prove the mysteries, is sufficient to prove the miracles as facts, and, when so proved, they are evidence to us in the same manner and in the same degree that they were to those who witnessed them. It does not, therefore, follow that we must prove, without them, all we want proved, before they can be evidence to us.

But this by the way. The author in his *dictum* asserts either that Christianity is not provable at all, or that it is provable without miracles; but no Christian can assert either the one or the other. The former is absurd, if Christianity came from God and is intended for reasonable beings. God, as the author of reason, cannot require us to believe, and we as reasonable beings cannot believe, without reason, or authority sufficient to satisfy reason. The latter cannot be said without reducing Christianity to the mere order of nature; for a supernatural religion is, in the nature of things, provable only by supernaturally accredited witnesses, and witnesses cannot be supernaturally accredited without miracles of some sort. To deny the necessity of miracles as motives of credibility, or to assert the provability of Christianity without them, is to deny the supernatural character of Christianity, and therefore to deny Christianity itself; for Christianity is essentially and distinctively supernatural. Without the miracles, Christianity is provable only as a philosophy, and as a philosophy it must lie wholly within the order of nature; since philosophy, by its very definition, is the science of principles cognizable by the light of natural reason. Rationalism turns for ever within the limits of nature, and, do its best, it can never overleap them. It can never rise to Christianity; all it can do is, by rejecting or explaining away the mysteries, discarding all that transcends reason, to bring Christianity down to itself,—a fact we commend to the serious consideration of all who pretend that our religion, even to its loftiest mysteries, is rationally or philosophically demonstrable. The Christianity they can prove as a philosophy is no more the Christianity of the Gospel than the Neoplatonism of Proclus and Plotinus was the Christianity of the Gregories, the Basils, and the Augustines.

The author also betrays the unchristian character of his order of thought in his third discourse, entitled *Spiritual Despotism and the Reformation*. He says, indeed, in this part of his work, some very handsome things—in his own estimation—of the Church; but, as he says them from the humanitarian point of view, on the hypothesis that she is a purely human institution, and therefore a gigantic imposition upon mankind, we cannot take them as evidences of his Christian mode of thinking. If the Church is what we hold her to be, these humanitarian compliments and apologies are impertinent; and if what he holds her to be, they betray on his part a very unchristian laxity of moral principle. An infallible Church, the Church of God, needs no apologies; man's Church, or the Synagogue of Satan, deserves none. But, although the author maintains that the Church was very necessary from the fifth to the fifteenth century,—that she preserved our holy religion, and without her Christian faith and piety would have been lost, Christianity would have been unable to fulfil her mission, and the European nations would have remained uncivilized, ignorant, illiterate, ruthless barbarians,—he yet holds that she was a spiritual despotism, and the Protestant Reformation was inevitable and necessary to emancipate the human mind from her thraldom, and to prepare the way for mental and civil freedom.

According to the author, the spiritual despotism of the Church consisted in her claiming and exercising authority over faith and morals,—over the minds, the hearts, and the consciences of the faithful. If we catch his meaning, which does not appear to lie very clear or distinct even in his own mind, the despotism is in the authority itself, not simply in the fact that the Church claims and exercises it. It would be equally despotism, if claimed and exercised by any one else, because it is intrinsically hostile to the rights of the mind and to the principles of civil liberty. Consequently, he objects not merely to the *claimant*, but to the thing *claimed*, and rejects the authority, let who will claim it, or let it be vested where or in whom it may.

But this is obviously unchristian. If we suppose Christianity at all, we must suppose it as an external revelation from God, a definite and authoritative religion, given by the Supreme Lawgiver to all men as the Supreme Law, binding upon the whole man, against which no one has the right to think, speak, or act, and to which every one is bound to conform in thought, word, and deed. All this is implied in the very conception of Christianity, and must be admitted, if we admit the Christian religion at all. The authority objected to is therefore included in the fundamental conception of the Christian revelation, and consequently we cannot denominate it a spiritual despotism without denominating Christianity itself a spiritual despotism, which, we need not say, would be any thing but Christian.

The author's order of thought would carry him even farther. If the authority of the Church is a spiritual despotism for the reason he assigns, the authority of God is also a spiritual despotism. The principle on which he objects to the Church is, that the mind and the state are free, and that any authority over either is unjust. The essence of despotism is not that it is authority, but that it is authority without right, will without reason, power without justice. We cannot suppose the existence of God without supposing the precise authority over the mind and the state objected to. If this authority, claimed and exercised in his name by the Church, is despotism, it must be, then, because he has no right to it; if no right to it, he is not sovereign; if not sovereign, he does not exist. If God does not exist, there is no conscience, no law, no accountability, moral or civil. To this conclusion the author's notions of mental freedom and civil liberty, pushed to their logical consequences, necessarily lead.

Every Christian is obliged to recognize, in the abstract, to say the least, the precise authority claimed and exercised by the Church over faith and morals, over the intellect and the conscience, in spirituals and in temporals; and it is a well-known fact, that all Christian sects, as long as they retain any thing distinctively Christian, do claim, and, as far as able, exercise it, and never practically abandon it, till they lapse into pure Rationalism, from which all that is distinctively Christian disappears. It cannot be otherwise; because Christianity is essentially law, and the Supreme Law, for the reason, the will, the conscience, for individuals and nations, for the subject and for the prince. If our author's order of thought were Christian, he could not object to authority in itself; he would feel himself obliged to assert and vindicate it somewhere for some one; and and if he objected to the Church at all, he would do so, not because of the authority, but because it is not rightfully hers, but another's,—which would be a legitimate objection, and conclusive, if sustained, as of course it cannot be, by the facts in the case. His failure to object on this ground is a proof that his thought is not Christian.

The author's notions of authority and liberty are not only unchristian, but exceedingly unphilosophical and confused. He has no just conception of either, and is evidently unable to draw any intelligible distinction between authority and despotism on the one hand, or between liberty and license on the other. He can conceive of authority and liberty only as each is the antagonist or the limitation of the other; he ingenuously confesses that he is unable to reconcile them, and presents their reconciliation as a problem that Protestantism has yet to solve. "To adjust the respective limits of these antagonists,—Liberty of thought and Ecclesiastical authority,—and bring about a lasting treaty of peace between them, is the yet unsolved problem of the Reformation. The Reformers attempted to solve it, and strove in vain to confine the torrent they had set in motion, within certain dikes of their own construction. The spring-tide of free inquiry, not yet perhaps at its flood, is sweeping away their barriers, and ages may elapse before it subsides into its proper channel, after cleansing the earth of a thousand follies and abuses." (p. 160.) All this proves that his order of thought is unchristian, and that his conceptions of authority and of liberty are not taken from the Gospel. No intelligent Christian, no sound philosopher even, ever conceives of authority and liberty as antagonists, as limiting one the other, or admits that their conciliation is an unsolved problem, or even a problem at all.

The Christian, even the philosopher, derives all from God, and nothing from man, and therefore escapes the difficulty felt by our author and the Reformers. He knows that authority is not authority, if limited, and liberty is not liberty, if bounded. Consequently, he never conceives of the two in the same sphere, but distributes them in separate spheres, where each may be supreme. God is the absolute, underived, and unlimited Sovereign and Proprietor of the universe. Here is the foundation of all authority, and also of all liberty. Before God we have no liberty. We are his, and not our own. We are what he creates us, have only what he gives us, and lie completely at his mercy. We hold all from him, even to the breath in our nostrils, and he has the sovereign right to dispose of us according to his own will and pleasure. In his presence, and in presence of his law, we have duties, but no rights, and our duty and his right is the full, entire, and unconditional submission of ourselves, soul and body, to his will. Here is authority, absolute, full, entire, and unbounded,—as must be all authority, in order to be authority.

In the presence of authority there is no liberty; where, then, is liberty? It is not before God, but it is between man and man, between man and society, and between society and society. The absolute and plenary sovereignty of God excludes all other sovereignty, and our absolute and unconditional subjection to him excludes all other subjection. Hence no liberty before God, and no subjection before man; and therefore liberty is rightly defined, full and entire freedom from all authority but the authority of God. Here is liberty, liberty in the human sphere, and liberty full and entire, without restraint or limit in the sphere to which it pertains. Man is subjected to God, but to God only. No man, in his own right, has any, the least, authority over man; no body or community of men, as such, has any rightful authority either in spirituals or temporals. All merely human authorities are usurpations, and their acts are without obligation, null and void from the beginning. If the parent, the pastor, the prince has any right to command, it is as the vicar of God, and in that character alone; if I am bound to obey my parents, my pastor, or my prince, it is because my God commands me to obey them, and because in obeying them I am obeying him. Here is the law of liberty, and here, too, is the law of authority. Understand now why religion must found the state, why it is nonsense or blasphemy to talk of an alliance between religion and liberty, a reconciliation between authority and freedom. Both proceed from the same fountain, the absolute, underived, unlimited sovereignty of God, and can be no more opposed one to the other than God can be opposed to himself. Hence, absolute and unconditional subjection to God is absolute and unlimited freedom. Therefore says our Lord, "If the Son makes you free, you shall be free indeed."

The sovereignty of God does not oppose liberty; it founds and guaranties it. Authority is not the antagonist of freedom; it is its support, its vindicator. It is not religion, it is not Christianity, but infidelity, that places authority and liberty one over against the other, in battle array. It is not God who crushes our liberty, robs us of our rights, and binds heavy burdens upon our shoulders, too grievous to be borne; it is man, who at the same time that he robs us of our rights robs God of his. He who attacks our freedom attacks his sovereignty; he who vindicates his sovereignty, the rights of God, vindicates the rights of man; for all human rights are summed up in the one right to be governed by God and by him alone, in the duty of absolute subjection to him, and absolute freedom from all subjection to any other. Maintain, therefore, the rights of God, the supremacy in all departments of the Divine law, and you need not trouble your heads about the rights of man, freedom of thought or civil liberty; for they are secured with all the guaranty of the Divine sovereignty. The Divine sovereignty is, therefore, as indispensable to liberty as to authority.

We need not stop to show that the Divine sovereignty is not itself a despotism. The essence of despotism, as we have said, is not that it is authority, but that it is authority without right, will without reason, power without justice, which can never be said of God; for his right to universal dominion is unquestionable, and in him will and reason, power and justice are never disjoined, are identical, are one and the same, and are indistinguishable save in our manner of conceiving them. His sovereignty is rightful, his will is intrinsically, eternally, and immutably just will, his power just power. Absolute subjection to him is absolute subjection to eternal, immutable, and absolute justice. Hence, subjection to him alone is, on the one hand, subjection to absolute justice, and, on the other, freedom to be and to do all that absolute justice permits. Here is just authority as great as can be conceived, and true liberty as large as is possible this side of license; and between the two there is and can be in the nature of things no clashing, no conflict, no antagonism. How mean and shallow is infidel philosophy!

Taking this view along with us, a view which is alike that of Christianity and of sound philosophy, we cannot fail to perceive that the objection urged against the Church is exceedingly ill-chosen. The Church, if what she professes to be,—and we have the right here to reason on the supposition that she is,— represents the Divine sovereignty, and is commissioned by God to teach and to govern in his name. Her authority, then, is his authority, and it is he that teaches and governs in her and through her; so far, then, from being hostile to liberty in one department or another, she must be its support and safeguard in every department. The ground and condition of liberty is the presence of the Divine sovereignty, for in its presence there is no other sovereignty, no other authority, consequently no slavery. The objection, that the Church is a spiritual despotism, is grounded on the supposition that all authority is despotism and all liberty license,—that is, that liberty and authority are antagonist forces,—which would require us to deny both, for neither despotism nor license is defensible. Authority and liberty are only the two phases of one and the same principle; suppose the absence of authority, you suppose the presence of license or despotism, which, again, are only the two phases of one and the same thing. To remove license or despotism, you must suppose the presence of legitimate authority. The Church being the representative of the Divine sovereignty on the earth, introduces legitimate authority, and by her presence necessarily displaces both despotism and license, that is, establishes both order and liberty.

The difficulty which Protestants and unbelievers suppose must exist in conforming reason, which is not always obedient to will, to the commands of authority, arises from their overlooking the nature of authority. The authority is not only an order to believe, but it is authority *for* believing. The authority of reason in the natural order is derived from God, not from man; and the obligation to believe the axioms of mathematics or the definitions of geometry arises solely from the fact, that reason, which declares them, does, thus far, speak by Divine authority. If it did not, reason would be no reason for believing or asserting them. The same Divine authority in a higher order, speaking through the Church, cannot be less authoritative, or a less authority for believing what the Church teaches. Hence the command of the Church is at once authority for the will and for the reason, an injunction to believe and a reason for believing. The absolute submission of reason to her commands is not, as some fancy, the abnegation of reason. Reason does not, in submitting, fold her hands, shut her eyes, and take a doze, like a fat alderman after dinner, but keeps wide awake, and exercises her highest powers, her most sacred rights, according to her own nature. What more reasonable reason for believing than the command of God?—since, in the order of truth, his sovereignty is identically his veracity. To suppose a Catholic mind can have any difficulty in bringing reason to assent to the teachings of the Church, believed to be God's Church, is as absurd as to suppose that an American who has never been abroad can have any difficulty in believing that there is such a city as Paris, or that Louis Napoleon Bonaparte has recently been elected President of the French Republic; or as to suppose that the logician finds a difficulty in bringing his reason to assent to the proposition that the same is the same, that the same thing cannot both be and not be at the same time, or that two and two make four.

It is not the Church that establishes spiritual despotism; it is she who saves us from it. Spiritual despotism is that which subjects us, in spiritual matters, to a human authority, whether our own or that of others,—for our own is as human as another's; and the only redemption from it is in having in them a divine authority. Protestants themselves acknowledge this, when they call out for the pure word of God. The Church teaches by Divine authority; in submitting to her, we submit to God, and are freed from all human authority. She teaches infallibly; therefore, in believing what she teaches, we believe the truth, which frees us from falsehood and error, to which all men without an infallible guide are subject, and subjection to which is the elemental principle of all spiritual despotism. Her authority admitted excludes all other authority, and therefore frees us from heresiarchs and sects, the very embodiment of spiritual despotism in its most odious forms. Sectarianism is spiritual despotism itself; and to know how far spiritual despotism and spiritual slavery may go, you have only to study the history of the various sects and false religions which now exist, or have heretofore existed.

In the temporal order, again, the authority claimed and exercised by the Church is nothing but the assertion over the state of the Divine sovereignty, which she represents, or the subjection of the prince to the Law of God, in his character of prince as well as in his character of man. That the prince or civil power is subject to the law of God, no man who admits Christianity at all dares question; and, if the Church be the Divinely commissioned teacher and guardian of that law, as she certainly is, the same subjection to her must be conceded. But this, instead of being opposed to civil liberty, is its only possible condition. Civil liberty, like all liberty, is in being held to no obedience but obedience to God; and obedience to the state can be compatible with liberty only on the condition that God commands it, or on the condition that he governs in the state, which he does not and cannot do, unless the state holds from his law and is subject to it. To deny, then, the supremacy of the Church in temporals is only to release the temporal order from its subjection to the Divine sovereignty, which, so far as regards the state, is to deny its authority, or its right to govern, and, so far as regards the subject, is to assert pure, unmitigated civil despotism. All authority divested of the Divine sanction is despotic, because it is authority without right, will unregulated by reason, power disjoined from justice. Withdraw the supremacy of the Church from the temporal order, and you deprive the state of that sanction, by asserting that it does not hold from God and is not amenable to his law; you give the state simply a human basis, and have in it only a human authority, which has no right to govern, which I am not bound to obey, and which it is intolerable tyranny to compel me to obey. "Let every soul," says the blessed Apostle Paul, the Doctor of the Gentiles, "be subject to the higher powers; for there is no power but from God; and those that are, are ordained of God. Therefore he that resisteth power resisteth the ordinance of God. . . . . . Wherefore be subject of necessity, not only for wrath, but for conscience' sake." (Rom. xiii. 1-5.) Here the obligation of obedience is grounded on the fact that the civil power is the ordinance of God, that is, as we say, holds from God. But, obviously, this, while it subjects the subject to the state, equally subjects the state to the Divine sovereignty. Take away the subjection of the state to God, and you take away the reason of the subjection of the subject to the state; and we need not tell you that to subject us to an authority which we are not bound to obey is tyranny. See, then, what you get by denying the supremacy of the Church in temporals!

The Church and the state, as administrations, are distinct bodies; but they are not, as some modern politicians would persuade us, two coördinate and mutually independent authorities. The state holds under the law of nature, and has authority only within the limits of that law. As long as it confines itself within that law, and faithfully executes its provisions, it acts freely, without ecclesiastical restraint or interference. But the Church holds from God under the supernatural or revealed law, which includes, as integral in itself, the law of nature, and is therefore the teacher and guardian of the natural as well as of the revealed law. She is, under God, the supreme judge of both laws, which for her are but one law; and hence she takes cognizance, in her tribunals, of the breaches of the natural law as well as of the revealed, and has the right to take cognizance of its breaches by nations as well as of its breaches by individuals, by the prince as well as by the subject, for it is the supreme law for both. The state is, therefore, only an inferior court, bound to receive the law from the supreme court, and liable to have its decisions reversed on appeal.

This must be asserted, if we assert the supremacy of the Christian law, and hold the Church to be its teacher and judge; for no man will deny that Christianity includes the natural as well as the supernatural law. Who, with any just conceptions, or any conceptions at all, of the Christian religion, will pretend that one can fulfil the Christian law and yet violate the natural law?—that one is a good Christian, if he keeps the precepts of the Church, though he break every precept of the Decalogue? —or that Christianity remits the catechumen to the state to learn the law of nature, or what we term natural morality? Grace presupposes nature. The supernatural ordinances of God's law presupposes the natural, and the Church, which is the teacher and guardian of faith and morals, can no more be so without plenary authority with regard to the latter than the former. Who, again, dares pretend that the moral law is not as obligatory on emperors, kings, princes, commonwealths, as upon private individuals?—upon politicians, as upon priests or simple believers? Unless, then, you exempt the state from all obligation even to the law of nature, you must make it amenable to the moral law as expounded by the Church, divinely commissioned to teach and declare it.

Deny this, and assert the independence of the political order, and declare the state in its own right, without accountability to the Christian law, of which it is not the teacher or guardian, supreme in temporals, and you gain, instead of civil liberty, simply, in principle at least, civil despotism. If you deny that the Church is the teacher and guardian of the law of God, you must either claim the authority you deny her for the state, or you must deny it altogether. If you claim it for the state, you, on your own principles, make the state a spiritual despotism, and on ours also; for the state obviously has not received that authority, is incompetent in spirituals, is no teacher of morals, or director of consciences. If you deny it altogether, you make the state independent of the moral order, independent of the Divine sovereignty, the only real sovereignty, and establish pure, unmitigated *civil* despotism.

There is no escaping this conclusion; and hence we see the folly and madness of those who assert in the name of liberty the independence of the political order, and exclaim, in a tone of mock heroism, "Neither priest nor bishop shall interfere with my political opinions as long as I am able to resist him!" Bravo! my young Liberal; but did you know what you are doing, you would see that you are laying the foundation, not of liberty, but of despotism. Hence, too, we see that our author must be mistaken, when he asserts that the Protestant Reformation, in its essential principle, was "a revolt of free spirits against profligate despotism." It was no such thing. Its objections to the Church, reduced to their substance, were simply, the Church is a spiritual despotism because she claims supremacy over reason, conscience, and the state; and it objected to her, not because it was she who claimed that supremacy, but because it rejected the supremacy itself, let it be claimed by whom it might. This our author himself concedes, contends, and proves. Its argument was, the Church of God cannot claim supremacy over reason, conscience, and the state. But the Church does claim this supremacy, therefore she cannot be the Church of God. The principle of the argument is, that God could not delegate the authority to any Church. But if he could not, it must have been because he himself did not possess it. Therefore the essential principle of the Reformation, in the last analysis, was the denial, on the one hand, of the sovereignty of God over reason, conscience, and the state, and on the other, the assertion of the absolute independence of man and the temporal order, which is either pure license or pure despotism, according to the light in which you choose to consider it. The real character of the Reformation was the substitution of human sovereignty for the Divine; and hence, in its developments, wherever it is free to follow its own law, we see it result either in pure humanism or pure pantheism, as it does or does not combine with religious sentiment. And either is the denial of both authority and liberty; for all authority is in the Divine sovereignty, and all liberty in being bound to it alone, that is, in freedom from all human government resting merely on a human basis, whether ourselves, the one, the few, or the many, as every one would see, if it were understood that authority over myself, emanating from myself, is as human, and therefore as illegitimate, as much of the essence of despotism, as authority over me emanating from other men. Is it not said in all languages that a man may be the slave of himself, of his own passions, his own ignorance, or his own prejudices? Under Protestantism we may have civil and spiritual despotism, or civil and spiritual license, the only two things that man can found, without a divine commission and subjection to the divine law; but authority and liberty are possible and can be practically secured only under the divine order represented by the Church, or an institution precisely similar to what she professes to be, the divinely commissioned teacher and guardian of both the natural and the revealed law.

That this conclusion will be acceptable to our politicians, young or old, we are not quite so simple as to suppose; but we are not aware that it is necessary to consult their pleasure. They have in these, as they had in other times, the physical power to do with us as seems to them good. They can decry us, they can pull out our tongue, cut off our right hand, and at need burn our body, or cast it to the wild beasts; but this will not alter the nature of things, make wrong right, or right wrong. Civil and spiritual despotism is not the less despotism because practised by them, and in the name of humanity and the people. We desire to have all due respect for them; but we must confess that we have not yet seen their title-deeds, the papers which prove them to have a chartered right from Almighty God to be the sole governors of mankind. We have no authority for pronouncing them infallible or impeccable; we have seen no reason for supposing their ascendency, freed from the restraints of the Divine law, is either honorable to God or serviceable to man; we have not found them always exempt from the common infirmities of our nature; and we think we have seen, at least heard of, politicians who were ambitious, selfish, intriguing, greedy of power, place, emolument even. In a word, we have no reason to believe that they monopolize all the wisdom, the virtue, the generosity and disinterestedness of the community, or that they never need looking after, and therefore never need a power above them, under the immediate and supernatural protection of Almighty God, to look after them, and to compel them to keep within their own province, to respect religion, and to refain from inflicting irreparable injuries upon society. Even should they, then, clamor against us, or do worse, it would not greatly move us, and would tend to confirm us in the truth of our doctrine, rather than lead us to distrust its soundness or its necessity.

We need hardly say that we advocate no amalgamation of the civil and ecclesiastical administrations. They are in their nature, as we have said, distinct, and the supremacy of the Church which we assert is by no means the supremacy of the clergy as politicians. We have no more respect for clergymen turned politicians than we have for any other class of politicians of equal worth, perhaps not quite so much; for we cannot forget that they, in becoming politicians, descend from their sacerdotal rank, as a judge does in descending from the bench to play the part of an advocate. We have had political priests ever since there was a Christian state, and many of them have made sad work of both politics and religion. We have nothing to say of them, but that they were politicians, and their censurable acts were not performed in their character of priests. The principle we assert does not exact that the Church should turn politician, and thus from the Church become the state, or that the clergy should turn politicians; it exacts that both she and they should not. The clergy as politicians fall into the category of all politicians, and their supremacy as politicians would still be the supremacy of the state, not of the Church. The state is supreme, if politicians as such be supreme, let them be selected from what class of the community they may. The principle exacts, indeed, the supremacy of the clergy, but solely as the Church, in their sacerdotal and pastoral character as teachers, guardians, and judges of the law of God, natural and revealed, supreme for individuals and nations, for prince and subject, king and commonwealth, noble and plebeian, rich and poor, great and small, wise and simple; not as politicians, in which character they have and can have no preëminence over politicians selected from the laity, and must stand on the same level with them. We do not advocate—far from it—the notion that the Church must administer the civil government; what we advocate is her supremacy as the teacher and guardian of the law of God,—as the supreme court, which must be recognized and submitted to as such by the state, and whose decisions cannot be disregarded, whose prerogatives cannot be abridged or usurped by any power on earth, without rebellion against the Divine majesty, and robbing man of his rights. As Christians, we must insist on this supremacy; as Catholics, it is not only our duty, but our glorious privilege, to assert it, and to understand and practise our religion as God himself, through his own chosen organ, promulgates and expounds it.

We know how hateful this doctrine is to politicians, to the world, and to the devil, who seek always to find a rival in the state to the kingdom of God. We know that the representatives of the state in nearly all ages of Christendom, and in nearly all nations, have resisted it, and been encouraged, sustained, in their resistance, by ambitious priests and courtly prelates. We know that it is now resisted by every civil government on earth, that the kings of the earth stand up, the princes conspire together, the nations rage, and the people imagine vain things, against the Lord and against his Christ, saying, Let us break their bonds asunder, let us cast away their yoke from us; but we cannot help that. We know the truth, and dare assert it; we know the rights of God, and dare not betray them. We cannot be false, because others are,—shrink from proclaiming the supremacy of the moral order, because now more than ever it is necessary to proclaim it. We do not understand the heroism that goes always with the popular party, or the loyalty that deserts to the enemy the moment that his forces appear to be the most numerous. We know the moral order is supreme, and shall we fear to say it, lest sinners tremble, the wicked gnash their teeth, and the multitude threaten? We know our Church is God's Church; that she is the judge of God's law, and has the right to denounce, as from the judgment-seat of the Almighty, whoever violates it, and to place king or peasant under her anathema, if he refuses to obey it. She has the right, the divine right, to denounce moral wrong, spiritual wrong, political wrong, tyranny and oppression, wheresoever or by whomsoever they are practised, and to vindicate the rights of God, and, in so doing, the rights of man, let who will dare threaten or invade them. We are subject to God, but to him only; and are we afraid to assert the fact? Are we not free before all men?

The Church is the Divinely appointed guardian of truth, virtue, liberty, because she is the representative of the Divine sovereignty on earth. Kings and potentates, commonwealths and mobs, may rise up, as they have often risen up, against her; politicians may murmur or denounce, the timid may quake, the faint-hearted may fail, the cowardly shrink away, and the disloyal join her persecutors; but that can neither justify them, nor unmake her rights, nor depose her from her sovereignty under God,—cannot make it not true that she represents the moral order, and that the moral order is supreme. That supremacy is a fact in God's universe, an eternal and primal truth; and let no man dare deny it, who would not be branded on his forehead traitor to God, and therefore to man ; and let him who fears to assert it in the hour of thickest danger be branded poltroon. It is the glory of the Church that she has always asserted it. She asserted it in that noble answer of her inspired Apostles to the magistrates,—" We must obey God rather than men ;" she asserted it in her glorious army of martyrs, who chose rather to die at the stake, in the amphitheatre, under the most cruel and lingering tortures, than to offer incense to Jupiter or to the statue of Cæsar ; she asserted it by the mouth of holy Ambrose, Archbishop of Milan, when he forbade the emperor Theodosius the Great to enter the Church till he had done public penance for his tyrannical treatment of his subjects, and drove him from the sanctuary, and bade him take his place with the laity, where he belonged ; she asserted it in the person of her sovereign Pontiff, St. Gregory the Seventh, when he made the tyrant and brutal Henry the Fourth of Germany wait for three days shivering with cold and hunger at his door, before he would grant him absolution, and when he finally smote him with the sword of Peter and Paul for his violation of his oaths, his wars against religion, and his oppression of his subjects; and she asserted it, again, in the person of her glorious Pontiff, Gregory the Sixteenth, who, standing with one foot in the grave, confronted the tyrant of the North, and made the Autocrat of all the Russias tremble and weep as a child. Never for one moment has she ceased to assert it in face of crowned and uncrowned heads,—Jew, Pagan, Arian, Barbarian, Saracen, Protestant, Infidel, Monarchist, Aristocrat, Democrat ; and gloriously is she asserting it now in her noble confessor, the Bishop of Lausanne and Geneva, and in her exiled Pontiff, Pius the Ninth.

You talk of religious liberty. Know you what the word means ? Know ye that religious liberty is all and entire in the supremacy of the moral order ? The Church is a spiritual despotism, is she ? Bold blasphemer, miserable apologist for tyrants and tyranny, go trace her track through eighteen hundred years, and behold it marked with the blood of her free and noble-hearted children, whom God loves and honors, shed in defence of religious liberty. From the first moment of her existence has she fought, ay, fought as no other power can fight, for liberty of religion. Every land has been reddened with the blood and whitened with the bones of her martyrs, in that sacred cause; and now, rash upstart, you dare in the face of day proclaim her the friend of despotism! Alas! my brother, may God forgive you, for you know not what you do.

But we have said enough to show the unchristian as well as the unphilosophical character of our author's thought, which we are willing to believe he does not fully comprehend, and from the logical consequences of which, were he to see them, we are anxious to believe he is prepared to recoil with horror. His thought is unphilosophical, because it conceives authority and liberty as antagonists ; it is unchristian, because it reduces Christianity to mere Rationalism, and revives Alexandrian Gentilism; because it denies the Divine sovereignty, and the supremacy in all things of the spiritual or moral order; because it denies moral accountability, and involves unmitigated despotism or unbounded license as the inevitable doom of the human race. As a philosopher, we hold his work in contempt; as an historian, we deny its authenticity; as a Christian, we abhor it; as a friend of liberty, civil and religious, we denounce its principles, as fit only for despots or libertines.

There are matters of detail in the work to which we seriously object, but, as we have shown the unsoundness of the book in its principles, it is not worth while to waste time or argument in exposing them. The author has expended no inconsiderable thought and labor in constructing his work, but, like all the works which rank under the head of *philosophy of history*, it is shallow, vague, confused, worthless. The writers of philosophy of history may have great natural talents, they may have varied and extensive learning, but they start wrong, they attempt what is impossible, and never go to the bottom of things or rise to their first principles. They never reach the ultimate ; they never attain to science; and only amuse or bewilder us with vague generalities, crude speculations, or unmeaning verbiage. There is an order of thought of which they have no conception, infinitely more profound than theirs, which, when once attained to, makes all their views appear heterogeneous, confused, weak, and childish.

We have no disposition to treat our young Kentuckian rudely, or to discourage him by an unkind reception. We know him only through his book. His book is bad, but we every day receive works which are far worse. We do not believe that he means to be a Pagan; we do not believe that he even means to be a Rationalist; we are sure that he does not mean to deny the moral order; and this is much for him personally, but it is nothing for his book. In judging the man, we look to his intention; in judging the author, we look only to the principles he inculcates. If these are unsound or dangerous, we have no mercy for the author, though we may abound in charity for the man. Mr. Nourse does not understand his own principles; he has not seen them in all their relations, and does not suspect their logical consequences. He has undertaken, without other guide than a few books which, themselves unsafe guides, he has read, but not digested, to do. after the study of a few months, what no mortal man could accomplish with all the libraries in the world, were he to live longer than the world has stood. How could he expect to succeed? We hold him accountable for his rashness in undertaking such a task, not for having failed in its accomplishment.

POLITICAL CONSTITUTIONS.*

OCTOBER, 1847.

COUNT JOSEPH DE MAISTRE was among the most distinguished men of his age. He was born at Chamberri in Savoy, 1753, was a senator of Piedmont at the time of the French invasion in 1792, and resided at St. Petersburg, as the ambassador of the king of Sardinia, from 1804 to 1817, in which last year he returned to Turin, where he died in 1821. Though not a subject of France, he was descended from a French family; was peculiarly French in his genius as well as his language, and his works were all written in reference to French ideas and affairs at the time of their composition. No one among those who labored during the first years of this century to revive and restore French literature, perverted by the philosophers, and nearly destroyed by the Revolution, deserves a more honorable mention, or exerted a more salutary influence in exposing the popular fallacies of the day, and in recalling men's minds to deeper and sounder religious and political doctrines.

As a theologian, some may think that he placed too much reliance on the analogies his profound and varied erudition supplied him with between the principles of our holy religion and those which were acknowledged in the old heathen world, that he was more fond than is prudent in these times of citing pagan authorities for his doctrines, and that he gave an almost unorthodox application to the dictum of St. Vincent of Lerins, *quod semper, quod ubique, et ab omnibus;* but it cannot be denied that his works were peculiarly adapted to the temper of the times in which they were written, and admirably fitted to excite and engage the attention of a lively people grown weary

---

* Essay on the Generative Principle of Political Constitutions Translated from the French of M. LE COMPTE JOSEPH DE MAISTRE. Boston: Little & Brown. 1847. 16mo. pp. 173.

indeed of infidelity, anarchy, and military despotism, but not yet recovered from the habits of incredulity and impiety, of sneering at the priest and the altar, and of regarding Christianity as old and effete; or that, if they contain some things local and temporary in their interest, they still contain much that is universal and permanent, which may be profitably studied in every age and country. No one acquainted with them can hesitate to regard them as peculiarly appropriate to our own country, and worthy the serious attention of our people, whether Catholic or Protestant.

The analogies between the principles of our holy religion and those of the ancient world, on which Count de Maistre lays great stress in all his works, are undeniable; but if we adduce them without taking great care to mark their precise nature, and the precise purpose for which we adduce them, we are in danger of giving occasion to an argument unfavorable to Christianity. German neologists and their American followers, it is well known, appeal to these analogies, and attempt from them to construct an argument against Christianity as a positive revealed religion, or against the special divine inspiration of the Holy Scriptures, and in favor of their pernicious error, that inspiration, so far as it is to be admitted at all, is a universal phenomenon, not peculiar, unless it be in degree, to certain individuals, but common to all men in all countries and ages of the world,—that God speaks objectively to no one, but reveals subjectively, in their spiritual nature, reason, conscience, sentiment, the same great truths to all. Hence they conclude that all religion is *natural*, if we consider the fact that it is common to all men, and resulting spontaneously from universal humanity,— or *supernatural*, if we consider the fact that our nature lives and operates only in God, and through the creative and upholding power and wisdom of God, who is himself above nature. All religions, say they, are therefore at bottom one and the same, natural or supernatural according to the point of view from which we choose to consider them; and they differ as concrete religions only according to, and in consequence of, the differing degrees of mental and moral culture of mankind in different ages, countries, and individuals. To get at the perfect form of religion, we must eliminate whatever is local, temporary, peculiar to this or that individual, to this or that age or country, and seize upon that which has been held always, everywhere, and by all. What we thus obtain, the residuum which remains after this analysis, will be absolute religion; that is to say, all religions in general, and no religion in particular, like man without men, the race without individuals!

No man was ever farther from adopting this gross absurdity, or of countenancing this religious nihilism, than Count de Maistre; but we sometimes feel, while reading his learned and brilliant pages, that he has not been always careful to guard against it, and that he says many things which could, without much difficulty, be construed in its favor. He does not appear to us to state clearly always the precise purpose for which he adduces these analogies, or the precise grounds on which he ascribes to them the value he evidently supposes them to possess. In a word, he does not appear to have marked with precision the place which belongs to the *consensus hominum*, and seems at times to hold it to be the ground of certainty, and to favor the notion that the Church is authoritative for the reason that she is the organ through which the universal consent of the race expresses itself, and therefore to favor the heresy taught a short time after by De Lammenais. Yet it is only in appearance; for in his thought, though not always sufficiently guarded in his expression, we are sure he was sound and orthodox.

If we appeal to these analogies to show what has always been the reason or belief of mankind, and, from the fact that mankind have always assented to principles identical with the principles of Christianity, or analogous to them, conclude the truth of the Christianity as a divinely revealed religion, we fall into the error of De Lammenais, condemned as heretical; because we then make the *consensus hominun* the ground of certainty, the authority for believing, instead of the veracity of God, as required by faith. But, if we adduce them as authorities, not for faith, but for what is and always has been the practical reason or common sense of mankind, and therefore as proofs that the principles of our holy religion are not unreasonable, but reasonable, our method is perfectly legitimate, and perhaps the very best that can be adopted against the unbeliever. It is only in this latter sense, we are confident, that Count de Maistre, in reality, appeals to the *consensus hominum* and adduces the analogies in question.

The unbeliever, born and bred in Christian lands, professes to meet the Christian on the ground of reason, and from reason alone to disprove the Christian religion; that is, he objects that Christianity is contrary to reason. But in order to sustain his objection, he must prove that Christianity is contradicted, either by the pure or demonstrative reason, or by the practical or moral reason; that is, either by reason as the principle of metaphysical certainty, or by reason as the principle of moral certainty. The first is out of the question; for reason in the former sense,—the speculative reason of Kant,—as Kant himself has shown in his *Kritik der reinen Vernunft*, cannot affirm or deny any thing on the subject. Moreover, it has been proved, over and over again, that there is nothing in Christianity which contradicts any principle of speculative reason; and all the chiefs of the modern infidel school, Bayle, Voltaire, D'Alembert, Hume, and Thomas Paine, concede that it is impossible to prove any thing, metaphysically, against Christianity. "They themselves," says Benjamin Constant, an unsuspicious authority on this point, "acknowledge that reasoning can authorize only doubt." *
They can only say they do not believe it, or that there is no sufficient reason for believing it; but no one of them ventures to say that it must necessarily be false, or that, after all, it may not be true. So far as regards the speculative reason, it is certain, that, if reason cannot, as we concede it cannot, pronounce a judgment in favor of our religion, it cannot pronounce a judgment against it. It can and must concede its metaphysical possibility, and this is as far as it can go, either one way or the other.

* *De la Religion*, Tom. I. p. 7. Paris, 1824.

The unbeliever, then, must leave the speculative reason, and show that our religion is condemned by the practical reason, or withdraw his objection. But the criterion of the practical reason is the *consensus hominum*. In speculative reason the individual needs not to go out of himself, for the speculative reason *in se* is as perfect in one as it is in all men; and when I have demonstrated that the three angles of the triangle are equal to two right angles, I have no need of the assent of the race, and their assent can add nothing to the demonstration, or to the certainty of the fact. But in regard to the practical reason it is not so; for this may be warped or perverted by individual idiosyncrasies, ignorance, education, position, passions, prejudices. Here the individual reason must be rectified or verified by the reason of the race, and that only is the reason of the race which is held always, everywhere, and by all. Hence we say the *consensus hominum* is the criterion of the practical reason, and the authority on which this or that is to be taken,—not as divine revelation, for that is the error to be avoided, but as practical reason; for certainly that is not unreasonable, contrary to the practical reason, which the race universally assents to, but must be in accordance with it, and demanded by it; or else the race would not and could not have universally assented to it. The *consensus hominum* is not the ground for believing this or that to be revealed, but simply for believing it approved by the practical reason; and if it is approved by the practical reason, we believe it on the authority of that reason,—not *fide divina*, indeed, but *fide humana*,—and must do so, or prove ourselves unreasonable, be ourselves condemned by reason.

Now if the unbeliever fails, as he does, to show that there is something essential to the Christian religion repugned by the practical reason, he fails entirely to sustain his objection. He boasts of common sense, but common sense is only another name for what we call the practical reason. He says our religion contradicts common sense. But his assertion is worth nothing, unless he proves it by showing the contradiction; which he never does and never can do. But if, on the other hand, we prove to him that every one of the principles of our religion has the authority of common sense, or that in believing our religion we assent to nothing not assented to in principle always and everywhere by the race, we prove that our religion in principle is reasonable, that the unbeliever cannot object that it is unreasonable, and that he, if he denies its principles, is himself unreasonable, obnoxious to the precise objection which he brings against us.

This last is what Count de Maistre has done. He proves, by admirable philosophical analysis and rare erudition, that there is in our holy religion no principle which the race has not always and everywhere assented to, and therefore, that, in refusing to believe it, in rejecting its principles, we are rejecting not merely the word of God as handed down to us by the Church, but also the practical reason or common sense of mankind, and by doing so place ourselves in direct hostility to the reason we boast, and whose authority we acknowledge. He thus turns the tables upon the loud-boasting and conceited infidel, and shows him that it is he, not the Christian, who must humble himself before reason, and beg pardon for the outrages he offers her. The unbeliever, in fact, builds never on reason, but always on unreason. Reason disowns him, scorns him, nay, holds him, intellectually considered, in perfect derision. Poor thing! she says, he has lost his wits; send him to the lunatic asylum.

Having established, as Count de Maistre has done, that all the principles of our religion have the *consensus hominum*, we have established that they are approved by reason. We must now assume that they are principles inherent in reason itself, immediately ascertainable by reason, or that they have been derived from some other source. If we say either of the former, they are authoritative for reason, and reason must assent to them on the peril of ceasing to be reason. If we say they are not inherent in reason, nor immediately ascertainable by reason, we must attribute them—since the practical reason by approving pronounces them pure, sacred, good—to some source above reason, that is, the supernatural, and therefore either immediately or mediately to God himself. Then they are unquestionably true, and we must believe them, or again prove ourselves unreasonable; for nothing is more reasonable than to believe God, and therefore what he reveals. So, on either supposition, we must assent to them or deny reason itself. Consequently, the analogies alleged against us by the enemies of our religion fully establish the reasonableness of Christianity in principle, and that reason must assent to it in principle or abdicate itself.

Yet we pretend not that by these analogies and pagan authorities we prove the absolute truth of Christianity as a positive revealed religion. We simply remove all objections *a priori* which can be conceived against it, and establish the reasonableness, the truth, for the practical reason, of its principles ; but we leave the fact of Christianity as a supernaturally revealed religion to be proved or not proved by the testimony in the case. The argument thus far shows the possible truth of the religion, the actual truth for the reason of its principles, and places it as a positive religion in the category of facts which may be proved by testimony. If the actual testimony appropriate in the case be equal to what satisfies the reason in the case of ordinary historical facts, to what is sufficient in the ordinary affairs of life to render assent prudent, it is proved as a positive revealed religion to the full extent that reason does or can demand ; and he who does not assent and act accordingly abdicates his title to be considered a reasonable being. The appropriate testimony in the case is unquestionably equal to this,—is all that reason, unless it ceases to be reason, requires or can require. Whoever, then, witholds his assent from the Christian religion, unless through sheer ignorance, denies reason. True, the assent thus yielded or warranted is only the assent of reason, and by no means the assent of faith, in the proper Christian sense ; something more is undoubtedly demanded for faith ; but·that, whatever it be, is to be sought, not from reason, but from divine grace, which is freely given to all who do not voluntarily resist it.

The Count's method of argument, properly understood, is

therefore triumphant against the unbeliever, as the neologists themselves have proved over and over again. The objection of the neologist which we have stated is met,—1. by the fact that the analogies adduced extend to the principles, not to the positive doctrines, of Christianity; and consequently, before the neologists can be entitled to their conclusion, they must rebut the positive testimony in favor of Christianity as a supernaturally revealed religion, and also prove that the principles without the doctrines are sufficient, neither of which they do or can do; and, 2. by the fact that the principles in question, between which and Christianity there is the relation of analogy or identity, are not themselves originally derived from simple natural reason, or from an interior subjective revelation made immediately to each man in particular, but from the primitive revelation made to our first parents, and preserved and diffused by tradition. We, as well as they, find Christian elements in the old heathen poets and philosophers; and perhaps in general the heathen world, under each of its various religions, retained more of Christian principle—we say not of Christian doctrine—than is retained by our modern sects. Under veils and symbols more or less transparent, we find not seldom, not only Christian principles, but a very near approach to some one or more of the Christian Mysteries themselves. Indeed, the type after which all religions have been fashioned is evidently the Christian religion, and there is scarcely a single Christian *idea*, if we may use the term, which is not to be found out of the Christian Church. This, however, presents no difficulty to the Christian;—not, indeed, because he supposes all has been derived from the Holy Scriptures and intercourse with the Jews, as some have thought,—though more may have been derived from this source than many in our days are willing to acknowledge, but because it was contained in the primitive revelation to our first parents, and formed the common patrimony of the race. What we thus find is revealed truth, truth pertaining to the Christian revelation, pure in its source, but in the lapse of time corrupted and mixed up with fables by the nations, as they multiplied and spread themselves over the face of the earth. The fountain was pure and supernatural, but the streams which flowed from it became gradually corrupt by receiving waters flowing from other fountains. Thus, what we find in consonance with our religion as supernatural we attribute to the primitive revelation preserved by tradition; what we find repugnant to it we attribute to men speaking from themselves, their own darkened understandings and corrupt hearts.

The Christian revelation is not, strictly speaking, a new revelation; Judaism as such, though a divine institution for a special purpose, was not a dogmatic revelation, and contained no revealed truths not contained in the primitive revelation. The primitive revelation contained in substance the whole Christian revelation, and the only difference between the faith of the Fathers from the beginning, before Christ, and that of the Fathers since, is, that those before believed in a Christ to come, and those since believe in a Christ that has come, and that in many things our faith is clearer and more explicit than was theirs. From the beginning till now, the revelation believed has been ever one and the same revelation, the faith has always been one and the same faith. Our Lord and his Apostles introduced no new religion, no new faith, made no new revelation, except to clear up and render more explicit what had been revealed and believed by the faithful from the first. It is not the true view to look upon our Lord as coming into the world to found a new religion, or to reveal even new dogmas, as do many of our modern sects. He came to make the Atonement, to perform the work of redemption, to open the door for the admission of the just into heaven, and to establish a new order, the order of grace in place of the Law, that we might have life, and have it more abundantly.

Due consideration of this fact would correct the errors of our Liberal Christians, and enable them to get over some of the difficulties they now find, or imagine they find. They read the New Testament, and find in it no creed formally drawn out, and therefore conclude that none is enjoined or necessary. They find some one asking what he shall do to be saved, and an Apostle in his answer requiring him simply to believe in the Lord Jesus Christ, and therefore they conclude only the simple belief in Jesus as the Messiah, whether as God, as a superangelic being, or as man only, it matters not, is all the faith the Gospel requires. But they forget that they to whom the Apostle so answers are supposed to be already instructed in the faith, and to lack nothing of the true Christian faith, but to believe that the Christ that was to come has come, and is this same Jesus whom they crucified, and whom God has raised from the dead. The simple article enjoined was all the addition or modification their previous faith required. But to conclude from this that nothing more was required at all is very bad logic.

This fact attended to furnishes us one of the reasons why the faith is always assumed or presupposed in the Holy Scriptures, instead of being distinctly and formally taught. The sacred writers always address themselves to believers, to persons supposed to have already received the faith, and therefore not in need of being formally and systematically taught the whole creed. They write, not to propose the creed, but simply, under the relation of faith, to correct the errors of believers, or to enlighten them on some particular points of doctrine. Nothing is more illogical than to conclude, from the absence of all distinct and formal statement from their pages of the several articles of the creed, that no formal creed was proposed, believed, or required.

The recognition of the primitive revelation is necessary, also, to account for the sublime truths we often meet with in ancient pagan writers, Oriental and Occidental, in juxtaposition with mere puerilities, gross absurdities, and abominations. Any one who has read Plato will understand what we mean. There are passages in this writer hardly unworthy of a Christian Father, which are admirable for the truth and sublimity of the thought, for their lofty religious conception and pure morality; and there are others childishly weak, obviously absurd, and grossly impure, as, for instance, some passages in the *Banquet*, the *Timæus*, and the *Republic*. Take Socrates himself. What more noble than his speech on his trial? He speaks of God, of virtue, and immortality with his disciples, while awaiting his execution, almost as a Christian, and more worthily than many who call themselves Christians do or can speak; and yet, just before his death, he can order a cock to be sacrificed to Æsculapius. Through nearly all heathen antiquity we find similar phenomena constantly recurring. How explain them? The mind capable of producing from its own resources the true, the pure, the sublime, and beautiful thoughts and sentiments we find, could never have produced or tolerated those of a totally different character, invariably mixed up with them. The only possible explanation is, that in the former they spake from tradition, from the sublime wisdom of the ancients, derived from a primitive revelation, as they themselves always acknowledge; just as the only explanation of what we find agreeable to the purity, truth, and sublimity of the Gospel in the writings and discourses of modern heretics is that it is derived not from their heresy or their own minds, but retained from the Gospel itself, is the reminiscence of the true faith, not yet wholly lost in the crude mass of their own errors and speculations.

But we have suffered ourselves to be carried too far away by a topic only incidental to our present purpose. While acknowledging the danger to which Count de Maistre's method of reasoning for religion against an unbelieving and scoffing age is exposed, when not duly guarded, we have wished, in passing, to show that it is substantially sound, and may be used with great propriety and effect. The influence his writings have exerted on France are a proof of it. When he first appeared, religion was out of fashion, and her voice failed to arrest the attention of the reading public. It required no ordinary degree of moral courage at that time to avow one's self a Christian, a firm believer in the Church of God, and ready to do battle for the faith. For more than half a century the whole literary taste had been perverted; the philosophers and their followers, Voltaire and his school, reigned supreme in the world of letters, in the public acts, and the saloons of fashion. But

Count de Maistre did not hesitate to raise his voice, and, seconded by De Lammenais, not yet fallen, and by the Restoration and its friends, he succeeded, by the grace of God, in bringing up religion once more to men's thoughts and affections, and of showing to faith and purity—what is never to be doubted—that they have no cause to blush before the pretended worshippers of reason, even in the temple of reason herself. France is no longer what she was. The French works best known and most generally read by the people of this country are the groans, writhings, and contortions of a party in its agony. They proceed not from the mind or the heart of the real, living, progressive France of to-day. Sans-culottism in religion, morals, or politics is not at present precisely a Parisian mode, and it is no longer incompatible with good taste and admission into good society to cover one's nakedness with the robe of justice and piety.

Of the several works of Count de Maistre, there is no one which, at the present moment, could be circulated or read with more advantage amongst us, than the one now before us, or better fitted to the actual wants of our politicians, whether Catholics or Protestants; for, unhappily, a very considerable portion of our Catholic population are as unsound in their politics as their Protestant neighbors. Both classes, with individual exceptions, have borrowed their political notions from the school of Hobbes, Locke, Jean Jacques Rousseau, and Thomas Paine, and forget, or have a strong tendency to forget, that Divine Providence has something to do with forming, preserving, amending, or overthrowing the constitutions of states. We say nothing new, when we say that modern politics are in principle, and generally in practice, purely atheistic. Even large numbers, who in religion are sound orthodox believers, and would suffer a thousand deaths sooner than knowingly swerve one iota from the faith, may be found, who do not hesitate to vote God out of the political constitution, and to advocate liberty on principles which logically put man in the place of God. It is to such as these the little work before us is addressed, and they cannot study it without perceiving the capital mistake they have made —not in seeking political freedom, but in seeking to base it on atheistical principles. The man who advocates political liberty on Protestant principles can stop short of atheism only at the expense of his logic.

Count de Maistre is no doubt a stanch monarchist, and holds hereditary monarchy, tempered by a due admixture of aristocracy and democracy, to be the best of all possible forms of government; but it is not for this we commend him, for this is by no means a necessary conclusion from the great generative principle of political constitutions he insists upon. That principle we may accept without any disposition to be monarchists, for it is as true and as applicable in the case of a republican constitution as in that of a monarchical constitution. Where the existing legitimate order is monarchical, it undoubtedly requires us to support monarchy, and forbids us to seek to substitute another order in its place; but, for the same reason, where the existing legitimate order is the republican, it requires us to support republicanism, and forbids us to seek to introduce monarchy. In this country the existing legal order is republican, and the principle the Count insists upon commands us, whatever may or may not be our private convictions as to the best form of government *in se*, to support it, and to resist with our lives every attempt to subvert it. It may or may not be, we may or we may not believe it, the best of all possible forms of government in the abstract; but that has nothing to do with the question. It is the form which God in his providence has established here, and therefore it is the best for *us*; it is the law, and therefore we must obey it, and cannot resist it without resisting God, from whom is all power, by whom kings reign and legislators decree just things.

There are two grounds on which we may seek support for our republican institutions;—the one, opinion; the other, conscience; —that is, either because we believe them the best *in se*, or because they are the law. Our modern politicians, who uniformly mistake falsehood for truth, and substitute the feebler for the stronger, the worse for the better reason, as a matter of course place all their reliance on the former, and regard those who prefer the latter as the enemies of our free institutions. But nothing is more fluctuating, precarious, or uncertain than opinion. The multitude may be of one opinion to-day, and of another to-morrow. To-day they may hurrah for democracy; to-morrow they may throw up their caps for some military hero, and cry, Long live the king! To rely on mere opinion is to lean on a broken reed. The opinion may change, and the moment it does, we have no reason, if it has been our reliance, to urge for sustaining the present order, or why the people should not subvert it, and substitute some other order; and we may be sure the opinion will change, whenever the present order proves, or attempts to prove, itself a government by restraining popular passion and caprice, or anything more than a by-law of a voluntary association;—

> "For no man ever feels the halter draw
> But with a mean opinion of the law."

But if we place their support on the ground that they are the legal order, the law, we make our appeal, not to opinion, but to conscience. Conscience uniformly and invariably commands us to obey the law, but does not command us always to obey opinion. Opinions may vary as to what is the law; but when this or that is decided to be law, conscience, which is not opinion, without any variation or the least hesitation, commands us to submit to it, and all who regard at all the voice of conscience do so. When we place the obligation to support our institutions on the notion we may have that they are the best, we give them only an intellectual basis, and can enlist only the intellect in their behalf; but when we demand obedience to them on the ground that they are the law, we base them on morality, and place them under the protection of religion. We demand then obedience as a *duty*, not merely as a sound judgment, and make loyalty not merely a sentiment, but a virtue. It was only the folly or delusion of the last century that could, for a moment, have hesitated between conscience and opinion, or even pretended to doubt which is the more reasonable and solid basis of government.

We suspect, however, that our politicians will continue to prefer opinion to conscience; for it is not the preservation of our institutions, but the facility of changing them, that they wish to secure. It is not government they want, but the liberty to make the government any thing they please; or if they ask for government, it is not that it may govern them, but that they may govern it. They want, not a fixed and permanent order, but a loose and flexible order, yielding without the least resistance to their passions, caprices, or supposed interests. They regard, and for this reason will continue to regard, all those who would make our institutions sacred, place them under the protection of religion and morals, and support them on the ground that they are the law, and that the law must be obeyed, as the enemies of the people, and to be denounced as anti-republican and anti-American. They are willing to appeal to opinion and sentiment, but they cannot endure that we should appeal to religion and morals, to conscience, or the sense of duty. For on the former ground there is liberty to change, modify, subvert, at will; but on the latter there is a strict obligation to preserve the institutions as they are, and to resist unto death every one who would seek to subvert them. It is not monarchy or aristocracy against which the modern spirit fights, but against *loyalty;* what it hates is not this or that form of government, but *legitimacy,* and it would rebel against democracy as quick as against absolute monarchy, if democracy were asserted on the ground of legitimacy.

The modern spirit is in every thing the direct denial of the practical reason. It reverses every thing which has received the sanction of the race. In former times, it was universally held that authority was a good, indeed a necessity, and in all things men sought for an authority, something which could and had the right to command. They inquired always for the law, and law was always held to be imperative. Religion was the highest law, and authoritative, and no individual or nation had a right to dispute its dominion ; morals were binding, were the law imposed by religion ; politics were referred to the sovereign authority, to the majesty of the prince, or the state. The greatest evil conceivable was supposed to be that of being without law, without religious, moral, and political authority having the right to exact and the ability to secure submission. Man's glory, according to the ancient spirit, was in obedience to law. But the modern spirit reverses all this. It seeks not the authority which men are bound to obey, and to induce them to obey it, but it claims for man himself the authority in all things to make the law. It asserts the universal and absolute supremacy of man, and his unrestricted right to subject religion, morals, and politics to his own will, passion, or caprice. There is no denying this. Its direct aim and tendency is to place the subject over the sovereign, and to give to the subject in religion, morals, or politics the right to put a rope round his sovereign's neck, as the Chinese sometimes do around the neck of their idol, and drag him from his throne, and through the streets, and apply the bamboo whenever he chances not to conform himself to their will and pleasure. It calls government government, because it is *not* government ; morals morals, because they are *not* morals, that is, not obligatory upon the will ; religion religion, because it is *not* religion, that is, does *not* bind man to God ; law law, because it is *not* law ; and reason reason, because it is *not* reason. Marvellous is the age we live in ! Marvellous the light and progress of the modern world ! We have extinguished the light of reason, and therefore are reasonable ; reduced wisdom to folly, and therefore are wise ; substituted nonsense for sense, and therefore are intelligent, and have the right to call all who went before us fools and madmen, which assuredly they were,— unless we are.

The political mania of the last century, and a mania not yet much abated, was that a political constitution may be written and clapped into one's pocket. Men not in a lunatic hospital, men who were regarded by their contemporaries as great men, learned men, profound philosophers and statesmen, in open day, in elaborate treatises, in grave deliberative assemblies, actually contended that the political constitution is a thing which may be made as one makes a handcart or a wheelbarrow, or drawn up beforehand as one draws up a note of hand; and, what is stranger still, they were believed, and whole nations thrilled at the wonderful discovery, and, leaving all other business, engaged heart and soul, might and main, in the manufacture and sale of constitutions. We ourselves opened a shop for the business, or pretended to do so; but France opened an establishment on a much larger scale, and carried on the business to an extent which differed only a step from the sublime. The facility and rapidity with which the lively French, for a series of years, turned out ready-made constitutions, for home consumption and exportation, can be compared to nothing better than to the facility with which a Connecticut Yankee turns out wooden clocks, wooden bowls, wooden nutmegs, cut-nails, clothes-pins, or loco-foco matches. The delusion was all but universal for a time, and can be accounted for not without attributing it in part to demoniacal agency. Men not drawn down below the rank of their own nature, not made worse than human in their passions, and less than human in their reason and understanding, could never have been so wildly and madly carried away.

In the work before us, Count de Maistre attacks with all his erudition, philosophy, experience, and wit, this terrible delusion, —a delusion which even Carlyle has mercilessly ridiculed, and against which, our readers will bear us witness, we ourselves have argued and declaimed with all our might, ever since we began to address the public on political subjects. De Maistre shows, beyond the possibility of doubt or cavil, that the political constitution of a state is not and cannot be made; that whatever it is, whatever its form, if it be a constitution at all, it is generated, not made; that it grows up by Divine Providence, and is never framed beforehand, drawn up deliberately, and put into operation by those who live or are to live under it. It is never the work of deliberation, but always the work of Divine

Providence, using men and circumstances as his instruments. It is always immediately or mediately—mediately in all cases, perhaps, except one—imposed by God himself, is the expression of the Divine will, and therefore legitimate, sacred, and suited to the nation. This is the leading principle of the Essay before us. The generative principle of all political constitutions which are such is Divine Providence, never the deliberate wisdom or will of men.

This doctrine is unquestionably conservative; for it makes the constitution sacred. It is monarchical, where monarchy is the constitution of the state; it is also republican, where, as with us, the constitution is republican. It would forbid the subjects of a monarchy to throw off monarchy and attempt to create a republic; it would also forbid the citizens of a republic to throw off republicanism and attempt to found a monarchy. If we are destructives or revolutionists on principle, and are resolved to be always able to govern the government when we please and as we please, this doctrine must offend us, and we cannot but resist it; but if we are attached to our institutions, hold our constitution to be law, not a mere regulation, and wish to preserve it, this is the very doctrine we need, and must heartily embrace. For our own part, we hold the republican constitution of this country to be the legitimate order, and ourselves bound in conscience to submit to it, whether we believe it the best possible form of government for every people on earth or not. IT IS THE BEST POSSIBLE FORM FOR US. We wish to preserve it intact, in all its life and vigor, and therefore we wish to see the doctrine in question embraced and cherished by every American citizen.

But when we speak of the American constitution, our readers must not imagine that we mean the written instrument usually denominated the constitution. The written constitution may sometimes be a memorandum of the real constitution, but is never that constitution itself; and it is always a mere cobweb, save so far as it is also written on the hearts, and in the habits, the manners and customs of the people, as our own daily experience abundantly proves. The constitution is the living soul of the nation, that by virtue of which it is a nation, and is able to live a national life, and perform national functions. You can no more write it out on parchment, and put it into your pocket, than you can the soul of man. It is no dead letter, which when interrogated is silent, and when attacked is impotent; it is a living spirit, a living power, a living providence, and resides wherever the nation is, and expresses itself in every national act. Written constitutions are never resorted to, when the real constitution is in full vitality and vigor, and the state performs freely its normal functions; and the most beautiful period in the history of every nation is the period prior to the attempt to reduce its constitution and laws to writing. The written instrument is invariably a proof that the constitution has suffered violence, has been enfeebled, and its existence endangered. It is resorted to as a means of preservation, in the hope that by writing it the constitution may be strengthened, and further encroachment prevented. But when it is in its full vigor, and has suffered no violence, men no more think of writing it, than the housewife thinks each morning of reducing to writing her arrangements for her household during the day.

The people of this country have not made, and could not make, our political constitution. It was imposed by a competent authority, and has grown to be what it is, through the providence of God. The people have never had the control of it. It was not their foresight, wisdom, convictions, or will, that made it republican. The constitution was republican from the first, and we established no monarchy or nobility at the close of the war of Independence, for the simple reason that neither was in our constitution. The royalty and nobility we knew prior to Independence were English, not American. Mr. Bancroft has well remarked, in his history of the Colonization of the United States, that royalty and nobility did not emigrate. Since they did not emigrate, they remained at home, and were not here; not being here, they were not in our political constitution. The commons alone emigrated, and consequently our constitution recognized only commons. When, therefore, the foreign authority was thrown off, and we were left to our own constitution, we had only the government of the commons, that is to say, the representative democracy, or the elective aristocracy, if we may use the term, which we brought here from the mother country. Our government is simply the British House of Commons, without the king and House of Lords, divided for the sake of convenience into an upper and lower chamber, and with such few changes and modifications as were necessary to provide for an executive authority. The constitution was determined for us by the providence of God, which so ordered it that only the commons emigrated, and so created and arranged circumstances as to compel us from sheer necessity to live under a government from which royalty and nobility are excluded.

Count de Maistre not only contends that the constitution is never made, or drawn up by the people with deliberation and forethought, that it is always the work of Providence using men and circumstances to effect or express his will, but that it can never be essentially changed by the people or the nation, deliberately or otherwise, without the destruction of the nation itself. If God determines and fixes the political constitution of a people, it follows that the constitution exists by the divine will and authority; to seek to subvert or essentially change it is, then, to war against God, and we need not labor to prove that no individual or nation can ever rebel against God with success or impunity. Nations and individuals who conspire against God, and seek to make their will prevail instead of his, are sure to be destroyed. They separate themselves from the source of life, from the fountain of strength, and can but wither and die, as the branch severed from the vine.

This conclusion, which we know by infallible faith to be true, is, moreover, verified by all history. Our wise politicians seek a thousand reasons to explain the different results which national independence has produced here, from those which it has produced in Spanish America. There can be no question that in every one of the Spanish American states republicanism has proved a complete failure; yet with us it is thought to have succeeded. Whence the difference? It is idle to look for the cause in the superiority of the Anglo-Saxon over the Spanish race, for this superiority is perfectly imaginary; and the Spanish American colonies, as colonies, were in real prosperity and genuine civilization in advance of the Anglo-American. The difference of religion, too, has been immensely in favor of Spanish America; because, while Protestantism tends to render men disorderly, insubordinate, impatient of restraint, and indifferent to the sacred obligations of law, Catholicity generates habits of order, subordination, and reverence for law. Yet the attempt to establish republicanism in Spanish America has resulted very nearly in the dissolution of all society. The cause of the difference is in the fact that republicanism with us was from the first the constitution, but was never the constitution of the Spanish American colonies. In them royalty and nobility settled; and the whole constitution of the mother country, not merely that of the commons, was transferred to the New World. Royalty and nobility were integral elements in their constitution from the outset. We in declaring independence made no revolution in the government; we only threw off what was foreign, while we retained all that was indigenous, and the removal of the foreign or English authority only enabled the indigenous to manifest and exert itself in open day, in full and unimpeded life and vigor. But in Spanish America independence was not merely throwing off the foreign element, the authority of the mother country, but was a revolution, a subversion of the existing constitution, and the attempt to establish a new and a totally different political order. The cause of the failure is precisely in this attempt to change essentially the political constitution. If Spanish America had simply declared herself independent of Old Spain, but retained intact her domestic constitution, there can be no reason to doubt that her prosperity would, at least, have kept pace with ours. Portuguese America, Brazil, has succeeded the best, after us, of all the American States, for she did not essentially change her original constitution.

We can easily suppose what would have been our success, if

we had attempted to introduce and establish monarchy and nobility. There were among us distinguished men—the most distinguished, perhaps, and firm patriots, too—who had no confidence in republicanism, and were pretty well persuaded that a government without king and nobles must prove a failure. But we had no royalty and nobility. Neither was here, and neither could be introduced without a social revolution. Suppose we had attempted to introduce them, to constitute the three estates, and retain the whole constitution of the mother country; who can doubt that the result would have been similar to what has been in Spanish America the attempt to introduce republicanism? Neither being in the constitution, both would have been resisted by the whole force of American society, and could have triumphed only by overcoming that force, and destroying the whole existing social order, that is, the state itself.

France sought to change from a monarchy to a republic. She was great, powerful, intellectual, and enthusiastic. Never could the attempt have been made under more favorable auspices. She was aided, or not impeded, in the outset, by the very orders in the state which had the greatest privileges to lose; the surrounding nations, the whole world sympathized with her, and applauded her movement; and yet her failure was striking, and no man can doubt, if he has ordinary judgment, that, if she had not returned to her old constitution, or in part returned, she would ere this have been blotted out from the chart of Europe as an independent nation. Her present uneasiness, her present unsettled and ominous state, and all the difficulties she has to encounter grow out of her return having been partial, instead of complete. The most glorious period of French history since the reign of Louis the Fourteenth, perhaps since St. Louis, is that of Charles the Tenth,—a man and a prince to whom history is not likely to do justice. The Bourbons committed great faults, and they deserved, and drew down upon their guilty heads the vengeance of Almighty God; but if the family had, before the breaking out of the Revolution, or in its first stages, listened to the Count d'Artois, or if France had been wise enough to understand his character and appreciate the firmness of his principles when he became Charles the Tenth, she would now have been in the possession of her ancient constitution and of all her ancient glory. There would have been no "glorious three days," no *programme de Hôtel de Ville*, no such anomaly as a "citizen king,"—a king by virtue of the *Bourse*, it is true, but only so much the better. The same impossibility of changing the constitution without destroying social order we see in the recent history of Spain and Portugal. Each of these kingdoms, Spain especially, played at no distant date a distinguished part among the kingdoms of Europe; but both are now fallen so low that there are few so poor as to do them reverence. It is not difficult to trace their present degradation, we say not to efforts at social amelioration, but to efforts to ameliorate their social condition by organic changes, or fundamental changes in the political constitution of the state, that is, to revolutionism, and they must return substantially to their old national constitutions, lapse into anarchy and barbarism, or be absorbed by their more powerful neighbors.

We have found in our historical reading no instance of a fundamental change of the national constitution that was successful. Never does a republic become a monarchy, or a monarchy a republic, without the virtual destruction of the state. Athens was originally monarchical, tempered, we suspect, by both aristocracy and democracy. The democratic element finally gained the mastery; but it retained the ascendency for only one hundred and four years. Solon himself saw the Pisistratidæ, and the whole period was one of political turmoil, of change, and usurpation, and the government was almost always in the hands of a single chief, who ruled, with or without law, during his ascendency, very much as he pleased. The smaller Grecian cities, which adopted the republican order with scarcely an exception, in brief space, fell under the rule of tyrants or usurpers. We make no account of Rome, because her constitution was originally patrician, a modification of the patriarchal, and the royal authority acted not really on the people, but simply on the patrician, or head of the *gens*. The abolition of the royal and the substitution of the consular authority were no fundamental change in the constitution; nor was the establishment, at a later period, of the tribunitial veto; for the positive power of the state continued where it had been placed by Romulus, in the patrician body. The change to the imperial government was perhaps more fundamental, and makes decidedly for the doctrine we maintain; for just in proportion as the constitution was changed under the emperors, and they usurped the functions of the Senate, Rome declined, and continued to decline, till it was no more.

In fact, if we may credit at all the lessons of history, the change of the original constitution of a state, if fundamental and permanent, is always and inevitably the destruction of the state itself. It is as easy to extract the soul from the body, and give to the body another soul, without causing death, as to take from a state its original constitution and give it a new one, and still retain the life of the nation. If the original constitution has died out, the nation is dead, and you can no more give it a new constitution and restore it to life, than you can give to a dead body a new soul, and render it once more a living body. The new constitution must come in with a new people, which subjects and takes the place of the old, as is clearly evinced in the case of the downfall of the old Roman empire, and the rise of the modern states of Europe. Even religion herself cannot prevent it; she may delay the catastrophe, but she has no power to avert it. Constantine, Theodosius, Justinian, cannot prevent the doom of Rome, old or new. The Northern barbarian executes it upon the one, the Turk upon the other. The vast populations of Asia have no indigenous power to rise from their degradation, and they will be restored never, unless conquered and subjected by a people already living, already in possession of a constitution in its life and vigor, because their old political constitutions are effete, and they now subsist as populations rather than as states.

God, by giving in his providence a particular constitution to a particular people, has fixed its law, the law of its life, its prosperity, and its duration. No people survives its constitution. The overthrow of our republican constitution would be our political death. Spanish America, if it does not reëstablish its original monarchical and aristocratic order, must either lapse into complete barbarism, or be absorbed by us. The Canadas have foolishly attempted once, perhaps may attempt again, independence of the mother country, in view of establishing the republican regime; they have thus far failed, for they have royalty and nobility in their constitution. If Lower Canada had not had, she would, in what we call our Revolution, have made common cause with us, gained her independence, and become a member of our confederacy. Some Young Irelanders appear to us also to dream of republicanism or democracy for Ireland. They could not be madder. The constitution of Ireland is not, never was, and never can be, republican. Royalty and nobility are essential elements of it.

But let no one be so silly as to imagine that the conservative principle contended for by Count de Maistre is hostile to such social meliorations and such administrative changes as time and its vicissitudes may render necessary or expedient. But the true social reformer is the state physician, and proceeds in regard to the state precisely as the medical doctor does in regard to the human body. He seeks always to heal the disorders of the state without destroying or impairing the constitution, and by the application of such remedies as are peculiarly adapted to the constitution. If the constitution is already broken up and become incurable, he knows there is no effectual remedy, and that complete dissolution, sooner or later, must inevitably ensue. But if he finds the constitution still sound at bottom, he seeks simply to restore it to its normal state, and to guard against whatever would tend to impair its healthy and vigorous action. In other words, he restores, but does not seek to create; develops, but does not attempt to institute.

On this principle we see our present Holy Father introducing administrative changes in the temporal government of the States of the Church. How far the reforms he has introduced or proposed extend, we are not able to say; and how far they will effect the end intended, and serve to tranquillize the turbulent spirits, the unprincipled and ambitious, among his subjects, it is not for us to judge, or even to inquire. But we can easily believe that in an old government, like that of the Roman States, some administrative abuses may with the lapse of time have crept in, and that the alterations which for the last hundred years have been taking place around them have rendered some administrative changes expedient. As a wise and judicious prince, as a watchful and tender father, the Pope seems to believe such to be the fact, and to be determined to correct the former and to introduce the latter; and for this he has been applauded to the echo, rather in the hope of inducing him to go farther, we apprehend, than from any real satisfaction felt for what he has thus far done or proposed. But we confess, that, notwithstanding the shouts which ring in our ears, and the loud praises he has secured from those whose praise is always suspicious, we have seen in him not the least conceivable tendency to countenance the misnamed Liberalism now so rife in the European populations. They who flatter themselves that the Sovereign Pontiff of Christendom, is about to place himself at the head of the Liberals, as their leader in the war against legitimacy, will find their shouts have been premature, and their hopes fallacious. That Pius the Ninth is the father of his people, that his sympathies are with the oppressed and down-trodden of all nations, that he is the uncompromising enemy of injustice and arbitrary rule, whether of kings or peoples, is no doubt true, and in saying so we only say he is Pope; but *because* this is true, we have the fullest assurance that nothing can be farther from his thoughts and intentions than to countenance, even in the remotest degree, the mad and ruinous radicalism or socialism of the day, or that it has aught to hope from him but his anathema.

We know the enemies of law and order have rejoiced; we know that even some Catholics, placing their politics, unconsciously no doubt, before their religion, have flattered themselves that our Holy Father seeks to effect an alliance between Catholicity and modern socialism; but he is the Vicar of Jesus Christ, not a pupil from the school of the apostate De Lamennais, and can no more form an alliance with socialism than with despotism. One Pope is not in the habit of reversing, in what involves a principle, the decisions of another. We all know the doctrine of the *l'Avenir;* we all know that after the revolution of July, 1830, De Lamennais sought to persuade the Church to make common cause with the European populations against their political sovereigns, to throw herself into the arms of the people, and trust for her support to their holy instincts; and we all know the answer he received from Rome. The Church throws herself into the arms of neither the people nor the sovereigns; she relies for support on no power foreign to herself. She rests on God alone, who has promised to be with her all days unto the consummation of the world. She forms no alliances. The sects may trim their sails to the breeze, and appeal now to despotism and now to liberalism, now seek to avail themselves of a temperance excitement, and now of an Abolitionist or a socialist movement, for they are all impotent in themselves, and can subsist only by means of supplies drawn from abroad. But the Church draws all her support and all her motive power from within, from God himself. Her ensign is the cross, the cross alone, and her battle-cry, from the first to the last, is *Deus vult.* As she withstood the despotic tendency of kings and emperors in the Middle Ages, and taught the sovereigns that they held their power as a trust from God, and were bound to exercise it for the good of their subjects, so will she withstand the popular tendencies towards license and anarchy, and teach the people that their duty and their interest are in the maintenance of the order Almighty God has established for them, and in frank and conscientious submission to law.

Nothing could be madder, on the part of Catholics with us, than to adopt the radicalism of the country. Our only security here is in the supremacy of the law, and the prevailing sense of its sacredness, without which its supremacy is impossible. The Catholic who does not wish to pave the way for the confiscation of the property of his Church, and for the suppression of his worship in these States, must beware how he binds himself to the extreme *liberalism* of the country, and aids the tendency now so active, under the name of progress, to sweep away all the guaranties of law. It is natural that persons who have during their whole lives felt only the pressure of government, and known government only in its abuses, should on coming here be disposed to adopt extreme views, and think only of restricting the sphere and diminishing the power of government; and it is natural also, that, finding their religion generally unpopular, they should seek to conciliate favor for it, or to acquire popularity for themselves, by falling in with the popular political current, and showing themselves enthusiastic in their support of the dominant tendency of the country; but in doing either they are as far from consulting their true interest as they are their duty as Catholics. Majorities may protect themselves; minorities have no protection but in the sacredness and supremacy of law. The law is right as it is; we must study to keep it so; and if we do, we shall always throw our influence on the conservative side, never on the radical side.

It may be objected, that the doctrine we contend for is opposed to progress; but it is opposed to progress in no sense in which progress is not a delusion. There is progress of individuals, but no progress of human nature,—a progress of particular nations, but none of the race. Nations are like individuals; they are born with their peculiar constitutions and capacities, which determine all that they can be. They grow up like individuals, attain their growth, their maturity, decline into old age, become enfeebled, and die, and pass away. It is the universal law, and there is no *elixir vitæ* for nations any more than for individuals. The Rosicrucians pretended that it is possible in the case of the individual to ward off death and maintain perpetual youth, and Godwin, and Balzac, and Bulwer have made the notion the theme of interesting romances, as all know who have read *St. Leon*, *Le Centenaire*, and *Zanoni*, and our modern politicians try to persuade us to believe the same is possible with regard to the state; but, in either case, it is a mere dream of the fancy or a delusion of the devil. The limits of our national progress are fixed by the inherent principles of our constitution, and it is madness to dream of passing beyond them.

In conlusion, we would express our thanks to the translator of the excellent little work which we have made the text of our remarks. He has done his task with taste and fidelity, and the notes he has annexed to the work add to its permanent value. There is one thing, however, the translator has not done; but as he knows what it is, and as it concerns him personally, we say no more. Disagreeing with De Maistre as to his monarchical views, at least so far as concerns our own country, and avowing it as our full and settled conviction that the destiny of our country is inseparable from the destiny of its republican constitution, we yet recommend his Essay as worthy of general study, and as almost the only sensible political pamphlet that has ever been published amongst us. Our politicians may slight it, may denounce it, and denounce us for recommending it; but if they do, so much the worse for them, so much the worse for the country.

WAR AND LOYALTY.*

OCTOBER, 1846.

OUR orators have invested the Fourth of July with so many disturbing associations, that our citizens are gradually becoming less and less disposed to greet its annual return with those festivities which it was the hope of our fathers would continue to

* An Oration delivered before the Authorities of the City of Boston in the Tremont Temple, July 4, 1846. By FLETCHER WEBSTER Boston: Eastburn. 1846. 8vo. pp. 33.

mark it through all generations to come. Still, it is a day sacred in the affections of every American citizen, and it cannot come round without exciting lively emotions of gratitude and joy in every American heart. The birth of a nation is an event to be remembered, and the day on which it takes its rank in the family of independent nations is well deserving to be set apart by some service, at once joyous and solemn, recounting the glory which has been won, the blessings which have been received, and pointing to the high destiny and grave responsibilities to which the new people are called.

The orations ordinarily given on our national anniversary are of that peculiar sort which it is said neither gods nor men can tolerate. They are tawdry and turgid, full of stale declamation about liberty, fulsome and disgusting glorification of ourselves as a people, or uncalled-for denunciations of those states and empires that have not seen proper to adopt political institutions similar to our own. Yet we may, perhaps, be too fastidious in our taste, and too sweeping in our censures. Boys will be boys, and dulness will be dulness, and when either is installed "orator of the day," the performance must needs be boyish or dull. But when the number of orations annually called forth by our national jubilee, from all sorts of persons, throughout the length and breadth of the land, is considered, we may rather wonder that so many are produced which do credit to their authors, and fall not far below the occasion, than that there are so few. All are not mere school-boy productions; all are not patriotism on tiptoe, nor eloquence on stilts. Every year sends out not a few, which, for their sound sense, deep thought, subdued passion, earnest spirit, manly tone, and chaste expression, deserve an honorable place in our national literature. There are—and perhaps as large a proportion as we ought to expect—Fourth of July orators, who, while they indulge in not unseemly exultations, forget to disgust us with untimely rant about self-government, the marvellous virtue and intelligence of the masses, and the industrial miracles they are daily performing; who show by their reserve, rather than by their noisy declamation, that they have American hearts, and confidence in American patriotism and American institutions. A people not factitiously great has no occasion to speak of its greatness; and true patriotism expresses itself in deeds, not words. The real American patriots are not those shallow brains and gizzard hearts which are always prating of the American spirit, American genius, American interests, American greatness, and calling for an American party; but those calm, quiet, self-possessed spirits who rarely think of asking themselves whether they are Americans or not, and who are too sincere and ardent in their patrotism to imagine it can be necessary to parade its titles. Their patriotism has no suspicions, no jealousies, no fears, no self-consciousness. It is too deep for words. It is silent, majestic. It is where the country is, does what she bids, and, though sacrificing all upon her altars, never dreams that it is doing any thing extraordinary. There is, perhaps, more of this genuine patriotism in the American people than strangers, or even we ourselves, commonly suppose. The foam floats on the surface, and is whirled hither and thither by each shifting breeze; but below are the sweet, silent, and deep waters.

Among the orations delivered on our great national festival, which we would not willingly forget, the one before us by Mr. Fletcher Webster, eldest son of the Hon. Daniel Webster, deserves a high rank. It is free from the principal faults to which we have alluded, simple and chaste in its style and language, bold and manly in its tone and spirit, and, in the main, sound and just in doctrine and sentiment. It frequently reminds us of the qualities which mark the productions of the author's distinguished father, and which have placed him at the head of American orators; and it bears ample evidence, that, with time, experience, and effort, the son need not be found unworthy of such a father.

Certainly, we do not subscribe to every sentiment, view, or argument of this eloquent oration; but we like its frank and manly tone, its independent and earnest spirit, and we accept without reserve the leading doctrine it was designed to set forth. We are also grateful to Mr. Webster for having had the moral courage to assert great truths in a community where they can win little applause, and to administer a well merited rebuke to certain dangerous ultraisms when and where it was not uncalled for. He has proved that he is not unworthy to be reckoned a freeman and a patriot, and he deserves and will receive the approbation of all who can distinguish between words and things, and prefer sound sense and solid wisdom to mad fanaticism and hollow cant. It is cheering to find our young men rising above the tendencies of the age and country, and manifesting some respect for the wisdom and virtue of their ancestors, and indicating that they have some suspicion that all that is wise and just was not born with the new generation and possibly may not die with it. It permits us to hope things may not have gone quite so badly with us as we had feared; that the people are less unsound at the core than we had dared believe; that, after all, there is a redeeming spirit at work among them; and that our noble experiment in behalf of popular institutions may not be destined to a speedy failure.

Our great danger lies in the radical tendency which has become so wide, deep, and active in the American people. We have, to a great extent, ceased to regard any thing as sacred or venerable; we spurn what is old; war against what is fixed; and labor to set all religious, domestic, and social institutions afloat on the wild and tumultuous sea of speculation and experiment. Nothing has hitherto gone right; nothing has been achieved that is worth retaining; and man and Providence have thus far done nothing but commit one continued series of blunders. All things are to be reconstructed; the world is to be recast, and by our own wisdom and strength. We must borrow no light from the past, adopt none of its maxims, and take no *data* from its experience. Even language itself, which only embodies the thoughts, convictions, sentiments, hopes, affections, and aspirations of the race, cannot serve as a medium of intercourse between man and man. It is not safe to affirm that **black is black**, for the word *black* only names an idea which the past entertained, and most likely a false idea. With such a tendency, wide and deep, strong and active, we cannot but apprehend the most serious dangers. With it there can be no permanent institutions, no government, no society, no virtue, no well-being.

There is much to strengthen this radical tendency. It is natural to the inexperienced, the conceited, and the vain; and it can hardly fail to be powerful in a community where these have facilities for occupying prominent and commanding positions. Young enthusiasts, taught to "remember, when they are old, not to forget the dreams of their youth," that is, not to profit by experience, and not doubting that what they were ignorant of yesterday was known by no one, and that they must needs be as far in advance of all the world as they are of their own infancy, bring benevolent affection, disinterested zeal, and conscientiousness to its aid; political aspirants, reckless of principle and greedy of place, appeal to it as their most facile means of success; and the mass of the people, finding their passions flattered, and their prejudices undisturbed, are thrown off their guard, presume all is right, and cherish unconsciously the enemy that is to destroy them. A factitious public opinion grows up, becomes supreme, to which whoever wishes for some consideration in the community in which he lives, must offer incense, and which he must presume on no occasion to contradict. The majority of the people, indeed, may not be represented by this opinion,—may, it is true, not approve it; but they are isolated one from another, minding each their own affairs, and ignorant of their numbers and strength; while the few, by their union, mutual acquaintance, concert, and clamor, are able to silence any single voice not raised in adulation of their idol. Political parties conspire to the same end. One party to-day, ambitious of success, courts this factitious public opinion as a useful auxiliary, and succeeds; the other must do so to-morrow, or abandon all hopes of succeeding. Then follows a strife of parties, which shall bid highest, and *outradical* the other. The radical tendency is thus daily exaggerated by those who in reality disapprove it, and in their feelings have no sympathy with it. Hence, the evil goes ever from bad to worse. Unhappily, this is no fancy sketch. We have seen it, and we see it daily pass under our own eyes, and not, we confess, without lively alarm for our beloved country and her popular institutions.

It is, therefore, with more than ordinary pleasure that we see among our young men, in whose hands are the destinies of our country, whose views and passions and interests must be consulted by any party aspiring to power and place, some symptoms of an opposing tendency. Right glad are we that the young "sovereigns" show some signs of beginning to take sounder and more practical views, and to cherish a reaction against the ultraisms of the day. This oration, and some other indications, which have not escaped our notice, prove to us that there is a returning respect for the wisdom of experience, and that the reign of the Garrisons, the Parkers, the Sumners, the O'Sullivans, the Channings, the Abby Folsoms, *et id omne genus*, approaches its termination, and that henceforth practical sense and wise experience will at least dispute the throne with fanatic zeal, blind enthusiasm, and bloated conceit.

In preparing this oration, Mr. Webster must have been conscious that he was running athwart the views of many whom most of us have been accustomed to hold in high esteem, and that, in venturing to assert the lawfulness of war and the obligation of the citizen to obey the government, he would be attacking every class of fanatics in the land, and could not fail to incur the unmitigated wrath and hostility of the whole modern "Peace" party. Yet his courage did not fail him. He does not appear to have had any misgivings before even the awful shade of the late Noah Worcester, founder of the American Peace Society, and he has dared consult his relations as a man and a citizen, and to lay it down as his rule of action, that he is responsible, not to the self-created associations of the day, to the reigning cant of the time and place, but solely to his God and his country. For this, however much he may be condemned by fanatical reformers, we honor him, and for this every right-minded man will honor him; for in this he has asserted his independence, and set an example worthy of imitation.

The main topic of this oration is the lawfulness of war, and the duty of the citizen to obey the government,—a topic at all times interesting and important; and especially so at this time, when we are actually engaged in a war with a neighboring republic, the necessity of which is questioned by many of our citizens; and when there is widely prevalent a notion that the citizen is under no moral obligation to obey the law, if it does not chance to coincide with his own private convictions of justice and expediency. We agree in the main with the view of this topic which the author takes, and gladly avail ourselves of the occasion to make some additional remarks of our own, which may tend to illustrate and confirm it, though the readers of the oration may, perhaps, consider them quite superfluous.

The war of 1812, declared by this country against Great Britain, as is well known, was exceedingly unpopular in the New England States,—not, indeed, in consequence of any especial partiality for Great Britain herself, nor because they were less patriotic than the other members of the confederacy, but because the chief burdens of the war fell upon them, in the ruin it brought to their commerce and its dependent interests, then their principal interests. It is not for us to pronounce any opinion on the justice or expediency of that war; but we cannot censure with extreme severity the New England people for being strongly opposed to it. Yet there can be no question, that, in the madness of the moment, the opposition was carried to wholly unjustifiable lengths, and, though we willingly acquit it of all treasonable intentions, it in reality stopped only this side of treason. Some weak-minded but well disposed New England ministers, incapable of taking comprehensive views and of seeking to remedy an evil by attacking it in its principle, seeing the danger to the union, to the stability of our institutions, occasioned by the opposition to the war, which they never thought of censuring or attempting to moderate, lamenting the very serious evils suffered by their friends and neighbors, and taking it for granted that the war was wholly unnecessary and unjust, made the grand discovery in moral theology that war is *malum in se*, is always unnecessary, and can never be lawful. They without much delay proceeded, *more suo*, to form an association against war, and to preach, lecture, and issue tracts in favor of universal peace. They appealed to the prejudices against the actual war, and to general philanthropy. New Englanders, especially Bostonians, are rarely insensible to the appeal to philanthropy. Since the softening down of some of the asperities of their primitive Puritanism, which took place in the latter half of the last century, they have been justly remarkable for their philanthropy,—no people in the world more so. Industrious, frugal, economical, they certainly are ; but mean, sordid, miserly, they are not, and are incapable of being. They are, in truth, open, frank, generous, and liberal, with a sort of passion for world reform, which is one of their foibles. The unpopularity of the war of 1812, and the popularity of the appeal to philanthropy, gave to the peace movement a speedy and strong support, till peace became a sort of cant among us, and it was hazardous to one's reputation to intimate that war, terrible as may be its evils, is nevertheless sometimes just and necessary.

But the genuine Yankee is never satisfied with doing only one thing at a time. He is really in his glory only when he has some dozen or more irons all in the fire at once. The simple question of peace could by no means absorb his superabundant zeal and philanthropy, so he invented and set on foot antislavery and various other movements, all of which adopted the "peace principle ;" for the chief actors in one were, for the most part, prominent actors in all. By means of agitation, froth and foam, declamation and rant, of conventions, agents, tracts, lectures, sermons, periodicals, a new code of morals has been gradually framed among us ; all that was once regarded as settled is now called in question ; what was approved by the generations which preceded us is now pronounced low, earthly, sensual, devilish; the fairest reputations are blackened; our own patriots and heroes are calumniated, and even Washington himself has been publicly branded as an "inhuman butcher." We are cast completely adrift. There was no true morality in the world before these modern societies sprung from the womb of night, and we are required to look to a few canting ministers, strolling spinsters, and beardless youths, as the sole authoritative expounders of the precepts of the divine law. We are unable to determine what it is safe to eat or to drink, when to rise up or sit down, unless some of these self-constituted guides condescend to inform us. Sin and death hover everywhere; poison lurks in every thing, even in the bread made from the finest wheat, and in the purest water from the fountain; and there seems to be no possible means of living but to go naked and cease to eat or drink. It is a wonder how the world has contrived, for six thousand years, to get on, how men and women have contrived to be born, to live, to grow, and to persuade themselves that they enjoy a tolerable share of health and vigor, both of mind and body.

The joke, in fact, becomes serious. Many of the rising generation are beginning to take it, not as a dull jest, but as downright earnest. It interferes quite too much with the social and domestic business of life, and, if continued much longer, will reduce the great mass of us to mere automata. It is, therefore, high time for what sober sense, for what decency, there may have been left in the community to speak out, send these fanatics back to their native inanity, and let it be known, that, though for a time we have suffered ourselves to be made fools of, after all, we are not quite so stupid, so vain or conceited, as to imagine that nobody understood or practised the moral virtues till our modern associations burst from darkness to teach them; that we really have not sunk so low as to lose all respect for our ancestors, all reverence for the awful past, over which has flowed the tide of human joy and human sorrow, and to be wholly unable to serve our own generation without calumniating those which have placed us in the world and made us what we are.

He is a foolish as well as a wicked son who curses the mother that bore him. There has been, from the first, a Providence that has watched over and ruled in the affairs of men ; our distant forefathers had eyes, ears, hands, intellects, hearts, as well as we, and knew how to use them, and did use them, not always ineffectually. How, indeed, would the hoary Past, were it not that experience has made it wise and taught it to make allowances for the follies and pranks of youth, laugh at our solemn airs and grave decisions! How should we hang our heads and blush, even to the tips of our ears, could we but for one moment see ourselves as it sees us! "The son," says the proverb, "*thinks* his father a fool ; the father *knows* his son to be one." The more we study what has been, the less disposed shall we be to exult in what is. Happily, we begin to discover some symptoms that there are those among us, who have, now and then, at least, a suspicion that change is not always progress, and that it is more creditable to be able to revere wisdom than to contemn it.

War, against which nearly all our modern fanatics declaim so much, and which in the new moral code is utterly prohibited, is, of course, not a thing to be sought for its own sake. Its necessity must always be lamented, as we must always lament that there are crimes to be redressed, or criminals to be punished, or diseases to be cured. But because we must always lament that there are offenders to be punished, it does not follow that to punish them is never necessary, or that their punishment is an evil, and morally wrong ; or because it is to be regretted that there are diseases, that we must treat the physician and his drugs as a nuisance. The father weeps that he has occasion to chastise his child, but knows that "to spare the rod is to spoil the child ;" nor does it necessarily follow, because war involves terrible evils, and is to be avoided whenever it can be without sacrificing the public weal, that it is in itself wrong, and may never be resorted to without violating the law of God. Its necessity is an evil, but, as a remedy, it may be just and beneficial. Disease is an evil, but not, therefore, the medicine that restores to health. War is a violent remedy for a violent disease, and as such may, when all other remedies prove or must prove ineffectual, be resorted to without sin. We, therefore, venture to maintain, in the very face of our modern fanatics, that war declared by the sovereign authority of the state, for a just cause, and prosecuted with right intentions, is not morally wrong, and may be engaged in with a safe conscience.

That war is not morally wrong, in itself, is evident from the fact, that Almighty God has himself, on several occasions, as in the case of the ancient Israelites, actually commanded or approved it. But God cannot command or approve what is morally wrong, without doing wrong himself; which is absurd and impious to suppose. It cannot be in itself morally wrong, unless prohibited by some law; but there is no law which prohibits it. It is not prohibited by the law of nature. By the law of nature, the individual has the right to defend and avenge himself. Justice not only forbids wrong to be done, but requires that the wrong done be avenged. In a state of nature where there is no established government, but each individual is left to his own sovereignty, each one has the right of defending and avenging himself in his own hands. If this be true of a private person, it must also be true of the state or nation; for nations have precisely the same rights in relation to one another that individuals have. They then, who admit no law but the law of nature, must concede that war is not prohibited.

Nor is war prohibited by the divine law. This all will readily grant to be true, so far as concerns the old law, which nowhere condemns war, and not frequently presents us God himself as commanding or approving it. It is also true, so far as concerns the new law, or Christian law. "If Christian discipline," says St. Augustine, "condemned all wars, the Gospel would have given this counsel of salvation to the soldiers who asked what they should do, that they should throw away their arms and withdraw themselves from the military service altogether. But it says to them, 'Do violence to no man, calumniate no one, and be content with your wages.' St. Luke iii. 14."

Surely it does not prohibit the military service to those whom it commands to be contented with its wages." *

Our Lord, St. Matt. viii. 10, commends the faith of a centurion who had soldiers under his command, says he had not found so great faith in Israel, and yet does not order him to throw away his arms, or abandon the military service. Cornelius, Acts x. 2, " a centurion of the band which is called Italian," is commended as " a religious man, fearing God ; " and the blessed Apostle Paul, Heb. xi. 32–34, praises Gedeon, Barac, Samson, and others, " who through faith subdued kingdoms, became valiant in war, put to flight the armies of foreigners." These considerations show that war is not prohibited by the Christian law. Then it is prohibited by no law, and therefore is not necessarily sinful, but may be just and expedient.

But it is objected, that there are certain passages in the New Testament which, if not expressly, yet by implication, evidently deny the lawfulness of war. 1. " All that take the sword shall perish by the sword." St. Matt. xxvi. 52. But to take the sword is to use the sword without the order or consent of the proper authority. He who only *uses* the sword by order or consent of the proper authority, that is, of the political sovereign, if he be a private person, or of God, if he be a public person or sovereign prince, does not *take* the sword, but simply uses the sword committed to him. Nor are we to understand that all who take the sword on incompetent authority will be literally slain, but that they will perish by their own sword, that is, be punished eternally for their sin, if they do not repent.†

2. "I say unto you, not to resist evil ; but if any man strike

---

* " Nam si Christiana disciplina omnia bella culparet, hoc potius militibus consilium salutis petentibus in Evangelio diceretur, ut abjicerent arma, seque omnino militiæ subtraherent. Dictum est autem eis, *Neminem concusseritis, nulli calumniam feceritis ; sufficiat vobis stipendium vestrum.* Quibus proprium stipendium sufficere debere præcepit, militare utique non prohibuit." Epist. V., *Ad Marcellinum*, c. 2. 15. n.

† See St. Augustine, *Contra Faustum*, lib. 22, c. 70, and St. Thomas, *Summa*, 2. 2, Q. 40, a. 1.

thee on thy right cheek, turn to him the other also." St. Matt. v. 39. War is resistance of evil; but this text forbids the resistance of evil; therefore it forbids war. But the precept refers to the interior disposition, and commands that preparation of the heart which does not resist evil by rendering evil for evil, but endures patiently whatever wrongs or injuries are necessary for the honor of God and the salvation of men. It is not to be understood to the letter, for our Lord, who fulfilled it, when struck in his face, did not turn the other cheek, but defended himself by reasoning. It commands patience under wrongs and insults, and forbids us to seek to avenge ourselves on our own authority; but it does not prohibit the redress of wrongs by the proper authorities; because we know from the testimony of St. Paul that the magistrate is "the minister of God, an avenger to execute wrath upon him that doeth evil." Rom. xiii. 4. Wrongs, when redressed by the proper authority, may be redressed without any malignant feelings, and, indeed, with the most benevolent intentions towards the wrong-doer. Wrongs are not, in all cases, to go unavenged, otherwise God would not have appointed a ministry to avenge them. It is often the greatest of evils to suffer offences to go unpunished, and one of the most certain methods of preventing them is for the magistrate to let it be known and understood that they cannot be committed with impunity.*

* " Sunt ergo ista præcepta patientiæ semper in cordis præparatione retinenda, ipsaque benevolentia, ne reddatur malum pro malo, semper in voluntate complenda est. Agenda sunt autem multa, etiam cum invitis benigna quadam asperitate plectendis, quorum potius utilitati consulenda est quam voluntati. . . . . . Nam in corripiendo filio quamlibet aspere, nunquam amor paternus amittitur. Fit tamen quod no lit et doleat, qui etiam videtur dolore sanandus. Ac per hoc si terrena ista respublica præcepta Christiana custodiat, et ipsa bella sine benevolentia non gerentur, ut ad pietatis justitiæque pacatam societatem victis facilius consulatur. Nam cui licentia iniquitatis eripitur, utiliter, vincitur; quoniam nihil est infelicius felicitate peccantium, qua pœnalis nutritur impunitas, et mala voluntas velut hostis interior roboratur." S. Aug. *ubi sup. et de Serm. Domini,* lib. 1, c. 19, and also St. Thomas, *ubi sup.*

3. "Revenge not yourselves, my dearly beloved, but give place to wrath; for it is written, Vengeance is mine, and I will repay, saith the Lord." Rom. xii. 19. This, though relied on by the peace party, is not to the purpose, for it speaks of private revenge, which every body admits is condemned by the Christian law. It is of the same import with the text we have just dismissed. It simply commands patience under injuries, forbearance towards those who do us wrong, and forbids us to seek redress of wrongs done us in a resentful spirit, or by our own hands or authority. But it does not necessarily imply that the public authority, which is the minister of God, may not redress them, or that the commonwealth may not repel or vindicate attacks upon itself, whether they come from within or from without. To avenge wrongs is not in itself wrong, because it is said the Lord "will repay;" nor is it wrong for the magistrate to avenge them, for "he is the minister of God, an avenger," as we have seen, "to execute wrath upon him that doeth evil;" and it is wrong for the individual to do it only because in civil society his natural right to do so is taken away, and because it is made his duty to leave it to God or the minister God in his providence appoints.

4. "For the weapons of our warfare are not carnal, but powerful through God." 2 Cor. x. 4. But St. Paul is speaking, not of the sword which the magistrate bears, nor of that which the sovereign state, as the minister of God to execute wrath, may put into the hands of its servants, but of the weapons to be used in the conversion of infidels and sinners. These, indeed, are not carnal, but spiritual, and powerful through the virtue God confers on them. Carnal weapons are unlawful in the work of conversion, for conversion is not conversion unless voluntary. God says to the sinner, "Give me thy heart," that is, thy will; and this carnal weapons can force no man give. It can be subdued only by spiritual arms, rendered effectual through divine grace. But this says nothing against the lawfulness of repelling or avenging injustice whether from subjects or foreigners, by the proper authorities. These several texts, then, make

nothing against our general conclusion, that war is not, in all cases, prohibited by the Christian law.

But we are told, still further, that war is opposed to peace; yet the Gospel is a Gospel of peace, commands peace, and pronounces a blessing on peacemakers. "*Beati pacifici, quoniam filii Dei vocabuntur.*" St. Matt. v. 9. War, undertaken for its own sake, looking to itself as the end, is opposed to peace, and unlawful, we grant; but war, undertaken for the sake of obtaining a just and lasting peace, is not opposed to peace, but may be the only means possible of restoring and securing it. Peace is then willed the intentions are peaceful, and war, as a necessity, becomes itself a peacemaker, and as such is lawful, and its prosecutors are not necessarily deprived of the blessing pronounced on peacemakers. Hence, St. Augustine says,— "*Pacem habere debet voluntas, bellum necessitas, ut liberet Deus a necessitate, et conservet in pace. Non enim pax quæritur ut bellum excitetur, sed bellum geritur ut pax acquiratur. Esto ergo etiam bellando pacificus, ut eos quos expugnas, ad pacis utilitatem vincendo perducas.*"* The peace is broken, not by the just war, but by the previous injustice which has rendered the war necessary. The war itself is, necessarily, no more repugnant to the virtue of peace than medicine is to health. The mission of our Saviour is not opposed to peace, because followed by certain evils of which he speaks, St. Matt. x. 34–36, and which were not the end for which he came into world. The preaching of the Gospel is not inconsistent with the virtue of peace, because, through the depravity and wickedness of men, it often occasions discord, divisions, and even wars; nor do they who faithfully preach it any the less "follow after the things which make for peace."

In asserting that war is not necessarily unlawful, we are far from pretending that all wars are just, or that war may ever be waged for slight and trivial offences. The nation is bound studiously to avoid it, to forbear till forbearance ceases to be a virtue, and appeal to arms only as the last resort, after all other

* Epist. 205, *Ad Bonifacium Comitem.*

appeals have failed, or it is morally certain that they must fail. But when its rights are seriously invaded, when the offender will not listen to reason, and continues his injustice, the nation may appeal to arms, and commit its cause to the God of battles. The responsibility of the appeal rests on the offender whose injustice has provoked it.

It may be said that war is unjustifiable, because, if all would practise justice, there could be no war. Undoubtedly, if all men and nations were wise and just, wars would cease. We might then, in very deed, "beat our swords into ploughshares and our spears into pruning-hooks," and learn war no more. We should, not in vision only, but in reality, possess universal peace. So, if all individuals understood and practised the moral and Christian virtues in their perfection, there would be no occasion for penal codes, and a police to enforce them. If no wrongs or outrages were committed, there would be none to be repressed or punished. If there were no diseases, there would be none to cure. If the world were quite another world than it is, it—would be. But so long as the world is what it is, so long as man fails to respect the rights of man, the penal code and police will be necessary; so long as diseases obtain, the physician and his drugs, nauseous as they are, will be indispensable; and so long as nation continues to encroach on nation, the aggrieved party will have the right and be compelled to defend and avenge itself by an appeal to arms, terrible as that appeal may be, and deplorable as may be the necessity which demands it.

The evils of war are great, but not the greatest. It is a greater evil to lose national freedom, to become the tributaries or the slaves of the foreigner, to see the sanctity of our homes invaded, our altars desecrated, and our wives and children made the prey of the ruthless oppressor. These are evils which do not die with us, but may descend upon our posterity through all coming generations. The man who will look tamely on and see altars and home defiled, all that is sacred and dear wrested from him, and his country stricken from the roll of nations, has as little reason to applaud himself for his morals-as for his manhood. No doubt, philanthropy may weep over the wounded and the dying; but it is no great evil to die. It is appointed unto all men to die, and, so far as the death itself is concerned, it matters not whether it comes a few months earlier or a few months later, on the battle-field or in our own bedchambers. The evil is not in dying, but in dying unprepared. If prepared,—and the soldier, fighting by command of his country in her cause, *may* be prepared,—it is of little consequence whether the death come in the shape of sabre-cut or leaden bullet, or in that of disease or old age. The tears of the sentimentalist are lost upon him who is conscious of his responsibilities, that he is commanded to place duty before death, and to weigh no danger against fidelity to his God and his country. Physical pain is not worth counting. Accumulate all that you can imagine, the Christian greets it with joy when it lies in the pathway of his duty. He who cannot take his life in his hand, and, pausing not for an instant before the accumulated tortures of years, rush in, at the call of duty, where "blows fall thickest, and blows fall heaviest," deserves rebuke for his moral weakness, rather than commendation for his "peaceable dispositions."

Wars, we have been told, cost money; and we have among us men piquing themselves on their lofty spiritual views, accusing the age of being low and utilitarian, and setting themselves up as moral and religious reformers, who can sit calmly down and cast up in dollars and cents the expenses of war, and point to the amount as an unanswerable argument against its lawfulness. War unquestionably costs money, and so do food and clothing. But the sums expended in war would, if applied to that purpose, found so many schools and universities, and educate so many children! The amount expended for food and clothing would found a larger number of schools and universities, and educate a larger number of children. You should ask, not, Will it cost money? but, Is it necessary, is it just? Would you weigh gold in the balance with duty, justice, patriotism, heroism? If so, slink back to your tribe, and never aspire to the dignity of being contemptible.

But having established that war may be necessary and just, the question comes up, What is the duty of the citizen or subject, when his government is actually engaged in war? This is a question of some moment, especially at the present time, when there are so many among us who entertain very loose notions of allegiance, and hardly admit that loyalty is or can be a virtue. We may answer, in general terms, that, when a nation declares war, the war is a law of the land, and binds the subject to the same extent and for the same reason as any other law of the land. The whole question is simply a question of the obligation of the citizen to obey the law. So far as the subject is bound to obey the law, so far he is bound to render all the aid in prosecuting the war the government commands him to render, and in the form in which it commands it.

If the government leaves it optional with the citizen whether to take an active part in the war or not, he is unquestionably bound to remain passive, if he believes the war to be unjust. Consequently, no foreigner, owing no allegiance to the sovereign making the war, can volunteer his services, if he entertains any scruples about its justice. But the subject, though entertaining doubts about the justice of a given war in its incipient stages, believing his government too hasty in its proceedings, and not so forbearing as it might and should have been, yet after the war has been declared, after his country is involved in it, can retreat only by suffering grievous wrongs, and seeks now to advance only for the purpose of securing a just and lasting peace, may, no doubt, even volunteer his active services, if he honestly believes them to be necessary; for the war now has changed its original character, has ceased to be aggressive, and become defensive and just. In such a case, love of country, and the general duty of each citizen to defend his country, to preserve its freedom and independence, override the scruples he felt with regard to the war in its incipient stages, and enable him to take part in it with a safe conscience. But, however this may be, it is clear, that, when the government has actually declared war, and actually commands the services of the subject, he is bound in conscience, whatever may be his private convictions of the justice of the war, to render them, on the ground that he is bound in conscience to obey the law. If he takes part in obedience to the command of the government, he takes part, even though his private conviction is against the war, with a good conscience; because the motive from which he acts is not to prosecute a war he does not regard as just, but to obey his sovereign, which he is not at liberty not to do, and which he must do for conscience' sake.

The law binds in conscience, because all legitimate government exists by divine appointment, and has a divine right to make laws. For the same reason, then, that we are bound in conscience to obey God, we are bound in conscience to obey the law. The sovereignty resides in the nation, but is derived from God. *Per me reges regnant, et legum conditores justa decernunt.* " By me kings reign and lawgivers decree just things." Prov. viii. 15. "Let every soul be subject to the higher powers; for there is no power but from God; and the powers that are, are ordained of God. Therefore he that resisteth the power resisteth the ordinance of God, and they that resist purchase damnation to themselves." Rom. xiii. 1, 2. Since, then, the nation is sovereign by divine appointment, it follows necessarily, that, when the sovereign authority of the nation declares war, and commands the services of the subject, he is held, on his allegiance to God, who is the King of kings and Sovereign of sovereigns, to render them, and cannot refuse without purchasing damnation to himself.

The nation is not constituted sovereign by the assent of the individuals of which it is composed, for it must be a sovereign nation before individuals have or can have the right of assenting or dissenting. The error of Rousseau and of some of our own politicians is in assuming that the sovereignty, the authority to institute government, to make and execute laws, inheres primarily in the people distributively, as equal, independent individuals, and is subsequently possessed by the people collectively, as a political organism or person, by virtue of the assent of the people taken distributively. The motive for advocating this view in twofold: the first is, to make the basis of sovereignty purely human; and the second, to take from actually existing governments all claims to inviolability, and thus establish a sort of legal right on the part of subjects to rebel against the constituted authorities, whenever they judge it to be expedient. The doctrine is the offspring of an age disposed to revolt from both God and the state, and can be regarded only with horror by the Christian and the patriot. The true doctrine is, that every nation, that is, every people taken collectively, as a moral unity, as a collective individual, is, by the fact that it is a nation, sovereign, and sovereign by the ordinance of God. Being thus invested by the divine will with the political sovereignty, the nation acting in its sovereign capacity has, saving the divine law, the right to institute such forms of government, or to adopt such methods for the expression of its sovereign will, as it in its prudence judges best. It may institute a monarchy, an aristocracy, or a pure democracy; it may combine these three forms, or any two of them, in any proportion and degree, and establish such mixed governments as it pleases; or it may reject all these forms, and, as with us, establish representative government, to be carried on through the medium of popular election. Which is wisest and best is for each nation to decide for itself. In point of fact, we suppose all are best where they fit, and worst where they do not fit. But however individuals may speculate, and whatever preferences as simple individuals they may have, the nation acting in its sovereign capacity is the sovereign arbiter, and alone decides which shall be adopted, and having once decided, that form which it adopts is legitimate, exists by divine right, and its legitimate acts are laws, and bind in the interior as well as in the exterior court.

This is as true of the actual American governments as of any others. The American people were created by their colonial governments, established by legitimate authority, bodies corporate and politic subject to the crown of Great Britian. But the charters granted by the crown, creating the colonial governments, and reserving the allegiance of the colonies, expressed or necessarily implied reciprocal obligations. There was an express or implied contract between the crown and the colonies. When the crown, on its part, broke the contract, as we alleged it did, it forfeited its rights, and the colonies were *ipso facto* absolved from their allegiance, and necessarily became *ipso facto* free and independent states or nations, as Great Britiain herself subsequently acknowledged them to be. As independent nations, they possessed by the ordinance of God, who makes every nation, in that it is a nation, sovereign, the right of self-government, and were free to devise and adopt such forms of government, not repugnant to the divine law, as they in the exercise of their sovereign wisdom judged to be most expedient. They, in the exercise of the right given them by Almighty God, established the representative form of government, under a federal head. This form of government, therefore, exists with us by divine right, is an ordinance of God. As such it is sovereign and inviolable; as such it has from God authority to enact laws for the common good. Then, since we are all bound in conscience to obey God, we are bound to obey the government, and when it enacts war, just the same as when it enacts any thing else.

Ignorant, conceited, and unbelieving politicians, who would be free to rule, but not bound to obey, may affect to be startled, whenever there is speech of the divine right of government; but we really say nothing that militates in the least conceivable degree against popular sovereignty. Our real offence consists, not in denying the popular sovereignty, but in asserting for it a divine sanction. What, indeed, is it we say? Simply, that the nation, that is, the people as a moral unity, or collective individual, as distinguished from the people taken distributively, is sovereign by the ordinance of God; from which it follows, that the people taken distributively owe allegiance to the nation, and are bound to obey all the sovereign enactments of the government, not merely because it is human government, but because it is human government governing by divine right. This abridges no right of the sovereign people, but confirms its rights by the highest of all possible sanctions. It leaves the nation free to adopt, if it chooses, a pure democracy, and commands us, even though individually disapproving that form of government, to obey it for conscience' sake. In a word, the doctrine we lay down makes the nation—that is, the whole people taken collectively—sovereign and inviolable, and the form of government it adopts, legitimate and sacred, as the ordinance of God. It no doubt, therefore, stamps with the divine as well as the national displeasure what by a strange perversion is termed sometimes "the sacred right of insurrection," and utterly condemns all attempts at rebellion or resistance to establish government, in the legitimate exercise of its legitimate functions, as so many attacks on the inviolability of the nation, and therefore on the inviolability of God himself, who ordains that every nation, in that it is a nation, shall be sovereign and inviolable. It can tolerate no efforts of any portion of the people to change by violence any established form of government for the sake of establishing another form which they may believe to be more for the common good. But it leaves individuals perfectly free to labor through legal forms, in an orderly manner, for the amelioration of the laws and institutions of the country, and the nation itself, when acting in its sovereign capacity, as we did at the epoch of what we call our Revolution, or as we do through the legal conventions of the people, to change even the form of the government, and to ordain such new methods for the expression of its sovereign will as it may believe to be most for the common good.* It leaves the people as the commonwealth and the people as individuals all the freedom there is this side of license, and forbids nothing that is compatible with national sovereignty and inviolability. It can be objected to, then, by none who are not prepared to object to all government, all law, and all order.

* See St. Th., *Summa*, 1. 2, Q. 97, a. 1, and St. Aug., *De Libero Arbitrio*, I., c. 6.

The duty of obedience to law is precisely the same under a republican government as under any other form of government. For though the people make the law, yet it is not in the same sense as that in which they are held to obey it. They make the law in their collective sense, as a moral unity, or public person; they are held to obey in their distributive capacity, as simple individuals. In their quality of electors, acting through legal forms prescribed by sovereign authority, the people with us make the law, but it is only when so acting that they make it, have any voice in making it, or incur any responsibility, be the law what it may. As individuals acting in any other capacity, they are subjects, and in the same sense and to the same extent as they would be in case they enjoyed no elective franchise at all. The law is as imperative with us as it is under any other form of government, and can no more be resisted with a safe conscience than elsewhere.

This assumed, the individual in his quality of subject stands here in relation to the law precisely as he does in those countries where there is no elective franchise. He incurs, indeed, as elector, a responsibility for the law, and cannot be exempted from blame, if he have not done all in his power to make the law just and useful; but when the proper authorities have enacted and promulgated the law, he in his quality of subject incurs no responsibility by obeying it, in consequence of his responsibility as an elector in making it. The act of making the law was not his individual act, and he is responsible for it, providing he acted with proper motives, only so far as he went to make up the collective unity that enacted it. But the act of obedience or of disobedience is purely his individual act, and is unaffected, as obedience or disobedience, by any act of his performed in another capacity, in which he acts not as an individual, but as a part of a whole. Suppose, then, I look upon the war declared by my government as unjust or uncalled for. This may be a good reason why I should exert myself in my quality of elector to get the law declaring it repealed, but it leaves me in my quality of subject precisely where I should be in case I had no elective franchise. I am just as much bound to obey the law declaring the war, and incur no more blame for aiding in prosecuting it. The citizen, when he believes a law unjust, is doubtless bound as an elector to seek its repeal; but till repealed, he is as much bound to obey as he would be if he were no elector, and only a simple subject; and being so bound, incurs no blame in obeying it, that he would not then also incur.

But is there no limit to this obedience to law? Have I not the right to judge the acts of authority, and decide for myself whether they are such as I ought or ought not to obey? That is, Does or does not the law depend on the assent of the governed for its validity? It is a sort of maxim with us Americans, that no man can be justly held to obey a law to which he has not assented. This, taken absolutely, is not admissible. The sovereign authority resides in the people as a whole, taken collectively, not in the people distributively, and is derived not from the people as individuals, as Rousseau dreamed, but from God, as we have before proved from the Holy Scriptures. Moreover, to make the law depend on the assent of the governed, that is, on the assent of the subject, is to deny that the law is law, that the subject is a subject, and to assert that one is bound by no law, but free to do as he pleases. There can be no legitimate government unless it have the right to govern, and there can be no right to govern where there is not a correlative obligation to obey. If the law cannot bind the subject till he gives his assent, and he is free to give or withhold his assent, he is, and can be, under no obligation to obey unless he chooses, and then there is no right on the part of the government to enforce obedience; then no right to govern; and then no government. To make the law depend for its validity on the assent of the governed is, then, the denial of all government. But government exists by divine right. It has from God the right to command. Then it is not under the necessity of entreating or requesting the subject to be so complacent as to obey. The law, then, is complete, the moment it is enacted and promulgated by the proper authority. If the law is then complete, the subject has no assent to give or withhold, no judgment to form, no decision to take, but that to obey.

Nevertheless, there is a sense, in this country, and perhaps in all countries, in which it is true that the assent of the governed is essential to the validity of the law; but this is the assent they give in their quality of electors, through the medium of their representatives in enacting the law, not an assent which they give as subjects to the law after it is enacted and promulgated. The distinction is obvious and important. It is only in our quality of electors, through the medium of our representatives, that we have any legislative authority, any assent, to give or to withhold. But in this quality we have already assented to the law, otherwise it could not have been enacted, since there is no power with us but the people in this quality and through this medium that does or can make the law. Having thus assented, nay, enacted the law, we have no more assent to give, and it would be absurd to seek, after this, the assent of the people in their capacity of simple individuals, in which they are simply subjects, and have no legislative voice whatever. Having spoken once in our legislative capacity, as electors, through our representatives, we must obey, till, by speaking again in the same capacity and through the same medium, we repeal the law. That is, when the people have made the law, they must obey it, till they, through the forms through which they made it, repeal it.

But laws may undoubtedly be unjust. Am I bound to obey unjust laws? We will let St. Thomas answer this question for us. "Laws imposed by human authority may be either just or unjust. If they are indeed just, they bind in conscience, by the eternal law from which they are derived, according to Prov. viii. 15,—'*Per me reges regnant, et legum conditores justa decernunt.*' They are just when they ordain what is for the common good, when enacted by an authority which does not exceed its powers, and when they distribute in equal proportions the burdens they impose upon the subjects for the common good. For, since each man is a part of the multitude, every man belongs to the multitude in that which he is and in that which he has, in like manner as the part belongs in what it is to the whole, and hence nature allows a certain detriment to the part that the whole may be saved. Consequently, laws of this kind, which proportion equally the burdens imposed, are just, bind in conscience, and are legal laws. But laws may be unjust in two senses. 1. By contrariety to *human* good, in the respects just mentioned. They are unjust, when a prince imposes burdens on his subjects, not for the common good, but rather for his own glory or cupidity, when they exceed the commission or the authority which ordains them, and when the burdens they impose, even though for the common good, are not equally proportioned. Such acts are violences rather than laws, as St. Augustine says, *De Lib. Arb.*, I., c. 5.—' *Lex esse non videtur, quæ justa non fuerit.*' Laws of this kind do not bind in conscience, unless, perchance, for the avoiding of scandal or disorder, for which a man must forego his own rights, according to St. Matt. v. 40, 41,—' *Qui angariaverit te mille passus, vade cum eo alia duo ; et qui abstulerit tibi tunicam, da ei et pallium.*' 2. Laws may be unjust by contrariety to *divine* good, as the edicts of tyrants commanding idolatry or other things forbidden by the divine law. Such laws are to be observed in no sense whatever, since, Acts iv., it is necessary to obey God rather than men." *

The principle is, that all just laws bind in conscience ; but, with regard to unjust laws, we must distinguish between those which are unjust because they ordain what is repugnant to human good, and those which are unjust because they ordain what is repugnant to the divine law. The latter do not bind, but we are bound in conscience to refuse to obey them at all hazards ; the former, when they only require us to suffer wrong,—and if they go farther and command us to do wrong, they are identical with the latter,—we may obey, and are bound to obey, when our disobedience would cause scandal or breed disturbance in the state.

But who is to determine whether the laws are just or unjust?

* *Summa*, 1. 2, Ques. 96, a. 4.

Not absolutely in all cases the state, for that would make the distinction between just and unjust laws nugatory, since the state, in enacting a law, decides that it is just; not the individual, for that would make the law depend on the assent of the subject for its legality, which we have seen is not the fact, and cannot be the fact, if we are to have government at all. There is here, to many minds, no doubt, a serious difficulty; but, without considering it in a light which would involve a controversy foreign to our present purpose, we may answer the question by laying down the principle, that authority is always *presumptively* in the right, and the law *primà facie* evidence of justice. The *onus probandi* rests on the shoulders of the subject, who must prove the law to be unjust, before he can have the right to refuse it obedience. For this his own private judgment or conviction can never suffice. If he can allege nothing against the law but his own individual persuasion of its injustice, he is bound, by his general obligation to obey the laws, to obey it. No one, then, can ever be justified in disobeying on his own private authority. He must sustain his refusal to obey by an authority higher than his own, higher than that of the state, or else he will be guilty of resisting the ordinance of God, and, therefore, purchase damnation to himself. Hence, where there is no infallible authority to decide, the subject must always presume the law to be just, and faithfully obey it, unless it manifestly and undeniably ordains what is wrong in itself, and prohibited by the law of God.

This rule may strike some as too stringent, but, if examined, closely, it will be found to allow all the liberty to the subject compatible with the existence of government. If, for instance, the government should command me to lie, to steal, to rob, to bear false witness, or any thing else manifestly against the law of nature or the law of God, I should hold myself bound to disobey, and to take the consequences of my disobedience. So, also, if my government should declare war against an unoffending state, manifestly for the purpose of stripping it of its territory, destroying its independence, and reducing its people to slavery, or for the purpose of overthrowing the Christian religion and substituting a false religion, and should command me to aid it in its nefarious designs, I should hold myself bound in conscience to refuse at all hazards; for such a war would be manifestly and palpably unjust, not in my judgment only, but in that of all sound-minded men. Such a case would be clear, and duty would be so plain that no question could arise. But in a case less clear and manifest, in a case where there was room for doubt, for an honest difference of opinion, I should hold myself bound to obey the orders of the government, for conscience' sake, leaving the responsibility with it, sure of incurring no blame myself.

In conclusion, we say, that, though we have defended the lawfulness of war, when declared by the sovereign authority, for a just cause, and prosecuted with right intentions, we have no sympathy with that restless and ambitious spirit that craves war for the sake of excitement or glory. Only a stern necessity can ever justify the resort to arms, and that necessity does not in reality often exist. In most cases, the war, with a little prudence, a little forbearance, a little use of reason, might be avoided; and a terrible responsibility rests upon rulers when they unnecessarily plunge two nations in the horrors of war. Yet it belongs to the sovereign authority to judge of the necessity of the war, no less than to declare it; and when not manifestly and undeniably for that which is wrong in itself, the subject is bound to obey, and give his life, if need be, for his country. But the subject can, with a good conscience, fight only under the national banner. He can never justly fight under the blood-red flag of the factionist or of the revolutionist. The loyal subject hears no call to the battle-field but that of his sovereign. This sovereign he hears, by him he stands, for him he is ready to fight against any enemies, from within or from without. But there he stops. He can join with no faction, with no party, against the legitimate authorities of his country. No dreams of free institutions, of popular government, of an earthly paradise can make him raise the parricidal hand, and seek by violence to overthrow legitimate government, and introduce a new political order. No, dearly as we love liberal institutions, and as ready as we are to spill our blood in their defense where they are the legal order, we would rush to the side of authority, and spill the same blood against them, if there were an attempt by violence to introduce them. True freedom is only where the law is supreme, and the law is supreme only where the people reverence it, and feel themselves bound by their duty to God to obey it.

THE HIGHER LAW.*

JANUARY, 1851.

PROFESSOR STUART appears to have written this pamphlet from patriotic motives, with an earnest desire to allay the uncalled for popular agitation on the subject of negro slavery, and to contribute his share towards the maintenance of domestic peace, and the preservation of the Union. His chief purpose appears to have been to remove the scruples of some of his friends, by showing that a man may with a good conscience support the Federal Constitution although it recognizes slavery, and requires the slave escaping into a non-slaveholding State to be given up on the demand of his owner; and though he is no great proficient in moral theology, and his style is prolix, prosy, and at times even garrulous, he has shown this to the satisfaction of all but mere factionists and cavillers.

We do not think that the learned Professor has made out his case as conclusively as he might have done. He is a man of respectable ability and attainments, but not remarkable for the strength or acuteness of his logical powers. He makes now and

---

* Conscience and the Constitution, with Remarks on the recent Speech of the Hon. Daniel Webster in the Senate of the United States on the Subject of Slavery. By MOSES STUART. Boston: Crocker & Brewster. 1850. 8vo. pp. 119.

then a slip, of which an uncandid critic might take advantage. He is strongly opposed to slavery, but wishes at the same time to prove that the Christian may with a good conscience be a slave-holder. In order to prove this, he asserts and proves that slavery is not *malum in se*, and therefore, if a sin at all, it is so only accidentally. But in order to justify his sincere aversion to slavery, he maintains that it is always and everywhere an evil, and excuses the old patriarchs for holding slaves only on the ground of invincible ignorance! In the darkness of those early ages men knew and could know no better! This we need not say is in contradiction to his assertion that slavery is not *malum in se*. But passing over slips of this sort,—somewhat common in all Professor Stuart's writings that have fallen under our notice,—and looking only to the main design and argument of the pamphlet, we can very cheerfully commend it to our Protestant readers.

For ourselves, we agree with Professor Stuart that slavery is not *malum in se*. We hold that in some cases at least slavery is justifiable, and to the slave even a blessing. To the slave it is always good or evil according as he wills it to be one or the other, or according to the spirit with which he bears it. If he regards it as a penance, and submits to it in a true penitential spirit, it is a blessing to him, a great mercy,—as are on the same condition to every one of us all the sufferings and afflictions of this life. We should covet in this world, not happiness, but suffering, and the more grievous our afflictions, the more should we rejoice and give thanks. Christianity does not teach carnal Judaism, but condemns it, and commands its opposite as the condition of all real good, whether for this world or for that which is to come. To the master, slavery is not an evil, when he does not abuse it; when he has not himself participated in reducing those born free to servitude; when he treats his slaves with kindness and humanity, and faithfully watches over their moral and religious well-being. The relation of master and man, as to the authority of the former and the subjection of the latter, differs in nothing from the relation of father and son while the son is under age, and there is nothing which necessarily makes the relation less advantageous to either party in the one case than in the other.

That slavery as it exists in our Southern States is an evil, we do not doubt; but it is so accidentally, not necessarily. The evil is not in the relation of slavery itself, but in the fact that the great body of the masters do not bring up their slaves in the Church of God, and train or suffer them to be trained to observe the precepts of the Divine law. The mass of the slaves in this country grow up in heresy or heathenism, to the everlasting destruction of their souls. Here is the evil we see and deplore,—an evil, however, which none but Catholics do or can feel with much vividness. It is an evil which does not and cannot weigh much with Protestants, for the slaves in general are as little heathen and fully as orthodox as their masters. If the masters were good Catholics, as they ought to be, and are under the condemnation of God for not being, and brought up, as they are bound to do, their slaves in the belief and practice of the Catholic religion, there would be no evil in negro slavery to disturb us. The only evils we see in it are moral and spiritual, inseparable from heresy and heathenism. The physical and sentimental evils, or pretended evils, about which Abolitionists and philanthropists keep up such a clamor do not move us in the least. We place not the slightest value on what the men of this world call liberty, and we are taught by religion that poverty and suffering are far more enviable than riches and sensual enjoyment.

But conceding the evil of slavery as it exists in this country, it is far from certain that it is an evil that would be mitigated by emancipation, or that emancipation would not be even a greater evil. The negroes are here, and here they must remain. This is a "fixed fact." Taking the American people as they are, and as they are likely to be for some time to come, with their pride, prejudices, devotion to material interests, and hatred or disregard of Christian truth and morals, it is clear to us that the condition of the negro as a slave is even less evil than would be his condition as a freedman. The freed negroes amongst us are as a body, to say the least, no less immoral and heathen than the slaves themselves. They are the pests of our Northern cities, especially since they have come under the protection of our philanthropists. With a few honorable exceptions, they are low and degraded, steeped in vice and overflowing with crime. Even in our own city, almost at the moment we write, they are parading our streets in armed bands, for the avowed purpose of resisting the execution of the laws. Let loose some two or three millions like them, and there would be no living in the American community. Give them freedom and the right to vote in our elections, and the whole country would be at the mercy of the lowest and most worthless of our demagogues. With only Protestantism, indifferentism, infidelity, or savage fanaticism to restrain them, all their base and disorderly passions would be unchained, and our community would be a hell upon earth. No; before we talk of emancipation, before we can venture upon it with the least conceivable advantage to the slaves, we must train them, and train the white American people also, to habits of self-denial and moral virtue under the regimen of the Catholic Church, which alone has power to subdue the barbarous elements of our nature, and to enable men of widely different races, complexions, and characteristics to live together in the bonds of peace and brotherhood. We cannot, therefore, agree with Professor Stuart in his demand for emancipation, and we are decidedly opposed, for the present at least, not only to the fanatical proceedings set on foot by our miserable Abolitionists and philanthropists to effect emancipation, but to emancipation itself. In the present state of things, emancipation would be a greater evil than slavery, and of two evils we are bound to choose the least. We have heard enough of liberty and the rights of man; it is high time to hear something of the duties of men and the rights of authority.

We write very deliberately, and are prepared for all the obloquy which may be showered upon us for what we write. The cry of liberty has gone forth; we, as well as others, have heard it; it has gone forth and been echoed and reëchoed from every quarter, till the world has become maddened with it. The voice of law, of order, of wisdom, of justice, of truth, of experience, of common sense, is drowned in the tumultuous shouts of Liberty, Equality, Fraternity!—shouts fit, in the sense they are uttered, only for assembled demons declaring war upon the Eternal God. But this should be our shame, not our boast. It ought not to be, and, if the world is to continue, must soon cease to be. Society cannot subsist where the rights of authority are forgotten, and loyalty and obedience are foresworn. There is no use in multiplying words on the subject. Man is a social being, and cannot live without society; society is impracticable and inconceivable without government; and government is impossible where its right to command is denied, or the obligation to obey it is not recognized. It is of the essence of government to restrain, and a government that imposes no restraint, that leaves every one free to do whatever seemeth right in his own eyes, is no government at all. The first want of every people is strong and efficient government,—a regularly constituted authority, that has the right and the power to enforce submission to its will. No matter what the form of your government, no matter in whose hands the power is lodged,—in the hands of the king, of the lords, or the commons,—it must, in so far as government at all, be sovereign, clothed, under God, with supreme authority, and be respected as such, or society is only Bedlam without its keeper.

This is the great truth the American people, in their insane clamor about the rights of man and the largest liberty, that is to say, full license to every man, lose sight of, or in reality deny; and it is on this truth, not on liberty, for which all are crying out, that it is necessary now to insist, both in season and out of season. There may be times and countries when and where the true servants of God must seek to restrict the action of government, and lessen the prerogatives of power; but assuredly here and now our duty is not to clamor for liberty or emancipation, but to reassert the rights of authority and the majesty of law. You will be decried, if you do so. No doubt of it. But what then ? When was it popular to insist on the special truth demanded by one's own age ? When was it that one could really serve his age or country without falling under its condemnation ? When was it that the multitude were known to applaud him who rebuked them for their errors, exposed to them the dangers into which they were running by following their dominant tendencies, and presented them the truth needed for their salvation ? What great or good man ever proposed to himself to serve his fellow-men by following their instincts, flattering their prejudices, and inflaming their passions ? Who knows not that error and sin come by nature, and that virture is achieved only by effort, by violence, by heroic struggle against even ourselves ? Is not the hero always a soldier ? Let then, the multitude clamor, let the age denounce, let the wicked rage, let earth and hell do their worst, what care you, heroic soldier of the King of kings ? Go forth and meet the enemy. Charge, and charge home, where your Immortal Leader gives the word, and leave the responsibility to him. If you fall, so much the greater glory for you, so much the more certain your victory, and your triumph.

But we are straying from the point we had in mind when we set out. Our purpose was, to offer some remarks on what is termed " the higher law" to which the opponents of the recent Fugitive Slave Law appeal to justify their refusal to execute it. The Hon. Mr. Seward, one of the Senators from New York, in the debate in the Senate during the last session of Congress on the Fugitive Slave Bill, refused to vote for the measure, although necessary to carry out an express constitutional provision, on the ground that to give up a fugitive slave is contrary to the law of God ; and the Abolitionists and Free Soilers refuse to execute the law, and even in some instances resist its execution, on the same ground. When the honorable Senator appealed from the Constitution to the law of God, as a higher law, he was told by the advocates of the bill, that, having just taken his oath to support the Constitution, he had debarred himself from the right, while retaining his seat in the Senate, to appeal from it to any law requiring him to act in contravention of its provisions. The Abolitionists and Free Soilers immediately concluded from this that the advocates of the bill denied the reality of any law higher than the Constitution, and their papers and periodicals teem with articles and essays to prove the supremacy of the law of God. The question is one of no little gravity, and, to our Protestant friends, of no little perplexity. We may, therefore, be allowed to devote a few pages to its consideration.

We agree entirely with Mr. Seward and his Abolition and Free Soil friends, as to the fact that there is a higher law than the Constitution. The law of God is supreme, and overrides all human enactments, and every human enactment incompatible with it is null and void from the beginning, and cannot be obeyed with a good conscience, for "we must obey God rather than men." This is the great truth statesmen and lawyers are extremely prone to overlook, which the temporal authority not seldom practically denies, and on which the Church never fails to insist. This truth is so frequently denied, so frequently outraged, that we are glad to find it asserted by Mr. Seward and his friends, although they assert it in a case and for a purpose in which we do not and cannot sympathize with them.

But the concession of the fact of a higher law than the Constitution does not of itself justify the appeal to it against the Constitution, either by Mr. Seward or the opponents of the Fugitive Slave Law. Mr. Seward had no right, while holding his seat in the Senate under the Constitution, to appeal to this higher law against the Constitution, because that was to deny the very authority by which he held his seat. The Constitution, if repugnant to the law of God, is null and void, is without authority, and as Mr. Seward held his seat by virtue of its authority, he could have no authority for holding his seat, after having declared it to be null and void, because the Constitution is a mere compact, and the Federal Government has no existence independent of it, or powers not created by it. This is an inconvenience he does not appear to have considered. The principle that would have justified his refusal to obey the Constitution would have deprived him of his seat as a Senator. Moreover, the question of the compatibility or incompatibility of the Constitution with the law of God was a question for him to have raised and settled before taking his senatorial oath. Could he conscientiously swear to support the Constitution? If he could, he could not afterwards refuse to carry out any of its imperative provisions, on the ground of its being contrary to the higher law; for he would in swearing to support the Constitution declare in the most solemn manner in his power, that in his belief at least it imposed upon him no duty contrary to his duty to God, since to swear to support a constution repugnant to the Divine law is to take an unlawful oath, and to swear with the deliberate intention of not keeping one's oath is to take a false oath. After having taken his oath to support the Constitution, the Senator had, so far as he was concerned, settled the question, and it was no longer for him an open question. In calling God to witness his determination to support the Constitution, he had called God to witness his conviction of the compatibility of the Constitution with the law of God, and therefore left himself no plea for appealing from it to a higher law. If he discovered the incompatibility of the imperative provisions of the Constitution only after having taken his oath, he was bound from that moment to resign his seat. In any view of the case, therefore, we choose to take, Mr. Seward was not and could not be justified in appealing to a law above the Constitution against the Constitution while he retained his seat under it and remained bound by his oath to support it. It is then perfectly easy to condemn the appeal of the Senator, without, as Abolitionists and Free Soilers pretend, falling into the monstrous error of denying the supremacy of the Divine law, and maintaining that there is no law above the Constitution.

What we have said is conclusive against the honorable Senator from New York, but it does not precisely apply to the case of those who resist or refuse to obey the Fugitive Slave Law now that it has been passed. These persons take the ground that the law of God is higher than any human law, and therefore we can in no case be bound to obey a human law that is in contravention of it. Such a law is a violence rather than a law, and we are commanded by God himself to resist it, at least passively. All this is undeniable in the case of every human enactment that really does command us to act contrary to the law of God. To this we hold, as firmly as man can hold to any thing, and to this every Christian is bound to hold even unto death. This is the grand principle held by the old martyrs, and therefore they chose martyrdom rather than obedience to the state commanding them to act contrary to the Divine law. But who is to decide whether a special civil enactment be or be not repugnant to the law of God? Here is a grave and a perplexing question for those who have no divinely authorized interpreter of the Divine law. The Abolitionists and Free Soilers, adopting the Protestant principle of private judgment, claim the right to decide each for himself. But this places the individual above the state, private judgment above the law, and is wholly incompatible with the simplest conception of civil government. No civil government can exist, none is conceivable even, where every individual is free to disobey its orders whenever they do not happen to square with his private convictions of what is the law of God. The principle of private judgment, adopted by Protestants in religious matters, it is well known, has destroyed for them the church as an authoritative body, and put an end to every thing like ecclesiastical authority; transferred to civil matters, it would equally put an end to the state, and abolish all civil authority, and establish the reign of anarchy or license. Clearly, if government is to be retained, and to govern, the right to decide when a civil enactment does or does not conflict with the law of God cannot be lodged in the individual subject. Where then shall it be lodged? In the state? Then are you bound to absolute obedience to any and every law the state may enact; you make the state supreme, absolute, and deny your own principle of a higher law than the civil law. You have then no appeal from the state, and no relief for conscience, which is absolute civil despotism. Here is a sad dilemma for our uncatholic countrymen, which admirably demonstrates the unsuitableness of Protestant principles for practical life. If they assert the principle of private judgment in order to save individual liberty, they lose government and fall into anarchy. If they assert the authority of the state in order to save government, they lose liberty and fall under absolute civil despotism, and it is an historical fact that the Protestant world perpetually alternates between civil despotism and unbridled license, and after three hundred years of experimenting finds itself as far as ever from solving the problem, how to reconcile liberty and authority. Strange that men do not see that the solution must be sought in God, not in man! Alas! reformers make a sad blunder when they reject the Church instituted by God himself for the express purpose of interpreting his law,—the only protector of the people, on the one hand, against despotism, and of government, on the other, against license!

But the people cannot avail themselves of their own blunder to withdraw themselves from their obligation to obey the laws. Government itself is a divine ordinance, is ordained of God. " Let every soul be subject to the higher powers; for there is no power but from God; and the powers that be are ordained of God. Therefore he that resisteth the power resisteth the ordinance of God. And they that resist purchase to themselves damnation." We do not say that all the acts of government are ordained of God; for if we did, we could not assert the reality of a law higher than that of the state, and should be forced to regard every civil enactment as a precept of the Divine law. In ordinary government, God does not ordain obedience to all and every of its acts, but to those only of its acts which come within the limits of his own law. He does not make civil government the supreme and infallible organ of his will on earth, and therefore it may err, and contravene his will; and when and where it does, its acts are null and void. But government itself, as civil authority, is a divine ordinance, and, within the law of God, clothed with the right to command and to enforce obedience. No appeal, therefore, from any act of government, which in principle denies the divine right of government, or which is incompatible with the assertion and maintenance of civil authority, can be entertained. Since government as civil authority is an ordinance of God, and as such the Divine law, any course of action, or the assertion of any principle of action, incompatible with its existence as government, is necessarily forbidden by the law of God. The law of God is always the equal of the law of God, and can never be in conflict with itself. Consequently no appeal against government as civil authority to the law of God is admissible, because the law of God is as supreme in any one of its enactments as in another.

Now it is clear that Mr. Seward and his friends, the Abolitionists and Free Soilers, have nothing to which they can appeal from the action of government but their private interpretation of the law of God, that is to say, their own private judgment or opinion as individuals; for it is notorious that they are good Protestants, holding the pretended right of private judgment, and rejecting all authoritative interpretation of the Divine law. To appeal from the government to private judgment is to place private judgment above public authority, the individual above the state, which, as we have seen, is incompatible with the very existence of government, and therefore, since government is a divine ordinance, absolutely forbidden by the law of God,—that very higher law invoked to justify resistance to civil enactments. Here is an important consideration, which condemns, on the authority of God himself, the pretended right of private judgment, the grossest absurdity that ever entered the heads of men outside of Bedlam, and proves that, in attempting to set aside on its authority a civil enactment, we come into conflict not with the human law only, but also with the law of God itself. No man can ever be justifiable in resisting the civil law under the pretence that it is repugnant to the Divine law, when he has only his private judgment, or, what is the same thing, his private interpretation of the Sacred Scriptures, to tell him what the Divine law is on the point in question, because the principle on which he would act in doing so would be repugnant to the very existence of government, and therefore in contravention of the ordinance, therefore of the law, of God.

Man's prime necessity is society, and the prime necessity of society is government. The question, whether government shall or shall not be sustained, is at bottom only the question, whether the human race shall continue to subsist or not. Man is essentially a social being, and cannot live without society, and society is inconceivable without government. Extinguish government, and you extinguish society; extinguish society, and you extinguish man. Inasmuch as God has created and ordained the existence of the human race, he has founded and ordained government, and made it absolutely obligatory on us to sustain it, to refrain in principle and action from whatever would tend to destroy it, or to render its existence insecure. They who set aside or resist the Fugitive Slave Law on the ground of its supposed repugnance to the law of God are, then, no more justifiable than we have seen was the honorable Senator from New York. In no case can any man ever be justified in setting aside or resisting a civil enactment, save on an authority higher than his own and that of the government. This higher authority is not recognized by the Abolitionists and Free Soilers; they neither have nor claim to have any such authority to allege; consequently, they are bound to absolute submission to the civil authority, not only in the case of the Fugitive Slave Law, but in every case, however repugnant such submission may be to their private convictions and feelings, or what they call their conscience, for conscience itself is respectable only when it is authorized by the law of God, or is in conformity with it.

That this is civil despotism, that is, the assertion of the absolute supremacy of the state, we do not deny; but that is not our fault. If men, by rejecting the divinely authorized interpreter of the law of God, voluntarily place themselves in such a condition that they have no alternative but either civil despotism or resistance to the ordinance of God, the fault is their own. They must expect to reap what they sow. They were warned betimes, but they would heed no warning; they would have their own way; and if they now find that their own way leads to death, they have only themselves to blame. It is not we who advocate despotism, but they who render it inevitable for themselves, if they wish to escape the still greater evil of absolute license. As Catholics we wash our hands of the consequences which they cannot escape, and which any man with half an eye might have seen would necessarily follow the assertion of the absurd and ridiculous, not to say blasphemous, principle of private judgment. We have never been guilty of the extreme folly of proclaiming that principle, and of superinducing the necessity of asserting civil despotism as the only possible relief from anarchy. We are able to assert liberty without undermining authority, and authority without injury to liberty; for we have been contented to let God himself be our teacher and our legislator, instead of weak, erring, vain, and capricious men, facetiously ycleped *reformers*. As Catholics, we were not among those who undertook to improve on Infinite Wisdom, and to reform the institutions of the Almighty. We are taught by a divinely authorized Teacher, that government is the ordinance of God, and that we are to respect and obey it as such in all things not repugnant to the law of God; and we have an authority higher than its, higher than our own, to tell us, without error, or the possibility of error,—because by Divine assistance and protection rendered infallible,—when the acts of government conflict with the law of God, and it becomes our duty to resist the former in obedience to the latter. Civil authority is respected and obeyed when respected and obeyed in all things it has from God the right to do or command; and liberty is preserved inviolate when nothing can be exacted from us in contravention of the Divine law, and we are free to disobey the prince when he commands us to violate the law of God. We then do and can experience none of the perplexity which is experienced by our uncatholic countrymen. We have an infallible

Church to tell us when there is a conflict between the human law and the Divine, to save us from the necessity, in order to get rid of despotism, of asserting individualism, which is the denial of all government, and, in order to get rid of individualism, of asserting civil despotism, that is, the supremacy of the state, the grave of all freedom. We have never to appeal to the principle of despotism nor to the principle of anarchy. We have always a public authority, which, as it is inerrable, can never be oppressive, to guide and direct us, and if we resist the civil law, it is only in obedience to a higher law, clearly and distinctly declared by a public authority higher than the individual, and higher than the state. Our readers, therefore, will not accuse us of advocating civil despotism, which we abhor, because we show that they who reject God's Church, and assert private judgment, have no alternative but despotism or license. They are, as Protestants, under the necessity of being slaves and despots, not we who are Catholics. We enjoy, and we alone enjoy, the glorious prerogative of being at once freemen and loyal subjects.

There is no principle on which the Abolitionists and Free Soilers can justify their resistance to the Fugitive Slave Law. They cannot appeal to the law of God, for, having no authority competent to declare it, the law of God is for them as if it were not. It is for them a mere unmeaning word, or meaning only their private or individual judgment, which is no law at all, and if it were would at best be only a human, and the lowest conceivable human law. The highest human law is unquestionably the law of the state, as the state is the highest human authority conceivable. No appeal can then lie from the state to another human authority, least of all to the individual; for appeals do not go downwards, do not lie from the higher to the lower, as ultra democracy would seem to imply. The highest conceivable human authority has passed the law in question, and in so doing has declared it compatible with the law of God; and as its opponents have only a human authority at best to reverse the judgment of the state, nothing remains for them but to yield it full and loyal obedience.

We have dwelt at length on this point, because it is one of great importance in itself, and because we are anxious to clear away the mist with which it has been surrounded, and to prevent any denial on the one hand, or misapplication on the other, of the great principle of the supremacy of the Divine law. The misapplication of a great principle is always itself a great and dangerous error, and often, perhaps always, leads to the denial of the principle. Mr. Seward and his friends asserted a great and glorious principle, but misapplied it. Their opponents, the friends of the Constitution and the Union, seeing clearly the error of the application, have, in some instances at least, denied the principle itself, and their papers North and South are filled with sneers at *the higher law* doctrine. The one error induces the other, and we hardly know which, under existing circumstances, is the most to be deprecated. Each error favors a dangerous popular tendency of the times. We have spoken of the tendency, under the name of liberty, to anarchy and license; but there is another tendency, under the pretext of authority, to civil despotism, or what has been very properly denominated *Statolatry*, or the worship of the state, that is, elevating the state above the Church, and putting it in the place of God. Both tendencies have the same origin, that is, in the Protestant rejection of the spiritual authority of the Church on the one hand, and the assertion of private judgment on the other; and in fact, both are but the opposite phases or poles of one and the same principle. The two tendencies proceed *pari passu*, and while the one undermines all authority, the other grasps at all powers and usurps all rights, and modern society in consequence is cursed at once with the opposite evils of anarchy and of civil despotism. The cry for liberty abolishes all loyalty, and destroys the principle and the spirit of obedience, while the usurpations of the state leave to conscience no freedom, to religion no independence. The state tramples on the spiritual prerogatives of the Church, assumes to itself the functions of schoolmaster and director of consciences, and the multitude clap their hands, and call it liberty and progress! We see this in the popular demand for state education, and in the joy that the men of the world manifest at the nefarious conduct of the Sardinian government in breaking the faith of treaties and violating the rights of the Church. When it concerns the Church, the supremacy of the state is proclaimed, and when it concerns government or law, then it is individualism that is shouted. Such is our age, our boasted nineteenth century.

Now there is a right and a wrong way of defending the truth, and it is always easier to defend the truth on sound than on unsound principles. If men were less blind and headstrong, they would see that the higher law can be asserted without any attack upon legitimate civil authority, and legitimate civil authority and the majesty of the law can be vindicated without asserting the absolute supremacy of the civil power, and falling into statolatry,—as absurd a species of idolatry as the worship of stocks and stones. The assertion of the higher law, as Abolitionists and Free Soilers make it, without any competent authority to define and declare that law, leads to anarchy and unbridled license, and therefore we are obliged, as we value society, law, order, morality, to oppose them. On the other hand, the denial of the higher law as the condition of opposing them asserts the supremacy in all things of the state, and subjects us in all things unreservedly to the civil power, which is statolatry, and absolute civil despotism. No wise and honest statesman can do either. But—here is the difficulty—the Protestant statesman is obliged to do one or the other, or both, at one moment one, at the next moment the other. This is what we have wished to make plain to the dullest capacity. Protestantism is clearly not adapted to practical life, and its principles are as inapplicable in politics as in religion. There is no practical assertion of true liberty or legitimate authority on Protestant principles, and neither is or can be asserted but as men resort, avowedly or otherwise, to Catholic principles. Hence the reason why we have been unable to discuss the question presented, and give a rational solution of the difficulty, without recurring to our Church. In recurring to her, we have, no doubt, offended the friends of the Constitution and the Union, the party with whom are our sympathies, as much as we have their enemies; but this is no fault of ours, for we cannot go contrary to what God has ordained. He has not seen proper so to constitute society and endow government that they can get on without his Church. She is an integral, an essential element in the constitution of society, and it is madness and folly to think of managing it and securing its well-being without her. She is the solution of all difficulties, and without her none are solvable.

For us Catholics, the Fugitive Slave Law presents no sort of difficulty. We are taught, as we have said, to respect and obey the government as the ordinance of God, in all things not declared by our Church to be repugnant to the Divine law. The law is evidently constitutional, and is necessary to carry out an express and imperative provision of the Constitution, which ordains (Art. IV. Sect. 2), that "No person held to service or labor in one State, under the laws thereof, escaping into another, shall, in consequence of any law or regulation therein, be discharged from such service or labor, but shall be delivered up on claim of the party to whom such service or labor may be due." This is imperative, and with regard to its meaning there is no disagreement. By this the slaveholders have the right to claim their fugitive slaves in the non-slaveholding States, and the non-slaveholding States are bound to deliver them up, when claimed. For the purpose of carrying out this constitutional provision, Congress passed a law, in 1793, which has proved ineffectual, and it has passed the recent law, more strigent in its provisions, and likely to prove efficient, for the same purpose. We can see nothing in the law contrary to the Constitution, and, as high legal authority has pronouced it constitutional, we must presume it to be so. Nobody really regards it as unconstitutional, and the only special objection to it is,—what is no objection at all,—that it is likely to answer its purpose. Now as the law is necessary to secure the fulfilment of the obligations imposed by the Constitution, and as our Church has never decided that to restore a fugitive slave to its owner is *per se* contrary to the law of God, we are bound to obey the law, and could not, without resisting the ordinance of God and purchasing to ourselves damnation, refuse to obey it. This settles the question for us.

As to Protestants who allege that the law is contrary to the law of God, and therefore that they cannot with a good conscience obey it, we have very little in addition to say. There are no principles in common between them and us, on which the question can be decided. We have shown them that they are bound to obey the civil law till they can bring a higher authority than the state, and a higher than their own private judgment, to set it aside as repugnant to the law of God. This higher authority they have not, and therefore for them there is no higher law. Will they allege the Sacred Scriptures? That will avail them nothing till they show that they have legal possession of the Scriptures, and that they are constituted by Almighty God a court with authority to interpret them and declare their sense. As this is what they can never do, we cannot argue the Scriptural question with them. We will only add, that there is no passage in either the Old Testament or the New that declares it repugnant to the law of God, or law of eternal justice, to deliver up the fugitive slave to his master; and St. Paul sent back, after converting him, the fugitive slave Onesimus to his master Philemon. This is enough; for St. Paul appears to have done more than the recent law of Congress demands; he seems to have sent back the fugitive without being requested to do so by his owner; but the law of Congress only requires the fugitive to be delivered up when claimed by his master. It will not do for those who appeal to the Sacred Scriptures to maintain either that St. Paul was ignorant of the law of God, or that he acted contrary to it. This fact alone concludes the Scriptural question against them.

But we have detained our readers long enough. We have said more than was necessary to satisfy the intelligent and the candid, and reasoning is thrown away upon factionists and fanatics, Abolitionists and philanthropists. There is no question that the country is seriously in danger. What, with the sectionists at the North and the sectionists at the South, with the great dearth of true patriots, and still greater dearth of statesmen, in all sections of the Union, it will go hard but the Union itself receive some severe shocks. Yet we trust in God it will be preserved, although the American people are far from meriting so great a boon. After the humiliation of ourselves, and prayer to God, we see nothing to be done to save the country, but for all the friends of the Union, whether heretofore called Whigs or Democrats, to rally around the Union, and form a grand national party, in opposition to the sectionists, factionists, and fanatics, of all complexions, sorts, and sizes. It is no time now to indulge old party animosities, or to contend for old party organizations. The country is above party, and all who love their country, and wish to save the noble institutions left us by our fathers, should fall into the ranks of one and the same party, and work side by side, and shoulder to shoulder, for the maintenance of the Union and the supremacy of law. We see strong indications that such a party is rapidly forming throughout the country, and we say, let it be formed,—the sooner the better. Let the party take high conservative ground, against all sorts of radicalism and ultraism, and inscribe on its banner, THE PRESERVATION OF THE UNION, AND THE SUPREMACY OF LAW, and it will command the support, we doubt not, of a large majority of the American people, and deserve and receive, we devoutly hope, the protection of Almighty God, who, we must believe, has after all great designs in this country. Above all, let our Catholic fellow-citizens in this crisis be faithful to their duty, even though they find Mr. Fillmore's administration and our Protestant countrymen madly and foolishly hostile to them; for on the Catholic population, under God, depend the future destinies of these United States. The principles of our holy religion, the prayers of our Church, and the fidelity to their trusts of the Catholic portion of the people, are the only sure reliance left us.

CATHOLICITY NECESSARY TO SUSTAIN POPULAR LIBERTY.

OCTOBER, 1845.

By popular liberty, we mean democracy; by democracy, we mean the democratic form of government; by the democratic form of government, we mean that form of government which vests the sovereignty in the people as population, and which is administered by the people, either in person or by their delegates. By sustaining popular liberty, we mean, not the introduction or institution of democracy, but preserving it when and where it is already introduced, and securing its free, orderly, and wholesome action. By Catholicity, we mean the Roman Catholic Church, faith, morals, and worship. The thesis we propose to maintain is, therefore, that without the Roman Catholic religion it is impossible to preserve a democratic government, and secure its free, orderly, and wholesome action. Infidelity, Protestantism, heathenism may institute a democracy, but only Catholicity can sustain it.

Our own government, in its origin and constitutional form, is not a democracy, but, if we may use the expression, a limited *elective* aristocracy. In its theory, the representative, within the limits prescribed by the Constitution, when once elected, and during the time for which he is elected, is, in his official action, independent of his constituents, and not responsible to them for his acts. For this reason, we call the government an elective aristocracy. But, practically, the government framed by our fathers no longer exists, save in name. Its original character has disappeared, or is rapidly disappearing. The Constitution is a dead letter, except so far as it serves to prescribe the modes of election, the rule of the majority, the distribution and tenure of offices, and the union and separation of the functions of government. Since 1828, it has been becoming in practice, and is now, substantially, a pure democracy, with no effective constitution but the will of the majority for the time being. Whether the change has been for the better or the worse, we need not stop to inquire. The change was inevitable, because men are more willing to advance themselves by flattering the people and perverting the Constitution, than they are by self-denial to serve their country. The change has been effected, and there is no return to the original theory of the government. Any man who should plant himself on the Constitution, and attempt to arrest the democratic tendency,—no matter what his character, ability, virtues, services,—would be crushed and ground to powder. Your Calhouns must give way for your Polks and Van Burens, your Websters for your Harrisons and Tylers. No man, who is not prepared to play the demagogue, to stoop to flatter the people, and, in one direction or another, to exaggerate the democratic tendency, can receive the nomination for an important office, or have influence in public affairs. The reign of great men, of distinguished statesmen and firm patriots, is over, and that of the demagogues has begun. Your most important offices are hereafter to be filled by third and fourth-rate men,—men too insignificant to excite strong opposition, and too flexible in their principles not to be willing to take any direction the caprices of the mob—or the interests of the wire-pullers of the mob —may demand. Evil or no evil, such is the fact, and we must conform to it.

Such being the fact, the question comes up, How are we to sustain popular liberty, to secure the free, orderly, and wholesome action of our practical democracy? The question is an important one, and cannot be blinked with impunity.

The theory of democracy is, Construct your government and commit it to the people to be taken care of. Democracy is not properly a government; but what is called the government is a huge machine contrived to be wielded by the people as they shall think proper. In relation to it the people are assumed to be what Almighty God is to the universe, the first cause, the medial cause, the final cause. It emanates from them; it is administered by them, and for them; and, moreover, they are to keep watch and provide for its right administration.

It is a beautiful theory, and would work admirably, if it were not for one little difficulty, namely,—*the people are fallible, both individually and collectively, and governed by their passions and interests, which not unfrequently lead them far astray, and produce much mischief.* The government must necessarily follow their will; and whenever that will happens to be blinded by passion, or misled by ignorance or interest, the government must inevitably go wrong; and government can never go wrong without doing injustice. The government may be provided for; the people may take care of that; but who or what is to take care of the people, and assure us that they will always wield the government so as to promote justice and equality, or maintain order, and the equal rights of all, of all classes and interests?

Do not answer by referring us to the virtue and intelligence of the people. We are writing seriously, and have no leisure to enjoy a joke, even if it be a good one. We have too much principle, we hope, to seek to humbug, and have had too much experience to be humbugged. We are Americans, American born, American bred, and we love our country, and will, when called upon, defend it, against any and every enemy, to the best of our feeble ability; but, though we by no means rate American virtue and intelligence so low as do those who will abuse us for not rating it higher, we cannot consent to hoodwink ourselves, or to claim for our countrymen a degree of virtue and intelligence they do not possess. We are acquainted with no salutary errors, and are forbidden to seek even a good end by any but honest means. The virtue and intelligence of the American people are not sufficient to secure the free, orderly, and wholesome action of the government; for they do not secure it. The government commits, every now and then, a sad blunder, and the general policy it adopts must prove, in the long run, suicidal. It has adopted a most iniquitous policy, and its most unjust measures are its most popular measures, such as it would be fatal to any man's political success directly and openly to oppose; and we think we hazard nothing in saying, our free institutions cannot be sustained without an augmentation of popular virtue and intelligence. We do not say the people are not capable of a sufficient degree of virtue and intelligence to sustain a democracy; all we say is, they cannot do it without virtue and intelligence, nor without a higher degree of virtue and intelligence than they have as yet attained to. We do not apprehend that many of our countrymen, and we are sure no one whose own virtue and intelligence entitle his opinion to any weight, will dispute this. Then the question of the means of sustaining our democracy resolves itself into the question of augmenting the virtue and intelligence of the people.

The press makes readers, but does little to make virtuous and intelligent readers. The newspaper press is, for the most part, under the control of men of very ordinary abilities, lax principles, and limited acquirements. It echoes and exaggerates popular errors, and does little or nothing to create a sound public opinion. Your popular literature caters to popular taste, passions, prejudices, ignorance, and errors; it is by no means above the average degree of virtue and intelligence which already obtains, and can do nothing to create a higher standard of virtue or tone of thought. On what, then, are we to rely?

"On Education," answer Frances Wright, Abner Kneeland, the Hon. Secretary of the Massachusetts Board of Education, and the Educationists generally. But we must remember that we must have virtue *and* intelligence. Virtue without intelligence will only fit the mass to be duped by the artful and designing; and intelligence without virtue only makes one the abler and more successful villain. Education must be of the right sort, if it is to answer our purpose; for a bad education is worse than none. The Mahometans are great sticklers for education, and, if we recollect aright, it is laid down in the Koran, that every believer must at least be taught to read; but we do not find their education does much to advance them in virtue and intelligence. Education, moreover, demands educators, and educators of the right sort. Where are these to be obtained? Who is to select them, judge of their qualifications, sustain or dismiss them? The people? Then you place education in the same category with democracy. You make the people through their representatives the educators. The people will select and sustain only such educators as represent their own virtues, vices, intelligence, prejudices, and errors. Whether they educate mediately or immediately, they can impart only what they have and are. Consequently, with them for educators, we can, by means even of universal education, get no increase of virtue and intelligence to bear on the government. The people may educate, but where is that which takes care that they educate in a proper manner? Here is the very difficulty we began by pointing out. The people take care of the government and education; but who or what is to take care of the people, who need taking care of quite as much as either education or government?—for, rightly considered, neither government nor education has any other legitimate end than to take care of the people.

We know of but one solution of the difficulty, and that is in RELIGION. There is no foundation for virtue but in religion, and it is only religion that can command the degree of popular virtue and intelligence requisite to insure to popular government the right direction and a wise and just administration. A people without religion, however successful they may be in throwing off old institutions, or in introducing new ones, have no power to secure the free, orderly, and wholesome working of any institutions. For the people can bring to the support of institutions only the degree of virtue and intelligence they have; and we need not stop to prove that an infidel people can have very little either of virtue or intelligence, since, in this professedly Christian country, this will and must be conceded us. We shall, therefore, assume, without stopping to defend our assumption, that religion is the power or influence we need to take care of the people, and secure the degree of virtue and intelligence necessary to sustain popular liberty. We say, then, if democracy commits the government to the people to be taken care of, religion is to take care that they take proper care of the government, rightly direct and wisely administer it.

But what religion? It must be a religion which is above the people and controls them, or it will not answer the purpose. If it depends on the people, if the people are to take care of it, to say what it shall be, what it shall teach, what it shall command, what worship or discipline it shall insist on being observed, we are back in our old difficulty. The people take care of religion; but who or what is to take care of the people? We repeat, then, what religion? It cannot be Protestantism, in all or any of its forms; for Protestantism assumes as its point of departure that Almighty God has indeed given us a religion, but *has given it to us not to take care of us, but to be taken care of by us.* It makes religion the ward of the people; assumes it to be sent on earth a lone and helpless orphan, to be taken in by the people, who are to serve as its nurse.

We do not pretend that Protestants say this in just so many words; but this, under the present point of view, is their distinguishing characteristic. What was the assumption of the Reformers? Was it not that Almighty God had failed to take care of his Church, that he had suffered it to become exceedingly corrupt and corrupting, so much so as to have become a very Babylon, and to have ceased to be his Church? Was it not for this reason that they turned reformers, separated themselves from what had been the Church, and attempted, with such materials as they could command, to reconstruct the Church on its primitive foundation, and after the primitive model? Is not this what they tell us? But if they had believed the Son of Man came to minister and not to be ministered unto, that Almighty God had instituted his religion for the spiritual government of men, and charged himself with the care and maintenance of it, would they ever have dared to take upon themselves the work of reforming it? Would they ever have fancied that either religion or the Church could ever need reforming, or, if so, that it could ever be done by human agency? Of course not They would have taken religion as presented by the Church as the standard, submitted to it as the law, and confined themselves to the duty of obedience. It is evident, therefore, from the fact of their assuming to be reformers, that they, consciously or unconsciously, regarded religion as committed to their care, or abandoned to their protection. They were, at least, its guardians, and were to govern it, instead of being governed by it.

The first stage of Protestantism was to place religion under the charge of the civil government. The Church was condemned, among other reasons, for the control it exercised over princes and nobles, that is, over the temporal power; and the first effect of Protestantism was to emancipate the government from this control, or, in other words, to free the government from the restraints of religion, and to bring religion in subjection to the temporal authority. The prince, by rejecting the authority of the Church, won for himself the power to determine the faith of his subjects, to appoint its teachers, and to remove them whenever they should teach what he disapproved, or whenever they should cross his ambition, defeat his oppressive policy, or interfere with his pleasures. Thus was it and still is it with the Protestant princes in Germany, with the temporal authority in Denmark, Sweden, England, Russia,—in this respect also Protestant,—and originally was it the same in this country. The supreme civil magistrate makes himself sovereign pontiff, and religion and the Church, if disobedient to his will, are to be turned out of house and home, or dragooned into submission. Now, if we adopt this view, and subject religion to the civil government, it will not answer our purpose. We want religion, as we have seen, to control the people, and through its spiritual governance to cause them to give the temporal government always a wise and just direction. But, if the government control the religion, it can exercise no control over the sovereign people, for they control the government. Through the government the people take care of religion, but who or what takes care of the people? This would leave the people ultimate, and we have no security unless we have something more ultimate than they, something which they cannot control, but which they must obey.

The second stage in Protestantism is to reject, in matters of religion, the authority of the temporal government, and to subject religion to the control of the faithful. This is the full recognition in matters of religion of the democratic principle. The people determine their faith and worship, select, sustain, or dismiss their own religious teachers. They who are to be taught judge him who is to teach, and say whether he teaches them truth or falsehood, wholesome doctrine or unwholesome. The patient directs the physican what to prescribe. This is the theory adopted by Protestants generally in this country. The congregation select their own teacher, unless it be among the Methodists, and to them the pastor is responsible. If he teaches to suit them, well and good; if he crosses none of their wishes, enlarges their numbers, and thus lightens their taxes and gratifies their pride of sect, also well and good; if not, he must seek a flock to feed somewhere else.

But this view will no more answer our purpose than the former; for it places religion under the control of the people, and therefore in the same category with the government itself. The people take care of religion, but who takes care of the people.

The third and last stage of Protestantism is Individualism. This leaves religion entirely to the control of the individual, who selects his own creed, or makes a creed to suit himself, devises his own worship and discipline, and submits to no restraints but such as are self-imposed. This makes a man's religion the effect of his virtue and intelligence, and denies it all power to augment or to direct them. So this will not answer. The individual takes care of his religion, but who or what takes care of the individual? The state? But who takes care of the state? The people? But who takes care of the people? Our old difficulty again.

It is evident, from these considerations, that Protestantism is not and cannot be the religion to sustain democracy; because, take it in which stage you will, it, like democracy itself, is subject to the control of the people, and must command and teach what they say, and of course must follow, instead of controlling, their passions, interests, and caprices.

Nor do we obtain this conclusion merely by reasoning. It is sustained by facts. The Protestant religion is everywhere either an expression of the government or of the people, and must obey either the government or public opinion. The grand reform, if reform it was, effected by the Protestant chiefs, consisted in bringing religious questions before the public, and subjecting faith and worship to the decision of public opinion,—public on a larger or smaller scale, that is, of the nation, the province, or the sect. Protestant faith and worship tremble as readily before the slightest breath of public sentiment, as the aspen leaf before the gentle zephyr. The faith and discipline of a sect take any and every direction the public opinion of that sect demands. All is loose, floating,—is here to-day, is there to-morrow, and, next day, may be nowhere. The holding of slaves is compatible with Christian character south of a geographical line, and incompatible north; and Christian morals change according to the prejudices, interests, or habits of the people,—as evinced by the recent divisions in our own country amoug the Baptists and Methodists. The Unitarians of Savannah refuse to hear a preacher accredited by Unitarians of Boston.

The great danger in our country is from the predominance of material interests. Democracy has a direct tendency to favor inequality and injustice. The government must obey the people; that is, it must follow the passions and interests of the people, and of course the stronger passions and interests. These with us are material, such as pertain solely to this life and this world. What our people demand of government is, that it adopt and sustain such measures as tend most directly to facilitate the acquisition of wealth. It must, then, follow the passion for wealth, and labor especially to promote worldly interests.

But among these worldly interests, some are stronger than others, and can command the government. These will take possession of the government, and wield it for their own especial advantage. They will make it the instrument of taxing all the other interests of the country for the special advancement of themselves. This leads to inequality and injustice, which are incompatible with the free, orderly, and wholesome working of the government.

Now, what is wanted is some power to prevent this, to moderate the passion for wealth, and to inspire the people with such a true and firm sense of justice, as will prevent any one interest from struggling to advance itself at the expense of another. Without this the stronger material interests prodominate, make the government the means of securing their predominance, and of extending it by the burdens which, through the government, they are able to impose on the weaker interests of the country.

The framers of our government foresaw this evil, and thought to guard against it by a written Constitution. But they intrusted the preservation of the Constitution to the care of the people, which was as wise as to lock up your culprit in prison and intrust him with the key. The Constitution, as a restraint on the will of the people or the governing majority, is already a dead letter. It answers to talk about, to declaim about, in electioneering speeches, and even as a theme of newspaper leaders, and political essays in reviews; but its effective power is a morning vapor after the sun is well up.

Even Mr. Calhoun's theory of the Constitution, which regards it not simply as the written instrument, but as the disposition or the constitution of the people into sovereign states united in a federal league or compact, for certain purposes which concern all the states alike, and from which it follows that any measure unequal in its bearing, or oppressive upon any portion of the confederacy, is *ipso facto* null and void, and may be vetoed by the aggrieved state,—this theory, if true, is yet insufficient; because, 1. It has no application within the State governments themselves; and because, 2. It does not, as a matter of fact, arrest what are regarded as the unequal, unjust, and oppressive measures of the Federal government. South Carolina, in 1833, **forced a compromise, but in 1842, the obnoxious policy was** revived, is pursued now successfully, and there is no State to attempt again the virtue of State interposition. Not even South Carolina can be brought to do so again. The meshes of trade and commerce are so spread over the whole land, the controlling influences of all sections have become so united and interwoven, by means of banks, other moneyed corporations, and the credit system, that henceforth State interposition becomes practically impossible. The Constitution is practically abolished, and our government is virtually, to all intents and purposes, as we have said, a pure democracy, with nothing to prevent it from obeying the interest or interests which for the time being can succeed in commanding it. This, as the Hon. Caleb Cushing would say, is a "fixed fact." There is no restraint on predominating passions and interests but in religion. This is another "fixed fact."

Protestantism is insufficient to restrain these, for it does not do it, and is itself carried away by them. The Protestant sect governs its religion, instead of being governed by it. If one sect pursues, by the influence of its chiefs, a policy in opposition to the passions and interests of its members, or any portion of them, the disaffected, if a majority, change its policy; if too few or too weak to do that, they leave it and join some other sect, or form a new sect. If the minister attempts to do his duty, reproves a practice by which his parishioners "get gain," or insists on their practising some real self-denial not compensated by some self-indulgence, a few leading members will tell him very gravely, that they hired him to preach and pray for them, not to interfere with their business concerns and relations; and if he does not mind his own business, they will no longer need his services. The minister feels, perhaps, the insult; he would be faithful; but he looks at his lovely wife, at his little ones. These to be reduced to poverty, perhaps to beggary,—no, it must not be; one struggle, one pang, and it is over. He will do the bidding of his masters. A zealous minister in Boston ventured, one Sunday, to denounce the modern spirit of trade. The next day, he was waited on by a committee of wealthy merchants belonging to his parish, who told him he was wrong. The Sunday following, the meek and humble minister publicly retracted, and made the *amende honorable.*

Here, then, is the reason why Protestantism, though it may institute, cannot sustain popular liberty. It is itself subject to popular control, and must follow in all things the popular will, passion, interest, ignorance, prejudice, or caprice. This, in reality, is its boasted virtue, and we find it commended because under it the people have a voice in its management. Nay, we ourselves shall be denounced, not for saying Protestantism subjects religion to popular control, but for intimating that religion ought not to be so subjected. A terrible cry will be raised against us. "See, here is Mr. Brownson," it will be said, "he would bring the people under the control of the Pope of Rome. Just as we told you. These Papists have no respect for the people. They sneer at the people, mock at their wisdom and virtue. Here is this unfledged Papistling, not yet a year old, boldly contending that the control of their religious faith and worship should be taken from the people, and that they must believe and do just what the emissaries of Rome are pleased to command; and all in the name of liberty too." If we only had room, we would write out and publish what the anti-Catholic press will say against us, and save the candid, the learned, intellectual, and patriotic editors the trouble of doing it themselves; and we would do it with the proper quantity of Italics, small capitals, capitals, and exclamation points. Verily, we think we could do the thing up nearly as well as the best of them. But we have no room. Yet it is easy to foresee what they will say. The burden of their accusation will be, that we labor to withdraw religion from the control of the people, and to free it from the necessity of following their will; that we seek to make it the master, and not the slave, of the people. And this is good proof of our position, that Protestantism cannot govern the people,—for they govern it,—and therefore that Protestantism is not the religion wanted; for it is precisely a religion that can and will govern the people, be their master, that we need.

If Protestantism will not answer the purpose, what religion will? The Roman Catholic, or none. The Roman Catholic religion assumes, as its point of departure, that it is instituted not to be taken care of by the people, but to take care of the people; not to be governed by them, but to govern them. The word is harsh in democratic ears, we admit; but it is not the office of religion to say soft or pleasing words. It must speak the truth even in unwilling ears, and it has few truths that are not harsh and grating to the worldly mind or the depraved heart. The people need governing, and must be governed, or nothing but anarchy and destruction await them. They must have a master. The word must be spoken. But it is not our word. We have demonstrated its necessity in showing that we have no security for popular government, unless we have some security that the people will administer it wisely and justly; and we have no security that they will do this, unless we have some security that their passions will be restrained, and their attachments to worldly interests so moderated that they will never seek, through the government, to support them at the expense of justice; and this security we can have only in a religion that is above the people, exempt from their control, which they cannot command, but must, on peril of condemnation OBEY. Declaim as you will; quote our expression,—THE PEOPLE MUST HAVE A MASTER,—as you doubtless will; hold it up in glaring capitals, to excite the unthinking and unreasoning multitude, and to doubly fortify their prejudices against Catholicity; be mortally scandalized at the assertion that religion ought to govern the people, and then go to work and seek to bring the people into subjection to your banks or moneyed corporations through their passions, ignorance, and worldly interests, and in doing so, prove what candid men, what lovers of truth, what noble defenders of liberty, and what ardent patriots you are. We care not. You see we understand you, and, understanding you, we repeat, the religion which is to answer our purpose must be *above* the people, and able to COMMAND them. We know the force of the word, and we mean it. The first lesson to the child is, *obey ;*

the first and last lesson to the people, individually or collectively, is, OBEY ;—and there is no obedience where there is no authority to enjoin it.

The Roman Catholic religion, then, is necessary to sustain popular liberty, because popular liberty can be sustained only by a religion free from popular control, above the people, speaking from above and able to command them,—and such a religion is the Roman Catholic. It acknowledges no master but God, and depends only on the divine will in respect to what it shall teach, what it shall ordain, what it shall insist upon as truth, piety, moral and social virtue. It was made not by the people, but for them ; is administered not by the people, but for them ; is accountable not to the people, but to God. Not dependent on the people, it will not follow their passions ; not subject to their control, it will not be their accomplice in iniquity ; and speaking from God, it will teach them the truth, and command them to practise justice. To this end the very constitution of the Church contributes. It is Catholic, universal; it teaches all nations, and has its centre in no one. If it was a mere national church, like the Anglican, the Russian, the Greek, or as Louis the Fourteenth in his pride sought to make the Gallican, it would follow the caprice or interest of that nation, and become but a tool of its government or of its predominating passion. The government, if anti-popular, would use it to oppress the people, to favor its ambitious projects, or its unjust and ruinous policy. Under a popular government, it would become the slave of the people, and could place no restraint on the ruling interest or on the majority ; but would be made to sanction and consolidate its power. But having its centre in no one nation, extending over all, it becomes independent of all, and in all can speak with the same voice and in the same tone of authority. This the Church has always understood, and hence the noble struggles of the many calumniated popes to sustain the unity, Catholicity, and independence of the ecclesiastical power. This, too, the temporal powers have always seen and felt, and hence their readiness, even while professing the

Catholic faith, to break the unity of Catholic authority; for, in so doing, they could subject the Church in their own dominions, as did Henry the Eighth, and as does the emperor of Russia, to themselves.

But we pray our readers to understand us well. We unquestionably assert the *adequacy* of Catholicity to sustain popular liberty, on the ground of its being exempted from popular control and able to govern the people; and its *necessity*, on the ground that it is the only religion, which, in a popular government, is or can be exempted from popular control, and able to govern the people. We say distinctly, that this is the ground on which, reasoning as the statesman, not as the theologian, we assert the adequacy and necessity of Catholicity; and we object to Protestantism, *in our present argument*, solely on the ground that it has no authority over the people, is subject to them, must follow the direction they give it, and therefore cannot restrain their passions, or so control them as to prevent them from abusing their government. This we assert, distinctly and intentionally, and so plainly, that what we say cannot be mistaken.

But in what sense do we assert Catholicity to be the master of the people? Here we demand justice. The authority of Catholicity is spiritual, and the only sense in which we have here urged or do urge its necessity is as the means of augmenting the virtue and intelligence of the people. We demand it as a religious, not as a political power. We began by defining democracy to be that form of government which vests the sovereignty in the people. If, then, we recognize the sovereignty of the people in matters of government, we must recognize their political right to do what they will. The only restriction on their will we contend for is a *moral* restriction; and the master we contend for is not a master that prevents them from doing politically what they will, but who, by his moral and spiritual influence, prevents them from willing what they ought not to will. The only influence on the political or governmental action of the people which we ask from Catholicity, is that which it exerts on the mind, the heart, and the conscience;—an influence which it exerts by enlightening the mind to see the true end of man, the relative value of all worldly pursuits, by moderating the passions, by weaning the affections from the world, inflaming the heart with true charity, and by making each act in all things seriously, honestly, conscientiously. The people will thus come to see and to will what is equitable and right, and will give to the government a wise and just direction, and never use it to effect any unwise or unjust measures. This is the kind of master we demand for the people, and this is the bugbear of "Romanism" with which miserable panders to prejudice seek to frighten old women and children. Is there anything alarming in this? In this sense, we wish this country to come under the Pope of Rome. As the visible head of the Church, the spiritual authority which Almighty God has instituted to teach and govern the nations, we assert his supremacy, and tell our countrymen that we would have them submit to him. They may flare up at this as much as they please, and write as many alarming and abusive editorials as they choose or can find time or space to do,—they will not move us, or relieve themselves of the obligation Almighty God has placed them under of obeying the authority of the Catholic Church, Pope and all.

If we were discussing the question before us as a theologian, we should assign many other reasons why Catholicity is necessary to sustain popular liberty. Where the passions are unrestrained, there is license, but not liberty; the passions are not restrained without divine grace; and divine grace comes ordinarily only through the sacraments of the Church. But from the point of view we are discussing the question, we are not at liberty to press this argument, which, in itself, would be conclusive. The Protestants have foolishly raised the question of the influence of Catholicity on democracy, and have sought to frighten our countrymen from embracing it by appealing to their democratic prejudices, or, if you will, convictions, We have chosen to meet them on this question, and to prove that democracy without Catholicity cannot be sustained. Yet in our own minds the question is really unimportant. We have proved the insufficiency of Protestantism to sustain democracy. What then? Have we in so doing proved that Protestantism is not the true religion? Not at all; for we have no infallible evidence that democracy is the true or even the best form of government. It may be so, and the great majority of the American people believe it is so; but they may be mistaken, and Protestantism be true, notwithstanding its incompatibility with republican institutions. So we have proved that Catholicity is neccessary to sustain such institutions. But what then? Have we proved it to be the true religion? Not at all. For such institutions may themselves be false and mischievous. Nothing in this way is settled in favor of one religion or another, because no system of politics can ever constitute a standard by which to try a religious system. Religion is more ultimate than politics, and you must conform your politics to your religion, and not your religion to your politics. You must be the veriest infidels to deny this.

This conceded, the question the Protestants raise is exceedingly insignificant. The real question is, Which religion is from God? If it be Protestantism, they should refuse to subject it to any human test, and should blush to think of compelling it to conform to any thing human; for when God speaks, man has nothing to do but to listen and obey. So, having decided that Catholicity is from God, save in condescension to the weakness of our Protestant brethren, we must refuse to consider it in its political bearings. It speaks from God, and its speech overrides every other speech, its authority every other authority. It is the sovereign of sovereigns. He who could question this, admitting it to be from God, has yet to obtain his first religious conception, and to take his first lesson in religious liberty; for we are to hear God, rather than hearken unto men. But we have met the Protestants on their own ground, because, though in doing so we surrendered the vantage-ground we might occupy, we know the strength of Catholicity and the weakness of Protestantism. We know what Protestantism has done for liberty, and what it can do. It can take off restraints, and introduce license, but it can do nothing to sustain true liberty. Catholicity depends on no form of government; it leaves the people to adopt such forms of government as they please, because under any or all forms of government it can fulfil its mission of training up souls for heaven; and the eternal salvation of one single soul is worth more than, is a good far outweighing, the most perfect civil liberty, nay, all the wordly prosperity and enjoyment ever obtained or to be obtained by the whole human race.

It is, after all, in this fact, which Catholicity constantly brings to our minds, and impresses upon our hearts, that consists its chief power, aside from the grace of the sacraments, to sustain popular liberty. The danger to that liberty comes from love of the world,—the ambition for power or place, the greediness of gain or distinction. It comes from lawless passions, from inordinate love of the goods of time and sense. Catholicity, by showing us the vanity of all these, by pointing us to the eternal reward that awaits the just, moderates this inordinate love, these lawless passions, and checks the rivalries and struggles in which popular liberty receives her death blow. Once learn that all these things are vanity, that even civil liberty itself is no great good, that even bodily slavery is no great evil, that the one thing needful is a mind and heart conformed to the will of God, and you have a disposition which will sustain a democracy wherever introduced, though doubtless a disposition that would not lead you to introduce it where it is not.

But this last is no objection, for the revolutionary spirit is as fatal to democracy as to any other form of government. It is the spirit of insubordination and of disorder. It is opposed to all fixed rule, to all permanent order. It loosens every thing, and sets all afloat. Where all is floating, where nothing is fixed, where nothing can be counted on to be to-morrow what it is to-day, there is no liberty, no solid good. The universal restlessness of Protestant nations, the universal disposition to change, the constant movements of the populations, so much admired by shortsighted philosophers, are a sad spectacle to the sober-minded Christian, who would, as far as possible, find in all things a type of that eternal fixedness and repose he looks forward to as the blessed reward of his trials and labors here. Catholicity comes here to our relief. All else may change, but it changes not. All else may pass away, but it remains where and what it was, a type of the immobility and immutability of the eternal God.

LEGITIMACY AND REVOLUTIONISM.

october, 1848.

We take, in our political essays, unwearied pains to make ourselves understood, and to guard against being misapprehended; but, through our own fault or that of our readers, our success has rarely corresponded to our efforts. On all sides, from all quarters, we are charged with being hostile to liberty and favorable to despotism,—the enemy of the people, and the friend of their oppressors. We could smile at this ridiculous charge, were it not that some honest souls are found who appear to believe it, and some moon-struck scribblers make it the occasion of exciting unjust prejudices against our friends, and of placing them, as well as ourselves, in a false position before the public. Injustice to us personally is of no moment, and demands of us no attention; but when, owing to our peculiar position, it can hardly fail to work injustice to others, we are bound to notice and to repel it.

The age in which we live is an age of theoretical, and, to a great extent, of practical anarchy. Its ideas and movements are marked by impatience of restraint, denial of law, and contempt of authority. We have seen this, and have felt it our duty to protest against it, and to do what we could, in our limited sphere, to recall men to a sense of the necessity of government, and to the fact of their moral obligation to uphold the supremacy of law. This is our offence. Yet one would naturally suppose that people of ordinary intelligence, somewhat acquainted with our past history, might, without much difficulty, believe that in this our motive has been to serve the cause of freedom, not that of despotism. We, in fact, have done it, because liberty is impossible without order, order is impossible without government, and government in any worthy sense of the term is impossible without a settled conviction on the part of the people of its legitimacy, and of their obligation in conscience to obey it. Nothing deserving the name of government can be founded on the sense of the agreeable or of the useful. Governments, so called, which appeal to nothing higher, more catholic, and more stable, are mere creatures of passion or caprice, and must follow the lead of popular folly and excess, instead of restraining them, and directing the general activity to the public good. They are not governments, but mere instruments for the private gain or aggrandizement of the adroit and scheming few who contrive to possess themselves of their management. It is philosophically and historically demonstrable, that the permanence and stability of government, and its wise and just administration for the common weal,—the only legitimate end of its institution,—are impracticable, unless the government is held to rest on the universal and unalterable sense of duty, under the protection of religion.

This truth, though, in fact, a very commonplace truth, our age overlooks, or, if it does not overlook, it rejects. Hence the danger with which liberty in our times is threatened. We have believed it, therefore, not improper to guard against this danger, and in order to do so, we have traced government back to its source, and to the foundation of its authority. We have found its origin, not in the people, but in God, from whom is all power; and we have concluded from this its divine right, within its legitimate province, to our allegiance. It has, since it derives its authority from God, a divine right to command, and, if so, we must be bound in conscience to obey it. Then it rests, not on the sense of the agreeable or of the useful, to fluctuate as these fluctuate, but on the sense of duty,—and not merely duty to our country or to mankind, but duty to God,—a duty founded in the unalterable relations of man to his Maker. This raises political allegiance and obedience to the law to the rank of moral virtue, and declares their violation to be a sin against God, to whom we belong, all we have, and all we are. Hence, in its legitimate province, even civil government becomes sacred and inviolable; and therefore we assert, on the one hand, our duty to obey it, and, on the other, deny the right of revolution, what Lafayette calls "the sacred right of insurrection."

Here, in general terms, is the doctrine we have endeavored to inculcate. That it is hostile to the political atheism now so rife, we concede. We are Christians, and do not understand the possibility of being Christians, and yet atheists in politics. We have but one set of principles, and these are determined by our religion. We cannot adopt one set of principles in our religion and a contradictory set in our politics, saying "Good Lord" in the one, and "Good Devil" in the other. We are too far behind the age for that. But that this doctrine is hostile to liberty or favorable to despotism, we do not concede,—nay, positively deny. In setting it forth, we have dwelt on that phase of it directly opposed to the dangerous tendencies of the age, because it was not necessary to guard against tendencies from which we have nothing to apprehend, and because we presumed that our readers would of themselves see that it had another phase equally opposed to the opposite class of tendencies. But for the hundredth time in our short life we have learned that the writer who presumes any thing on the intelligence or discrimination of the bulk of readers presumes too much, and will assuredly be disappointed. The doctrine protects the government against radicals, rebels, and revolutionists; but it protects, also, the people against tyrants and oppressors. The fears of our politicians on this last point, whether real or affected, do little credit to their sagacity. The monsters which affright them a little more light would enable them to see are as harmless as the charred stump or decaying log which the benighted traveller mistakes for bear or panther.

When we assert the doctrine of legitimacy, we are understood to assert passive obedience and non-resistance to tyrants; but needs it any extraordinary intellectual power and cultivation to perceive that legitimacy, while it smites the rebel or the revolutionist, must equally smite the tyrant or usurper? If the doctrine asserts the right of legitimate, it must deny the right of illegitimate government; if it denies the right to disobey the legitimate authority, it must also deny the right of illegitimate authority to command; if it disarms the subject before the legal authority, it must equally disarm the illegal authority before the subject. How, then, from the fact that we are forbidden to resist or to subvert legitimate government, the legal constitution of the state, conclude that we are forbidden to resist or to depose the tyrant? Tyranny, oppression, is never legal, and therefore no tyrant or oppressor ever is or can be the legitimate sovereign. To resist him is not to resist the legitimate authority, and therefore demands for its justification no assertion of the revolutionary principle. How is it, then, that you do not see that the doctrine of legitimacy gives a legal right to resist whatever is illegal, and therefore lays a solid foundation for liberty?

People, we know, are prejudiced against the doctrine which asserts the divine origin and right of government, but it is because they misapprehend the doctrine, and because they identify liberty with democracy. The doctrine, undoubtedly, does assert the sacredness, inviolability, and legitimacy of every actual political constitution, whatever its form, and that the monarchical or aristocratic order, where it is the established order, is as legitimate as the democratic. But, if liberty and democracy are one and the same thing, since the monarchical order is that which is actually the established order in most states, liberty in most states is precluded, and the people are and must be slaves. Yet is it true that liberty and democracy are identical or convertible terms? Democracy, whose expression is universal suffrage, intrusts every citizen with a share in the administration of the government, which is and can be done by no other political order. But the elective franchise is a trust, not a right, and therefore to withhold it is not to withhold freedom. Liberty is in the possession and exercise of our natural rights. We have none of us any natural right to govern; for under the law of nature all men are equals, and no one has the right to exercise authority over others. The franchise is a municipal grant, and depends on the will of the political sovereign. Liberty, unless the question be between nation and nation, is not a predicate of the government, but of the subject, and of the subject not in his quality of a constituent element of the sovereignty, but in his quality of subject. As subject he may be free, without being intrusted with authority to govern, and therefore may be free under other forms of government than the democratic.

In fact, democratic politicians never attain to the conception of liberty. The basis of their theory of government is despotism. They make the right to govern a natural right, and differ from the confessedly despotic politicians only in claiming for every man what these claim for only one. They make government a personal right, incident to manhood, inalienable, and inamissible, —not a solemn trust which the trustee is bound to hold and exercise according to law, and for which he is accountable. Hence it is that democracy always sooner or later terminates in despotism or autocracy. We deny that government is ever a personal right, whether of the one, the few, or the many, and therefore deny that a man has a natural right to a share in the administration. He only has the right to whom the power is delegated by the competent authority, and he holds it, not as a personal right, but as a trust. Consequently, we do not concede that the establishment of the democratic *régime* is at all essential to the establishment or maintenance of liberty. He is free, enjoys his liberty, who is secured in the possession and enjoyment of all his natural rights; and this is done wherever the legitimate authority governs, and governs according to the principles of justice. We are aware of no form of government that cannot so govern, or which cannot also govern otherwise, if it choose.

We are republicans, because republicanism is here the established order, but we confess that we do not embrace, and never have embraced, as essential to liberty, or even as compatible with liberty, the popular democratic doctrine of the country. We beg leave to introduce here some remarks on *Democracy* which we wrote in 1837, and published in the first number of *The Boston Quarterly Review*, January, 1838.

"Democracy . . . . . is sometimes asserted to be the sovereignty of the people. If this be a true account of it, it is indefensible. The sovereignty of the people is not a truth. Sovereignty is that which is highest, ultimate; which has not only the physical force to make itself obeyed, but the moral right to command whatever it pleases. The right to command involves the corresponding duty of obedience. What the sovereign may command, it is the duty of the subject to do.

" Are the people the highest ? Are they ultimate ? And are we· bound in conscience to obey whatever it may be their good pleasure to ordain ? If so, where is individual liberty ? If so, the people, taken collectively, are the absolute master of every man taken individually. Every man, as a man, then, is an absolute slave. Whatever the people, in their collective capacity, may demand of him, he must feel himself bound in conscience to give. No matter how intolerable the burdens imposed, painful and needless the sacrifices required, he cannot refuse obedience without incurring the guilt of disloyalty ; and he must submit in quiet, in silence, without even the moral right to feel that he is wronged.

" Now this, in theory at least, is absolutism. Whether it be a democracy, or any other form of government, if it be absolute there is and there can be no individual liberty. Under a monarchy, the monarch is the state. ' *L'Etat, c'est moi*,' said Louis the Fourteenth, and he expressed the whole monarchieal theory. The state being absolute, and the monarch being the state, the monarch has the right to command what he will, and exact obedience in the name of duty, loyalty. Hence absolutism, despotism. Under an aristocracy, the nobility are the state, and consequenly, as the state is absolute, the nobility are also absolute. Whatever they command is binding. If they require the many to be 'hewers of wood and drawers of water' to them, then 'hewers of wood and drawers of water' to them the many must feel it their duty to be. Here, for the many, is absolutism as much as under a monarchy. Every body sees this.

"Well, is it less so under a democracy, where the people, in their associated capacity, are held to be absolute? The people are the state, and the state is absolute; the people may therefore do whatever they please. Is not this freedom? Yes, for the state; but what is it for the individual? There are no kings, no nobilities, it is true; but the people may exercise all the power over the individual that kings or nobilities may; and consequently every man, taken singly, is, under a democracy, if the state be absolute, as much the slave of the state, as under the most absolute monarchy or aristocracy.

"But this is not the end of the chapter. Under a democratic form of government, all questions which come up for the decision of authority must be decided by a majority of voices. The sovereignty which is asserted for the people must, then, be transferred to the ruling majority. If the people are sovereign, then the majority are sovereign; and if sovereign, the majority have, as Miss Martineau lays it down, the absolute right to govern. If the majority have the absolute right to govern, it is the absolute duty of the minority to obey. We who chance to be in the minority are then completely disfranchised. We are wholly at the mercy of the majority. We hold our property, our wives and children, and our lives even, at its sovereign will and pleasure. It may do by us and ours as it pleases. If it take it into its head to make a new and arbitrary division of property, however unjust it may seem, we shall not only be impotent to resist, but we shall not even have the right of the wretched to complain. Conscience will be no shield. The authority of the absolute sovereign extends to spiritual matters, as well as to temporal. The creed the majority is pleased to impose, the minority must in all meekness and submission receive; and the form of religious worship the majority is good enough to prescribe, the minority must make it a matter of conscience to observe. Whatever has been done under the most absolute monarchy or the most lawless aristocracy may be reënacted under a pure democracy, and what is worse, legitimately too, if it be once laid down in principle that the majority has the absolute right to govern.

"The majority will always have the physical power to coerce the minority into submission; but this is a matter of no moment, in comparison with the doctrine which gives them the right to do it. We have very little fear of the physical force of numbers, when we can oppose to it the moral force of right. The doctrine in question deprives us of this moral force. By giving absolute sovereignty to the majority, it declares whatever the majority does is right, that the majority can do no wrong. It ligitimates every possible act for which the sanction of a majority of voices can be obtained. Whatever the majority may exact it is just to give. Truth, justice, wisdom, virtue, can erect no barriers to stay its progress ; for these are the creations of its will, and may be made or unmade by its breath. Justice is obedience to its decrees, and injustice is resistance to its commands. Resistance is not crime before the civil tribunal only, but also *in foro conscientiæ*. Now this is what we protest against. It is not the physical force of the majority that we dread, but the doctrine that legitimates each and every act the majority may choose to perform ; and therefore teaches them to look for no standard of right and wrong beyond their own will. . . . . .

" The effects of this doctrine, so far as believed and acted on, cannot be too earnestly deprecated. It creates a multitude of demagogues, pretending a world of love for the *dear* people, lauding the people's virtues, magnifying their sovereignty, and with mock humility professing their readiness ever to bow to the will of the majority. It tends to make public men lax in their morals, hypocritical in their conduct; and it paves the way for gross bribery and corruption. It generates a habit of appealing, on nearly all occasions, from truth and justice, wisdom and virtue, to the force of numbers, and virtually sinks the man in the brute. It destroys manliness of character, independence of thought and action, and makes one weak, vacillating,—a time-server and a coward. It perverts inquiry from its legitimate objects, and asks, when it concerns a candidate for office, not, Who is the most honest, the most capable ? but, Who will command the most votes ? and when it concerns a measure of policy, not, What is just ? What is for the public good ? but, What can the majority be induced to support ?

" Now, as men, as friends to good morals, we cannot assent to a doctrine which not only has this tendency, but which declares this tendency legitimate. That it does have this tendency needs not to be proved. Every body knows it, and not a few lament it. Not long since it was gravely argued by a leading politician, in a Fourth of July oration, that Massachusetts ought to give Mr. Van Buren her votes for the Presidency, because, if she did not, she would array herself against her sister States, and be compelled to stand alone, as the orator said with a sneer, 'in solitary grandeur.' In the access of his party fever, it did not occur to him that Massachusetts was in duty bound, whether her sister States were with her or against her, to oppose Mr. Van Buren, if she disliked him as a man, or distrusted his principles as a politician or a statesman. Many good reasons, doubtless, might have been alleged why Massachusetts ought to have voted for Mr. Van Buren, but the orator would have been puzzled to select one less conclusive, or more directly in the face and eyes of all sound morals, than the one he adduced. The man who deserves to be called a statesman never appeals to low or demoralizing motives, and he scorns to carry even a good measure by unworthy means. There is within every man, who can lay any claim to correct moral feeling, that which looks with contempt on the puny creature who makes the opinions of the majority his rule of action. He who wants the moral courage to stand up 'in solitary grandeur,' like Socrates in the face of the Thirty Tyrants, and demand that right be respected, that justice be done, is unfit to be called a statesman, or even a man. A man has no business with what the majority think, will, say, do, or will approve; if he will be a man, and maintain the rights and dignity of manhood, his sole business is to inquire what truth and justice, wisdom and virtue, demand at his hands, and to do it, whether the world be with him or against him,—to do it, whether he stand alone 'in solitary grandeur,' or be huzzaed by the crowd, loaded with honors, held up as one whom the young must aspire to imitate, or be sneered at as singular, branded as a 'seditious fellow,' or crucified between two thieves. Away, then, with your demoralizing and debasing notion of appealing to a majority of voices! Dare be a man, dare be yourself, to speak and act according to your own solemn convictions, and in obedience to the voice of God calling out to you from the depths of your own being. Professions of freedom, of love of liberty, of devotion to her cause, are mere wind, when there wants the power to live and to die in defence of what one's own heart tells him is just and true. A free government is a mockery, a solemn farce, where every man feels himself bound to consult and to conform to the opinions and will of an irresponsible majority. Free minds, free hearts, free souls, are the materials, and the only materials, out of which free governments are constructed. And is he free in mind, heart, soul, body, or limb, he who feels himself bound to the triumphal car of the majority, to be dragged whither its drivers please? Is he the man to speak out the lessons of truth and wisdom when most they are needed, to stand by the right when all are gone out of the way, to plead for the wronged and downtrodden when all are dumb, he who owns the absolute right of the majority to govern?

"Sovereignty is not in the will of the people, nor in the will of the majority. Every man feels that the people are not ultimate, are not the highest, that they do not make the right or the wrong, and that the people as a state, as well as the people as individuals, are under law, accountable to a higher authority than theirs. What is this Higher than the people? The king? Not he whom men dignify with the royal title. Every man, by the fact that he is a man, is an accountable being. Every man feels that he owes allegiance to some authority above him. The man whom men call a king, is a man, and, inasmuch as he is a man, he must be an accountable being, must himself be under law, and therefore cannot be the highest, the ultimate, and of course not the true sovereign. His will is not in itself law. Then he is not in himself the sovereign. Whatever authority he may possess is derived, and that from which he derives his authority, and not he, in the last analysis, is the true sovereign. If he derive it from the people, then the people, not he, is the sovereign; if from God, then God, not he, is the sovereign.

"Are the aristocracy the sovereign? If so, annihilate the aristocracy, and men will be loosed from all restraint, released from all obligation, and there will be for them neither right nor wrong. Nobody can admit that right and wrong owe their existence to the aristocracy. Moreover, the aristocracy are men, and, as men, they are in the same predicament with all other men. They are themselves under law, accountable, and therefore not sovereign in their own right. If we say they are above the people, they are placed there by some power which is also above them, and that, not they, is the sovereign.

"But if neither people, nor kings, nor aristocracy are sovereign, who or what is? What is the answer which every man, when he reflects as a moralist, gives to the question, Why ought I to do this or that particular thing? Does he say, Because the king commands it,—the aristocracy enjoin it,—the people ordain it,—the majority wills it? No. He says, if he be true to his higher convictions, Because it is right, because it is just. Every man feels that he has a right to do whatever is just, and that it is his duty to do it. Whatever he feels to be just he feels to be legitimate, to be law, to be morally obligatory. Whatever is unjust he feels to be illegitimate, to be without obligation, and to be that which it is not disloyalty to resist. The absolutist, he who contends, for unqualified submission on the part of the people to the monarch, thunders, therefore, in the ears of the absolute monarch himself, that he is bound to be just; and the aristocrat assures his order that its highest nobility is derived from its obedience to justice; and does not the democrat, too, even while he proclaims the sovereignty of the people, tell this same sovereign people to be just? In all this, witness is borne to an authority above the individual, above kings, nobilities, and people, and to the fact, too, that the absolute sovereign is justice. Justice, is then, the sovereign, the sovereign of sovereigns, the king of kings, lord of lords, the supreme law of the people, and of the individual.

"This doctrine teaches that the people, as a state, are as much bound to be just as is the individual. By bounding the state by justice, we declare it limited, we deny its absolute sovereignty, and therefore save the individual from absolute slavery. The individual may on this ground arrest the action of the state, by alleging that it is proceeding unjustly; and the minority has a moral force with which to oppose the physical force of the majority. By this there is laid in the state the foundation of liberty; liberty is acknowledged as a right, whether it be possessed as a fact or not.

"A more formal refutation of the sovereignty of the people, or vindication of the sovereignty of justice, is not needed. In point of fact, there are none who mean to set up the sovereignty of the people above the sovereignty of justice. All, we believe, when the question is presented as we have presented it, will and do admit that justice is supreme, though very few seem to have been aware of the consequences which result from such an admission. The sovereignty of justice, in all cases whatsoever, is what we understand by the doctrine of democracy. True democracy is not merely the denial of the absolute sovereignty of the king, and that of the nobility, and the assertion of that of the people; but it is properly the denial of the absolute sovereignty of the state, whatever the form of government adopted as the agent of the state, and the assertion of the absolute sovereignty of justice. . . . . .

"Sovereignty may be taken either absolutely or relatively. When taken absolutely, as we have thus far taken it, and as it ought always to be taken, especially in a free government, it means, as we have defined it, the highest, that which is ultimate, which has the right to command what it will, and which to resist is crime. Thus defined, it is certain that neither people, nor kings, nor aristocracies, are sovereign, for they are all under law, and accountable to an authority which is not theirs, but which is above them and independent of them.

"When taken relatively, as it usually is by writers on government, it means the state, or the highest civil or political power of the state. The state, we have seen, is not absolute. It is not an independent sovereign. It is not, then, in strictness, a sovereign at all. Its enactments are not in and of themselves laws, and cannot be laws, unless they receive the signature of absolute justice. If that signature be witheld, they are null and void from the beginning. Nevertheless, social order, which is the indispensable condition of the very existence of the community, demands the creation of a government, and that the government should be clothed with the authority necessary for the maintenance of order. That portion of sovereignty necessary for this end, and, if you please, for the promotion of the common weal, justice delegates to the state. This portion of delegated sovereignty is what is commonly meant by sovereignty. This sovereignty is necessarily limited to certain specific objects, and can be no greater than is needed for those objects. If the state stretch its authority beyond those objects, it becomes a usurper, and the individual is not bound to obey, but may lawfully resist it, as he may lawfully resist any species of injustice,—taking care, however, that the manner of his resistance be neither unjust in itself, nor inconsistent with social order. For instance, the state assumes the authority to allow a man to be seized and held as property; the man may undoubedetly assert his liberty, his rights as a man, and endeavour to regain them; but he may not, in doing this, deny or infringe any of the just rights of him who may have deemed himself his master or owner."—pp. 37-45.

When we wrote this, we had the reputation of being one of the stanchest friends of liberty and the most ultra radicals in the country,—a fact which we commend to those of our former friends who are now so ready to represent us as having gone over to the side of despotism. We should not now call the doctrine of the extract Democracy, as we did when we wrote it, nor should we use certain locutions, to be detected here and there in the extract, dictated by an erroneous theology; but the doctrine itself is our present doctrine, as clearly and as energetically expressed as we could now express it. It seems to us to contain an unanswerable refutation of the popular democratic principle, and a triumphant vindication of the sovereignty of justice,— therefore, of the divine origin and right of government; for justice, in the sense the writer uses it, is identical with God, who alone is absolute, immutable, eternal, and sovereign Justice.

The purpose of the writer was evidently to obtain a solid foundation for individual freedom. If he, in order to do this, found and proved it necessary to assert the divine origin and right of government, to rise above the sovereignty of kings, of nobles, and even of the people, to the eternal and underived sovereignty of God, King of kings, and Lord of lords, how should we suspect ourselves of being hostile to liberty, when asserting the same doctrine in defence of the rights of government? Having for years proved the doctrine to be favorable to liberty, how could we believe the public would be so unjust to us as to accuse us of favoring despotism, because we undertook to prove it equally favorable to civil government? Why are we to be classed as hostile to freedom, because we defend in the interests of authority the doctrine which we have uniformly asserted as the only solid foundation of freedom? Whether we are right or wrong in the doctrine itself, or in its application, would it be any remarkable stretch of charity to give us credit for believing ourselves no less favorable to liberty in bringing the doctrine out in defence of authority, than we were in bringing it out in defence of the rights of the subject? Are liberty and authority necessarily incompatible one with the other? Or is it a blunder to derive both from the same source, and to suppose that what establishes the legitimacy of authority must needs establish also the legitimacy of liberty?

But is the doctrine of the divine origin and right of government hostile to liberty? If government derives its existence and its right from God, it can have no power but such as God delegates to it. But God is just, justice itself, and therefore can delegate to the government no power to do what is not just. Consequently, whenever a government exercises an unjust power, or its powers unjustly, it exceeds its delegated powers, and is an usurper, a tyrant, and as such forfeits its right to command. Its acts are lawless, because contrary to justice, and do not bind the subject, because he can be bound only by the law. If they do not bind, they are null, and the attempt to enforce obedience to them may be resisted. Is it difficult, then, to understand, that, while the doctrine asserts the obligation in conscience of obedience to legitimate authority, to the government as long as it does not command any thing unjust, it condemns all illegal authority, and deprives the government of its right to exact obedience the moment it ceases to be just? What is there in this hostile to liberty? Is my liberty abridged when I am required to obey justice? If so, be good enough to tell me whence I obtain the right to do wrong.

Modern politicians assert, in opposition to the sovereignty of God, the sovereignty of the people. The will of the people is with them the ultimate authority. Is it they or we who are the truest friends of liberty? Liberty cannot be conceived without justice, and wherever there is justice there is liberty. Liberty, then, must be secured just in proportion as we secure the reign of justice. This is done in proportion to the guaranties we have that the will which rules shall be a just will. Is there any one who will venture to institute a comparison between the will of the people and the will of God? No one? Then who can pretend that the doctrine which makes the will of the people the sovereign is as favorable to liberty as the doctrine which makes the will of God the sovereign? The will of God is always just, because the Divine will is never separable from the Divine reason; but the will of the people may be, and often is, unjust, for it is separable from that reason, the only fountain of justice. We make the government a government of law, because we found it on will and reason; these modern politicians make it one of mere will, for they have no assurance that the will of the people will always be informed by reason. By what right, then, do they who maintain the very essence of despotism charge us with being hostile to liberty? Wherefore should we not, as we do denounce them as the enemies, nay, the assassins of liberty,—men who salute her, and at the same instant smite her under the fifth rib?

But, it is gravely argued, if you deny the popular origin and right of government, you are a monarchist or an aristocrat. We deny the conclusion. If people would pay a little attention to what we actually say, before conjuring up their objections, they would, perhaps, reason less illogically. We raise no question between the sovereignty of kings and nobles and that of the people. What we deny is the *human* origin and right of government. We deny all undelegated sovereignty on earth, whether predicated of the king, the nobility, or the people. The question we are discussing lies a little deeper and a little farther back than our modern politicians are aware. They are political atheists, and recognize for the state no power above the people; we are Christians, and hold that all power, that is, all legal authority, is from God; therefore we deny that kings, nobilities, or the people have any authority in their own right, and maintain that the state itself, however constituted, has only a delegated authority, and no underived sovereignty. They place the people back of the state, and maintain that it derives all its powers from the people, and is therefore bound to do their will; we tell them that the people themselves are not ultimate—have no power to delegate, except the power which Almighty God delegates to them, and this power they, as trustees, are bound to exercise according to his will, and are, therefore, not free to exercise it according to their own. They are desirous mainly of getting rid of kings and nobles, and, to do so, they assert the sovereignty of the popular will; we wish to get rid of despotism and to guard against all unjust government, and we assert the sovereignty of God over kings, nobles, and people, as well as over simple private consciences. Is this intelligible? Who, then, is the party hostile to liberty?

But, reply these same politicians, we do not mean to deny the sovereignty of God; we only mean that the authority he delegates is delegated to the people, and not to the king or the nobility. If by people you understand the people as the nation with its political faculties and organs, and not the people as mere isolated individuals, who disputes you? Who denies that kings and nobilities hold their powers, if not from, at least for, the people, and forfeit them the moment they refuse to exercise them for the common good of the people? What are you dreaming of? Do you suppose all men have lost their senses because you have lost yours? Who born and brought up under a republic, who acquainted with and embracing the teachings of Catholic theologians, is likely to hold the slavish doctrine, that the people are for the government, not the government for the people? Do you suppose that the republican and Catholic advocate the divine right of kings, and passive obedience,—the invention of Protestant divines, set forth and defended by that pedantic Scotchman, the so-called English Solomon? Who that has meditated on the saying of our Blessed Lord, "Let him that would be greatest among you be your servant," can hold that a prince receives power, or has any right to power, but for the public good? We do not deny the responsibility of kings and nobles to the nation, or that the nation may, under certain circumstances, and observing certain forms, call them to an account of their stewardship. But if this removes your objections to our doctrine, it by no means removes ours to yours. We complain of you, not because you make princes responsible to the people, that is, to the nation, but because you leave the people irresponsible, and make them subject to no law but their own will. You simply transfer the despotism from the one or the few to the many, and deny liberty by resting in the arbitrary will of the people. You stop with the people, and, if you do not deny, you at least fail to assert, the sovereignty of God; you tell them their will is sovereign, without adding that they have only a delegated sovereignty, and are bound to exercise it in strict accordance with and in obedience to the will of God. Here is your original sin. On your ground, no provision is made for liberty, none for resistance to tyranny, without resorting to the revolutionary principle, the pretended right to resist legitimate government, a contradiction in terms, and alike hostile to liberty and to authority. On our ground, the right to resist tyranny or oppression is secured without detriment to legitimate government; because the prince who transgresses his authority and betrays his trust forfeits his rights, and having lost his rights, he ceases to be sacred and inviolable.

But we are told, once, more, that practically it can make no difference whether we say the will of God is sovereign, or the will of the people; for the will of the people is the true expression of the will of God, according to the maxim, *Vox populi, vox Dei*. We deny it. The will of God is eternal and immutable justice, which the will of the people is not. The people may and do often actually do wrong. We have no more confidence in the assertion, "The people can do no wrong," than we have in its brother fiction, "The king can do no wrong." The people must be taken either as individuals or as the state. As individuals, they certainly are neither infallible nor impeccable. As the state, they are only the aggregate of individuals. And are we to be told, that from an aggregation of fallibles, we can obtain infallibility? Show us a promise from Almighty God, made to the people in one capacity or the other, that he will preserve them from error and injustice, before you talk to us of their infallibility. The people in their collective capacity, that is, the state popularly constituted, never surpass the general average of the wisdom and virtue of the same people taken individually; and as this falls infinitely below infallibility, let us hear no more of the infallibility of the people. For very shame's sake, after denying, as most of you do, the possibility of an infallible Church immediately constituted and assisted by Infinite Wisdom, do not stultify yourselves by coming forward now to assert the infallibility of the people. If the people are infallible, what need of constitutions to protect minorities, and of contrivances for the security of individual liberty, which even we in our land of universal suffrage find to be indispensable?

But we return to our original position. All power is of God.

By him kings reign and princes decree just things. Government is a sacred trust from him, to be exercised according to his will, for the public good. The government which he in his providence has instituted for a people, and which confines itself to its delegated powers, for the true end of government, is legitimate government, whatever its form, and cannot be resisted without sin. But the government which is arbitrarily imposed upon a people, or which betrays its trust, or usurps powers seriously to the injury of its subjects, is illegitimate, and has no claim to our allegiance. Such a government may be lawfully resisted, and sometimes to resist it becomes an imperative duty.

But who is to decide whether the actual government has transcended its powers, and whether the case has occurred when we are permitted or bound to resist it? This is a grave question, because, if the fact of illegitimacy be not established by some competent authority, they who resist run the hazard of resisting legitimate government, and of ruining both their own souls and their country. Evidently the individual is not to decide for himself by his own private judgment; for that would leave every one free to resist the government whenever he should choose, which would be whenever it should command any thing not to his liking. If he had the right thus to resist, the government would have no right to coerce his obedience, and there would be an end of all government. Evidently, again, not the people, for we must take the people either as the state, or as outside of the state. Outside of the state they are simple individuals, and, as we have seen, have not, and cannot have, the right to decide. As the state, they have no faculties and no organs but the government which is to be judged, and therefore can neither form nor express a judgment. Who, then? Evidently the power whose function it is to declare the law of God. Since the government derives its authority from God, and is amenable to his law, evidently it can be tried only under that law, and before a court which has authority to declare it, and to pronounce judgment accordingly.

But what shall be done in case there be no such court of competent jurisdiction? We reject the supposition. Almighty God could never give a law without instituting a court to declare it, and to judge of its infractions. We, as Catholics, know what and where that court is, and therefore cannot be embarrassed by the question. If there are nations who have no such court, or who refuse to recognize the one Almighty God has established, that is their affair, not ours, and they, not we, are responsible for the embarrassments to which they are subjected. They, undoubtedly, are obliged either to assert passive obedience and non-resistance, or to deny the legitimacy of any government by asserting the right of revolution; that is, they have no alternative but anarchy or despotism, as their history proves. But this is not our fault. We are not aware that we are obliged to exclude God and his Church from our politics in order to accommodate ourselves to those who blaspheme the one and revile the other. We are not aware that we are obliged to renounce our reason, and reject the lessons of experience, because, if we admit them, they prove that Almighty God has made his Church essential to the maintenance of civil authority on the one hand, and of civil liberty on the other,—because they prove that the state can succeed no better than the individual, without religion. We have never supposed that a man could be a Christian and exclude God from the state, and we have no disposition to concede, or to undertake to prove, that he can be. If the Church is necessary as a teacher of piety and morals, she must be necessary to decide the moral questions which arise between prince and prince, and between prince and subject, and to maintain the contrary is only to contradict one's self. Politics are nothing but a branch of general ethics, and ethics are simply practical theology. If there is any recognized authority in theology, that authority must have jurisdiction of every ethical question, that is, every question which involves considerations of right and wrong, in whatever department of life they may arise. You may fight against this as you please, but you cannot change the unalterable nature of things. It is useless as well as hard to kick against the pricks. The question of resistance, presents a case of conscience, a moral question, and as such belongs by its very nature to the spiritual order, and then necessarily falls under the jurisdiction of the legitimate representative of that order. All the great principles of politics and law are ethical, and treated as such by both Catholic and Protestant theologians. How, then, can we dispense with the agency of the Church in politics, any more than in private morals or in faith itself? And are we to forego civil government, are we to submit passsively to tyrants, or to rush into anarchy, because the madness or blindness of others leaves them no other alternative? Must we reject or refrain from using the infallible means which we possess for determining what is the law of God, because others discard them and attempt to get on without them? Must we strip ourselves and run naked through the streets, because some of our brethren obstinately persist in being Adamites? Really, this were asking too much of us.

But let no one be frightened out of his propriety, for we really say no more for our Church than every sectarian claims for his sect,—no more in principle than was claimed last year by the Presbyterians, when they officially condemned the Mexican war, or by the Unitarians, when, as officially as was possible with their organization or want of organization, they did the same. The Church, in the case we have supposed, decides only the morality or immorality of the act done or proposed to be done. And is there a Protestant who belongs to what is called a church who does not take his church as his moral teacher? When Philip of Hesse found his wife unsatisfactory to him, and wished to take unto himself another, did he not submit the question to Luther and the pastors of the new religion? What are your Protestant ministers, if not, in your estimation, among other things, teachers of morals? And in case of doubt, to whom would you apply for its resolution but to your church, such as it is? Do you say you would not? To whom, then? To your politicians? What! do you regard politicians as safer moral guides than your pastors? To the state? So you hold the state more competent to decide questions of morals than your church! But the state is the party accused; would you suffer it to be judge in its own cause? Then you are at its mercy, and are a slave. Trust your own judgment? But you are a party interested, and what right have you to be judge in your own cause?

The fact is, every man who admits religion at all must admit its jurisdiction over all moral questions, whether in their individual or in their social application, and therefore does and must defer in them to that authority which represents for him the spiritual order. The state has no commission as a teacher of morals or as a director of consciences, and unless you blend church and state, and absorb the spiritual in the temporal, you cannot claim authority for the state in any strictly moral question. The theory of our own institutions is the utter incompetency of the state in spirituals. But spirituals include necessarily every question of right and wrong, whether under the natural law or the revealed law,—a fact too often overlooked, and not sufficiently considered by some even of our nominally Catholic politicians and newspaper-writers and editors. If this be so, the ligitimate province of the state is restricted to matters which pertain to human prudence and social economy. Within the limits of the law of God, that is, providing it violate no precept of the natural or revealed law, it is, as we have said in our reply to Mr. Thornwell, independent and free to pursue the policy which human wisdom and prudence suggest as best adapted to secure the public good. To give it a wider province would be to claim for it a portion at least of that very authority which Protestants make it an offence in us to claim even for the Church of God. We claim here no direct temporal authority for the Church, but we do claim, and shall, as long as we retain our reason, continue to claim for her, under God, supreme and exclusive jurisdiction over all questions which pertain to the spiritual order.

The conservative doctrine which we have contended for, and which does not happen to please some of our readers, follows necessarily from this doctrine of the divine origin and right of government. No one particular form of government exists by divine right for every people, but every form so exists for the particular nation of which it is the established order. The established order, the constitution of the state, which God in his providence has given to a particular people, which is coeval with that people, has grown up with it, and is identified with its whole public life, is the legitimate order, the legal constitution, and therefore sacred and inviolable. If sacred and inviolable, it must be preserved, and no changes or innovations under the name of progress or reform, that would abolish or essentially alter it, or that would in any degree impair its free, vigorous, and healthy action, can be tolerated.

This is the doctrine we have maintained, and this is asserted to be hostile to liberty and favorable to despotism. However this may be, the doctrine is not a recent doctrine with us, not one which we have embraced for the first time since our conversion to Catholicity. We held and publicly maintained it during that period of our life when we were regarded as a liberalist, and denounced by our countrymen as a radical, a leveller, and a disorganizer. Thus, in October, 1838, we oppose it to the mad proceedings of the Abolitionists, and maintain that it is a sufficient reason for condemning those proceedings, that they are unconstitutional and revolutionary.

" We would acquit the Abolitionists, also, of all wish to change fundamentally the character of our institutions. They are not, at least the honest part of them, politicians ; but very simple-minded men and women, who crave excitement, and seek it in Abolition meetings, and in getting up Abolition societies and petitions, instead of seeking it in ball-rooms, theatres, or places of fashionable amusement or dissipation. Politics, properly speaking, they abominate, because politics would require them to think, and they wish only to feel. Doubtless some of them are moved by generous sympathies, and a real regard for the well-being of the Negro ; but the principal moving cause of their proceedings, after the craving for excitement, and perhaps notoriety, is the feeling that slavery is a national disgrace. Now this feeling, as we have shown, proceeds from a misconception of the real character of our institutions. This feeling can be justified only on the supposition that we are a consolidated republic. Its existence is therefore a proof, that, whatever be the conscious motives in the main of the Abolitionist, their proceedings strike against our Federal system.

"Well, what if they do? replies the Abolitionist. If Federalism, or the doctrine of State sovereignty, which you say is the American system of politics, prohibits us from laboring to free the slave, then down with it. Any system of government, any political relations, which prevent me from laboring to break the yoke of the oppressor and to set the captive free, is a wicked system, and ought to be destroyed. God disowns it, Christ disowns it, and man ought to disown it. If consolidation, if centralization, be the order that enables us to free the slave, then give us consolidation, give us centralization. It is the true doctrine. It enables one to plead for the slave. The slave is crushed under his master's foot; the slave is dying; I see nothing but the slave; I hear nothing but the slave's cries for deliverance. Away with your paper barriers! away with your idle prating about State rights! clear the way! let me run to the slave! Any thing that frees the slave is right, is owned by God.

"We express here the sentiment and use very nearly the language of the Abolitionists. They have no respect for government as such. They, indeed, are fast adopting the ultra-radical doctrine, that all government is founded in usurpation, and is an evil which all true Christians must labor to abolish. They have, at least some of them, nominated Jesus Christ to be President of the United States; as much as to say, in the only practical sense to be given the nomination, that there shall be no President of the United States but an idea, and an idea without any visible embodiment; which is merely contending, in other words, that there shall be no visible government, no political institutions whatever. They have fixed their minds on a given object, and, finding that the political institutions of the country and the laws of the land are against them, they deny the legitimacy of all laws and of all political institutions. Let them carry their doctrines out, and it is easy to see that a most radical revolution in the institutions of the country must be the result.

"Now, we ask, has a revolution become necessary? Is it no longer possible to labor for the progress of Humanity in this country, without changing entirely the character of our political institutions? Must we change our Federal system, destroy the existing relations between the States and the Union and between the States themselves? Nay, must we destroy all outward, visible government, abolish all laws, and leave the community in the state in which the Jews were, when 'there was no king in Israel, and every man did that which was right in his own eyes?' We put these questions in soberness, and with a deep feeling of their magnitude. The Abolition ranks are full of insane dreamers, and fuller yet of men and women ready to undertake to realize any dream, however insane, and at any expense. We ask, therefore, these questions with solemnity, and with fearful forebodings for our country. We rarely fear, we rarely tremble at the prospect of evil to come. The habitual state of our own mind is that of serene trust in the future; and if in this respect we are thought to have a fault, it is in being too sanguine, in hoping too much. But we confess, the proceedings of the Abolitionists, coupled with their vague speculations and their crude notions, do fill us with lively alarm, and make us apprehend danger to our beloved country. We beg, in the name of God and of man, the Abolitionists to pause, and if they love liberty, ask themselves what liberty has, in the long run, to gain by overthrowing the system of government we have established, by effecting a revolution in the very foundation of our Federal system.

"For ourselves, we have accepted with our whole heart the political system adopted by our fathers. . . . . . We take the American political system as our starting-point, as our primitive data, and we repulse whatever is repugnant to it, and accept, demand whatever is essential to its preservation. We take our stand on the Idea of our institutions, and labor with all our soul to realize and develop it. As a lover of our race, as the devoted friend of liberty, of the progress of mankind, we feel that we must, in this country, be *conservative*, not *radical*. If we demand the elevation of labor and the laboring classes, we do it only in accordance with our institutions and for the purpose of preserving them, by removing all discrepancy between their spirit and the social habits and condition of the people on whom they are to act and to whose keeping they are intrusted. We demand reform only for the purpose of preserving American institutions in their real character; and we can tolerate no changes, no innovations, no alleged improvements, not introduced in strict accordance with the relations which do subsist between the States and the Union and between the States themselves. Here is our political creed. More power in the Federal government than was given it by the Convention which framed the

Constitution would be dangerous to the States, and with less power the Federal government would not be able to subsist. We take it, then, as it is. The fact, that any given measure is necessary to preserve it as it is, is a sufficient reason for adopting that measure; the fact, that a given measure is opposed to it as it is, and has a tendency to increase or diminish its power, is a sufficient reason for rejecting that measure."—*The Boston Quarterly Review*, 1838, Vol. I. pp. 492-495.

The same doctrine we had inculcated in the Review for the previous July of the same year.

"Our government, in its measures and practical character, should conform as strictly as possible to the ideal or theory of our institutions. Nobody, we trust, is prepared for a revolution; nobody, we also trust, is bold enough to avow a wish to depart very widely from the fundamental principles of our institutions; and everybody will admit that the statesman should study to preserve those institutions in their simplicity and integrity, and should seek, in every law or measure he proposes, merely to bring out their practical worth, and secure the ends for which they were established. Their spirit should dictate every legislative enactment, every judicial decision, and every executive measure. Any law not in harmony with their genius, any measure which would be likely to disturb the nicely adjusted balance of their respective powers, or that would give them, in their practical operation, a character essentially different from the one they were originally intended to have, should be discountenanced, and never for a single moment entertained.

"We would not be understood to be absolutely opposed to all innovations or changes, whatever their character. It is true, we can never consent to disturb the settled order of a state, without strong and urgent reasons; but we can conceive of cases in which we should deem it our duty to demand a revolution. When a government has outlived its idea, and the institutions of a country no longer bear any relation to the prevailing habits, thoughts, and sentiments of the people, and have become a mere dead carcass, an encumbrance, an offence, we can call loudly for a revolution, and behold with comparative coolness its terrible doings. But such a case does not as yet present itself here. Our institutions are all young, full of life, and the future. Here, we cannot be revolutionists. Here, we can tolerate no innovations, no changes, which touch fundamental laws. None are admissible but such as are needed to preserve our institutions in their original character, to bring out their concealed beauty, to clear the field for their free operation, and to give more directness and force to their legitimate activity. Every measure must be in harmony with them, grow, as it were, out of them, and be but a development of their fundamental laws."—Vol. I. pp. 334, 335.

Undoubtedly, we here recognize a case in which a revolution would be justifiable; but not a case in which it would be lawful to subvert the constitution; for the case supposed is one in which the constitution has already been subverted, and ceased to be living and operative. The doctrine is nowise different from our present doctrine on the subject, only what we called revolution then we should call by another name now. The movements of a people to depose the tyrant, to throw off the illegitimate and to restore the legitimate authority, are not a revolution in the sense in which we deny the right of revolution. It is essential to our idea of a revolution, that it should involve, in some respect, an effort or intention to subvert the legal authority of a state. If, for instance, it be conceded that Ireland is an integral part of the British empire, or, rather, of the British state, an effort on the part of Irishmen to sever her from the British state, and erect her into an independent nation, would be revolutionary and unjustifiable. But if it be conceded that she is a separate state, that she has never been merged in the British state, and has been bound to it only by a mutual compact, and if it be conceded or established that England has broken the compact or not complied with its conditions, a like effort at separation and independence would involve no revolutionary principle, and, if prudent or expedient, would be justifiable, even though it should lead to a fearful and protracted war between the two nations.

It is clear, however, from these extracts, that, as long ago as 1838, we were, in relation to our own country, decidedly conservative. Here is another extract from the same Review, for October, 1841, which proves that we, while still regarded as a radical, generalized it and extended it to all countries.

"In this matter of world-reforming, it is our misfortune to disagree with our radical brethren. The reforms which can be introduced into any one country are predetermined by its geographical position, the productions of its soil, and the genius of its people and of its existing institutions. Any reform which requires the introduction or the destruction of a fundamental element is precluded. All reforms must consist in, and be restricted to, clearing away anomalies and developing already admitted principles."—Vol. IV. p. 532.

Here is the conservative doctrine stated as broadly and as distinctly as we state it now, and we could easily show that we entertained it at a much earlier date. Doubtless there are many things to be found in *The Boston Quarterly Review* not easily reconcilable with this doctrine; for we had not, at the time of conducting it, reduced all our ideas to a systematic and harmonious whole. Moreover, we wrote with less care than we do now; for we wrote more for the purpose of exciting thought than of establishing conclusions. But the discrepancies to be detected are in general more apparent than real; for we, unhappily, adopted the practice of using popular terms in an unpopular sense, which often gave us the appearance of advocating doctrines we by no means intended. Thus, we adopted the word *democracy*, but defined it in a sense of our own, very different from the popular sense. We did the same with many other terms. There was in this no intention to deceive. But we had a theory,—for in those times we were addicted to theorizing,—that the people used terms in a loose and vague sense, and that the business of the writer was to seize and define it,—to give in its precision what the people really mean by the term, if they could but explain their meaning to themselves. But we found by experience that we could not make the people attend to our definitions, and that they would, in spite of them, continue to use the popular term in its popular sense, and that, if we wished to express another sense, or the same sense somewhat modified, we must select another term. The mistake we fell into is fallen into by many who are not so fortunate as to detect it. Some of our friends have tried to find fault with our views on liberty, when their own views were the same as ours. They use the word *liberty* in relations in which we avoid it; but they, in using it, fail to convey their real meaning. The popular mind understands by liberty something very different from what they do. It is necessary to select terms with a view of denying what we do not mean, as well as of expressing what we do mean. Many of the inconsistencies we have been charged with have grown out of our former neglect of this rule, and not a few of the changes we are supposed to have undergone are really nothing but changes in our terminology, made for the purpose of getting our real meaning out to public apprehension. But this by the way. Versatile as we may have been, we have always had certain fixed principles, and what they were may be known by noting what we have cast off in our advance towards manhood, and what we have retained and still retain. The conservative principle is evidently one of these, and as we undeniably held it when nobody dreamed of charging us with hostility to liberty, we cannot see why our holding it now should be construed into proof that we are on the side of despotism.

But let us look at the doctrine itself. People hold it objectionable, because they suppose it commands us to preserve old abuses and forbids us to labor for the progress of civilization. But in this they assume two things:—1. That the legitimate constitution of a state is, or may be, an abuse; and, 2. That the progress of civilization is denied, if the right to subvert the constitution is denied.

The first involves a contradiction in terms. Nothing legal or legitimate is or can be, an abuse; An abuse is a misuse of that which is legal. The abuse is always contrary to the constitution, or at least some departure from it; and consequently conservatism, or the preservation of the constitution, instead of requiring us to conserve the abuse, imperatively commands us to redress it; because, if not redressed, it may in time undermine and destroy the constitution itself.

The second is equally unfounded. The destruction of the

constitution is the destruction of the state itself, its resolution into anarchy or despotism, either of which is fatal to civilization. What should we think of the physician who should undertake to restore a man to health, or to increase his soundness and vigor, by destroying his constitution? What we should think of him is precisely what we ought to think of the statesman who seeks to advance civilization by subverting the constitution of the state. The progress of civilization is inconceivable without the progress of the state, and the progress of the state is inconceivable without the existence of the state. How, then, can the subversion, that is, the destruction, of the state tend to advance civilization? If you will listen either to common sense or to the lessons of experience, you will grant that revolutions tend only to throw men into barbarism and savagism. The passions they call forth are the lowest, fiercest, and most brutal of our nature, and your patriot so called, he who seeks to advance his country by destroying its constitution, is usually a tiger for his ferocity.

But it is said that the existing constitution is destroyed only in order to make way for a new and better organization of the state. When you have shown us an instance, in the whole history of the world, in which the destruction of an existing constitution of a state has been followed by the introduction and adoption of a new and better one,—better for the particular nation, we mean,—we will give up the point, acknowledge that we have been in this whole matter consummate fools, and become as mad revolutionists as the best of you. But such an instance cannot be found. How often must we tell you that a constitution cannot be made as one makes a wheel-barrow or a steam-engine,—that of the constitution we must say, as we say of the poet, "Nascitur, non fit?" It is generated, not constructed, and no human wisdom can give to a state its constitution. The experiment has often been tried, and has just as often failed. Shaftesbury and Locke tried it for the Carolinas. They failed. France tried it in her old revolution; she is trying it again. Her former experiment resulted in anarchy, military despotism, and the restoration; her present experiment in four short months has reached military despotism. England has tried it, and sent out from her mills at home, along with her other manufactures, a constitution cut and dried for each of her colonies, and in what instance has the constitution not proved a curse to the colony for which it was made and on which it has been imposed? Who are these men who now come forward and ask us to credit them in spite of philosophy, of common sense, uniform experience, and experiment? Surely they must be prodigies of modesty, or else count largely on our simplicity and credulity.

But we are referred to our own country, to the American Revolution. Be it so. In reply, we might refer to the Spanish American revolutions, as a case much more in point. But our own country is the case on which the modern revolutionists chiefly rely for their justification. We do not contest the right of the Anglo-American colonies to separate from the mother country; we are not the men to condemn the Congress of 1776; and we cheerfully concede the prosperity which has followed the separation. But what is called the American Revolution was no revolution in the sense in which we deny the right of revolution, and in it there was no subversion of the state, no destruction of the existing constitution, and no assertion of the right to destroy it. The colonies were held by compact to the crown of Great Britain. The tyranny of George the Third broke that compact, and absolved the colonies from their allegiance. Absolved from their allegiance to the crown, they were, *ipso facto*, sovereign states, and the war which followed was simply a war in defence of their independence as such states. No abuse of terms can convert such a war into a revolutionary war. Then there was no civil revolution. The internal state of the colonies was not dissolved, and there was no war on the constitution of the American states. They retained substantially the very political constitutions with which they commenced, and retain them up to this moment. We have never undergone a revolution in any sense like the European revolutions which have followed since the war of our independence. Slight alterations have from time to time been, wisely or unwisely, effected in the State constitutions, but none which have struck at essential principles.

Nor was the formation of our Federal Constitution any thing like what the French National Assembly are attempting. It was similar in its character to what the German Diet at Frankfort have just done, or are still engaged in doing. It was not making and giving a constitution to a people who had just overthrown an old government, destroyed the old constitution, and resolved the state into its original elements, but was the act of free, sovereign states, already constituted, and exercising all the faculties of sovereign states. Here are vast differences, which are too often overlooked, and which should prevent our conduct in throwing off the crown of Great Britain and forming the Federal Union from being regarded as a precedent for those who would destroy an existing constitution for the purpose of reörganizing the state. We never did any thing of the sort, and from the fact that the result of what we did do has been great national prosperity it cannot be inferred that such will be the result of revolutions in the European states. Revolutionists both at home and abroad, especially abroad, do not sufficiently consider the wide difference between colonies already existing as bodies politic, exercising nearly all the functions of government, separating themselves politically, under the authority of their local governments, from the mother country, and setting up for themselves, and the insurrection of the mob against the existing constitution, destroying it, and attempting to replace it by one of their own making. We were children come to our majority, leaving our father's house to become heads of establishments of our own; the revolutionists are parricides, who knock their aged parent in the head or cut his throat in order to possess themselves of the homestead.

But however this may be, it is clear that the doctrine we put forth is not favorable to despotism; for despotism is as destructive of the legitimate constitution as revolutionism in favor of what is called Liberalism. Radicalism and despotism are only two phases of one and the same thing. Despotism is radicalism in place; radicalism is despotism out of place. Both are unconstitutional, and to preserve the constitution requires us to oppose the one as much as the other. Liberty demands the supremacy of the law, and law is will regulated by reason, restrained by justice; and to preserve law in this sense, we must resist every attempt, come it from what quarter it may, to substitute for it the government of arbitrary will.

Nobody denies the right to correct abuses. The doctrine we set forth not only concedes our right to correct abuses, but makes it, as we have seen, our duty to correct them. All that it forbids is our right to correct them by illegal, and therefore unjustifiable means. We must obey the law in correcting the abuses of the law, the constitution in repelling its enemies. This restriction is just, and good ends are never attainable by unjust means. Needs it be said again and again, that iniquity can never lead to justice, tyranny to liberty? But observing this restriction, you may go as far as you please. The doctrine we contend for does not, indeed, allow you to change a legal monarchy into a democracy, nor a democracy, where it is the legal order, as with us, into a monarchy; but it does allow you to change the individuals intrusted with the administration of the government. Kings, as long as they reign justly, reign by divine right; and in this sense, and in no other, we accept the doctrine of the divine right of kings; but when they cease to reign justly, become tyrannical and oppressive, they forfeit their rights, and the authority reverts to the nation, to be exercised, however, in accordance with its fundamental constitution. The nation may depose the tyrant, even dispossess, for sufficient reasons, the reigning family, and call a new dynasty to the throne; for no nation can be rightfully the property of a prince, or of a family, or bound to submit to eternal slavery. Thus far we go; for we hold with the great Catholic authorities, that the king is not in reigning, but in reigning justly.

But we have said enough to vindicate our doctrine from the charge of being hostile to liberty and favorable to despotism. We yield to no man in our love of liberty, but we have always felt that just ends are more easily gained by just than by unjust means, and that the truth is much more effectually defended by arguments drawn from sound than from unsound principles. It is not that we are indifferent to liberty, but that we reject the grounds on which modern politicians defend it, and disapprove of the means by which they seek to secure it. We have shown that those grounds are untenable, and that those means are fitted only to defeat the end for which they are adopted. He who wants more than justice will give him wants what he cannot have without injustice to others. Our doctrine will satisfy no such man, and we should be satisfied with no doctrine that would. He who wishes for liberty without obedience to law wishes for what never has been and never can be. An authority which does not restrain, which is only an instrument to be used when it serves our purpose, and to be cast off the moment it can no longer serve it, is no legitimate authority, is not a government at all. If we have government, it must govern, and we must obey it, even when to obey it may be a restraint on our private feelings and passions, for it is only at this price that we can purchase immunity from the private feelings and passions of others. Nothing is, then, in reality more unwise than to cherish an impatience of restraint and a spirit of insubordination. The sooner we learn the difficult lesson of obedience, the better will it be for us. We cannot, if we would, have every thing our own way; and perhaps it would not be to our advantage, if we could. Life has, and as long as the world stands will have, its trials, and, however impatient we may be, there is and will be much which we can conquer only by learning to bear it. It is easy to stir up a revolution, to subvert a throne or a dynasty; but to reëstablish order, to readjust the relations of man with man, of prince with subject and subject with prince, so as to remove all evils and satisfy every wish,—this is labor, this is work, which no mortal man has ever yet been equal to. A man could lose paradise, bring sin, death, and all our woe into the world; only a God could repair the damage, and restore us to the heaven we had forfeited.

Our doctrine, just at this moment, may be unpopular, and we know it will put no money into our pocket, and bring us no applause; but this is not our fault, nor a reason why we should withhold it. Having never yet pandered to popular prejudices, or sought to derive profit from popular passions and fallacies, we shall not attempt to do it now. We love our country, perhaps, as much as some others who make much more parade of their patriotism; and we love liberty, it may be, as well, and are likely to serve it as effectually, as our young revolutionists in whom reason "sleeps and declamation roars." We have, indeed, a tolerable pair of lungs, and if not a musical, at least a strong voice; we know and could use all the commonplaces of our young patriots, and reformers,—nay, we think we could, if we were to try, beat them at their own trade, grave and staid as we have become; but we have no disposition to enter the lists with them. We have never seen any good come from the declamatory speeches and fiery patriotism of boys just escaped the ferula of the pedagogue, and who can give utterance to nothing but puerile rant about liberty and patriotism. We have never seen good come to a country whose counsellors were young men with downy chins, and we set it down as a rule, that the country in which they can take the lead, whatever else it is fitted for, is not fitted for the liberty which comes through popular institutions.

We can weep as well as our juniors over a nation robbed of its rights, on whose palpitating heart is planted the iron heel of the conqueror, and have the will, if not the power, to strike, if we can but see a vulnerable spot, or a chance that the blow will tell upon the tyrant. But, as a general thing, we have a great distaste for the valor that evaporates in words, though they be great and high-sounding words, well chosen, skilfully arranged, and admirably pronounced; and an equal distaste even for deeds which recoil upon the actor, and aggravate his sufferings, already too afflicting to behold. We believe it wise to bide one's time, and to take council of prudence. In most cases, the sufferings of a people spring from moral causes beyond the reach of civil government, and they are rarely the best patriots who paint them in the most vivid colors, and rouse up popular indignation against the civil authorities. Much more effectual service could be rendered in a more quiet and peaceful way, by each one seeking, in his own immediate sphere, to remove the moral causes of the evils endured. St. Vincent of Paul was a far wiser and more successful patriot than the greatest of your popular orators, declaimers, and songsters. He, humble-minded priest, had no ambition to shine, no splendid scheme of world or state reform. He thought only of saving his own soul, by doing the work that lay next him; and he became the benefactor of his age and his country, and in his noble institutions of charity he still lives, and each year extends his influence and adds to the millions who are recipients of his bounty. O ye who would serve your country, relieve the suffering, solace the afflicted, and right the wronged, go imitate St. Vincent of Paul, and Heaven will own you and posterity revere you.

NATIVE AMERICANISM.*

JANUARY, 1845.

WE have read this pamphlet with pleasure and instruction. It is written in good temper, and with a good share of ability. It triumphantly refutes the oft repeated slander, that the Roman Catholic Church is incompatible with republican institutions and popular freedom; and, though it contains expressions, and, if by a Catholic, concessions, which we do not approve or believe warranted, we commend it to the American Protestant Society, and especially to the so-called Native American party. Neither can hardly fail to profit by its careful and diligent perusal.

* Catholicism compatible with Republican Government, and in full Accordance with Popular Institutions. By FENELON. New York: Edward Dunnigan. 1844. 8vo. pp. 48.

We have introduced this pamphlet simply as the text of some few remarks the subject of NATIVE AMERICANISM. We are ourselves native-born, and we hope not deficient in true love of country. Though not blind to the faults of our countrymen, and endeavoring on all occasions to place the love of God before the love of country, we believe we possess some share of genuine patriotic feeling. We know we have loved American institutions; and we are ready to vindicate them, with what little ability we may have, on any occasion, and against any and every sort of enemies. But we confess that we have and have had, from the first, no sympathy, with what is called Native Americanism. We have seen no necessity for a movement against foreigners who choose to make this land their home; and we have felt that such a movement, while it could lead to no good, might lead to results truly deplorable.

We have been accustomed to trace the hand of a merciful Providence in reserving this New World to so late a day for Christian civilization; we have been in the habit of believing that it was not without a providential design, that here was reserved an open field in which that civilization, disengaging itself from the vices and corruptions of the Old World, might display itself in all its purity, strength, and glory. We have regarded it as a chosen land, not for one race, or one people, but for the wronged and downtrodden of all nations, tongues, and kindreds, where they might come as to a holy asylum of peace and charity. It has been a cause of gratulation, of ardent thankfulness to Almighty God, that here was founded, as it were, a city of refuge, to which men might flee from oppression, be free from the trammels of tyranny, regain their rights as men, and dwell in security. Here all partition walls which make enemies of different races and nations were to be broken down; all senseless and mischievous distinctions of rank and caste were to be discarded; and every man, no matter where born, in what language trained, was to be regarded as man,—as nothing more, as nothing less. Here we were to be found, not a republic of Englishmen, of Frenchmen, of Dutchmen, of Irishmen, but of men; and to make the word *American* mean, not a man born on this soil or on that, but a free and accepted member of the grand republic of men. Such is what has been boasted as the principle and the destiny of this New World; and with this, we need not say, Native Americanism is directly at war.

The great principle of true *Americanism*, if we may use the word, is, that merit makes the man. It discards all distinctions which are purely accidental, and recognizes only such as are personal. It places every man on his own two feet, and says to him, Be a man, and you shall be esteemed according to your worth as a man; you shall be commended only for your personal merits; you shall be made to suffer only for your personal demerits. To each one according to his capacity, to each capacity according to its works. This is Americanism. It is this which has been our boast, which has constituted our country's true glory. It is this which we have inherited from our fathers; it is this which we hold as a sacred trust, and must preserve in all its purity, strength, and activity, if we would not prove " degenerate sons of noble sires;" and it is this, which *Native* Americanism, so called, opposes,—and because it opposes this, no true American can support it.

There is something grateful to all our better feelings in the thought, that here is a home to which the oppressed can come, and find the rights, the respect, and the well-being denied them in the land of their birth. The emigrant's condition is not a little improved by touching upon our shores; and the condition of his brother-laborers, whom he leaves behind, is also not a little ameliorated, and the general sum of well-being is greatly augmented. On the simple score of philanthropy, then, who would not struggle to keep our country open to the emigrant, and be prepared to welcome him as a brother, and to rejoice that another is added to the family of freemen?

But even as a question of our own interest as a people, we should welcome the foreigner. If we would sit down and reckon up what we lose and what we gain by foreigners coming to settle among us, we should find the gain greatly overbalances the loss. Naturalized citizens constitute no inconsiderable portion of our population, and by no means the least important portion. Without these, what would have been our condition now? Whose labor has cleared away many of our Western forests, dug our canals and railroads? and by whose labor and practical skill have we introduced our manufactures, and brought them to their present high state of perfection? In all the branches of manufactures, in nearly all branches of mechanical industry, the head workmen, if we have been rightly informed, are foreigners. And why foreigners, rather than native-born? Surely, not because there is any partiality for foreigners over native Americans, but because they are more thorough masters of their business. Then, who man our navy, of which we are so justly proud? and who constitute, in time of war, the rank and file of our army? Not all foreigners, truly; but not a few who were not born on American soil. No small portion of our hardy seamen are of alien birth; but they are none the less true to our flag on that account, nor any the less freely do they spill their blood for our national defence or national glory. We do not agree with the assertion said to have been made by a foreigner residing amongst us, that native Americans are *cowards*, and if we did, we have still too much of the old Adam, and of the narrow feeling of former times, to suffer him, without rebuke, to tell us so. Americans are not deficient in courage, and will, when necessary, face the enemy as boldly as any other people on the globe. Nevertheless, our ranks are not dishonored by foreigners, and no native-born citizens have ever done our country's flag more honor or fought more valiantly in its defence, than the brave and warm-hearted Irish; and none would do us more efficient service again, were we so unhappy as to be involved in a war. In the Revolution, we found men not born in America could fight manfully for us, and then they were not considered as in the way of the native-born. It was no loss to us to reckon in our army a Montgomery, a Gates, a De Kalb, a Steuben, a Pulaski, a Lafayette. No; man is man, wherever born; and every freeman is our brother, and we should clasp him to our bosom.

As a party movement, the Native American party is contemptible. As a movement of native American citizens against foreigners who come amongst us to claim the rights and to perform the duties of citizens, it is founded on low and ungenerous prejudices,—prejudices of birth, which we, as a people, profess to discard. We, as a people, recognize no nobility founded on birth; for our principle is, that all who are born at all are well-born. But what is the effort to confine the political functions incident to citizenship to native-born Americans, but the attempt to found an aristocracy of birth, even a political aristocracy, making the accident of birth the condition of political rights? Is this Americanism? The American who pretends it is false to his American creed, and has no American heart.

We, of course, do not oppose *Native* Americanism on the untenable ground, that every man has a *natural* right to be a citizen, and to take part in the administration of the government. The right of suffrage is a *municipal* right, not a natural right. But we, as a people, have adopted, with slight restrictions, the principle of universal suffrage. We, as a people, hold that the government is safest where all the people have a voice in saying what it shall be and who shall be its administrators. We adopt universal suffrage, not indeed as a right, but as a dictate of prudence. We hold that we select better men to rule us, and enact wiser and more equitable laws, by admitting the great body of the people to a participation of political sovereignty, than we should by confining the sovereignty to one man or to a few men. We hold that the people are best governed, when they constitute and manage the government themselves. This is the political creed of the country; and he is false to his country, who would abolish it, or defeat its practical application. Foreigners, who come here, have, then, in view of the acknowledged principles of the country, a right to be admitted to citizenship, to the rank and dignity of freemen; and could rightly complain of injustice, if not so admitted.

But we are told that the Native American party does not propose to exclude foreigners from the country, nor from citizenship. It only wishes to prevent them from coming here and exercising the rights of citizens before being properly instructed in the duties of citizens. This plea is specious, but not solid. It is the public ostensible plea; but not the private, real one. The real design is, to exclude foreigners, to prevent them from coming here, by denying them the right to become citizens. We have never conversed with an advocate of the party who did not avow this. But take the plea as publicly offered. It is contended that foreigners, brought up under monarchical or aristocratical governments, cannot be expected, on arriving on our shores, to understand the nature of our peculiar form of government, and that it is necessary for them to serve a long novitiate before they can be prepared to enter upon the duties of freemen. The necessity of intelligence, of understanding well our peculiar institutions, on the part of every man who is to exercise the rights and to discharge the duties of a citizen, we certainly shall not dispute, whether the man was born at home or abroad. But the ignorance of the foreigners who come here is greatly exaggerated. Brought up under monarchical or aristocratical governments, one would naturally expect them to be averse to our democracy, and in favor of institutions similar to those with which they had been accustomed. But no complaint of this kind is ever made against them. Foreigners who come here and condemn our institutions, show contempt for them, and wish to exchange them for institutions similar to those they have left behind, are in general cordially welcomed, and treated with great consideration. The complaint is the reverse of this, their offence is in being too democratic, and in wishing the government to be administered on strictly democratic principles. It is not their ignorance of the real nature of democracy, but their intelligence of it, that constitutes their disqualification.

But pass over this. The naturalization laws, as they now are, require a foreigner to reside in the country five years before he can become a citizen, or be legally naturalized. This is, in general, five years after the man has become of full age. Now, it is fair to presume that an emigrant to this country, intending to come here and to make this his home, has before coming made some inquiries respecting the country, the character of its people, its government, and laws; and he may be judged to know as much of them as in general one of our own boys at the age of sixteen. In most cases he knows much more, but assume that he knows as much. Then he and the native-born are placed on the same footing. Each must wait five years before entering upon the discharge of his duties as a citizen; and who will pretend to say that a man from the age of twenty-one to twenty-six cannot learn as much of what those duties are, as the boy from sixteen to twenty-one? The law, as it now stands, exacts in reality as long a novitiate of the foreign-born as of the native-born; and even on the ground of time to be instructed in one's duties, no more needs to be altered in the case of the one than of the other.

But, politically speaking, this objection is not the real one. The *political* leaders, of the Native American party, are opposed to naturalized citizens solely on the ground that these citizens do not uniformly vote on their side. We do not discover that our politicians of either party object to the votes of naturalized citizens when given for them, nor to naturalizing them, if they feel sure of their suffrages. Why not say so, then, and let the honest truth come out? Surely, honest men, high-minded men, the true nobility of the earth, as all our political leaders are, can have no objections to avowing their real intentions, and the real motives from which they act. Such men will never show false colors!

But the objection to foreigners is not exclusively political, nor chiefly political. Below this is another objection, which operates chiefly amongst the laboring classes. The mass of the people, especially of those who live on from father to son in the same position and pursuit, retain almost forever their primitive prejudices. These in this country are of English descent,—for we are all of foreign extraction; and they have inherited from their ancestors, and still retain, two strong prejudices,—contempt of the Irish and hatred of the French. There is no use in disguising the fact. The assistance the French rendered us in the Revolution has mollified our feelings somewhat towards them, but we still bear them no real good-will. But the national English contempt for the Irish has been reinforced in America. The Yankee hod-carrier, or Yankee wood-sawyer, looks down with ineffable contempt upon his brother Irish hod-carrier or Irish woodsawyer. In his estimation, "Paddy" hardly belongs to the human family. Add to this that the influx of foreign laborers, chiefly Irish, increases the supply of labor, and therefore apparently lessens the demand, and consequently the wages of labor, and you have the elements of a wide, deep, and inveterate hostility on the part of your Yankee laborer against your Irish laborer, which manifests itself naturally in your Native American party. But this contempt of the Irish, which we have inherited from our English ancestors, is wrong and ungenerous. The Irish do not deserve it, and it does not become us to feel it. It is a prejudice disgraceful only to those who are governed by it, and no words of condemnation are sufficiently severe for the political aspirant who would appeal to it. Every friend to his country, every right-minded man, must frown upon it, and brand as an incendiary, as a public enemy, the demagogue, whether in a caucus speech in old Faneuil Hall or elsewhere, whether admired by the whole nation for his transcendent abilities or not, who should seek to deepen it, or even to keep it alive.

But, after all, the competition, which our native American laborers so much dread, is far less than they imagine. The foreign laborers do not, in general, come directly into competition with them. A great part of the labor they perform is labor which native Americans could not or would not perform themselves. Then, the increased demand for labor in other branches of industry, caused by the works carried on mainly by the labor of foreigners, fully compensates, perhaps more than compensates, the native American laborers for any loss they may sustain in the few cases of competition which there really may be. Viewed in all its bearings, the influx of foreign laborers has very little, if any, injurious effect on our own native laborers. The immense internal improvements completed or in process of completion would never have been attempted, if the reliance had been solely on native labor, and, consequently, none of the additional labor employed in the various branches of industry, which these improvements have stimulated, would have been in demand. The laboring class, as a class, has really gained in the amount of employment by the increase of laborers, and of course, in the price of labor. Labor begets the demand for labor. Individuals may have suffered somewhat, in some particular branches, but upon the whole the laboring class has been benefited.

But the real objection lies deeper yet. The Native American party is not a party against admitting foreigners to the rights of citizenship, but simply against admitting a certain class of foreigners. It does not oppose Protestant Germans, Protestant Englishmen, Protestant Scotchmen, nor even Protestant Irishmen. It is really opposed only to *Catholic* foreigners. The party is truly an anti-Catholic party, and is opposed chiefly to the Irish, because a majority of the emigrants to this country are probably from Ireland, and the greater part of these are Catholics. If they were Protestants, if they could mingle with the native population and lose themselves in our Protestant sects, very little opposition would be manifested to their immigration or to their naturalization. But this they cannot do. They are Catholics. They adhere to the faith of their fathers, for which they have suffered these three hundred years more than any other people on earth. Being Catholics, they hold religion to be man's primary concern, and the public worship of God an imperative duty. They accordingly seek to settle near together, in a neighborhood, where the Church may rise in their midst, within reach of the altar where the "clean sacrifice" is offered up daily for the living and the dead, and where they can receive the inestimable services of the minister of God. Hence, they seem, because in this respect their habits differ from those of our Protestant countrymen, to be a separate people, incapable even in their political and social duties of fraternizing, so to speak, with their Protestant fellow-citizens. Here is the first and immediate cause of the opposition they experience.

But deeper yet lies the old traditionary hatred of Catholicity. The majority of the American people have descended from ancestors who were accustomed to pray to be delivered from the flesh, the world, the devil, and the *Pope ;* and though they have in a great degree rejected the remains of faith still cherished by their Protestant ancestors, they retain all their hatred of the Church. If they believe nothing else, they believe the Pope is Antichrist, and the Catholic Church the Scarlet Lady of Babylon. When the Catholic Church is in question, all the infidels and nothingarians are sure to sympathize with their Protestant brethren. Pilate and Herod are good friends, when it concerns crucifying the Redeemer of men. This is, perhaps, as it should be. Hence, the great mass of the American people, faithful to their traditions, are inveterately opposed to Catholicity, and it is this opposition that manifests itself in Native Americanism, and which renders it so inexcusable and so dangerous.

We presume there are few who will question this statement. The " Native Americans " with whom we have conversed, all, to a man, avow it, and the late disgraceful riots and murder and sacrilege in Philadelphia prove it. There, no harm was done to Protestant foreigners. Hostility was directed solely against Catholics. They were Catholics, who were shot down in the streets,—Catholic churches, seminaries, and dwellings, that were rifled and burnt. Even the most active members of the Native American party, if we may be pardoned the Hibernianism, are in many cases foreigners. The notorious ex-priest Hogan, a foreigner and an Irishman, deposed for his immoral conduct, is, if we are rightly informed, a most zealous *Native*, and has been lecturing in this city and vicinity in favor of Native Americanism, and we have heard no Nativist object to having men like him exercise the rights of an American citizen. The Orangemen, foreigners as they are, did the Natives substantial service in Philadelphia, as it has been said, and they threaten to do the same here, if occasion serve. All this proves that the opposition is not to foreigners, as such, but simply to Catholics, and especially to *Irish* Catholics.

Now against this, we hardly need say, we protest in the name of the Constitution, and the good faith of the country. The Constitution of this country does not merely tolerate different religious denominations, but it recognizes and guaranties to all men the free exercise of their religion, whatever it may be. It places all denominations, however great or however small, on the same footing, before the state, and recognizes the equal rights of all and of each. To this the faith of the country is pledged. We say to all, of all creeds, Come here and demean yourselves, in civil matters, as good citizens, and your respective faiths and modes of worship shall all alike be legally respected and protected. This is what we have professed; of this we make our boast; and this we consider our chief title to the admiration of the world. We have promised to all the fullest conceivable religious liberty. For this we have solemnly pledged our faith before the world and before Heaven. Are we prepared to break our faith?

But in getting up a party against any one religious denomination, are we not breaking our faith, and perjuring ourselves in the sight of God and of men? What matters it to honest men, whether we do this directly or indirectly? What is the difference in principle between passing a law excluding, under severe penalties, the exercise of the Catholic religion in this country, and, by our political and other combinations, rendering its exercise impossible? What is the difference between excluding Catholics directly, and treating them in such a manner that they will be forced to exclude themselves?

Then, again, the wisdom of the policy of combining for the expulsion or exclusion of Catholics may be gravely questioned. Where there is a multiplicity of denominations, there is safety for any one only so far as there is safety for all. Combine and suppress Catholicity to-day, and it may be some other one's turn to be suppressed to-morrow. The precedent established, the Catholics disposed of, a new combination may be formed against the Methodists, then against the Baptists, then against the Unitarians and Universalists, and then against the Episcopalians, or for the revival of the Classis of Amsterdam, or the Kirk of Scotland. Cannot all see that the safety of each is in protecting all, and suffering a combination to be formed against none?

Moreover, why should Protestants combine against Catholics? Have they not the Bible and private reason? and with these what has a Protestant to apprehend? Is he not abundantly able to meet and vanquish in the fair field of controversy the benighted and idolatrous Papist? Does he not believe that he has truth, reason, and revelation on his side? Does he not know that he has all the prejudices and nearly nineteen twentieths of the whole population of the country on his side? Are there not here odds enough in his favor? What, then, does he fear? With all these advantages, does he tremble before the Papist, and fear the meeting-house may give place to the church, the table to the altar, the bread and wine to the Real Presence? A sorry compliment this to Protestantism! a sorry compliment to reason, to distrust its encounter with error in open field and fair combat! Were we Protestants, as we once were, —but, God be praised, are no longer,—we should blush to appeal against *Popery* to any other arguments than Scripture and reason. If with these we could not resist the spread of Catholicity, we should be led to distrust the sacredness of our cause, and to fear, that, after all, we had not the Lord on our side. These political combinations betray the weakness of Protestantism, not its strength; the doubts, not the faith, of its upholders. If they are right in their premises, they need not these combinations to suppress Catholicity; if they are wrong in their premises, then they are warring, not against a superstition, an idolatry, as they pretend, but against God, and we leave it to them to decide what is the proper name by which they should be designated.

But we are told that Catholics are opposed, not because they are Catholics simply, but because, being Catholics, they owe allegiance to a foreign power, and therefore cannot be good citizens. No Catholic, it is assumed, since he owes allegiance to the Pope, can be bound by any obligation he may contract as a citizen. If we really supposed that any one among us could be so simple as to believe this, we would contradict it. But there are charges too absurd to need a reply. The Catholic does, indeed, owe allegiance to the Pope as the visible head of the Church, but not as visible head of the state. Whoever knows any thing at all of the obligation of the Catholic to the successor of St. Peter knows that it would be as absurd to conclude that the Christian, because he owes allegiance to God, cannot be a good citizen, nor true to the obligations he contracts as a citizen to the state, as to infer that a Catholic cannot be a good citizen because he owes allegiance to the visible head of his Church. So far as this allegiance is a fact, and so far as it is operative on the heart and conscience of a Catholic, it binds him to be a peaceful and obedient subject to the state, a faithful and conscientious citizen.

But the Roman Catholic religion, we are further told, is incompatible with republicanism, hostile to popular institutions; from which it is to be inferred, we suppose, that Protestantism, as the negative of Catholicity, is compatible with republican institutions and friendly to popular freedom. It would, perhaps, be difficult to prove this. The most despotic states in Europe are the Protestant, and in Switzerland, for instance, the Catholic cantons are the most democratic. Despotism was hardly known in Europe prior to the Reformation, save in that portion not in communion with the Church of Rome; and we very much doubt if there be at this moment as much popular freedom in the Protestant states of Europe as there was in the twelfth, thirteenth, and fourteenth centuries. There are really fewer checks on arbitrary power, and there is more heartless oppression.

In this country, the only republican government that Protestantism can pretend ever to have founded has been established, but it has not been founded solely by Protestantism. It owes its origin to the circumstances in which the first settlers came here, and to the impossibility, after independence of the crown of Great Britain was proclaimed, of establishing any other than a republican form of government. We have existed as a republic between sixty and seventy years. But it needs no very sharp observation to perceive that our republic has virtually failed to accomplish the hopes of its founders, and that it is, without some notable change in the people, destined either to a speedy dissolution, or to sink into a miserable timocracy, infinitely worse than the most absolute despotism. Protestantism, if it could originate, has not proved itself able to sustain it.

We need but glance at our electioneering contests, becoming fiercer and fiercer, more and more demoralizing, with each succeeding election, to be convinced of this. The election of our presidents costs us more than the whole civil list of Great Britain. We have heard it suggested that the election of General Harrison cost the Whigs more than fifty millions of dollars, the expenditures of the opposite party in attempting to reëlect Mr. Van Buren were no trifle. Hardly less has been expended in the campaign just closed. This is a tax no people can bear for any great length of time, without ruin, and the complete prostration of public and private morality.

Protestantism, by its principle,—liberty of private judgment,—may undoubtedly seem to favor civil freedom; and that it often attempts to establish free popular institutions we do not deny; but it wants the virtue to sustain them. By this same principle, it multiplies sects without number, and virtually destroys, by dividing, the moral force of the nation. We see this with ourselves. Religion has little force in controlling our passions or pursuits. No one of the sects possesses a commanding influence over the people. The great mass of the people are left, therefore, to the corrupt passions of their own depraved nature. They cease to live for God, and live only for the world,—to live for eternity, and live only for time. They become wedded to things of this world, their hearts bent only on wealth and honors. In business the ruling passion is to get rich, in public life to rise to places of honor and emolument, in private life to gain ease and pleasure. Now, how long can a government, which rests for its existence on the virtue and intelligence of the people, exist, or, if exist, answer its end, in a community where the great mass of the people are carried away by the dominant passions, wealth, place, and pleasure?

We may be told that enlightened self-interest will suffice,—that only instruct the people what is for their interest, and they will do it. This is plausible, but all experience proves to the contrary. Who does not know that it is for his real interest, both for time and eternity, to be a devout Christian? And yet are all devout Christians? The wisdom and prudence of men's conduct cannot be measured by their intelligence. A corrupt man uses his intelligence only as the minister of his corruption. The more you extend intelligence, unless you extend the moral restraints and influences of the gospel at the same time, the more do you sharpen the intellect for evil. The people of the United States are far more instructed than they were fifty years ago, and yet have not half so much of the virtue necessary to sustain a republican government. We are never to expect men to act virtuously, simply because their understandings are convinced that virtue is the best calculation. You must make them act from a higher motive. They must be governed by religion; act from the love and the fear of God,—from a deep sense of duty; be meek, humble, self-denying; morally brave and heroic; choosing rather to die a thousand deaths than swerve from right principle, or disobey the will of God; or they will not practise the virtues without which liberty is an empty name,—a mere illusion.

Now, Protestantism never has, and never can, produce the virtues without which a republican government can have no solid foundation. It may have good words; it may say wise and even just things; but it wants the unction of the spirit. It does not reach and regenerate the heart, subdue the passions, and renew the spirit. It has never produced a single saint, and the virtues it calls forth are of the sort exhibited by the old heathen moralists. It praises the Bible, but studies the Greek and Roman classics; boasts of spirituality, but expires in a vain formalism. For the three hundred years it has existed, it has proved itself powerful to destroy, but impotent to found; ready to begin, but never able to complete. Whatever it claims that is positive, abiding, it has inherited or borrowed from the ages and the lands of faith. Its own creations rise and vanish as the soap-bubbles blown by our children in their sports. It has never yet shown itself able to command human nature, or to say to the roused waves of passion, Peace, be still. It lulls the conscience with the forms of faith and piety; soothes vanity and fosters pride by its professions of freedom; but leaves the passions all their natural force, and permits the man to remain a slave to all his natural lusts. It never subdues or regenerates nature. Hence, throughout all Protestantdom, the tendency is, to reproduce heathen antiquity, with all its cant, hollowness, hypocrisy, slavery, and wretchedness,—to narrow men's views down to this transitory life and the fleeting shows of sense, and to make them live and labor for the meat that perisheth. We appeal to England, Sweden, Denmark, Protestant Germany, Holland, and our own country, for the truth of what we say. They were Protestant traders who trampled on the cross of Christ to gain the lucrative trade of Japan. It is in no spirit of exultation we allude to Protestant worldly-mindedness and spiritual impotency. Would to God the sketch were from fancy, or our own diseased imagination!

We do not mean to deny, that, in words, Protestantism teaches many, perhaps most, of the Christian virtues. It has even some good books on morals and practical religion. Its clergy give good exhortations, and labor, no doubt, in good faith, for the spiritual culture of their flocks! No doubt, much truth, much valuable instruction, is given from Protestant pulpits. The Protestant clergy take no delight in the state of things they see around them. They would gladly see Christ reign in the hearts of men; they, no doubt, would joyfully dispense the bread of life to their famished people; and they do dispense the best they have. But alas! how can they dispense what they have not received? The living bread is not on their communion table. They communicate, according to their own confession, only a figure, a shadow; and how shall the divine life be nourished with shadows? What we mean to say is, not that Protestantism does not aim to bring men to Christ, to make them pure and holy, but that it has no power to do it. It does not control human nature, and produce the fruits of a supernatural faith, hope, and charity. Its faith is merely an opinion or persuasion, its hope a wish, and its charity natural philanthropy. It necessarily leaves human nature as it finds it, and no pruning of that corrupt tree can make it bring forth good fruit. It is of the earth,—earthy; and it will bear fruit only for the earth. With unregenerated nature in full activity, we can have only sensuality and mammon-worship.

Hundreds and thousands among us, who are by no means favorably disposed to Catholicity, see this and deplore it. They say the age has no faith. They see the impotency of Protestantism; that under it all the vices are sheltered; that, in spite of it, all the dangerous passions rage unchecked; and they turn away in disgust from its empty forms and vain words. Witness the response the biting sarcasms and withering irony of Carlyle brings from thousands of hearts in this republic, the echoes which the chiselled words and marble sentences of Emerson also bring. Witness, also, the movements of the Come-outers, the Socialists, Fourierists, Communists. All these see that Protestantism has nothing but words, while they want life, realities, not vain *simulacra*. They err most egregiously, no doubt; they go from the dying to the dead; but their error proves the truth of what we advance.

Now, assuming our view of Protestantism to be correct, we demand how it is to sustain, or we, with it alone, are to sustain our republican government. Do we not see, in this growing love of place and plunder, with this growing devotion to wealth, luxury, and pleasure, with these fierce electioneering contests, one no sooner ended than another begins, each to be fiercer and more absorbing and more destructive than the last, and each drawing within its vortex nearly the whole industrial interest of the country, and touching almost every man in his honor and his purse, that we want the moral elements without which a republic cannot stand? A republic can stand only as it rests upon the virtues of the people; and these not the mere natural virtues of wordly prudence and social decency, but those loftier virtues which are possible to human nature only as elevated above itself by the infused habit of supernatural grace. This is a solemn fact to which it is in vain for us to close our eyes. Human nature left to itself tends to dissolution, to destruction, decay, death. So does every society that rests only on those virtues which have their origin, growth, and maturity in nature alone. This is the case with our own society. We have really no social bond; we have no true patriotism; none of that patience, that self-denial, that loyalty of soul, which is necessary to bind man to man, each to each, and each to all. Each is for himself. Save who can (*Sauve qui peut*), we exclaim. Hence a universal scramble. Man overthrows man, brother brother, the father the child, and the child the father, the demagogue all; while the devil stands at a distance, looks on, and enjoys the sport. Tell us, ye who boast of the glorious Reformation, if a republican form of government is compatible with this moral state of the people?

Even in matters of education we can do little but sharpen the wit, and render brother more skilful and successful in plundering brother. With our multitude of sects, we may instruct, but not educate. Our children can have no moral training, for morality rests on theology, and theology on faith. But faith is expelled from our schools, because it is sectarian, and there is no one faith in the country which can be taught without exciting the jealousy of the followers of a rival faith. Cut up into such a multitude of sects, there is and can be no common moral culture in the country, no true religious träining. We give a little instruction in reading, writing, arithmetic, grammar, geography, perhaps history, the Greek and Roman classics, and in the physical sciences; and send our children out into the world, to form their morals and their religion without other guide or assistant than their own short-sighted reason and perverted passions. How can we expect any thing from such a sowing, but what we reap? and how, under Protestantism, which broaches every thing, and settles nothing, raises all questions and answers none, and therefore necessarily giving birth to a perpetual succession of sects, each claiming with equal reason and justice to have the truth, and the claims of all equally respected, as they must be, by the government, is this terrible evil to be remedied? Protestantism is just a-going to remedy it; but, alas! it does not succeed. It reminds us of a remark by a lady eating vegetable oysters,—"I always seem, when I eat vegetable oysters, as if I was just a-going to taste of an oyster." So, when we examine Protestantism, hear its loud professions, witness its earnest strivings, and observe each new sect it gives birth to, we say it is the lady eating vegetable oysters. It seems to itself that it is just going to light upon the truth, and to hit upon some plan by which it can remove the terrible evils it sees and deplores, and call forth the virtues it owns to be necessary; but, alas! it is only just a-going to taste the oyster: *it never quite tastes it.*

These facts, which we mention, are seen and felt by large numbers in our midst. Quiet, peaceable, but observing and reflecting men look on and observe our doings, and say to themselves, "This republicanism, after all, is a mere delusion. It is all very fine, no doubt, in theory, but exceedingly hateful in practice. Washington, and Hamilton, and others, were wiser than Jefferson and Madison. So large a republic, with such frequency of elections, and so many thousands depending on the fate of an election for their very means of subsistence, so many *ins* afraid of being turned out, so many *outs* anxious to be turned in, and the number each year increasing with the extent and population of the country,—well, let the republic stand if it can, but a change to a monarchy will soon be inevitable." There are men who so reason, and they are neither few nor despicable; nor are they fairly answered by our Fourth of July glorifications, or hurrahs for Democracy, *Vive la Republique! Vive la Democratie! Vive la Liberté!* We do not agree with them;—far from it; but we should agree with them, if we saw nothing better for our republic than Protestantism. Protestants as they are, we say they reason correctly, and if the religion of the country remains Protestant for fifty years longer, facts will prove it.

But with Catholicity the republic may be sustained, not because the Catholic Church enjoins this form of government or that, but because she nourishes in the hearts of her children the virtues which render popular liberty both desirable and practicable. The Catholic Church meddles *directly* with no form of government. She leaves each people free to adopt such form of government as seems to themselves good, and to administer it in their own way. Her chief concern is to fit men for beatitude, and this she can do under any or all forms of government. But the spirit she breathes into men, the graces she communicates, the dispositions she cultivates, and the virtues she produces, are such, that, while they render even arbitrary forms of government tolerable, fit a people for asserting and maintaining freedom. In countries where there are no constitutional checks on power, she remedies the evil by imposing moral restraints on its exercise, by inspiring rulers with a sense of justice and the public good. Where such checks do exist, she hallows them and renders them inviolable. In a republic she restrains the passions of the people, teaches them obedience to the laws of God, moderates their desires, weans their affections from the world, frees them from the dominion of their own lusts, and, by the meekness, humility, loyalty of heart which she cherishes, disposes them to the practice of those public virtues which render a republic secure. She also creates by her divine charity a true equality. No republic can stand where the dominant feeling is pride, which finds its expression in the assertion " I am as good as you." It must be based on love ; not on the determination to defend our own rights and interests, but on the fear to encroach on the rights and interests of others. But this love must be more than the mere sentiment of philanthropy. This sentiment of philanthropy is a very unsubstantial affair. Talk as we will about its excellence, it never goes beyond love to those who love us. We love our friends and neighbors, but hate our enemies. This is all we do as philanthropists. All the fine speeches we make beyond—about the love of humanity, and all that—are fine speeches. Philanthropy must be exalted into the supernatural virtue of charity, before it can become that love which leads us to honor all men, and makes us shrink from encroaching upon the interests of any man, no matter how low or how vile. We must love our neighbor, not for his own sake, but for God's sake,—the child, for the sake of the Father ; then we can love all, and joyfully make the most painful sacrifices for them. It is only in the bosom of the Catholic Church that this sublime charity has ever been found or can be found.

The Catholic Church also cherishes a spirit of independence, a loftiness and dignity of soul, favorable to the maintenance of popular freedom. It ennobles every one of its members. The lowest, the humblest Catholic is a member of that Church which was founded by Jesus Christ himself; which has subsisted for eighteen hundred years ; which has in every age been blessed with signal tokens of the Redeemer's love ; which counts its saints by millions ; and the blood of whose martyrs has made all earth hallowed ground. He is admitted into the goodly fellowship of the faithful of all ages and climes, and every day, throughout all the earth, the Universal Church sends up her prayers for him, and all the Church above receive them, and, with their own, bear them as sweet incense up before the throne of the almighty and eternal God. He is a true nobleman, more than the peer of kings or Cæsars ; for he is a child of the King of kings, and, if faithful unto death, heir of a crown of life, eternal in the heavens, that fadeth not away. Such a man is no slave. His soul is free ; he looks into the perfect law of liberty. Can tyrants enslave him ? No, indeed ; not because he will turn on the tyrant and kill, but because he can die and reign for ever. What were a mere human tyrant before a nation of such men? Who could establish arbitrary government over them, or subject them to unwholesome or iniquitous laws?

Here is our hope for our republic. We look for our safety to the spread of Catholicity. We render solid and imperishable our free institutions just in proportion as we extend the kingdom of God among our people, and establish in their hearts the reign of justice and charity. And here, then, is our answer to those who tell us Catholicity is incompatible with free institutions. *We tell them that they cannot maintain free institutions without it.* It is not a free government that makes a free people, but a free people that makes a free government; and we know no freedom but that wherewith the Son makes free. You must be free within, before you can be free without. They who war against the Church, because they fancy it hostile to their civil freedom, are as mad as those wicked Jews who nailed their Redeemer to the cross. But even now, as then, God be thanked, from the cross ascends the prayer, not in vain, " Father, forgive them, for they know not what they do."

As to the effect this Native American party may have on the Church, or the cause of Catholicity in this country, we have no fears. We know it is a party formed for the suppression of the Catholic Church in our land. Protestantism, afraid to meet the champions of the cross in fair and open debate, conscious of her weakness or unskilfulness in argument, true to her ancient instincts, resorts to the civil arm, and hopes by a series of indirect legislation—for she dare not attempt as yet any direct legislation—to maintain her predominance. But this gives us no uneasiness. We know in whom we believe, and are certain. We see these movements, we comprehend their aim, and we merely ask in the words of the Psalmist, " Why have the Gentiles raged, and the people devised vain things? The kings of the earth stood up, and the princes met together, against the Lord, and against his Christ. Let us break their bands asunder, and let us cast their yoke from us. He that dwelleth in the heavens shall laugh at them, and the Lord shall deride them. Then shall he speak to them in his anger, and trouble them in his rage." Ps. ii. 1-5. They wage an unequal contest who wage war against the Church of the Living God, who hath said to its Head, "Thou art my Son, this day have I begotten thee. Ask of me and I will give thee the Gentiles for thy inheritance, and the utmost parts of the earth for thy possessions." Ib., 7, 8. These may combine to put down Catholicity, form leagues against it, enlist all the powers of the earth against it; but what then? Nero tried to crush it in its infancy. Diocletian tried it. And Nero and Diocletian have passed away, and their mighty empire has crumbled to pieces and dissolved, leaving scarce " a wrack behind;" yet the Church has lived on, and the successor of the fisherman of Galilee inherited a power before which that of Rome in her proudest day was merely the dust in the balance. Pagan and Saracen tried to crush it, but Pagan and Saracen are scattered before its glory as the morning mist before the rising sun. Heretic and schismatic have tried to exterminate it,—Luther, and Calvin, and Henry of England, like the great dragon whose tail drew after it a third part of the stars of heaven; and their own children are rising up and cursing their memory. The powers of the earth have tried to do it,—Napoleon, the Colossus who bestrided Europe, and made and unmade kings in mere pastime; but Napoleon, from the moment he dared lay his hand on the Lord's anointed, loses his power, and goes to die at last of a broken heart in a barren isle of the ocean. Jew, Pagan, Saracen, heretic, schismatic, infidel, and lawless power have all tried their hand against the Church. The Lord has held them in derision. He has been a wall of fire round about her, and proved for eighteen hundred years that no weapen formed against her shall prosper; for he guards the honor of his Spouse as his own. Let the ark appear to jostle, if it will; we reach forth no hand to steady it, and fear no harm that may come to it. The Church has survived all storms; it is founded upon a rock, and the gates of hell are impotent against it. It is not for the friends of the Church to fear, but for those who war against her, and seek her suppression. It is for them to tremble,—not before the arm of man,

for no human arm will be raised against them; but before that
God whose Church they outrage, and whose cause they seek to
crush. The Lord hath promised his Son the Gentiles for his
inheritance, and the utmost parts of the earth for his possession.
He must and will have this nation. And throughout all the
length and breadth of this glorious land shall his temples rise
to catch the morning sun and reflect his evening rays, and holy
altars shall be erected, and the "clean sacrifice" shall be offered
daily, and a delighted people shall bow in humility before them,
and pour out their hearts in joyous thanksgiving; for so hath
the Lord spoken, and his word shall stand.

So far as the spread of Catholicity in this country is concerned, we look upon this anti-Catholic party with no apprehension.
If we deprecate the formation of such a party, it is for the sake
of those misguided citizens who may unite to form it. It is
because we see the terrible injustice of which they render themselves guilty, and the awful judgments they may provoke.
We say to them, as St. Justin Martyr said to the Roman
emperors, "Take heed how you hearken only to unjust accusations; fear lest an excessive complaisance for superstitious
men, a haste as blind as rash, old prejudices which have no
foundation but calumny, may cause you to pronounce a terrible
sentence against yourselves. As for us, nobody can harm us,
unless we harm ourselves, unless we ourselves become guilty of
some injustice. You may indeed kill us, but you cannot injure
us." It is for our countrymen, who will render themselves
guilty of gross wrong, of terrible sin, that we fear. They are
engaged in an unholy cause, and, if they persist, cannot fail to
draw down the judgments of Almighty God upon their guilty
heads. They can shoot us down in the streets; they may break
up our schools and seminaries; they may desecrate and burn
our churches. Such things have been, and may be again; but
it becomes those who have been and may be the perpetrators
of such things to pause and ask themselves what manner of
spirit they are of; and how, in that day of solemn reckoning
which must come to us all, they will answer the inexorable

Judge for their abuse, their riots, their murder, and their sacrilege. As they love their own souls, and desire good, we entreat them to beware how they plunge deeper in sin, and rekindle the torch of persecution. For their sakes, not for ours, we pray them to pause before they go farther, and make their peace with the Son of God.

LABOR AND ASSOCIATION.*

JANUARY, 1848.

UNLESS the estimable and accomplished translator has greatly improved upon his author, M. Briancourt is one of the most agreeable writers attached to the school of Association with whom we are acquainted. He appears to be sincere, earnest, gentle, and philanthropic; and he writes with ability, ease, vivacity, and grace. His pages have, comparatively, little of that barbarous terminology which renders the writers of the Associationists, in general, so forbidding to all but adepts. If we had the least conceivable sympathy with his doctrines and schemes, we could read him with pleasure, and, at times, with admiration; and we cannot but regard his little work as the best summary of the plans and hopes of his school which has as yet appeared.

But the more able, skilful, and fascinating is a writer, the more dangerous and carefully to be eschewed are his writings, if devoted to the propagation of false and mischievous theories. Error, though reason be free to combat it, is never harmless, any more than poison, because its antidote may be known and at hand. It may, upon the whole, be more prudent to allow it free course, than, by attempting its suppression by force, to run the risk of also suppressing the truth; but however that may or

---

* Organization of Labor and Association. By MATH. BRIANCOURT. Translated by FRANCIS GEO. SHAW. New York: Wm. H. Graham. 1847. 16mo. pp. 103.

may not be, the publication of error is always an evil which no freedom of its contradictory truth can ever wholly prevent or overcome. No man ever puts forth a system of unmixed falsehood; and the currency his error gains is always by virtue of the truth he mixes with it, and which he misinterprets and misapplies. To unravel his web of sophistry, to pick out his tangled yarn, or separate what is true from what is false, is a task of no small difficulty, and requires a patience of investigation, habits of nice discrimination and of close and rigid reasoning, which can be expected only from the gifted and thoroughly disciplined few, and rarely even from these. An error may be stated in a few words, in a popular form, and clothed with a brilliant and captivating dress, which, nevertheless, is not to be refuted, nor its truth, which gives it currency, separated from the falsehood which renders it mischievous, without long, elaborate, and abstruse reasoning, subtle distinctions, and exact definitions, beyond the capacity of the generality, usually held by them in detestation, and of which they are always impatient. But even if the refutation could be presented in a popular form, the majority of those who have embraced the error would not profit by it. Having adopted the error and committed themselves to it, they are unwilling to listen to any thing which may be urged against it, lest perchance it may disturb the tranquillity of their conviction, mortify their pride, or affect unfavorably their reputation. Hence it is that nothing is more difficult than to recall or repress an error once fairly in circulation. Hence it is that we can never allow ourselves to commend a work, however kindly disposed we may be towards its author, which, in our judgment, or according to the rule of judgment we are bound to follow, teaches a false doctrine or proposes a visionary scheme. The reading of such works, when not absolutely hurtful, is unprofitable, and no man can justify it, unless it be to refute them, and guard the public against their dangerous tendencies. The Associationists, then, must not be surprised, if we notice Mr. Briancourt's work only to censure it.

That Mr. Briancourt's doctrine is unsound, no argument is

needed to prove. No man, who proposes a doctrine which reverses all that has hitherto been regarded as settled, is ever entitled even to a hearing. He who, on his own authority, gives the lie to all men, of all ages and nations, gives to every man the best of all possible human reasons for giving the lie to him. If reason is to be trusted, the reason of all ages and nations overrides his; if it is not to be trusted, he has no authority for what he proposes. He places himself in an awkward position, who, asserting the authority of reason, yet opposes his own reason to the reason of all men. He must be a bold man, a man of unbounded self-confidence, the very sublime of egotism, who dares pretend, that, on his reason alone, the whole world may be rationally convicted of having blundered. They have all the attributes he can claim; why, then, assume that they have all blundered, and that he alone has hit upon the truth? Truth is revealed to the humble and childlike, not to the proud and arrogant; and who is prouder or more arrogant than he who claims to be superior to all men, to be the only man of his race who has perceived what is true and good?

Discoveries, like the one Fourier professes to have made, are not in the order of human experience. There is nothing to be found in the experience of the race analogous to them. Discoveries, which reverse what the race had hitherto regarded as the settled order, have never yet, so far as history goes, been made in any department of life,—in religion, in morals, in politics, or in social and industrial arrangements. Every man, who has come forward with any such pretended discovery, has failed to gain a verdict in his favor, and in the judgment of mankind has been finally condemned either as deceiving or as deceived, or both at once. M. Charles Fourier, a man, if you will, of an extraordinary intellect, and of philanthropic aims,—although, we confess, we find in his writings only wild extravagance, and a pride, an egotism, which amount very nearly, if not quite, to insanity,—professes, not, indeed, to have *invented*, but to have *discovered*, the law of a new social and industrial world. This law he professes to have drawn out and scientifically established in all its ramifications; and he and his followers propose to reorganize society and industry according to its provisions. Similar pretensions have often been made, now in one department of life, now in another; but has one of them ever succeeded? Is there one of them that has not been finally adjudged, at best, to be only visionary? Is there on record a single instance of a fundamental reorganization of society, industry, or even of government, that has ever been effected? Have not all who have labored for such reörganization been opposed by their age and nation? And can the Associationists name an instance in which posterity has reversed the judgment of contemporaries? They cannot do it. We are aware of the instances they will cite; but not one of them is to the purpose. Why, then, suppose the whole order of human experience is reversed, or departed from, in the case of M. Charles Fourier? The fact is, *fundamental* changes in the religious, moral, social, political, or industrial order of mankind—changes which throw off the old order, and establish a new *order* in their place—never have been, and, it requires no great depth of philosophy to be able to say, never can be, effected, unless by the intervention of a supernatural cause. When attempted, they may go so far as to break up the old order, never so far as to introduce and establish a new order. Man can be a destroyer; he can never be a CREATOR.

But these considerations, however conclusive in themselves, will not, we are aware, have much weight with the Associationists. The Associationists are accustomed to other principles of reasoning; they have, underlying their speculations, a philosophy of man and society which creates in their minds a presumption in favor of Fourierism. With them, it is an argument in favor of a proposition, that it is novel; and an argument against it, that it is ancient. Nothing seems to them more reasonable beforehand, or more in accordance with what the order of human experience authorizes them to expect, than that such a discovery as Fourier's should be made, and that the changes he proposes should be practicable. It is useless, so far as they are concerned, to controvert them on this point,—and if we would reach them, with the hope of doing them any good, we must enter with them into an examination of their doctrine or scheme, upon its merits. This we willingly attempt; for several of the more distinguished Associationists in this country have been our intimate personal friends, and we regard them as sincere, and as honestly desirous of doing all in their power for the benefit of their fellow-men. We believe they are men who have a certain loyalty; and who have no bigoted attachment to this or that method of serving mankind, but are willing to change the method they now insist upon for another, the moment they see a good reason for doing so. We do not believe them unwilling to look upon the question as still an open question, or that they have much of that foolish pride which binds persons to a cause simply for the reason that they stand committed to it before the public. We propose, therefore, in what follows, to enter somewhat into the merits of their doctrine and schemes; and, as what we shall say is said in good faith, we trust they will receive it in good faith, and frankly accept it, or show us good reasons for rejecting it.

We begin by asking, What is the end the Associationists propose, or what is it they seek to effect? The means we understand very well; they are, the organization of labor and association, according to a given plan. But before we can decide on the means, we must understand the end proposed, so as to be able to determine whether the end is desirable, a good end. After that, we may proceed to determine whether the means are adequate, whether by adopting them we can, in all reasonable probability, secure the end. Unless we know what is the end proposed, and know whether it be good or not good, we walk by conjecture, not by science. But the Associationists propose their doctrine, not as a theory, or as a system of belief, but as a *science*. They must, then, in the outset, show us clearly the end proposed, and establish, not conjecturally, not hypothetically, but *scientifically*, that the end is good, and therefore, one which it is lawful to seek.

1. What, then, is the specific end they propose? We do not

find in their writings as clear, distinct, and specific an answer to this question as is desirable. They answer generally, not specifically. Their answer, as we collect it, is,—"The end we propose is, to remove the obstacles which now hinder the fulfilment, and to gather round man the circumstances which will enable him to fulfil, his destiny on this globe; or, in a word, to enable man to fulfil the purpose of his present existence." Thus stated we of course have no objection to the end proposed. The good of a being is its destiny, or the end for which it exists; and to seek to enable a being to fulfil its destiny, or gain that end, is to seek its good. So the end for which man exists in this world is his good in relation to his existence here; and to labor to enable him to gain that end is to labor for his good, and his only good here. Thus far, we have, and can have, no quarrel with the Associationists.

But a general answer to a specific question is no answer at all; for the general has formal existence only in the special. We must, therefore, ask again, What is the *specific* end proposed? To answer, To remove evil, and to secure good, is not enough; for the question remains, What *is* evil? what *is* good? Evil, you say, is that which prevents, or in some way hinders or retards, the fulfilment of one's destiny. Very true; but what is it that does that? This is the question we want answered. We find in the writings of the Associationists graphic descriptions of the actual state of society,—what they call *Civilization*,—and brilliant pictures of the life men will live in *Harmony*, or the new world they propose; and it is from these we must collect what, in their view, is evil, or opposed to man's destiny on this globe, and what they suppose is good, that is, its fulfilment, or favorable to its fulfilment. In regard to the latter, we find the chief place assigned to wealth and luxury, two things which Fourier asserts possitively, again and again, are absolutely indispensable to the fulfilment of our destiny; in regard to the former, we find enumerated, among the evils of civilization, the *poverty* of the great mass of the people, and *unattractive* labor. It is fair, then, to say, that poverty and unattractive labor are *evils*, in the judgment of the Associationists. Labor itself they cannot regard as evil, because they propose to continue it in their new world. The evil, then, is in its unattractiveness,—that is, in our being bound or forced to labor against our inclinations, or to do that to which we are more or less averse. But this can be evil only on condition that it is an evil to be under the necessity of acting against our inclinations. If this be accepted, good is in being free to follow our inclinations ; evil in being compelled or bound to act against them. On what authority does this principle rest?

Moreover, is it certain that poverty, in itself considered, is evil, or opposed to our destiny? Where is the proof? Wealth and poverty are both relative terms, unless the term poverty be restricted to those who have not even so much as their will which is their own, and then we should be obliged to predicate wealth of all who possess something, however little. But the Associationists do not so restrict the sense of the word, for they include, in the number of the poor, people who have something of their own, at least their will and bodily activity. What, then, is the real distinction between wealth and poverty? Where draw the line, so that the rich shall all be on one side, and all the poor on the other? John Jacob Astor is said, when told of a man who had just retired from business with half a million, to have remarked, that he had no doubt but the poor man might be just as happy as if he were rich! To John Jacob Astor, the man worth half a million was a poor man ; to most men, he would be a rich man. One man counts himself poor, in the possession of thousands ; another feels himself rich, if he have a coarse serge robe, a crust of bread, and water from the spring. Which of the two is the rich, which the poor man? If the Italian lazzaroni, the scandal of thrifty Englishmen and Yankees, have what contents them, or are contented with what suffices for the present moment, unsolicitous for the next, wherein are they poorer than our "merchant princes," who have a multitude of wants they cannot satisfy? and wherein would you enrich them, by increasing their possessions, if you increased their wants in the same ratio?

But pass over this difficulty. Suppose you have some invariable standard by which to determine who are the poor and who are the rich; whence does it follow that poverty is in itself an evil? Many emperors, kings, princes, nobles, and innumerable saints, have voluntarily abandoned wealth, and chosen poverty, even made a solemn vow never to have any thing to call their own. Is it certain that these have acted a foolish part, abandoned good, and inflicted evil on themselves? If not, how can you say poverty is in itself an evil? Do you say, poverty breeds discontent, and leads to vice and crime? Is that true? Does it do so in all men who are poor? Did it do so in St. Anthony, St. Francis of Assisium, St. John of God, St. Thomas of Villanova, St. Philip Neri, and thousands of others we could mention, who observed evangelical poverty to the letter? Are all the poor discontented, vicious, and criminal? No man dares say it. Then what you allege is not a necessary result of poverty, and must have its efficient cause elsewhere, in the person, or in some circumstance not dependent on wealth or poverty. In the world's history, povery, vice, and misery are far from being inseparable companions; and so are wealth, virtue, and happiness. Was wealth a good to the rich man mentioned in the Gospel? Was poverty an evil to the poor man that lay at his gate full of sores, begging to be fed with the crumbs that fell from his table?

We might go through the whole list of physical evils drawn up by the Associationists, and ask, in relation to each, so far as it is physical, the same or similar questions. Whence, then, the certainty that what they propose to remove, as evil, is evil? Whence, then, the proof that the end they propose is a good end? Suppose—and the case is supposable—that what are called physical evils are dispensed by a merciful Providence, designed to be invaluable blessings, and are such to all who receive and bear them with the proper dispositions; could we then pronounce them evils? Would it not follow, that in themselves they may be indifferent, and that the good or the evil results from the disposition with which they are received and borne? Now this may be the fact. If it is, then the good or the evil depends on ourselves, and we may make them either blessings or curses, as we choose. Then to remove evil would not necessarily be to remove them, but to cure that moral state which makes a bad, instead of a good, use of them.

It is easy to declaim, but it is important that we declaim wisely; and to be able to declaim wisely, we must know what to declaim against. It is easy to harrow up the feelings by eloquent descriptions of physical sufferings, and no doubt physical sufferings are often an evil of no small magnitude; but this is nothing to the purpose. Is the evil in the physical suffering itself, or in the moral state of him who causes or suffers it? Suppose we transport ourselves to the early ages of our era, and take our stand in proud, haughty, imperial, and pagan Rome; suppose we assist at the trial, tortures, and martyrdom of the persecuted Christians, behold them cast to the wild beasts in the amphitheatre, see them broiling slowly on gridirons, their flesh torn off with pincers, or their living bodies stuck full of splinters besmeared with pitch, lighted, and ranged along the streets of the city by night, as so many lamps. Here is physical pain. Ingenuity, aided by diabolical malice, has done its best to refine upon torture, to produce the greatest amount possible of physical suffering. Yet what is it that excites our horror? This pain beyond conception of the Christian martyrs? Not at all. We glory in it; we bless God for it; and so do the sufferers themselves. They *choose* it, voluntarily submit to it, and joy in the midst of it, and would not have it less for all the world. There is no joy on earth so sweet, so great, so ecstatic, as that of the martyr. The horror we feel is not at the physical suffering, but at the malice which inflicts it,—not at the fact that the martyrs are enabled heroically to win their crowns, but at the refined cruelty which delights to torture them. It is very possible, then, to conceive the most exquisite physical sufferings, the most excruciating tortures, and the most cruel death, as even a great and invaluable good to those who suffer them.

Their presence, then, is not necessarily an evil to the sufferer, and consequently exemption from them not necessarily a good. For the same reason, it does not necessarily follow that the wealth, and luxury, and other things you propose, are necessarily in themselves at all desirable. You must go farther; and before attempting to decide what is good or what is evil, tell us WHAT IS THE DESTINY OF MAN; for it is only in relation to his destiny, that we can pronounce this or that good or evil. "Am I not a happy man;" said Crœsus to Solon, after showing him his treasures. "Whether a man is happy or not," replied the Athenian sage, "is not to be known before his death."

What, then, according to the Associationists, is the destiny of man, his *final* cause, or the end for which he exists? They have much to say of man's destiny; but we do not find, in those of their writings which we have consulted, any very satisfactory or even intelligible answer to this question. We are told, at one time, that man's destiny is, to live in harmony,— that is, in association as they propose to organize it. But this is no answer; for it only asserts, in other words, that man is able or fitted by nature to adopt the means of fulfilling his destiny. Besides, it defines the destiny of the race rather than the destiny of the individuals, without which the race is only an abstraction. At other times, we are told that man's destiny is, to harmonize the globe which he inhabits with itself, to harmonize it with the sideral heavens, and the sideral heavens with the universe so that all discord shall cease, and there shall be universal harmony; that is, man's destiny is, to complete the works of the Creator, and give them their last finish! The final cause of man is, then, to assist the Creator in completing the work of creation, that is, that he may constitute a portion of the First Cause! This, however, we understand to be only a fanciful speculation, for which the school, as it exists in this country, does not hold itself responsible.

The more modest of the members leave these lofty speculations by the way, and tell us that their object, and their sole object is, by the organization of labor and association, to enable man to fulfil his destiny on earth. But what is this destiny? We can find no specific answer. But they lay down, as their grand principle, ATTRACTIONS PROPORTIONAL TO DESTINY. According to them, we may, therefore, conclude man's destiny in this world is that towards which he is attracted by his nature, or which is indicated by his natural inclinations and tendencies. If we understand them, they undertake to give the law of attaining our destiny, rather than any clear statement of what is that destiny itself. But as the attractions are natural, and as they are the index to the end, and the law of its attainment, the end must itself be natural. If, then, we assert that they hold, that, when man has developed and satisfied in harmony his primitive or fundamental passions, or *stimulants*, as M. Briancourt calls them, he has fulfilled his destiny in this world, we may presume that they will readily admit our assertion to be correct. Then the destiny of man in this world is, the harmonious or orderly development and satisfaction of his whole nature. We will strike out from this "the development of his nature," because development can never be an end, since, by its nature, it is necessarily only the means or process of gaining the end. Then the answer will be, simply, Man's destiny on earth is, to satisfy his nature; that is, to obtain and possess, in all their variety and fulness, the natural objects indicated by his nature, and towards which he is naturally stimulated. This is nothing but our old acquaintance, the Epicurean philosophy, decked out in the latest Parisian mode. We can now *east* ourselves, and take a fresh departure.

But, to be just to the Associationists, we must observe, that they understand by *nature*, not merely our sensual inclinations and tendencies, but also our intellectual, social, domestic, and æsthetic passions or tendencies. Moreover, they do not teach, that, in gaining the end to which we are attracted, we are to follow blindly our natural inclinations and tendencies, or that we are necessitated by them. They are the index and the law, and we have reason and free will, as instruments by which to follow the law and secure the end. Nor do they teach that it will do to follow without restraint all our inclinations and tendencies *as they are actually developed under Civilization;* for they are now developed disproportionately, in violation of harmony, and it may require several generations in association before it will do to give them all their full liberty.; nevertheless, the end is in the natural order, and is the orderly satisfaction of nature by natural objects.

But on what authority rests this assumption, that our destiny as human beings in this world is the natural satisfaction of our nature? We do not find this proved in any of the writings of the Associationists which have fallen under our notice. M. Briancourt asserts it, in asserting the central principle of the school,—" Attractions proportional to destiny;" and he no doubt supposes that he proves it, in proving this principle, the grand discovery of Fourier; but we do not find that this principle itself is proved, at least, in the case of human beings, the only order of beings concerned in the inquiry. The school may have proved it of minerals, vegetables, and the different orders of the animal kingdom; but that is nothing to their purpose; for we cannot conclude the attributes and destiny of one genus from those of another. Because this or that is true of a pig, for instance, we cannot say, it is *therefore* true of man; nor that the fact that it is true of the pig affords even a presumption that it is true of man; for man is essentially different from the pig. To say, because it is true of other genera, that attractions are proportional to destiny, it must be true of human beings, is either a plain *non-sequitur*, or the denial that there is any essential difference between man and them. If there is no essential difference between man and a mineral, a vegetable, a pig, we concede your conclusion; if there is, we deny it. But the former we are loath to admit; and although our modern philosophers have done their best towards making it at least practically true, we must as yet hold on to the old doctrine that man is generically distinguished from all other orders of creatures, although he may have many attributes in common with them all.

If, as we presume it will be conceded, man is essentially distinguishable from the animal world, if he forms a genus of his own, nothing can be concluded of him, in so far as he is peculiarly man, from any other order; consequently, whatever is affirmed of him must be specifically proved of him. It may be, that all other orders of creatures on this globe have a natural destiny, and yet the Creator have appointed him to a supernatural destiny. It may be, as the Church teaches, and the Christian believes, that the end for which God designed and made him is not that to which he is directed and drawn by his nature, even in its purity and integrity, but an end to which, since the fall, his nature is even averse, and which can be gained only by denying and crucifying his natural inclinations and tendencies. This may be,—that is, it is conceivable; and if true, it will not do to say, *a priori*, of man, that attractions are proportional to destiny, or that they at all indicate either it or the law of its attainment. Now it is possible that this constitutes, in part, the essential difference between man and animals. If so, the whole doctrine of the Associationists falls to the ground.

The Associationists must not misapprehend the question we raise. We are travelling no more than they out of life in this world. We understand them to confine their view to man's destiny here on this globe; we are not, at this moment, extending ours beyond it. We agree perfectly with them, in what we presume to be their principle, namely, that there is no contradiction between our destiny here and our destiny hereafter, and that the surest method of gaining our end in the world to come is faithfully to fulfil our destiny in the world where we now are. We raise no question between our present good and our future good; for we suppose the principle of both to be the same. Nor do we raise a question as to foregoing our good in this life, for the sake of gaining a good hereafter; for we have never been taught that our true good here is at all incompatible with beautitude in heaven. The Christian who denies himself, chastises, mortifies the flesh with its deeds, crucifies his natural inclinations, is not supposed to deprive himself of any good here, and he perhaps enjoys, even in this life, a hundred-fold more than the Associationists in their most brilliant and ravishing day-dreams even venture to promise. We suspect that the life they promise would have had very few attractions for St. Francis of Assisium, St. Anthony, St. Benedict, or St. Bernard, even as to this world. The question lies between *the life of nature,* as contended for by the Associationists, and *the supernatural life,* which the Christian professes to live. The Christian lives his supernatural life even in this world, and its enjoyment is an enjoyment here, as well as hereafter, Both lives may therefore be considered as lived on this globe, yet differing as to their principle and end. The Christian view is, that God made man, whether you speak of this world or of that which is to come, for a supernatural destiny; the Associationist view is, that man is made, at least so far as this world is concerned, for a natural destiny. The question is between the two. If the Christian is right, the Associationist is wrong, and his effort to provide for the gaining of a natural destiny, for a life in accordance with natural inclination and tendency, is directly at war with man's true destiny on this globe, and therefore with man's true good, not only his true good hereafter, but his true good here.

The Associationists, of course, do not believe the Church; but that is not the question. They profess to walk by sight, by science, and therefore they must demonstrate that she is wrong, or have no right to assert as science their doctrine, that man's destiny on this globe is a natural destiny, or that the end of our existence here is attained by living a natural life. But they have not demonstrated this; they have, at best, only proved that this is or may be true of various animal tribes; but they have not proved at all that it is true of man. At best, then, their doctrine is but an hypothesis, a belief, for which they do not, and cannot, even pretend to have infallible authority.

The Associationists tell us that they have proved their doctrine by analysis of human nature, and that therefore it is science. But proved what? Conceding them all they can pretend to have proved by analysis, it is only that the primitive passions or stimulants they assert are psychologically true,—from which, at best, they can conclude only what *would be* man's destiny, in case his destiny were natural; but that it is natural, the precise point to be proved, they have not proved, for it can never be concluded from nature. Nature can guide us only on the assumption that the end is natural. When the question comes up, Is the purpose of our existence natural, or supernatural? nature has nothing to say one way or the other. This is a question which science can never answer; for science can never travel out of nature. It is idle, then, for the Associationists to tell us their doctrine is scientifically established. Whether the end for which Almighty God placed us here is natural or supernatural it is impossible to know without a supernatural revelation, and to a supernatural revelation, declaring our destiny here to be natural, the Associationists do not pretend.

These remarks show clearly enough that the Associationists are unable to answer the first question in order, namely, What is man's destiny on this globe? Then they are unable to legitimate the end they propose ; then unable to say, that what they call good is good, or what they call evil is evil; and then, finally, whether, even by complete success, they would or would not benefit their fellow-men. This deserves their serious consideration. If, as we have said, what the Church teaches and the Christian believes is true, they are certainly wrong as to man's destiny here, as well as hereafter. It will not do for them to reply, that they do not believe the Church, and that her authority is not sufficiently proved to them; because they must be able to assert their system as a science, or they have no right to assert it at all. They must, then, disprove the teaching of the Church. So long as there is a possibility that the teaching of the Church may turn out to be true, they cannot assert their own doctrine; for, in the nature of the case, they can conclude its truth only from the distruction of the negative.

2. This uncertainty as to man's destiny here, which the Associationists do not and cannot remove, attaches of course, to the

means proposed to enable us to fulfil it. The school adopts, as we have seen, as its fundamental principle, "Attractions proportional to destiny." Hence, by ascertaining and providing for the attractions, they determine and provide for the destiny. On this principle rests their whole fabric of Association. If this be true, their Association may or may not be adequate; but if not true, the whole scheme is evidently altogether inadequate, because natural attractions can be proportional only to a natural end, never to a supernatural end. This is conclusive against the scheme, till its advocates are able, by a supernatural authority, to prove that our destiny in this world is a natural destiny; for it requires no argument to prove that Association, organized with express reference to a *natural* destiny, must be unavailing —if nothing worse—for a *supernatural* destiny.

But even if the end of man in this world were the satisfaction of his nature, the means proposed would be inadequate. The assumption of the Associationists is, that our nature can be satisfied by the possession of the natural objects to which it directs and draws us. But this is not true. The arguments on which the Associationists rely to prove the contrary are inconclusive, because they are all arguments from one genus to another. When the premises and conclusion are not in the same genus, nothing is concluded. It may be true, as M. Briancourt proves, that, if a pig gets what his nature seeks, he will be satisfied, stop squealing, and lie down and sleep, till renewed appetite awakes him; and the same would, no doubt, be true of man, if, man were a pig, and might become true of him, if he by some Circean art, could be transformed into a pig. But it so happens that man is not a pig, and cannot, if he is to retain his essential nature as man, be changed into one. We cannot predicate indifferently of the two. Man is never satisfied by the possession of the natural objects to which he is naturally drawn. All experience proves it; the experience of each particular man proves it; else wherefore this deep wail from the heart of every one who lives simply the life of nature, this outbreak of despair, *Vanitas vanitatum, et omnia vanitas?* Build man the most splendid palace; lavish on it all the decorations of the most perfect art; furnish it with the most exquisite and most expensive taste; lodge him in it on the soft, voluptuous couch; spread his table with the most delicate viands and the rarest fruits; refresh him with the most costly wines; regale him with the richest music; rain down upon him the most fragrant odors; ravish him with beauty; gratify every sense, every taste, every wish, as soon as formed; and the poor wretch will sigh for he knows not what, and behold with envy even the ragged beggar feeding on offal. No variety, no change, no art, can satisfy him. All that nature or art can offer palls upon his senses and his heart,—is to him poor, mean, and despicable. There arise in him wants which are too vast for nature, which swell out beyond the bounds of the universe, and cannot, and will not, be satisfied with any thing less than the infinite and eternal God. Never yet did nature suffice for man, and it never will.

This great and solemn fact, which it is vain to attempt to deny,—a fact deep graven on all hearts that have experience, that have lived the natural life,—should lead thoughtful men to ask,—nay, it does lead thoughtful men to ask,—if, after all, it be not a mistake to attempt to satisfy ourselves with the vain and perishing things of this world; if the inability to find our satisfaction in nature be not a strong presumption that our Creator did not design us for a natural destiny; if, in fact, he did not intend us for an end above nature; and therefore, that our precise error is in seeking a natural destiny in opposition to his design, in neglecting our true destiny for a false destiny, that is, neglecting true good and pursuing real evil. We should suppose that this universal experience of all men would have created, at least, a doubt, in the minds of our friends, as to the soundness of their assumption of the natural as the true destiny of man on this globe.

The Associationists, doubtless, will reply, that they do not mean to deny the supernatural destiny; that they leave to man all the satisfactions of religion; that there is no incompatibility between the supernatural life of the Christian and the natural life of *harmony*. But in this they are mistaken. The principle, the means, and the end of their life are natural; but the principle, the means, and the end of the other are supernatural, and no man can possibly live both lives at once. This is what our Lord meant, when he said, "You cannot serve God and mammon. No man can serve two masters." When you propose nature as the end, and organize Association expressly in reference to it, you do not leave man free to propose God as his end, and to live solely the supernatural life. Moreover, you exclude religion from the Association. You recognize nothing that has the least resemblance to religion. It has with you no substantive existence; for, as M. Briancourt defines it, it is nothing but the reflection in their harmonic relations of all the primitive stimulants, as light, which is itself no color, is the reflection of all the primitive colors in perfect harmony.

Furthermore, the Associationists cannot admit the necessity of religion without abandoning their system. Their system is founded on the principle, that attractions are proportional to destiny; and if what pertains to the natural order is inadequate to satisfy nature, their system is false. The admission of the necessity of any thing transcending nature as a principle, a means, or an end, would be the denial of the sufficiency of nature; therefore, that attractions are proportional to destiny; therefore, the denial of the whole scheme of Association. The Associationists are not at liberty, when we have shown them from experience that nature does not suffice for nature, to defend themselves by saying, Then bring in the supernatural; for they are not at liberty to abandon the essential principle of their system, and still continue to assert it.

And, finally, if the system is insufficient in itself, if under it, as under Civilization, our destiny is not attainable without the supernatural, the system is useless, for the supernatural alone is sufficient. The man who lives the supernatural life of the Christian has God, and therefore all. He despises the life your Association proposes. Your wealth and luxury, your palace and grounds, your flower-gardens and ball-rooms, your song and dance, your statues and pictures, your scientific reunions, and your "Æsthetic Teas," are to him vanity, yea, less than vanity, and nothing. He holds them in utter contempt, and tramples them beneath his feet, and weeps tears of pity and tender compassion over those poor creatures who can esteem them. The epicurean and the saint, though for different reasons, both exclaim of all the world can give, *Vanity of vanities, all is vanity!* The former, because he has grown weary of it, and found it impotent to fill up the vacuum in his heart; the latter, because he is full without it, because he has no need of it, because it can offer him nothing, and serves only to distract him from God, and hinder his divine life.

But we have objections to the adequacy of the means proposed, of a kind which will have more weight with our friends, the Associationists. The means proposed are intended, besides other things, to remove the evils of poverty, that is, the moral evils occasioned in the community by poverty; for of the physical evils we say nothing. There is no question but poverty occasions discontent, envy, and repining, and these again lead to crimes against both person and property. But it occasions these evils only when it is contrasted with wealth. There is no more discontent, envy, or repining, where all are alike poor, than where all are alike rich. The hovel is a hovel only as contrasted with the palace which rises by its side and overtops it. The remedy here is either internal or external. The internal is moral, religious, which raises the poor to the supernatural life, gives them all the most favored have or can have, and leads them to look upon all the distinctions of rank and wealth as of no value, and to trample the world beneath their feet. He who asks nothing from the world envies never those who possess it, and repines never that he is poor. This remedy is the one the Church approves, and labors always to apply; and it checks alike the envy and repining of the poor, and the pride and insolence of the rich, enabling both to live together in mutual peace and charity,—in harmony. But this remedy the Associationists reject, even with scorn. They propose an external remedy. But the external remedy can be a remedy only so far as it removes the occasion; and to do that it must establish an equality of fortunes, or at least, so arrange matters that wealth and poverty shall never be in juxtaposition, or seen in contrast.

But if we consult the plan of the Associationists, we shall see that they propose nothing of the kind. They recognize property and inequality of property in like manner as they are recognized in our present social order; and, what is still more to the purpose, they bring together the extremes of wealth and poverty in the same phalanx, and lodge them in the same phalanstery, so that one cannot go in or go out, rise up or sit down, without having the violent contrast forced upon his attention, to exalt his pride or madden his envy. That is, they propose to cure the evil by increasing what they regard as its cause!

It is of no avail to allege that none in Association will be very poor, that there will be none who cannot by their own labor procure all the necessaries and chief comforts of life; for the evil in question does not arise from the consideration that I have *little*, but that my neighbor has *more*. So long as in your Association one has *more* than another, you have not removed the occasion of the evil you deplore. No matter, if my plain apartments are sufficient for my protection, when only a little lathing and plaster divide them from the gay and elegant and luxuriously furnished apartments of my neighbors; no matter that my one dish suffices for my physical necessities, so long as, in the room next to mine, my neighbor—a stupid fellow, I may think, not half as good as I—sits down to his dinner of twenty dishes. Since all these violent contrasts, all the distinctions of wealth, exist in the Association, and are perpetually under the eye, in the face and nose, of every one, meeting him at every turn he takes, the occasion of the evils exists there in even a greater and a more offensive degree than it does in the present social state; and as long as you do not by the Association remove the occasion, how can you say that by it you cure the evil? Do not refer us to moral influences which may be operative, for that is to abandon your system, and fall back on that which you condemn and anathematize. Your system is, to correct the internal by the judicious organization of the external; and if you are obliged to appeal from the external to the internal, to supply the defects of the organization, you acknowledge what we are endeavoring to prove, namely, the inadequacy of your means.

Again; the mother evil of our present industrial system, according to the Associationists, is COMPETITION. Indeed, to read their writings, one is inclined to believe that they regard competition in business as the cause of nearly all the ills that flesh is heir to. Their grand argument for Association is, that it will entirely do away with competition and its attendant evils. Whether their view of competition is correct or the reverse is not now the question. The question is, Does Association, on their plan, remove it, or, what is the same thing, afford no motive or scope for it? If not, their means are inadequate. Competition results from the inequality of fortunes, the freedom and the desire to accumulate. Where these three causes coexist, competition is possible and inevitable. Association, then, to remove competition, must take away these causes, at least some one of them. The desire to accumulate can be suppressed by external means only by an organization in which wealth can secure, or aid in securing, to its possessor no personal or social advantage, or what is regarded as an advantage by him or by others. This can never be the case where wealth and luxury are held to be important, essential to the fulfilment of one's destiny, and where the proprietor has the free use of his property. Grant, then, the desire, and allow the freedom, to accumulate, and you have competition, because property is in its nature exclusive.

Now all these conditions of competition must coexist in Association, because the Association is based on individual and not common property. There is inequality of property, and of course the distinctions which always do and always must accompany it. There is freedom to possess and use, and there is freedom to acquire, to hoard, or to display. There are objects forbidden to the poor, and accessible only to the rich. There are, then, all the motives to accumulate, and the same opportunity to acquire individual property, and to purchase pleasures or distinctions by it, which are furnished by existing economical arrangements. What, then, is to hinder competition in the bosom of the phalanx itself?

But pass over this, and consider the phalanx as a copartnership, or a huge business firm. There must be buying and selling between it and other firms; for we do not understand the Associationists to propose to stop all exchange, all trade and commerce. What, then, is to hinder competition between phalanx and phalanx, any more than now between one business firm and another? Is competition between firms less injurious than between individuals?—between large firms than between small ones? Indeed, is it not notorious that the rivalry of large bodies is more unprincipled, altogether less scrupulous, than that of individuals? Who needs to be told that a man, sheltering himself under the shield of a corporation, will do, without scruple, what he would recoil from doing in his individual capacity? What, then, under your system, is to prevent perhaps the most ruinous competition the world has ever witnessed? Phalanx may seek to circumvent phalanx in business, and every few days we may hear the crash of one or another, each burying eighteen hundred or two thousand people under its ruins! There is nothing in your system, so far as we can see, to prevent this disastrous result. Men in the Association have the same passions as out of it, and these passions will operate in the same way, if they have the liberty and the occasion.

We are aware that the Associationists suppose that they will keep down the spirit of rivalry by the various intellectual, social, domestic, and æsthetic influences which they expect to be operative in Association. But they recognize the spirit of rivalry, or competition. Let this be remembered. True, they count on turning it into other channels. Thus, by making shoeblacks the Legion of Honor, they fancy that the ambition will be to be shoeblacks; just as if the cross of honor will not cease to be an object of ambition the moment it is conferred on the shoe-black! The cross of honor is valued because it is bestowed as the reward of honorable or heroic deeds. It does not confer the honor, it signalizes it; and never will men become shoe-blacks, for the sake of it. It is impossible, by any artificial methods, to raise menial arts to the rank of the liberal; or menial services to the rank of the heroic, by conferring on them the insignia of the heroic. If you want the liberal and refined to be willing to perform the most menial and disgusting duties, you must propose the Cross of Christ, not the Cross of the Legion of Honor; the crown of immortal life, not the crown of laurel.

The Associationists, whatever influences or arrangements they may depend upon, must allow the individual the dominion of himself, and the freedom to follow the bent of his genius. They must allow the former, or they reduce man to complete slavery, and make the phalanx the grave of the individual; and the latter, or deny their grand principle of attractions proportional to destiny, and also their other principle of attractive labor, since no labor or employment against one's natural bent is or can be attractive. They do allow the first, otherwise individual property would be a mockery; they allow the second, otherwise their distribution of the phalanx into groups and series would be an absurdity. Allow a man freedom to follow his natural bent, that is, the passion or group of passions which are naturally predominant in him, and that passion or group will grow by indulgence, and soon gain the complete mastery over all the rest, and subordinate them to itself. Besides, the whole tendency of the Association is to this result. Its grand principle is, to follow the natural order and the natural attraction. The harmonious development our friends speak of is not a precisely similar development in every individual, but the harmonious development of each individual in accordance with his naturally predominant tendency or tendencies. To understand it in any other sense would be to make them inconsistent with themselves. Consequently, whatever influences they may bring to bear on the individual, they must tend to harmonize all in him with his naturally predominant passion. If then, we suppose one whose strong natural tendency is to acquire property, his whole nature will be subordinated to this tendency, and he will follow it to the full extent of his freedom and capacity. If we suppose two such, we have competition.

As for social influences, these, in a community which starts with the assumption that wealth and luxury are absolutely indispensable to the fulfilment of our destiny, will not be likely to check or discourage the efforts without which wealth and luxury are not to be had. The domestic influences will be no less favorable to the accumulation of wealth than now; for the father bequeaths his property to his children, and where there are inequalities of fortune, wealth will confer distinction. The æsthetic influences are of no account for good. All the world are not artists, and it is by no means certain that every phalanx will be a school of art; and if it should be, it must be borne in mind that its art will be purely secular, and purely secular art leads to nothing better than effeminacy and licentiousness. It would, then, check the tendency to accumulate, if at all, only by producing no less an evil of another sort. It would be well for modern rhapsodists to recollect that the artistic epoch—we speak not of religious art—follows, but has never yet been known to precede or accompany, an heroic epoch. It marks a decline, and usually is or ushers in an age of corruption. The shrine of natural beauty stands always in the vestibule of the temple of Venus, when not in the temple itself. Avarice, again, is no unnatural pendant to voluptuousness. We place no confidence, therefore, in your æsthetic influences, even to restrain competition,—especially, since wealth will be needed as the minister of voluptuousness.

It is unnecessary to pursue farther this branch of the subject. All our primitive tendencies are exclusive, and mutually repellant. They almost always exist in excess, and every one of them grows by indulgence. Philosophy and experience alike testify that their harmonious action is never possible, unless by their subjection to reason. But this subjection is contrary to the principles of the Associationists; for they allow us reason and free will, not to control our passions and keep them in subjection to the law, but as their servants or instruments. The passions give the law; reason and free will provide for its fulfilment. Consequently, the harmony of the passions is impossible, on the principles of the Associationists; and without such harmony, their means are obviously inadequate.

3. Whoever reads the works of the Associationists must perceive that they place great reliance for the success of their scheme on the mutual love and good-will of the members of the phalanx. There is to be there no pride of birth, no haughtiness of rank, no insolence of wealth. Gentlemen and simplemen, rich and poor, learned and unlearned, are all to meet as brothers; and no bickerings, nor jars, no envyings, no jealousies, no aversions, rancors, or heartburnings, are ever to find admittance into the *harmonic* paradise. No serpent will ever find his way into the new garden of Eden. Every one will be courteous, affable, gentle, affectionate, forbearing, and eager to oblige; and men will say, "See how these phalansterians love one another!" Undoubtedly, without this, the Association will be torn by internal dissentions, and soon prove only a monument to the folly of its founders.

But by what right do Associationists count on this universal and never-failing mutual love and good-will? They propose no radical change and no supernatural elevation of human nature. Men enter Association with all the essential passions, and with all the diversity of character, taste, and temperament which they now have, and must exhibit in Association the same phenomena as out of it, so far as the occasion is not removed. There is no removal of the occasion; and there must be, as we have shown, just as much occasion for the exercise of all the bitter and mischievous passions of our nature in Association as in the present order? Whence, then, is to come this anticipated result, so widely different from our present experience? From the moral causes operative there? What are they? Nay, you cannot appeal to moral causes, for your system is to reach and modify the moral through the physical.

But pass over this. How is the degree of love necessary to set the machinery of Association in operation to be obtained prior to Association itself? It requires a greater degree of love to introduce than it does to preserve after introduction. If any thing is certain in philosophy, it is that the effect cannot exceed the cause. Hence, universal experience proves that the founders of human institutions are always superior to those who are formed under those institutions. The progress under human institutions is always downwards; the purest and noblest characters formed under them are the earliest. Man is always superior to his productions, and these are superior to *their* productions. Reverberations grow fainter and fainter in the distance. Mark the difference between the men who made our Revolution and the men of to-day. Between George Washington and James K. Polk there is a distance; and there would have been a greater distance still, if it had not been for the continued operation of causes not introduced or essentially affected by our Revolution. Certainly, then, no more love can be in the Association than there is in the cause introducing Association. Then the Associationists must get, under Civilization, without Association, all the love they can have with and under it. But if we can have the love without Association, then there is no need of Association; if not, Association is impracticable. Here is a conclusive argument, not only against Association, but against every scheme for effecting the real progress of man or society *by virtue of a purely human principle.* Proceeding on a purely human principle, man, it is easy to demonstrate, can no more be a *reformer* than an *institutor,*—that is, he can neither by way of reform, nor by way of institution, introduce or establish any thing superior to what he finds existing, or which, in fact, does not fall below it. His boasted improvements are such only in relation to the order he introduces, and consist solely in getting more and more rid of the contradictions to it retained at first from the preëxisting order. The departure on a human principle from the existing order is always a step towards something inferior or less perfect. Man can fall from the civilized state to the savage; he never rises spontaneously from the savage state to the civilized; and for the very good reason, that in the moral, no more than in the physical world, can the stream rise higher than the fountain.

Moreover, the love itself, which our Associationists rely upon, can never be adequate to their purpose. It is, at best, only human love, the natural *sentiment* of philanthropy. This answers very well, when the work to be done is simply to propose grand schemes, make brilliant and eloquent speeches, or when there are no disagreeable duties to be performed, no violent natural repugnances to be overcome; but it fails in the hour of severe trial. Your philanthropist starts with generous impulses, with a glowing enthusiasm; and so long as there are no great discouragements, no disgusting offices in his way, and he has even a small number of admiring friends to stimulate his zeal, applaud his eloquence, flatter his pride, and soothe him for the rebuffs he meets from the world, he may keep on his course, and continue his task. But let him find himself entirely alone, let him have no little public of his own, which is all the world to him, let him be thwarted on every point, let him be obliged to work in secret, unseen by all but the All-seeing Eye, encounter from men nothing but contradiction, contempt, and ingratitude, and he will soon begin to say to himself, Why suffer and endure so much for the unworthy? He who loves man for man's sake loves only a creature, a being of imperfect worth, of no more worth than himself, perhaps not so much; and why shall he love him more than himself, and sacrifice himself for him? The highest stretch of human love is, to love our neighbor *as* we love ourselves; and we do injustice to ourselves, when we love them more than we do ourselves.

Nay, philanthropy itself is a sort of selfishness. It is a sentiment, not a principle. Its real motive is not another's good, but its own satisfaction according to its nature. It seeks the good of others, because the good of others is the means of its own satisfaction, and is as really selfish in its principle as any other of our sentiments; for there is a broad distinction between the *sentiment* of philanthropy, and the *duty* of doing good to others,—between seeking the good of others from sentiment, and seeking it in obedience to a law which binds the conscience. The measure of the capacity of philanthropy, as a sentiment, is the amount of satisfaction it can bring to the possessor. So long as, upon the whole, he finds it more delightful to play the philanthropist than the miser, for instance, he will do it, but no longer. Hence, philanthropy must always decrease just in proportion to the increase of the repugnances it must encounter, and fail us just at the moment when it is most needed, and always in proportion as it is needed. It follows the law so observable in all human society, and helps most when and where its help is least needed. Here is the condemnation of every scheme, however plausible it may look, that in any degree depends on philanthropy for its success.

The principle the Associationists want for their success is not philanthropy,—the love of man for man's sake,—but divine charity, not to be had and preserved out of the Catholic Church. Charity is, in relation to its subject, a supernaturally infused virtue; in relation to its object, the supreme and exclusive love of God for his own sake, and man for the sake of God. He who has it is proof against all trials; for his love does not depend on man, who so often proves himself totally unamiable and unworthy, but on God, who is always and everywhere infinitely amiable and deserving of all love. He visits the sick, the prisoner, the poor, for it is God whom he visits; he clasps with tenderness the leprous to his bosom, and kisses his sores, for it is God he embraces and whose dear wounds he kisses. The most painful and disgusting offices are sweet and easy, because he performs them for God, who is love, and whose love inflames his heart. Whenever there is a service to be rendered to one of God's little ones, he runs with eagerness to do it; for it is a service to be rendered to God himself. "Charity never faileth." It is proof against all natural repugnances; it overcomes earth and hell;

and brings God down to tabernacle with men. Dear to it is this poor beggar, for it sees in him only our Lord who had "not where to lay his head;" dear are the sorrowing and the afflicted, for it sees in them Him who was "a man of sorrows and acquainted with infirmity;" dear are these poor outcasts, for in them it beholds Him who was "scorned and rejected of men;" dear are the wronged, the oppressed, the down-trodden, for in them it beholds the Innocent One nailed to the Cross, and dying to atone for human wickedness. And it joys to succour them all; for in so doing, it makes reparation to God for the poverty, sufferings, wrongs, contempt, and ignominious death which he endured for our sakes; or it is his poverty it relieves in relieving the poor, his hunger it feeds in feeding the hungry, his nakedness it clothes in throwing its robe over the naked, his afflictions it consoles in consoling the sorrowing, his wounds into which it pours oil and wine and which it binds up. "Inasmuch as ye did it unto the least of these my brethren, ye did it unto me." All is done to and for God, whom it loves more than men, more than life, and more than heaven itself, if to love him and heaven were not one and the same thing. This is the principle you need; with this principle, you have God with you and for you, and failure is impossible. But with this principle, Association is, at best, a matter of indifference; for this is sufficient of itself at all times, under any and every form of political, social, or industrial organization. He who has God can have nothing more.

But our gravest objection to Associationism is, that it implicates the justice of Almighty God. The Associationists tell us that their plan is indispensable to the fulfilment of our destiny on this globe. By man they must mean men, or else they are talking of an abstraction. The species has actual existence only in individuals, and the question relates only to actual existences. It is absurd to suppose that God cares for species, and not for individuals,—for the ideal, and not for the actual,—for the abstract, and not for the concrete. When, therefore, the organization of Labor and Association are proposed as indispensable to the fulfilment of our destiny,—when its friends tell us, as they do, that all the past has been only a preamble to it, a necessary preparation for it, they tell us in effect that no human being has, as yet, had within his reach the means of fulfiling his destiny. But it will not do to say this. God can create no being, and appoint him to a certain end, that is, make it his duty to gain that end, and not provide him with sufficient means of gaining it, if he chooses to avail himself of them, without contradicting his own justice, and thereby proving himself unjust. If there is a single individual of our race that fails to attain his destiny, either here or hereafter, through defect of means, not through his own fault, the blame is chargeable upon the Creator. But God is infinitely just, and we cannot accuse him of injustice without blasphemy. Then the means of fulfiling his destiny, whether here or hereafter, must *always* be within the reach of every man; and if any one fails to fulfil it, he has no one to blame but himself. Then Association never has been, is not, and never can be, necessary for the fulfilment of our destiny on this globe, or elsewhere; for man, every man, can fulfil his destiny, if he chooses, without it.

These are some few of the objections which seem to us conclusive against the views and schemes of the Associationists. They by no means exhaust our list of objections; but we stop with them, because we regard them as amply sufficient of themselves. But let not the Associationists imagine, for a moment, because we refuse to go with them, that we are better satisfied with the present condition of our fellow-men than they are, or that we any more despair of its amelioration than they do. When we deserted the movement party and took refuge in the Church, it was not because we had become indifferent to human suffering, or because we despaired of solacing it. Never did the young enthusiast, the fierce declaimer, the bold radical, feel more alive to every form of human suffering, or entertain a stronger hope of relieving it, than we did, when our kind Mother was pleased to receive us and own us as one of her children. It is true, we did not embrace the Church for the reason that she is a social reformer, for the reason that we believed her capable of effecting the good we had attempted, or which our friends were attempting without her. In view of what she promises her faithful and obedient children, all that we or they contemplated is not worth a moment's consideration. Nevertheless, she furnishes in abundance all the means necessary to remove all real evils, and to secure every possible good.

Let not the Associationists misapprehend us. We do not ask them to embrace the Church, because she is the proper agent for acquiring the good they seek for their fellow men; for we wish them to embrace her from higher and worthier motives. For ourselves, we have been, and are even now, loath to dwell on what the Church can do for us in this life, lest we should be interpreted as assigning false motives for yielding her the homage which is her due. We are unwilling to pursue a line of argument, which, however proper it may be in itself, ignorance or malice may torture even into the appearance of placing time before eternity, society before heaven, or man before or in competition with God. The Church must be embraced for a heavenly motive, or no advantage inures to us from embracing her. She is here to prepare us for heaven, and heaven is the only end that we can legitimately seek. The good she effects for this world is incidental, and should never be made the motive for becoming or remaining a Catholic. But, bearing this always in mind, we may without impropriety show that she can do enough for us, even in this world, to satisfy all reasonable men.

Some of the Associationists are already looking towards the Church, apparently despairing of success in their enterprise without her; but they are looking to her, we fear, rather with the wish to obtain her sanction for their plan, and her assistance to carry it out, than with any sincere disposition to submit themselves to her direction and discipline. If she will accept Fourierism, they are ready to accept her. But she will make no such agreement with them. She will be all, or she will be nothing. They must accept her unconditionally, or she will not accept them. She has her own method, and will not learn of them; they must learn of her.

But is her method adequate? Let us see. The men who have manifested, under their highest forms, the virtues which are required to remove all real evils and to procure every true good of which men in this world are capable, are undeniably to be found in the Catholic Church, and nowhere else. If all men were like, for instance, St. Raymond of Pennafort, St. John of God, St. Vincent de Paul, or even Fenelon, a great and good man, yet far below the standard of a Catholic Saint, there could and would be no lack of the good desirable, and no real evil could exist. There is not a form of evil in society, a single ill that flesh is heir to, which some one or more of our saints have not made provision for removing or solacing, and which they would not have removed or solaced, if they had been duly seconded, as you must know, if you have made yourselves but passably acquainted with the charitable institutions of the Church. Yet these saints did not go out of the Church, and did but come up to that standard of perfection which she proposes to all, and exhorts all her children to aspire to, and to which all may attain, by the grace of God, and that, too, without any change of the existing political, social, or industrial order. All may have, in the bosom of the Church whatever the external order, all the means needed for attaining to the highest perfection of which they are capable; and by attaining to that perfection, all is secured that is or can be desired for society.

But you say, all are not saints. True; but whose is the fault? It is not the fault of the political, social, or industrial order, otherwise, these of whom we speak could not have become saints; not the fault of the Church, for she proffers to all the same means and assistance she extended to these; nor precisely the fault of human nature, for these were no better by nature than others; and many of the saints have even been wild and dissolute in their youth. All may not be called by Almighty God to the same degree of heroic sanctity, nor is it necessary; but all are called to Christian perfection, and the means which have proved effectual in the case of those who have attained to it are extended to all, and must needs be, if adopted, equally effectual in the case of all. The fault, whenever any one falls below the standard of perfection, is his own, is in the fact that he refuses to comply with all the Church commands and counsels. The Church cannot take away free will; and as long as men retain it, they will, to a greater or less extent, abuse it. Do the Associationists propose to take it away, and reduce men to mere machines? We do not understand them to propose any such thing; and if they should, it would be an additional objection to their scheme. God himself respects our free will, and governs us only according to our *choice*. He gives us, naturally or supernaturally, the ability to will and to do as he wills, and motives sweet and attractive as heaven and terrible as hell to induce us to will as he wills; but he does not will for us; the will must be our own act. If the Church proposes perfection to all, exhorts all to aspire to it, furnishes them all the assistance they need to gain it, and urges them by all the motives which can weigh with them to accept and use them, the fault, if they do not, is theirs, not hers, and she is not to be accused either of inefficiency or of insufficiency; for she does all that, in the nature of the case, it is possible to do.

But even a far lower standard of Christian worth than we have been speaking of, and which is possible in the bosom of the Church to all, will suffice for the purpose of the Associationists. Suppose every one should do, not all the Church counsels, but simply what she commands, enjoins, as of precept, and which every one must do, or fall under her censure, what real evil could remain, or what desirable sociable good would be wanting? There would be no wars, no internal disorders, no wrongs, no outrages, no frauds, or deceptions, and no taking the advantage one of another. There would be no unrelieved poverty, no permanent want of the necessaries or even comforts of life; for the Church makes almsgiving a precept, and commands all her children to remember the poor. There would remain no ruinous competition ; for no one would set a high value upon the goods of this world. The real cause of all the social and industrial evils the Associationists deplore, so far as evils they are, is coveteousness, which is said to be the root of all evil; and coveteousness the Church condemns as a mortal sin. Eradicate coveteousness from the heart, and your reform, so far as desirable, is effected; and it is eradicated, or held in subjection, by every obedient Catholic. Hence, all that is needed is in the Church; let every one submit to her and follow her directions ; nothing more will be wanting. All can submit to her ; for God, in one way or another, gives to every one sufficient grace for that, if it be not voluntarily resisted ; and she herself is the medium through which is communicated all the strength any one needs to do all she commands. The way to destroy the tree of evil is, to lay the axe at the root; and this the Church does. She seeks always to purify the heart, out of which are the issues of life, and she never fails to do it in the case of any one who submits himself to her discipline.

But, you reply, there are evils in Catholic countries, and the result promised is as far from being attained there as elsewhere. This is too strongly expressed. There are evils in Catholic countries, but they are fewer and of a more mitigated character than in other countries, and, moreover, diminish always in proportion as the country is more truly Catholic and more exclusively under Catholic influence. This is evident by contrasting Italy with England, Protestant England with Catholic England, or Spain and Portugal, as they now are, with what they were, when thoroughly Catholic, before they were prostrated by the prevalence of revolutionary and infidel ideas. M. Briancourt virtually admits as much, when he contrasts the present state of things with that which formerly existed, before infidel governments, philosophers, and reformers had detached modern society from the control of the Church. Besides, all in Catholic countries are not good Catholics; and the evils complained of undeniably spring from the acts of those who do not faithfully comply with the requirements of the Church.

If all complied, the evils would be removed. The Church is to be tested, not by the effects of non-compliance, but by the effects of compliance. She is answerable only for those who comply with her demands and follow her directions. She cannot force men against their will to comply; and you would be among the first to cry out against her tyranny, were she even to attempt it. The objection implied in the existence of evils in Catholic countries is, therefore, of no weight. Men who reject the Church, or refuse to obey her, must not complain that she does not make all men good Catholics.

The Church, then, offers an easy and effectual method of removing all real evils, and of securing all that is really good in relation even to our present existence. She offers a feasible and an effectual way of serving our fellow-men,—of acquiring and of giving practical effect to the most unbounded charity. Submit to the Church, follow her directions, and you will need nothing more. You can secure all you desire, so far as wise in your desires, whatever be the form of the government or the social or industrial order under which you live. The internal can be rectified in every state and condition of life; and when the internal is right, you need have no fears for the external. This is a speedy way, and within the power of each individual, without his being obliged to wait for the coöperation of his brethren; for each can individually submit himself at any moment he chooses. It is an effectual way; for the reliance is not on human weakness and instability, but on the infinite and unchangeable God.

Let not our friends scorn this way, because it is old, simple, and easy. God's ways are not ours. David, to slay the giant, chose a simple sling and a smooth stone from the brook, not the armor and sword of the king. The prophet bade the Syrian simply, "Go wash and be clean." God's ways are always foolishness to human pride and human prudence; but whoso enters them finds them leading to life. Let not our friends scorn this way through pride. Others as learned, as philosophic, as high in station, as proud as they, and who once looked upon it with as much distrust and contempt as they can, have, through grace, entered it; and they have found "hidden riches" which they did not look for, and which make all that is promised from Association, multiplied a thousand times into itself, appear poor, mean, and despicable.

SOCIALISM AND THE CHURCH.*

JANUARY, 1849.

THIS handsomely printed volume, has been sent us "from the author," and we can do no less than acknowledge its reception. It is filled with the wild speculations and demoralizing theories hardly to be expected from "a Woman." In a literary point of view, it is beneath criticism, but it bears the marks of some reading, and even of hard, though ill-directed, thinking. Nature has treated the author liberally, and she will have much to answer for. The work could have proceeded only from a strong mind and a corrupt heart.

The work itself pertains to the Socialistic school, and, substantially, to the Fourieristic section of that school. According to it, the human race began its career in ignorance and weakness, and establish a false system of civilization. Modern society, dating from the fall of the Western Roman empire, has been engaged in a continual struggle to throw off that system, and to establish a true system in its place. It has been engaged, thus far, in the work of demolition, which it has finally terminated. It has prepared the ground for true civilization, and the human race now stand waiting, or did stand waiting on the first of

* England the Civilizer; her History developed in its Principles; with Reference to the Civilizational History of Modern Europe, (America inclusive), and with a View to the Dénouement of the Difficulties of the Hour. By a Woman. London. Simpkins, Marshall, & Co. January, 1848. 12mo. pp. 470.

January, 1848, the signal to introduce it, and to put an end for ever to all evils, moral, social, and physical.

The old civilization, now effete, committed the capital error of recognizing religion,—in the language of the author, *superstition*,—government, property, and "the ascendency of the male sex," or family,—for the family cannot subsist without that ascendency;—the new civilization will correct this error, and for religion substitute science; for government, federation; for law, instinct; for property, communal wealth; for family, love; and for the ascendency of the male sex, the administration of women. Consequently, the new civilization is to be a petticoat civilization, in which we must include the human race in those genera which are named after the female, as cows, geese, ducks, hens, &c.

Into the details of this new civilization, or the means by which it is to be introduced and preserved, we need not enter. Some things may be assumed to be settled; if not, the human race can settle nothing, and it is idle to examine the claims of a new theory. If any thing can be settled, it is that the man is the head of the woman,—that she is for him, not he for her; and that religion, government, family, property, are essential elements of all civilization. Without them man must sink below the savage, for in the lowest savage state we find, at least, some reminiscences of them. Any system which proposes their abolition or essential modification is by that fact alone condemned, and proved to deserve no examination. We do the Socialists too much honor when we consent to hear and refute their dreams. We have not at this late day to resettle the basis of society, to seek for unknown truth in religion or politics, in relation to public or domestic, private or social life; we have no new discoveries to make, no important changes to introduce; and all that we need attempt is to acertain the truth which has been known from the beginning, and to conform ourselves to it.

Nevertheless, the work before us is a pregnant sign of the times, and may afford food for much useful reflection to those prepared to digest it. People who attend to their own business, tread the routine their fathers trod, and attempt to discharge in peace and quiet the practical duties of their state, little suspect what is fermenting in the heated brains of this nineteenth century. They know next to nothing of what is going on around them. They look upon the doctrines contained in works like the one before us as the speculations of a few insane dreamers, and are sure that the good sense of mankind will prevent them from spreading, and confine their mischief to the misguided individuals who put them forth. They regard them as too ridiculous, as too absurd, to be believed. They can do no harm, and we need not trouble our heads about them. This is certainly a plausible view of the subject, but, unhappily, there is nothing too ridiculous or too absurd to be believed, if demanded by the dominant spirit or sentiment of an age or country; for what is seen to be demanded by that spirit or sentiment never appears ridiculous or absurd to those who are under its influence.

Nothing, to a rightly instructed mind, is more ridiculous or absurd than the infidelity which so extensively prevailed in the last century, and which under another form prevails equally in this. Yet when the philosophy which necessarily implied it first made its appearance, few comparatively took the alarm, and even learned and sound Churchmen were unable to persuade themselves that there was any serious danger to be apprehended. When the philosophers and literary men went farther, and, developing that philosophy, actually made free with the Scriptures, and even the mysteries of faith, the majority of those who should have seen what was coming paid little attention to them, jested at the incipient incredulity with great good humor, felt sure that no considerable number of persons would proceed so far as to deny not only the Church, but the very existence of God, and flattered themselves that the infidelity which was manifest would prove only a temporary fashion, a momentary caprice, which would soon become weary of itself, and evaporate. Nevertheless, all the while, the age was virtually infidel, and thousands of those who had persisted in believing there was no danger were themselves but shortly after driven into exile, or brought to the guillotine by its representatives. The same thing occurs now in regard to Socialism. The great body of those who have faith and sound principles look upon it as the dream of a few isolated individuals, as undeserving a moment's attention, and think it a waste of time and breath even to caution the public against it. Yet in one form or other it has already taken possession of the age, has armed itself for battle, made the streets of Paris, Berlin, Frankfort, Vienna, and other cities, run with blood, and convulsed nearly the whole civilized world. It is organized all through Europe and the United States; scarcely a book, a tract, or a newspaper is issued from a constantly teeming press, that does not favor it, and there is scarcely any thing else going that can raise a shout of applause from the people; and yet we are told, even by grave men, that is a matter which need excite no apprehension.

Nor is this the worst aspect of the case. Not a few of those who shrink with horror from Socialism, as drawn out and set forth by its avowed advocates, do themselves, unconsciously, adopt and defend the very principles of which it is only the logical development; nay, not only adopt and defend those principles, but denounce, as behind their age, as the enemies of the people, those who call them in question. Have we not ourselves been so denounced? If you doubt it, read the criticisms of *The Boston Pilot* on our review of Padre Ventura's *Oration*, or *The New York Commercial Advertiser's* notice of our censure of the Italian Liberals for their persecution of the Jesuits. Of course, these papers have no authority of their own, but they echo public opinion, and tell, as well as straws which way the wind blows. If the public condemned in no measured terms the "horrible doctrines" we a few years since put forth in an *Essay on the Laboring Classes*, it has not condemned, but through some of its leading organs commended, an article on *The Distribution of Property*, published in *The North American Review* for July, 1848, the most conservative periodical, except our own, in the country,—which defends at length, and with more ability than we ordinarily expect in that Journal, the very principles from which we logically derive them. We hold now in utter detestation the doctrines of the Essay referred to and which raised a terrible clamor against us throughout the country; but we proved, in our defence, and no one has yet, to our knowledge, ventured to maintain the contrary, that those doctrines were only legitimate conclusions from the Protestant and democratic premises held by the great body of our countrymen, and by what they do and must regard as the more enlightened portion of mankind. In fact, a very common objection to us was, that we were ahead of the age, that is, drew the conclusions before the people were ready to receive them. We did but reason logically from the principles we had imbibed from public opinion, from general literature, and the practical teachings of those we had been accustomed from our childhood to hear mentioned with honor, and had been required to revere, —principles, which we had never heard questioned, and never thought of questioning, till we undertook to explain to ourselves the universal outcry which had been raised against us. As we found our countrymen saying two and two, we thought we might innocently add, two and two *make four*, and complete the proposition. We were wrong, not in our logic, but in our principles. We had trusted the age; we had confided in its maxims, and received them as axioms. As the mists cleared away, as the gloss of novelty wore off, and the excitement of self-defence subsided, we saw the horrible nature of the doctrines we had put forth, and recoiled, not only from them, but from the principles of which they were the necessary logical development. But the age has not followed our example. The great body of the people continue to adhere to those principles, and will not suffer them to be questioned.

No doubt, the majority of numbers are as yet unprepared to adopt Socialism as developed by Owen, Fourier, Saint-Simon, Cabet, Proudhon, or by "A Woman" in the work before us; but no man who has studied the age can, if he have any tolerable powers of generalization, doubt that Socialistic principles are those now all but universally adopted. They are at the bottom of nearly all hearts, and at work in nearly all minds; and just in proportion as men acquire courage enough to say not only two and two, two and two, but that two and two *make four*, the age rushes to their practical realization,—accepts their logical developments, however horrible, however impious. There is an invincible logic in society which pushes it to the realization of the last consequences of its principles. In vain do moderate men cry out against carrying matters to extremes; in vain do practical men appeal to common sense; in vain do brave men rush before the movement and with their bodies attempt to interpose a barrier to its onward progress. Society no more —nay, less—than individuals recoils from the conclusions which follow logically from premises it holds to be sound and well established. It draws practically those conclusions, with a terrible earnestness, and a despotism that scorns every limitation. On it moves, heedless of what or of whom it may crush beneath the wheels of its ponderous car. Woe to him who seeks to stay its movement! Social evils grow as it advances, and these it lays to the charge of those who would hold it back, and result, it maintains, only from the fact that it has not yet reached its goal. The reform is not carried far enough. Put on more steam, carry it farther, carry it farther, is the loud cry it raises.

We see this in the Protestant Reformation. The Reformers did not fulfil their promises, did not secure to the people the good they had led them to expect. Everybody saw this, everybody felt it; for everybody found himself distracted and unsatisfied. What was the inference drawn? That the Reformers had erred in principle, and that the Reformation could not secure the good promised? By no means. The people had accepted its principle. The Reform, said they, is good, is just and true; but it has not been carried far enough; the Reformers were only half reformed; they stopped short of the mark. The Reform must not stop with Luther and Calvin; we must carry it farther. This is what the children of the Reformation said, as we all know; and they have been from the first struggling to carry it farther and farther, and have at length carried it to the borders, if not into the regions, of nihility. The evils remain, nay, every day increase, and each day a new party rises up in the bosom of the most advanced sect, and demands a further advance.

In the political world we see the same thing. Revolution has followed revolution, and no political reform goes far enough to satisfy its friends. In the last century, revolutions were *political*, and had for their object the establishment of political equality, or democracy. It was soon seen that political equality answers no purpose where there is *social* inequality. A writer, who could speak with as much authority on this subject as any of our contemporaries, thus expressed himself in 1841:—

"But democracy as a form of government, *political* democracy, as we call it, could not be the term of popular aspiration. Regarded in itself, without reference to any thing ulterior, it is no better than the aristocratic form of government, or even the monarchical. Universal suffrage and eligibility, the expression of perfect equality before the state, and which with us are nearly realized, unless viewed as means to an end, are not worth contending for. What avails it, that all men are equal before the state, if they must stop there? If under a democracy, aside from mere politics, men may be as unequal in their social condition as under other forms of government, wherein consists the boasted advantages of your democracy? Is all possible good summed up in suffrage and eligibility? Is the millennium realized, when every man may vote and be voted for? Yet this is all that political democracy, reduced to its simplest elements, proposes. Political democracy, then, can never satisfy the popular mind. This democracy is only one step—a necessary step —in its progress. Having realized equality before the state, the popular mind passes naturally to equality before society. It seeks and accepts *political* democracy only as a means to *social* democracy; and it cannot fail to attempt to realize equality in men's social condition, when it has once realized equality in their political condition."—*The Boston Quarterly Review*, January, 1841, pp. 113, 114.

Political democracy leaves the principal social evils unredressed, and the causes which led the reform thus far remain in all their force to carry it still farther. Hence we see in the present century the same party which in the last demanded political democracy attempting throughout nearly the whole civilized world a series of revolutions in favor of social democracy. The leaders in the late French Revolution tell you that it was a social revolution they sought, and that it was this fact which distinguished it from the Revolution of 1789. In Italy and Germany two revolutions are going on at once, a political revolution and a social revolution. Young Italy is socialistic; so is Young Germany; and it was its socialistic character that gave to the movement of Ronge and his associates its significance and its moderate success. The race, modern philosophers tell us, is progressive, and in a certain sense we concede it. It tends invariably to reach the end implied in the principles it adopts or the impulse it has received, and that tendency is never self-arrested. Its progress towards that end is irresistible; and when it happens to be downward, as at present, it is fearfully rapid, and becomes more fearfully rapid in proportion to the distance it decends.

The only possible remedy is, not declamation against the horrible results, the pernicious conclusions, at which the popular mind arrives,—the resource of weak men,—but the correction of the popular premises and recalling the people to sound first principles. Once concede that even political equality is a good, an object worth seeking, you must concede that social equality is also a good; and social equality is necessarily the annihilation of religion, government, property, and family. The same principle which would justify the Moderate Republicans of France in dethroning the king would justify M. Proudhon in making war on property, declaring every rich man a robber, and seeking to exterminate the *bourgeoisie*, as these have already exterminated the nobility. There is no stopping-place between legitimacy—whether monarchical or republican legitimacy— and the most ultra Socialism. Once in the career of political reform,—we say *political*, not *administrative*, reform,—we are pledged to pursue it to its last results. We are miserable cowards, or worse, if we shrink from the legitimate deductions from our own premises. There is not a meaner sin than the sin of inconsequence,—a sin against our own rational nature which distinguishes us from the mere animal world. If we adopt the Socialistic premises, we must go on with the Socialists in their career of destruction; nay, we shall be compelled to do so, or strew the battle-field with our dead bodies. If we recoil from the Socialistic conclusions, we must reëxamine our own premises, and reject distinctly, unreservedly, and heroically every Socialistic principle we may have unwittingly adopted, every Socialistic tendency we may have unintentionally cherished.

The people, it is well known, do not discriminate, do not perceive, until it is too late, the real nature and tendency of their principles. They mix up truth and falsehood, and can hardly ever be made to distinguish the one from the other. They adopt principles which appear to them sound and wholesome, and which under a certain aspect are so, and, unconscious of aiming at what is destructive, they place no confidence in any who tell them they expose themselves to danger. They see no connection between their principles and the conclusions against which we warn them, and which they at present, as well as we, perhaps view with horror; they therefore conclude that the connection we assert is purely imaginary, that we ourselves are deceived, or have some sinister purpose in asserting it; that we are wedded to the past, in love with old abuses, because, perhaps, we profit, or hope to profit, by them; that we do not understand our age, are narrow and contracted in our views, with no love or respect for the poorest and most numerous class. In a word, they set us down as rank conservatives or aristocrats. No age ever comprehends itself, and the people, following its dominant spirit, can never give an account of their own principles. They never trace them out to their last results, and are unable to follow the chain of reasoning by which horrible consequences are linked to premises which appear to them innocent. They never see whither they are going. Democratic philosophers themselves tell us as much, and defend their doctrine on the ground that the people are directed by divine instincts and obey a wisdom which is not their own. To this effect we may quote the writer already cited, and who, on this point, was among the more moderate of his class. In an article on *Philosophy and Common Sense*, which had the honor to be commended by Victor Cousin, he says :—

"Philosophy is not needed by the masses; but they who separate themselves from the masses, and who believe that the masses are entirely dependent on them for truth and virtue, need it, in order to bring them back and bind them again to universal Humanity. And they need it now, and in this country, perhaps, as much as ever. The world is filled with commotions. The massess are heaving and rolling, like a mighty river, swollen with recent rains, and snows dissolving on the mountains, onward to a distant and unknown ocean. There are those among us, who stand awe-struck, who stand amazed. What means this heaving and onward rolling? Whither tend these mighty masses of human beings? Will they sweep away every fixture, every house and barn, every mark of civilization? Where will they end? In what will they end? Shall we rush before them and attempt to stay their progress? Or shall we fall into their ranks and on with them to their goal? 'Fall into their ranks; be not afraid; be not startled; *a divine instinct guides and moves onward that heaving and rolling mass;* and lawless and destructive as it may seem to you, ye onlookers, it is normal and holy, pursuing a straight and harmless direction on to the union of Man with God.' So answers philosophy, and this is its glory. The friends of Humanity need philosophy, as the means of legitimating the cause of the people, of proving that it is the right, and the duty, of every man to bind himself to that cause, and to maintain it in good report and in evil report, in life and in death. They need it, that they may prove to these conservatives, who are frightened almost out of their wits at the movements of the masses, and who are denouncing them in no measured terms, that these movements are from God, and that they who war against them are warring against truth, duty, God, and Humanity. They need it, that they may no longer be obliged to make apologies for their devotion to the masses, their democratic sympathies and tendencies. They who are persecuted for righteousness' sake, who are loaded with reproach for their fidelity to truth and duty, who are all but cast out of the pale of Humanity, because they see, love, and pursue Humanity's true interests,—they need it, that they may comprehend the cause of the opposition they meet, forgive their enemies, silence the gainsayer, and give to him that asks it a reason for the hope that is in them. The friends of progress, here and everywhere, need it, that, having vindicated, legitimated progress, as philosophers, they may go into the saloons, the universities, the halls of legislation, the pulpit, and abroad among the people, and preach it, with the dignity and the authority of the prophet."—*The Boston Quarterly Review*, January, 1838, pp. 104, 105.

It is necessary to take this ground, or give up democracy, which Mr. Bancroft defines "Eternal Justice ruling through the people," as wholly indefensible; for it cannot be denied that popular movements are blind, and that in them the people are borne onward whither they see not, and by a force they comprehend not. Hence it is easy to understand, that, retaining in their memories traces of former instructions, they may recoil with horror from the last consequences of Socialism, and yet be intent only on developing Socialistic tendencies, and crushing all opposition to them.

Socialism is, moreover, presented in a form admirably adapted to deceive the people, and to secure their support. It comes in Christian guise, and seeks to express itself in the language of the Gospel. Men whom this age delights to honor have called our blessed Lord "the Father of Democracy," and not few or insignificant are those who tell us that he was "the first Socialist." In this country, the late Dr. Channing took the lead in reducing the Gospel to Socialism; and in France, the now fallen Abbé de la Mennais, condemned by Gregory the Sixteenth, of immortal memory, was the first, we believe, who labored to establish the identity of Socialism and Christianity. We gave in another place, in 1840, a brief notice of his views on this point, which it may not be uninstructive to reproduce:

" The most remarkable feature in the Abbé de la Mennais's doctrine of liberty is its connection with religion. It is well known, that for some time the friends of freedom in Europe have been opposed to the Church, and in general to all religion. The privileged orders have also taken great pains to make it widely believed, that religion requires the support of existing abuses, and that no one can contend for social meliorations without falling into infidelity. This has created a false issue, one which M. de la Mennais rejects. He has endeavored, and with signal success, to show that there is no discrepancy between religion and liberty; nay, more, that Christianity offers a solid foundation for the broadest freedom, and that, in order to be true to its spirit, its friends must labor with all their might to restore to the people their rights, and to correct all social abuses. He proves that all men are equal before God, and therefore equal one to another. All men have one Father, and are therefore brethren, and ought to treat one another as brothers. This is the Christian law. This law is violated, whenever distinction of races is recognized; whenever one man is clothed with authority over his equals; whenever one man, or a number of men, are invested with certain privileges, which are not shared equally by the whole. As this is the case everywhere, everywhere therefore is the Christian law violated. Everywhere therefore is there suffering, lamentation. The people everywhere groan and travail in pain, sighing to be delivered from their bondage into the glorious liberty of the sons of God. To this deliverance the people have a right. For it every Christian should contend; and they wrong their brethren, deny Christianity, and blaspheme God, who oppose it.

"This is a new doctrine in France. It is something new since the days of the *philosophes*, to undertake to show that Christianity is the religion which favors not kings and privileged orders, but the people, the poor and needy, the wronged and downtrodden. Hitherto the few have made the many submit to the grievous burdens under which they groaned, by representing it as irreligious to attempt to remove them. They have enlisted the clergy on their side, and made religion, the very essence of which is justice and love, contribute to the support of oppression. They have deterred the pious from seeking to better their condition, by denouncing all who seek the melioration of society as infidels. But the Abbé has put a stop to this unhallowed proceeding. He has nobly vindicated religion and the people. He has turned the tables upon the people's masters, and denounced their masters, not the people, as infidels. He has enlisted religion on the side of freedom; recalled that long

forgotten Gospel, which was glad tidings to the poor, and dared follow the example of Jesus, whom the common people heard gladly, and whom the people's masters crucified between two thieves. He speaks out for freedom, the broadest freedom, not in the tones of the infidel scoffer, but in the name of God, Christ, and man, and with the authority of a prophet. His 'Words of a Believer' has had no parallel since the days of Jeremiah. It is at once a prophecy, a curse, a hymn, fraught with deep, terrible, and joyful meaning. It is the doom of the tyrant, and the jubilee-shout of the oppressed. We know of no work in which the true spirit of Christianity is more faithfully represented. It proclaims, 'Blessed are the poor, for theirs is the kingdom of heaven;' and woe unto the rich oppressor, the royal spoiler, the Scribes and Pharisees, hypocrites, who bind heavy burdens and lay them on men's shoulders, while they themselves will not move them with one of their fingers."
—*The Boston Quarterly Review*, January, 1840, pp. 117, 119.

It may not be amiss to place by the side of this bold commendation of the *Words of a Believer*, the judgment pronounced upon that book and its doctrines by the Sovereign Pontiff, in his Encyclical Letter, dated June, 1834, which we find in the *Pièces Justificatives*, published by M. de la Mennais at the end of his volume entitled, *Affaires de Rome*, Bruxelles, 1837 :

" Horruimus sane, venerabiles Fratres, vel ex primo oculorum obtutu, auctorisque cæcitatem miserati intelleximus, quonam scientia prorumpat, quæ non secundum Deum sit, sed secundum mundi elementa. Enimvero contra fidem sua illa declaratione solemniter datam, captiosissimis ipse ut plurimum verborum, fictionumque involucris oppugnandam, evertendamque suscepit catholicam doctrinam, quam memoratis nostris litteris,* tum de debita erga potestates subjectione, tum de arcenda a populis exitiosa *indifferentismi* contagione, deque frenis injiciendis evaganti opinionum sermonumque licentiæ, tum demum de damnanda omnimodo conscientiæ libertate, teterrimaque societatum, vel ex cujuscumque falsæ religionis cultoribus, in sacræ et publicæ rei perniciem conflatarum conspiratione, pro auctoritate humilitati nostræ tradita definivimus.

"Refugit sane animus ea perlegere, quibus ibidem auctor vinculum quodlibet fidelitatis subjectionisque erga principes

* *Epistola Encyclica*, August 15, 1832.

disrumpere conatur, face undequaque perduellionis immissa, qua publici ordinis clades magistratuum contemptus, legum infractio grassetur, omniaque, et sacræ, et civilis potestatis elementa convellantur. Hinc novo et iniquo commento potestatem principum, veluti divinæ legi infestam, imo *opus peccati* et *Satanæ potestatem* in calumniæ portentum traducit, præsidibusque sacrorum easdem, ac imperantibus turpitudinis notas inurit ob criminum molitionumque fœdus, quo eos somniat inter se adversus populorum jura conjunctos. Neque tanto hoc ausu contentus omnigenam insuper opinionum, sermonum, conscientiæque libertatem obtrudit militibusque ad eam *a tyrannide*, ut ait, liberandam dimicaturis fausta omnia ac felicia comprecatur, cœtus ac consociationes furiali æstu ex universo qua patet Orbe advocat, et in tam nefaria consilia urgens atque instans compellit, ut eo etiam ex capite monita præscriptaque nostra proculcata ab ipso sentiamus.

" Piget cuncta hic recensere, quæ pessimo hoc impietatis et audaciæ fœtu ad divina humanaque omnia perturbanda congeruntur. Sed illud præsertim indignationem excitat, religionique plane intolerandum est, divinas præscriptiones tantis erroribus adserendis ab auctore afferri, et incautis venditari, eumque ad populos lege obedientiæ solvendos, perindè ac si a Deo missus et inspiratus esset, postquam in sacratissimo Trinitatis augustæ nomine præfatus est, Sacras Scripturas ubique obtendere, ipsarumque verba, quæ verba Dei sunt, ad prava hujuscemodi deliramenta inculcanda callide audacterque detorquere, quo fidentius, uti inquiebat S. Bernardus, *pro luce tenebras offundat, et pro melle vel potius in melle venenum propinet, novum cudens populis Evangelium, aliudque ponens fundamentum præter id quod positum est.*

" Verum tantam hanc sanæ doctrinæ illatam perniciem silentio dissimulare ab eo vetamur, qui speculatores nos posuit in Israel, ut de errore illos moneamus, quos Auctor et consummator fidei Jesus nostræ curæ concredidit.

" Quare auditis nonnullis ex venerabilibus fratribus nostris S. R. E. cardinalibus, motu proprio, et ex certâ scientia, deque Apostolicæ potestatis plenitudine memoratum librum, cui titulus : *Paroles d'un Croyant*, quo per impium Verbi Dei abusum populi corrumpuntur ad omnis ordinis publici vincula dissolveda, ad utramque auctoritatem, labefactandam, ad seditiones in imperiis, tumultus, rebellionesque excitandas, fovendas, roborandas, librum ideo propositiones respective falsas, calumniosas, temerarias, inducentes in anarchiam, contrarias Verbo Dei, impias, scandalosas, erroneas jam ab Ecclesia præsertim in Valdensibus, Wiclefitis, Hussitis, aliisque id generis hæreticis damnatas continentem, reprobamus, damnamus, ac pro reprobato et damnato in perpetuum haberi volumus, atque decernimus.

"Vestrum nunc erit, venerabiles Fratres, nostris hisce mandatis, quæ rei et sacræ et civilis salus et incolumitas, necessario efflagitat, omni contentioni obsecundare, ne scriptum istius modi e latebris ad exitium emissum eò fiat perniciosius, quo magis vesanæ novitatis libidini velificatur, et latè ut cancer serpit in populis. Muneris vestris sit, urgere sanam de tanto hoc negotio doctrinam, vafritiamque novatorum patefacere, acriusque pro Christiani Gregis custodia vigilare, ut studium religionis, pietas actionum, pax publica floreant et augeantur feliciter. Id sane a vestra fide, et ab impensa vestra pro communi bono instantia fidenter operimur, ut, eo juvante qui pater est luminum, gratulemur (dicimus cum S. Cypriano) *fuisse intellectum errorem, et retusum, et ideo prostratum, quia agnitum, atque detectum.*"—pp. 56–62.

We hope the judgment of the Holy Father will weigh as much with our readers as that of the Editor of *The Boston Quarterly Review*. We had for a time the unenviable honor of being ranked ourselves among those who attempted here and elsewhere to translate Christianity into Socialism. There are, perhaps, yet living, persons who remember the zeal and perseverance with which we preached, in the name of the Gospel, the most damnable radicalism. We cite a few paragraphs from an essay entitled *Democracy of Christianity*, published in *The Boston Quarterly Review*, October, 1838.

"In a civil and political sense, we cannot discover that the Church regards Christianity in any other light than that of a curb, a bit, a restraint, a means by which the people may be kept in order and in submission to their masters. The clergy, under this point of view, are a sort of constabulatory force at the service of the police, and meeting-houses a substitute for police offices, houses of correction, and penitentiaries. Far be it from us to deny the great worth of Christianity in this respect. We acknowledge the virtues of the Church, as an agent of the police; but we hope we may be allowed to believe that Christianity requires the Church to possess other and far higher virtues. It should not merely keep the people in subjection to an order of things which is, but fire them with the spirit and the energy to create a social order, to which it shall need no constabulatory force, lay or clerical, to make the millions submissive.

"*But if the Church, both here and in Europe, does not desert the cause of Absolutism, and make common cause with the people, its doom is sealed.* Its union with the cause of Liberty is the only thing which can save it. The party of the people, the democracy throughout the civilized world, is every day increasing in numbers and in power. It is already too strong to be defeated. Popes may issue their bulls against it; bishops may denounce it; priests may slander its apostles, and appeal to the superstition of the multitude; kings and nobilities may collect their forces and bribe or dragoon; but in vain; IT IS TOO LATE. Democracy has become a power, and sweeps on resistless as one of the great agents of Nature. Absolute monarchs must be swept away before it. They will fail in their mad attempt to arrest the progress of the people, and to roll back the tide of civilization. They will be prostrated in the dust, and rise no more for ever. Whoever or whatever leagues with them must take their fate. If the Altar be supported on the Throne, and the Church joined to the Palace, both must fall together. Would the Church could see this in time to avert the sad catastrophe! It is a melancholy thing to reflect on the ruin of that majestic temple which has stood so long, over which so many ages have passed, on which so many storms have beaten, and in which so many human hearts have found shelter, solace, and heaven. It is melancholy to reflect on the condition of the people deprived of all forms of worship, and with no altar on which to offer the heart's incense to God the Father. Yet assuredly churchless, altarless, with no form or shadow of worship will the people be, if the Church continue its league with Absolutism. The people have sworn deep in their hearts, that they will be free. They pursue freedom as a Divinity, and freedom they will have,—with the Church if it may be, without the Church if it must be. God grant that they who profess to be his especial servants may be cured of their madness in season to save the Altar!

"The people almost universally identify Christianity with the Church. They cannot reject the Church without seeming to themselves to be rejecting Christianity, and therefore not without regarding themselves as infidels. Will the clergy consent to drive the people into infidelity? Can they not discern the signs of the times? Will they persist in maintaining social doctrines more abhorrent to the awakening instincts of the people than atheism itself? A people, regarding itself as infidel, is in the worst plight possible to pursue the work of social regeneration. It is then deprived of the hallowed and hallowing influence and guidance of the religious sentiment; and it can hardly fail to become disorderly in the pursuit of order, and to find license instead of liberty, and anarchy instead of a popular government. For its own sake, then, and for the sake of liberty also, the Church should break its league with the despots and join with the people, and give them its purifying and ennobling influence.

"The Church must do this or die. Already is it losing its hold on the hearts of the people. Everywhere is there complaint of men's want of interest in religion; everywhere is there need of most extraordinary efforts, and various and powerful machinery, to bring people into the Church, and few are brought in, save women and children. The pulpit has ceased to be a power. Its voice no longer charms or kindles. It finds no echo in the universal heart. Sermons are thought to be dull and vapid; and when they call forth applause, it is the preacher that wins it, not the cause he pleads. Are we at any loss to account for this? The old doctrines, the old maxims, the old exhortations, the old topics of discussion, which the clergy judge it their duty to reproduce, are not those which now most interest the people. The dominant sentiment of the people is not what it was. Once it was thought that the earth was smitten with a curse from God, and happiness was no more to be looked for *on* it than *from* it. Then all thoughts turned to another world, and the chief inquiry was, how to secure it. To save the soul from hell hearafter was then the one thing needful; and the preacher, who could show how that was to be done and heaven secured, was sure to be listened to. It is different now. Men think less of escaping hell, have less fear of the Devil, more faith in the possibility of improving their earthly condition, and are more in earnest to extinguish the fires of that hell which has been burning here ever since the fall. The Church must conform to the new state of things. She cannot bring back the past. Yesterday never returns. If she would have her voice responded to, she must speak in tones that shall harmonize with the dominant sentiment of the age. *She must preach democracy,* and then will she wake an echo in every heart, and call forth a response from the depths of the universal soul of Humanity. *She can speak with power only when she speaks to the dominant sentiment, and command love and obedience only when she commands that which the people feel, for the time at least, to be the one thing needful.*

"In calling upon the Church, by which term we mean especially the clergy of all communions, to associate with the democracy, and to labor for the realization of that equality towards which the people are everywhere tending, we seem to ourselves to be merely recalling the Church to Christianity. We freely acknowledge the past services of the Church. She has done much, and done nobly. She has protected the friendless, fed the orphan, raised up the bowed-down, and delivered him who was ready to perish. She has tamed the ruthless barbarian, infused into his heart the sentiment of chaste love, and warmed him with admiration for the generous and humane; she has made kings and potentates, who trample on their brethren without remorse, and lord it without scruple over God's heritage, feel that there is a power above them, and that throne and diadem, sceptre and dominion, shall avail them naught in presence of the King of kings, before whom they must one day stand and be judged, as well as the meanest of their slaves; she has done a thousand times over more good for the human race than we have space or ability to relate, and blessings on her memory! eternal gratitude to God for that august assembly of saints, martyrs, and heroes, which she has nourished in her bosom, and sent forth to teach the world, by their lives, the divinity there is in man, one day to be awakened and called forth in its infinite beauty and omnipotent energy!

"But while we say this, we feel that the Church now, in both its Catholic and Protestant divisions, is unconscious of its mission, and has become false to its great Founder. Jesus was, under a political and social aspect, *the prophet of the democracy.* He came to the poor and afflicted, to the wronged and the outraged, to the masses, the downtrodden millions; and he spoke to them as a brother, in the tones of an infinite love, an infinite compassion, while he thundered the rebukes of Heaven against their oppressors. 'Ye serpents, ye generation of vipers,' says he to the people's masters, 'how can ye escape the damnation of hell?' His word was with power. Ay, was it, because he spoke to the common soul, because he spoke out for outraged Humanity, and because he did not fear to speak to the great, the renowned, the rich, the boastingly religious, in terms of terrible plainness and severity. Before his piercing glance earthborn distinctions vanish, and kings and princes, scribes and Pharisees, chief priests and elders, sink down below the meanest fisherman, or the vilest slave, and become less worthy to enter the kingdom of heaven than publicans and harlots. Their robes and widened phylacteries, their loud pretentions, their wealth, rank, refinement, influence, do not deceive him. He sees the hollow heart within them, the whited sepulchres they are, full of dead men's bones and all manner of uncleanness, vessels merely washed on the outside, all filthy within, and he denounces them in terms too terrible to be repeated. Here was the secret of his power. The great, the honored, the respectable, the aristocracy, social or religious, beheld in him a fearful denouncer of their oppressions, a ruthless unveiler of their hidden deformity; while the poor, the 'common people,' saw in him a friend, an advocate, a protector, ay, an avenger.

"Jesus declared that the spirit of the Lord was upon him, because he was anointed to preach the Gospel to the poor; and he gave, when asked by the disciples of John, the fact, that the Gospel was preached to the poor, as one of the principal proofs of his Messiahship. He chose his disciples from the lowest ranks of his countrymen; and they were the common people who heard him gladly. Was he not a prophet from God to the masses? Was he a prophet to them merely because he prepared the way for their salvation hereafter? Say it not. The earth he came to bless; on the earth he came to establish a kingdom; and it was said of him that he should not fail nor be discouraged till he had set judgment,—justice,—in the earth and the isles waited for his law. He was to bring forth victory unto truth. In his days the earth was to be blest; under his reign all the nations were to be at peace; the sword was to be beaten into the ploughshare and the spear into the pruning-hook; and war was to be no more. The wolf and the lamb were to lie down together, and they were not to hurt or destroy in all the holy mountain of the Lord. The wilderness was to rejoice and blossom as the rose, and the solitary place was to be glad. Every man was to sit under his *own* vine and fig-tree, with none to molest or to make afraid. On the earth was he to found a new order of things, to bring round the blissful ages, and to give to renovated man a fortaste of heaven. It was here, then, the millions were to be blessed with a heaven, as well as hereafter." *—pp. 464–469.

* The Christian reader will not fail to perceive that the writer here, in his blindness, takes precisely the view which was taken by the carnal Jews, for which they were cursed. Truly, there is nothing new

The general doctrine asserted in this last extract was not peculiar to the writer cited. He was never remarkable for his originality. He was remarkable, if for any thing, only for the care with which he studied the movement party of our times, seized its great principles, and abandoned himself to their direction. He accepted that party, and followed it, with a courage and perseverance worthy of a better cause. The views he put forth were those of his party. They were not peculiar to him then, and they are far less so now. During the last ten or twelve years they have made fearful progress, both at home and abroad. Affecting to be Christian, their advocates invoke the name of Jesus and appeal to the holy Scriptures, the texts of which, with a perverse ingenuity, they accommodate to their Socialistic purpose. May Almighty God forgive us the share we had in propagating what we called the *Democracy of Christianity!* We have nothing to palliate our offence or to hide our shame; for, if we knew no better at the time, we might have known better, and our ignorance was culpable. All we can say is, we followed the dominant sentiment of the age, which is a poor excuse for one who professed to be a preacher of the Gospel.

Veiling itself under Christian forms, attempting to distinguish

under the sun. The old carnal Jews misinterpreted the prophecies; they expected in the Messiah that was to come a temporal prince, who was to found a temporal kingdom, for the temporal happiness of mankind. They rejected and crucified our Saviour, because he did not come as such a prince, because he proposed a spiritual kingdom, and the spiritual welfare of his subjects. The *Christian* Socialists do the same. They interpret the promises precisely as they were interpreted by the carnal Jews,—expect from our Lord, like them, a temporal kingdom, and precisely the same order of prosperity,—and reject the Church as antichristian, precisely because she, like her Master, proposes for her children the virtues and happiness of the spiritual order. So the progress of the age consists solely in bringing its master spirits round to the point of view of the carnal Jews, to join with them in crucifying their God between two thieves! The sects will generally be found to be wedded to the carnal just in proportion as they fancy they have become spiritual.

between Christianity and the Church, claiming for itself the authority and immense popularity of the Gospel, denouncing Christianity in the name of Christianity, discarding the Bible in the name of the Bible, and defying God in the name of God, Socialism conceals from the undiscriminating multitude its true character, and, appealing to the dominant sentiment of the age and to some of our strongest natural inclinations and passions, it asserts itself with terrific power, and rolls on in its career of devastation and death with a force that human beings, in themselves, are impotent to resist. Men are assimilated to it by all the power of their own nature, and by all their reverence for religion. Their very faith and charity are perverted, and their noblest sympathies and their sublimest hopes are made subservient to their basest passions and their most grovelling propensities. Here is the secret of the strength of Socialism, and here, is the principal source of its danger.

The open denial of Christianity is not now to be dreaded; the incredulity of the last century is now in bad taste, and can work only under disguise. All the particular heresies which human pride or human perversity could invent are now effete or unfashionable. Every article in the Creed has been successively denied, and the work of denial can go no farther. The attempt to found a new sect on the denial of any particular article of faith would now only cover its authors with ridicule. The age laughs at Protestantism, and scorns sectarism. The spirit that works in the children of disobedience must, therefore, affect to be Christian, more Christian than Christianity itself, and not only Christian, but *Catholic*. It can manifest itself now, and gain friends, only by acknowledging the Church and all Catholic symbols, and substituting for the divine and heavenly sense in which they have hitherto been understood a human and earthly sense. Hence the religious character which Socialism attempts to wear. It rejects in name no Catholic symbol; it only rejects the Catholic sense. If it finds fault with the actual Church, it is because she is not truly Catholic, does not understand herself, does not comprehend the profound sense of her own doctrines, fails to seize and expound the true Christian idea as it lay in the mind of Jesus, and as this enlightened age is prepared to receive it. The Christian symbol needs a new and a more Catholic interpretation, adapted to our stage in universal progress. Where the old interpretation uses the words God, Church, and Heaven, you must understand Humanity, Society, and Earth; you will then have the true Christian idea, and bring the Gospel down to the order of nature and within the scope of human reason. But while you put the human and earthly sense upon the old Catholic words, be careful and retain the words themselves. By taking care to do this, you can secure the support of the adherents of Christianity, who, if they meet their old familiar terms, will not miss their old, familiar ideas; and thus you will be able to reconcile the old Catholic world and the new, and to go on with Humanity in her triumphant progress through the ages.

Since it professes to be Christian, and really denies the faith, Socialism is a heresy; and since by its interpretation it eviscerates the Catholic system of its entire meaning, it is the *résumé* of all the particular heresies which ever have been or can be. The ingenuity of men, aided by the great Enemy of souls, can invent no further heresy. All possible heresies are here summed up and actualized in one universal heresy, on which the age is proceeding with all possible haste to erect a counterfeit Catholicity for the reception and worship of Antichrist as soon as he shall appear in person.

"Descend," says De la Mennais, "to the bottom of things, and disengage from the wavering thoughts, vain and fleeting opinions, accidentally mingled with it, the powerful principle which, without interruption, ferments in the bosom of society, and what find you but Christianity itself? What is it the people wish, what is it they claim, with a perseverance that never tires, and an ardor that nothing can damp? Is it not the abolition of the reign of force, in order to substitute that of intelligence and right? Is it not the effective recognition and social realization of equality, inseparable from liberty, the necessary condition and essential form of which, in the organization of the state, is election, the first basis of the Christian community.

"What, again, do the people wish? What do they demand? The amelioration of the lot of the masses, everywhere so full of suffering; laws for the protection of labor, whence may result a more equitable distribution of the general wealth; that the few shall no longer exercise an exclusive influence for their own profit in the administration of the interests of all; that a legislation which has no bounds, the everlasting refuge of privilege, which it in vain attempts to disguise under lying names, shall no longer, on every side, drive the poor back into their misery; that the goods, destined by the Heavenly Father for all his children, shall become accessible to all; that human fraternity shall cease to be a mockery, and a word without meaning. In short, suscitated by God to pronounce the final judgment upon the old social order, they have summoned it to appear, and recalling the ages which have crumbled away, they have said to it, 'I was hungry, and ye gave me not to eat; I was thirsty, and ye gave me not to drink; I was a stranger, and ye took me not in; naked, and ye clothed me not; sick and in prison, and ye did not visit me.' I interrogate you on the law. Respond. And the old social order is silent, for it has nothing to answer; and it raises its hand against the people whom God has appointed to judge it. But what can it do against the people, and against God? Its doom is registered on high, and it will not be able to efface it with the blood which, for a brief period, it is permitted to shed.

"We cannot, then, but recognize in what is passing under our eyes the action of *the Christian principle*, which, having for long ages presided almost exclusively over individual life, seeks now to produce itself under a more general and perfect form, to incarnate itself, so to speak, in social institutions,—the second phase of its development, of which only the first labor as yet appears. *Something instinctive and irresistible pushes the people in this direction.* The few have taken possession of the earth; they have taken possession of it by wresting from all others even the smallest part of the common heritage; and the people will that men live as brothers according to the Divine commandment. They battle for justice and charity; they battle for the doctrine which Jesus Christ came to preach to the world, and which will save it in spite of the powers of the world."—*Affaires de Rome*, pp. 319–321.

This is as artful as it is bold. It wears a pious aspect, it has divine words on its lips, and almost unction in its speech. It is not easy for the unlearned to detect its fallacy, and the great body of the people are prepared to receive it as Christian truth. We cannot deny it without seeming to them to be warring against the true interests of society, and also against the Gospel of our Lord. Never was heresy more subtle, more adroit, better fitted for success. How skilfully it flatters the people? It is said, the saints shall judge the world. By the change of a word, the people are transformed into saints, and invested with the saintly character and office. How adroitly, too, it appeals to the people's envy and hatred of their superiors, and to their love of the world, without shocking their orthodoxy or wounding their piety! Surely Satan has here, in Socialism, done his best, almost outdone himself, and would, if it were possible, deceive the very elect, so that no flesh should be saved.

What we have said will suffice to show the subtle and dangerous character of Socialism, and how, although the majority may recoil from it at present, if logically drawn out by its bolder and more consistent advocates, the age may nevertheless be really and thoroughly Socialistic. We know that the age seeks with all its energy, as the greatest want of mankind, political and social reforms. Of this there is and can be no doubt. Analyze these reforms and the principles and motives which lead to them, which induce the people in our days to struggle for them, and you will find at the bottom of them all the assumption, that *our good lies in the natural order, and is not attainable by individual effort.* All we see, all we hear, all we read, from whatever quarter it comes, serves to prove that this is the deep and settled conviction of the age. If it were not, these revolutions in France, Italy, Germany, and elsewhere, would have no meaning, no principle, no aim, and would be as insignificant as drunken rows in the streets of our cities.

But the essence of Socialism is in this very assumption, that our good lies in the natural order, and is unattainable by individual effort. Socialism bids us follow nature, instead of saying with the Gospel, Resist nature. Placing our good in the natural order, it necessarily restricts it to temporal goods, the only good the order of nature can give. For it, then, evil is to want temporal goods, and good is to possess them. But, in this sense, evil is not remediable or good attainable by individual effort. We depend on nature, which may resist us, and on the conduct of others, which escapes our control. Hence the necessity of social organization, in order to harmonize the interests of all with the interest of each, and to enable each by the union of all to compel Nature to yield him up the good she has in store for him. But all men are equal before God, and, since he is just, he is equal in regard to all. Then all have equal rights, —an equal right to exemption from evil, and an equal right to the possession of good. Hence the social organization must be such as to avert equal evil from all, and to secure to each an equal share of temporal goods. Here is Socialism in a nutshell, following as a strictly logical consequence from the principles or assumptions which the age adopts, and on which it everywhere acts. The systems drawn out by Owen, Fourier, Saint-Simon, Cabet, Proudhon, or others, are mere attempts to realize Socialism, and may or may not be ridiculous and absurd; but that is nothing to the purpose, if you concede their principle. These men have done the best they could, and you have no right to censure them, as long as you agree with them in principle, unless you propose something better.

Now we agree with De la Mennais, that Christianity has a political and social character, and with the editor of *The Boston Quarterly Review*, that Christianity seeks the good of man in this life as well as in the life to come. We say with all our heart, "On the earth was he [our Lord] to found a new order of things, to bring round the blissful ages, and to give to renovated man a foretaste of heaven. It was here the millions were to be blessed with a heaven, as well as hearafter." No doubt of it. But *in* the new order and *by* it,—not out of it and independently of it. Out of the new order and independently of it, the millions are, to say the least, no better off than if it did not exist, and have no right to any portion of its blessings. The Socialists, when they attempt to press Christianity into their service, are bad logicians. They are right when they tell us that our Lord came to found a new order of things, for he certainly did come for that purpose; they are right when they tell us that it is Christian to seek a heaven on earth for the millions, for there is a Christian heaven here for all men, if they choose to accept it; but when they say this, they are bound to add that this heaven is in the new order established, and is to be sought in it, and by obedience to its principles. It is Christian to seek that order of happiness which Christianity proposes, by the means it prescribes; but to seek another order of happiness, and by other means, is not *therefore* necessarily Christian, and may even be antichristian. Here is the point they overlook, and which vitiates all their reasoning.

Let no one say that we allege that man must forego any good while in this world in order to gain heaven hereafter. It would be no great hardship, even if it were so; but our God deals much more liberally with us, and requires us to give up, in order to secure heaven hereafter, only what makes our misery here. The Socialist is right in saying that there is good for us even in this world; his error lies in placing that good in the natural order, and in making it unattainable by individual effort. Our good lies not in the natural order, but in the supernatural order, —in that new order which our Lord came to establish. In that order there is all the good we can conceive, and attainable by simple voluntary efforts. Out of that order there is no good attainable either by the efforts of individuals or by association, because out of it there is no good at all. Temporal goods, giving to the term the fullest possible sense, are not good, and, sought for themselves, are productive only of evil. Here is the first error of the Socialists. No evil is removable, no good is attainable, as long as any earthly or merely natural end is held to be, for its own sake, a legitimate object of pursuit. There is and can be good for no one, here or hereafter, save in seeking, *exclusively*, the end for which Almighty God has intended us, and by the means and in the way he himself has appointed. Now this end is neither in this world nor of this world, neither in nature nor of nature, and therefore can be gained, can be promoted, by no natural effort, by no natural means,—neither by political changes nor by social changes, neither by political democracy nor by social democracy. These things have and can have no necessary connection with it. It is a mistake, then, to regard them, in themselves, as ever in any degree desirable.

The Socialists are right when they say that the Christian law is the law of liberty, but not therefore necessarily right when they term the movements of the people for what they call liberty Christian movements, originating in Christian principle. Undoubtedly, the Christian law is the law of liberty. Our Saviour came to free us from bondage, and whom he makes free is free indeed. In the order he establishes, our highest good, our only good, whether for time or eternity, is entirely independent of the world. Nothing in the universe can hinder us, against our will, from attaining to it. We have only to will it and it is ours, and we are always and everywhere free to will. No one depends on nature or other men for the power to fulfil his destiny,—to gain the end for which he was intended. Here is the Christian doctrine of liberty, the glorious liberty which our religion reveals, and which we know by divine faith is no deception. But the liberty the Socialists commend, and which the people are seeking, is not Christian liberty, for it is not liberty at all. Socialism, by its very principle, enslaves us to nature and society, and subjects us to all the fluctuations of time and sense. According to it, man can attain to true good, can gain the end for which he was made, only in a certain political and social order, which it depends on the millions, whom the individual cannot control, to construct, and which, when constructed, may prove to be inconvenient and inadequate, and require to be pulled down and built up again. The individual, it teaches us, can make no advance towards his destiny but in proportion as he secures the coöperation of his race. All men must be brought down or brought up to the same level before I can go to the end for which my God made me; each man's true good is unattainable, till all men are prepared to take "a pull, a strong pull, a long pull, and a pull altogether," to attain theirs! This is slavery, not liberty. Nay, it denies the possibility of liberty, and makes slavery the necessary condition of all men. Is not he a slave who is chained to nature for his good, or to a social organization which does not exist, and which depends on the wisdom, the folly, the passions or instincts, the whims or caprices of other men to create or to destroy? Who can deny it? He only is free, he only knows what freedom is, who tramples the world beneath his feet, who is independent of all the accidents of time and space, of all created beings, and who has but to will and all heaven is his, and remains his, though the entire universe fall in ruins around him.

Undoubtedly Christianity requires us to remove all evil, and in seeking to remove evil we follow the Christian principle; but what the Socialists call evil, and the people in revolt are seeking to remove, is not evil. Nothing is evil but that which turns a man away from his end, or interposes a barrier to his advance towards it. Nothing but one's own sin can do that. Nothing, then, but sin is or can be evil, and that is evil only to him who commits it. Take all these things which Socialists declaim against,—monarchy, aristocracy, inequalities of rank, inequalities of riches, poverty, want, distress, hunger, starvation even,—not one of them, in itself considered, is necessarily evil; not one of them, nor all of them combined, can harm the just man, or prevent, except by his own will, any one from the fulfilment of his destiny. If one is prepared to die, he may as well die in a hovel as a palace, of hunger as a fever. Nothing can harm us, that does not separate or tend to separate us from God. Nothing but our own internal malice can so separate us, and it is always in our power, through grace, which is never withheld, to remove that at will.

Undoubtedly, also, Christianity requires us to seek not only to remove evil, but to promote good, and good in this world. Good is the object of the will, and we are always to propose it.

SOCIALISM AND THE CHURCH.

But the things the people in their insurrectionary movements are seeking after, and which Socialists commend, are not necessarily good. As there is no evil to the just, so is there no good to the sinner, while he continues in his sinful state. If the Socialists could secure to all men every thing they promise or dream of, they would secure them nothing to their advantage. Place every man at the highest social level that you can conceive; give him the most finished education you can devise; lavish on him in profusion this world's goods; lodge him in the most splendid palace that genius can construct, furnished in the most tasteful and luxurious manner; let him be surrounded by the most beautiful scenes of nature and the choicest specimens of art; and let him have ample leisure and opportunity for travel, for social intercourse, and for the fullest and most harmonious development of all his natural faculties;—you advance him not the millionth part of a hair's-breadth towards his destiny, avert from him no evil, secure him no conceivable good. It will be no consolation to the damned to recollect, that, while here, they were clothed in purple and fine linen, and fared sumptuously every day; and your rich men, your great and renowned men, your fine gentlemen and ladies, with their polished manners and fashionable dresses, their soft complexions and gentle speech, your accomplished artists, your brilliant poets, your eloquent orators, your learned scholars, your profound and subtile philosophers, as well as coarse artisans, ragged beggars, cross-grained old hags, and country bumpkins, will be damned, eternally damned, if they die without the grace of God; and that grace is as likely to find its way to the hovel as to the palace, to dwell beneath the beggar's gabardine as the embroidered mantle of the rich and refined. The bulk of the strong-minded and thrifty citizens of this republic, with all their political franchises, social advantages, universities, academies, common schools, meeting houses, external decorum, and material prosperity, are infinitely more destitute than those Neapolitan lazzaroni whose lot they deplore, and are in no rational sense one whit better off than the miserable miners and degraded populace of Great Britain. Their possessions will add nothing to the fullness of their joy, if, by a miracle of mercy, they gain heaven, and will only render fiercer the flames of their torment, if they are doomed to hell, as they have every reason to fear will be the case.

The Socialists fall into the fallacy of passing, in their reasoning, from one species to another. Nothing they call evil is evil; nothing they call good is good ; and hence, because Chistianity commands us to remove evil and seek good, it does not follow that we must associate with the disaffected populations to bring about political and social reforms. All that is in any sense good or worth having the individual can always, under any political or social order, secure by a simple effort of his will. Forms of government and forms of social organization, then, are at best indifferent ; Socialism is a folly, and Socicalists fools. The Creator is good, and Providence is wise and just. All external events take place by the express appointment of God. If, then, a single event were evil or the occasion of evil to a single individual, save through that individual's own fault, the goodness of the Creator would be denied, and the wisdom and justice of Providence could not be asserted. No doubt, there is evil in the world, far more heart-rending, far more terrific, than Socialists depict, or even conceive ; but to no man is there or can there be evil, but his own sin, which is purely his own creation. Since no man is obliged or compelled to sin, since sufficient grace is given unto every man to enable him to break off from sin and to become just, every man can, as far as himself is concerned, put an end to all evil, and secure all good, even the supreme Good itself, at any moment he pleases. Nothing, then, is more idle than to pretend that political and social reforms,— touching the organization of the state or of society, we mean, not those which touch administration—are or ever can be necessary as the condition of averting any evil or procuring any good.

We agree, as we have said, that our Lord came to found a new order of things,—new in relation to that which obtained among the heathen,—and that he contemplated the good of the millions here as well as hereafter; we agree, nay, we hold, that he did propose the amelioration of the lot of man even while in this world,—and not of one class only, but of all classes. But how? By his new order, or, irrespective of it, by merely calling upon the people themselves to do it through political and social organization? If you say the latter, you place him in the old order, and class him with the old heathen philosophers. If he asserts simply man's dependence on nature and social organization, he founds no new order, for this dependence was the precise basis of the old order. Mankind always had nature and social organization, and to tell them to look to these for their good was to tell them nothing new; for this was precisely what they had done, and were doing. The evil which oppressed the millions was in this very dependence, and what was needed was deliverance from it,—some method, so to speak, of attaining our true good in spite of nature and of social organization. If, then, he retains that dependence, and does not provide this method, what has he done, or what can he do, which a heathen philosopher might not have done? and wherein is what you call the Christian order different from Heathenism? You say, he came to found a new order for the amelioration of mankind; but how can you say this, if you are to look for the amelioration, which you say he authorizes you to seek, not from any new order, but from nature and social organization, which is precisely what the heathen themselves did?

If you say, on the other hand, as you must, if you assert the new order at all, that our Lord ameliorates the lot of mankind *by* his new order, then you must concede that it is only in and through that order that the amelioration is to be effected. Then you are to look for it only as you come into and conform to that order. Now, according to that order, the millions are to be blessed, are to find their true happiness, not in following nature, but in resisting it,—not in possessing temporal goods, but in renouncing them, not in pride and luxury, but in humility, poverty, and mortification,—not in being solicitous for what we shall eat, or what we shall drink, or wherewith we shall be clothed, " for after all these things do the heathen seek" (St. Matt. vi. 31–34),—in a word, not in seeking any of these things, but in seeking first, that is, as the end of all seeking, the kingdom of God, and his justice, and then "all these things shall be added unto us." This is the order which our Lord has established. He gives us all needed grace to come into this order and to comply with all its demands, and, if we come in and so comply, he promises us all good, a hundred fold in this world, and everlasting life in the world to come.

Now, as you concede that our Lord came to establish a new order of things, and must concede, that if he blesses the millions at all, it must be in and by this new order, you are bound to admit that it is only by complying with its requisitions and placing ourselves under its influence, that our good in this world, as well as in the next, is attainable. Then all your efforts by political and social changes, which imply a recurrence to the old order, a reliance on the principles of the heathen world, can only remove you farther and farther from your true good. The only way to attain that good must be to begin by an act of renunciation, the renunciation of heathenism, of the world, of self, or, what is the same thing, and act of unconditional surrender of ourselves to God. This, if you admit Christianity at all, is the indispensable condition of all good. The heathen sought their good from nature and social organization, and found only evil. We are to seek not even our own good, that is, for the simple reason that it is *our* good, but God himself, and God alone, and then we shall find our good in Him who is the sovereign good itself. No doubt, this complete renunciation of self is any thing but pleasing to self; but we are never required to do it in our own strength. God always gives us grace to make it easy, if we will accept it. Moreover, we are required, in this, to do, at least, no more for God than he has done for us. We are required to give up all for him. But he gave up all for us. He made himself man, took upon himself the form of a servant, became poor, and obedient unto death, even unto the death of the cross for us; and can we not, therefore, give up ourselves for him, especially when what we give up it were an injury to us to hold back? If we give ourselves to him, he gives himself to us. He can give no more than himself, and can we ask or expect more than an infinite God can give? Here is the condition, and it is only, under the order God has established, by complying with this condition that there is good for us here or hereafter; and we know, also, that, by complying, all evil is removed, and all conceivable and more than all conceivable good is obtained. The true course to be taken, then, is perfectly plain, and may be taken without hesitation; for He who has promised is able to fulfil, and will keep his word.

Of course we do not pretend, that, by conforming to the Christian order, the political and social equality contended for will be obtained; we do not pretend that there will be no more pain, no more sorrow, no more poverty, no more hunger or thirst. These things will remain, no doubt, as facts; but we have shown that they are not necessarily evils, and that their removal is not necessarily a good. These things have their uses in this world, or they would not be suffered to exist. To the just they are mercies, salutary penance, or occasions of merit,—purging the soul from the stains of past transgressions, or giving it an occasion to rise to higher sanctity and a higher reward. To the sinner they may be the occasion of evil; but, if so, only because he does not receive them in a proper disposition, and because by his malice he refuses to profit by them. But even to him they are no more hurtful than their opposites,—often not so hurtful. By conforming to the Christian order, all so-called temporal evils, in so far as evil, are removed, and all so-called temporal goods, in so far as good, are secured; and this is all that can be asked.

But we are told, this is all, no doubt, very well, very true, very pious; but the age does not believe it, the people will not receive it. The people demand political and social reforms; and we must conform ourselves to their state of mind, or we can have no influence with them. Let the Church sanction them in their movements for liberty, equality, and brotherhood, and then they will listen to her teaching, and profit by it.

If there is any truth in this, it proves what we have all along been endeavoring to establish,—that the age is Socialistic, and that Socialism is unchristian, nay, antichristian. Those, then, who urge the Church to make an alliance with the people in their movements, to baptize Socialism, and even give it Holy Communion, or who suppose they can without detriment to religion sympathize with these movements, we leave to defend themselves, as best they may. We have no skill to frame an apology for them, unless it be that they cherish the spirit of the age instead of the spirit of the Church, which is only a condemnation.

But suppose the sanction involved no violation of principle, and suppose the Church should make common cause with the so-called movement party, and enable it to effect the reforms it attempts,—what would be gained? These reforms, if effected, would content nobody, and a new series of reforms would be attempted, in their turn to be found equally unsatisfactory, and thus on *in infinitum*,—reforms giving birth to new reforms, bringing no relief, producing and perpetuating endless confusion, to the contentment, the satisfaction of nobody, but the arch enemy of mankind.

The Church is not of this world, and her principles are not those which govern the princes or the people of this world. She is the Spouse of God in this world, the mother of the faithful, the teacher of truth, and the dispenser of the Bread of Life to all who will receive it. They who are nursed with the milk from her bosom, who receive the Bread of Life from her hands and eat thereof, shall never hunger or thirst, shall never die, but shall live for ever. All she asks of governments and social institutions is that they leave her free, that is, violate in their administration no law of God. If the people grow discontented with the material order they find existing, she expounds to them the law; if in violation of the law, as she expounds it, they still persevere, and introduce a new order, be it what it may, she does not desert them; she continues to present herself in her divine character before them, and to discharge for them her sacred mission. She has truly a maternal heart, and seeks always and every where the true good of the people for time and for eternity; but she knows that Almighty God has made their good possible only on one condition, and therefore on that one condition she must insist. She explains it to the people, she exhorts and entreats them with divine tenderness to comply with it; but if they regard themselves as wiser than she, refuse to comply with the indispensable condition proposed, and will return to the old heathen order and seek their good from nature and human society, instead of seeking it from God and his Church, she grieves over them as our Lord grieved over Jerusalem devoted to destruction, but she can do no more. Their sin is on their own head, and they must reap the fruit of their own sowing. Themselves they may destroy,—her they cannot harm.

Here the discussion of our subject properly closes; but we fear that without additional remarks we may be misapprehended. These are times of jealousy, suspicion, and great uncharitableness, when men's passions are inflamed, and their heads more than ordinarily confused. What we say on one subject we are in danger of having understood of another; and because we oppose certain popular tendencies, they who cherish them will allege that we are the enemies of the people, opposed to political and social amelioration, and solicitous only to maintain the reign of injustice and brute force,—than which nothing is or can be farther from the truth. Because we assert that our good lies solely in the Christian order and is always and every where attainable at will, and therefore deny the necessity or the utility of political and social changes as a means of bettering our condition, the same persons will endeavor to bring us into conflict with the Holy Father, who, according to them, is a *Liberal* Pontiff, a sort of Socialistic Pope, opposed to monarchy, in favor of popular institutions, taking the side of the people against their rulers, and sanctioning the principle of their movements, by granting a constitutional government to his immediate temporal subjects. A few words to clear up this matter will not be unnecessary.

We have no occasion to make a profession of our respect for the Papal authority; for our doctrine on that subject is well known. If that authority is in any instance against us, it is sufficient to convince us that we are wrong, and it is against us in the present instance, if the view given of Pius the Ninth be the just one. But that view has no authority, except the childish fears of one party and the unhallowed wishes of another. Pius the Ninth is a noble-minded and generous-hearted man, an enlightened prince, an humble and devout Christian, an uncompromising Catholic, a tender and vigilant shepherd, the spiritual Father of Christendom, the visible Head of the Church, the Vicegerent of God on earth; and he can be no Liberal, no Socialist, no political and social reformer, in the sense of this age, —no prince to deserve the sympathy of a De la Mennais or a Horace Greely, any more than of a Ledru Rollin or a Proudhon. We know beforehand that he cannot sanction what we have presented as the principles and motives of the popular movements of the day; for the Church in General Council and through her Sovereign Pontiffs has repeatedly and unequivocally condemned them; and he himself has condemned them, in condemning *Communism*, only another name for Socialism, and in enjoining respect and obedience to princes,—as any one may see who will read the several Allocutions in which he has explained his policy.

No man has been more grossly misrepresented by pretended friends and real enemies than Pius the Ninth. The admirers of the old order,—few in number, however,—alarmed at the magnitude of his proposed changes in the government and administration of his temporal dominions, perhaps offended because he did not ask or follow their advice, very naturally opposed him and sought to make him appear to be carried away by the spirit of the age, and pursuing a policy which must hurry the world into the abyss of Radicalism; on the other hand, Radicals, Socialists, Freemasons, and Carbonari claimed him as one of themselves, because they wished to use the authority of his name and position to stir up the Catholic populations to rebellion, and to cover their own revolutionary and anarchical purposes. We share neither in the alarm of the former nor in the wish of the latter. We form our judgment of Pius the Ninth neither from Greeley's *Tribune*, nor from the Roman correspondence of the London *Morning News;* but from well-known Catholic principles, his obvious position, and his own official documents. Interpreted by these, he has only followed, with singular fidelity and firmness, the policy uniformly pursued by his predecessors.

As to his having sanctioned the principles and motives of the popular movements of the day, there is nothing in it. The thing, *in hac providentia*, is simply impossible. The Church, it is certain and undeniable, is wedded to no particular form of government or of social organization. She stakes her existence neither on imperialism nor on feudalism, neither on monarchy nor on democracy. To no one or other of them does she commit herself, and she declares each of them to be a legitimate form of government when and where it exists with no legal claimant against it. But the principle of these movements is exclusive democracy;—not that democracy is a legitimate form of government, which is true; not that in these times, the views of the age being what they are, it is, with some restrictions, the best form of government, which may not be false; but that the democratic is the *only* legitimate form of government, that all other forms are illegitimate, usurpations, tyrannies, to which the people owe no allegiance, and which they may, when they please, or believe it will be for their interest, conspire to overthrow. This is the principle implied in these movements, and which the Liberals pretend that Pius the Ninth has sanctioned. But he has done no such thing. The Church cannot accept this principle, because it would bind her to democracy, as her enemies a few years ago alleged that she was bound to monarchy, and compel her to declare all other forms of government illegal, and their acts null and void from the beginning. It would erect democracy into a dogma of faith. If the people now establishing democracies should hereafter become tired of them, and wish to reëstablish monarchy,—not an impossible supposition,—they would be obliged to renounce their religion before they could do it. The Church could make no concession to them, and would be compelled by the invariable nature of faith, to command them to return to democracy, on pain of losing their souls. She would then not only be herself enslaved to democracy, but would be obliged to enslave the people to it also, and to prohibit them under any circumstances and in every country from ever adopting any other form, how much soever they might desire it. Forms of government, like all things human, are changeable, and it is impossible to keep the people always and everywhere satisfied with any one form. What more unreasonable and more impolitic, then, than to bind them by religion always and everwhere to one and the same specific form?

We are opposing, we are advocating, no particular form of government. In themselves considered, forms of goverment are matters of indifference. The wise and just administration of government is always a matter of moment,—the form, abstractly considered, never. Man's true good is as attainable under one form of government or social organization as another; for it is obtained, if obtained at all, from a source wholly independent of the temporal order. That good the Church does and must seek, and its necessary condition is true liberty. To assume, as these social movements do, that this liberty is possible only under a given form of government and social organization would be to maintain that the Church can discharge her mission only where that particular form of government and social organization exists. The first thing her missionaries to a country where that form does not exist must attempt would then be to revolutionize the state and reorganize society. The American people, to a very considerable extent, suppose this to be the fact; and, supposing monarchy to be the favorite form, maintain that the spread of Catholicity here must essentially destroy our popular form of government, and introduce forms similar to those which the people in the Old World are now laboring to throw off. Substitute democracy for monarchy, and the doctrine we oppose is precisely that which our adversaries allege against us. Are we to adopt it? Are we to believe that Pius the Ninth adopts it, and requires us to understand that all but democratic nations are out of the way of salvation, placed out of the condition of attaining to any good here or hereafter?

Since we hold that forms of government are indifferent, that there is evil only in sin, and that our good comes exclusively from the Christian order, we deny the necessity of political and social changes; and since to seek our good from them is to seek it from the temporal order instead of the spiritual, which is in principle a rejection of Christianity and a return to heathenism, we censure them. But the minds of the people may be perverted and their hearts corrupted, and we, in consequence, unable to make them see where their true good lies, or to induce them even to give us their attention while we point it out to them. They may be intent on certain political changes, mad for them, and have ears, eyes, hearts, and hands, for nothing else. We may condemn their state of mind, the moral disposition in which we find them, but it is a fact we have to meet, and deal with as a fact. In such cases, if the concession of the changes demanded involves no departure from faith or morals, it is wise to make it, in some sense, necessary, as a means of removing the *prohibens*, as we use logic with an unbeliever in order to remove the obstacles he finds in his mind to the reception of the faith. When political or social changes for this purpose become necessary, it is never the part of wisdom to resist them; authority should always be free to concede them; and that it may be is one reason why it cannot and should not be bound to any particular form of government or social organization.

Pius the Ninth has evidently acted on the principle we here commend. He found, on his accession to the pontifical throne, his own immediate temporal subjects and the European populations generally mad for popular institutions, and not to be satisfied with any thing else. They were ripe for revolt, and pepared to attempt the acquisition of popular government in some form, at all hazards,—if necessary, by insurrection, violent and bloody revolution. They had lost all respect for their rulers, and would listen no longer to the voice of their pastors,—would listen to nothing in fact, that was opposed to their dominant passion. What was to be done? There were but two alternatives possible. Authority must either repress them by the strong arm of physical force, or attempt to tranquillize them and save them from civil war and anarchy by the concession of popular institutions. The former had been adopted, had been tried, was in actual operation, and it alienated still more and more the hearts of the people from their sovereigns, and from the Church, in consequence of her supposed sympathy with monarchy. Nothing was left that could be tried with much hope of a favorable issue, but the latter alternative. Pius the Ninth saw this, —indeed, most statesmen saw it,—and, anxious for the peace and order of his dominions, and to remove from the minds of all whatever accidental obstacles there might be to their listening to the lessons of religion, he resolved to adopt it; and accordingly proceeded to give his subjects a constitutional government, and, by his example at least, recommended to the European sovereigns to do as much for theirs, and to do it cheerfully, ungrudgingly, and in good faith. The policy came, indeed, too late to effect all the good that was hoped, and to avert all the evil that was threatened; yet that, under the circumstances, it was wise and prudent, nay, even necessary, there really seems to us no room to doubt. We may have regretted the circumstances which called for it, but we have never for a moment doubted, or thought of doubting, its wisdom or its necessity, although from the first we apprehended the consequences which have followed, and that it would hasten the outbreak of the European populations, which we knew the ill-disposed were preparing; and we have never believed its effect in pacifying the excited multitudes would be as great as some of our friends, whose confidence in the people is greater than ours, expected it would be.

The adoption of this policy, the policy of concession to the exigencies of the times, implies no sanction by the Holy Father of the principles and motives of those popular movements and demands which made it necessary or advisable, nor of the political and social changes we have spoken against. We have been addressing the people and endeavoring to show them what is proper for them to seek, not attempting to point out to authority what it should do; for we have no vocation to instruct authority in its duties. We are of the people, and we only point out what our religion enjoins upon them and us. It may be very just, very wise, nay, very necessary, at times, for authority to concede what it is very wrong, very foolish, on the part of the people to demand. The children of Israel, in the time of Samuel, afford us a case in point. They demanded of the Lord a king, that they might be like other nations. The Lord rebuked them, told them they knew not what they asked, and unrolled before them the oppressions to which a compliance with their request would subject them. Nevertheless, he complied with it, and gave them a king. The question before Pius the Ninth was not the question we have been discussing. The movements existed, the people demanded popular institutions, and were resolved, come what might, to attempt them. The simple question for him was, How shall this state of things be treated? He said to the princes in answer, "Give the people what they ask." This he was free to do, because the Church is wedded to no political or social order, to monarchy no more than to democracy, is as independent of the throne as of the tribune, and can be as much at home in a republic as anywhere else.

What is to be the result of the movements of the day we know not. The old monarchies may be swept away, or they may partially recover, and linger on for ages to come; but that does not disturb us. Old Imperial Rome and old Roman civilization were broken down by the irruption of the Northern barbarians, and the world was deluged with barbarism, but the Church remained standing, and did not become barbarian; the feudalism of the Middle Ages, a system, as somebody has said, too perfect for its time, fell beneath the combined attacks of kings and people, but the Church survived, and beheld undismayed its funeral pile; modern monarchy may follow, and all the world become democratic, still the Church will survive, and remain in all her integrity, shorn of none of her glory, and deprived of none of her resources. Over no changes of this sort do we weep. We have no fears for the Church; we fear only for men. If we saw the people making war on the old political system in consequence of its wars on religion, and struggling for popular institutions in order to rescue the Church from her bondage, and to secure her an open field and fair play for the future, we should hear the volleys of musketry and the roar of cannon, and witness the charge, the siege and sack of cities, with tolerable composure; for then the war would be one of vengeance on the old governments for the insults they have offered to the Immaculate Spouse of God, and for the freedom of worship, the only war in which real glory ever is or can be acquired. But, alas! we see nothing of all this. These enraged populations are moved by no regard for religion, they are to a fearful extent the bitter enemies of religious freedom, and governed by a malignant hatred of the Church. They are seeking only an earthly end, and they loathe the Christian order. Here is the source of our anxiety, the ground of our fears,—not for the Church, not for ourselves, but for them. They threaten to be more violent enemies to religion than any kings have been since the persecuting emperors of Pagan Rome; and the conduct of the Swiss radicals, the imprisonment of the noble Bishop of Lausanne and Geneva in the Castle of Chillon, and the persecution of the children of St. Alphonsus by the people of Vienna, reveal but too plainly the spirit which animates them, and tell us but too distinctly what, at least for a time, we are to expect from the triumph of the popular party. Nevertheless, a wise and just Providence rules, and these things are permitted only as mercies or judgments upon the nations. It is ours to humble ourselves and adore; and always have we this consolation, that no evil can befall us against our will, and that always and everywhere may we secure every good by unreserved submission to God in his Church.

FINIS.

The Romantic Tradition in American Literature

An Arno Press Collection

Alcott, A. Bronson, editor. **Conversations with Children on the Gospels.** Boston, 1836/1837. Two volumes in one.

Bartol, C[yrus] A. **Discourses on the Christian Spirit and Life.** 2nd edition. Boston, 1850.

Boker, George H[enry]. **Poems of the War.** Boston, 1864.

Brooks, Charles T. **Poems, Original and Translated.** Selected and edited by W. P. Andrews. Boston, 1885.

Brownell, Henry Howard. **War-Lyrics** and Other Poems. Boston, 1866.

Brownson, O[restes] A. **Essays and Reviews Chiefly on Theology, Politics, and Socialism.** New York, 1852.

Channing, [William] Ellery (The Younger). **Poems.** Boston, 1843.

Channing, [William] Ellery (The Younger). **Poems of Sixty-Five Years.** Edited by F. B. Sanborn. Philadelphia and Concord, 1902.

Chivers, Thomas Holley. **Eonchs of Ruby:** A Gift of Love. New York, 1851.

Chivers, Thomas Holley. **Virginalia;** or, Songs of My Summer Nights. (Reprinted from *Research Classics*, No. 2, 1942). Philadelphia, 1853.

Cooke, Philip Pendleton. **Froissart Ballads,** and Other Poems. Philadelphia, 1847.

Cranch, Christopher Pearse. **The Bird and the Bell,** with Other Poems. Boston, 1875.

[Dall], Caroline W. Healey, editor. **Margaret and Her Friends.** Boston, 1895.

[D'Arusmont], Frances Wright. **A Few Days in Athens.** Boston, 1850.

Everett, Edward. **Orations and Speeches,** on Various Occasions. Boston, 1836.

Holland, J[osiah] G[ilbert]. **The Marble Prophecy,** and Other Poems. New York, 1872.

Huntington, William Reed. **Sonnets and a Dream.** Jamaica, N. Y., 1899.

Jackson, Helen [Hunt]. **Poems.** Boston, 1892.

Miller, Joaquin (Cincinnatus Hiner Miller). **The Complete Poetical Works of Joaquin Miller.** San Francisco, 1897.

Parker, Theodore. **A Discourse of Matters Pertaining to Religion.** Boston, 1842.

Pinkney, Edward C. **Poems.** Baltimore, 1838.

Reed, Sampson. **Observations on the Growth of the Mind.** *Including,* **Genius** (Reprinted from *Aesthetic Papers,* Boston, 1849). 5th edition. Boston, 1859.

Sill, Edward Rowland. **The Poetical Works of Edward Rowland Sill.** Boston and New York, 1906.

Simms, William Gilmore. **Poems:** Descriptive, Dramatic, Legendary and Contemplative. New York, 1853. Two volumes in one.

Simms, William Gilmore, editor. **War Poetry of the South.** New York, 1866.

Stickney, Trumbull. **The Poems of Trumbull Stickney.** Boston and New York, 1905.

Timrod, Henry. **The Poems of Henry Timrod.** Edited by Paul H. Hayne. New York, 1873.

Trowbridge, John Townsend. **The Poetical Works of John Townsend Trowbridge.** Boston and New York, 1903.

Very, Jones. **Essays and Poems.** [Edited by R. W. Emerson]. Boston, 1839.

Very, Jones. **Poems and Essays.** Boston and New York, 1886.

White, Richard Grant, editor. **Poetry:** Lyrical, Narrative, and Satirical of the Civil War. New York, 1866.

Wilde, Richard Henry. **Hesperia:** A Poem. Edited by His Son (William Wilde). Boston, 1867.

Willis, Nathaniel Parker. **The Poems, Sacred, Passionate, and Humorous, of Nathaniel Parker Willis.** New York, 1868.

MUHLENBERG LIBRARY

3 1542 00130 3431